1996

Environmental Politics and

Theories and Evidence

Edited by James P. Lester

Duke University Press Durham and London 1989

Second impression, 1990

Printed in the United States of America
on acid-free paper. ∞
Library of Congress Cataloging-in-Publication Data
appear on the last printed page of this book.

Dedicated to
Lynton K. Caldwell, Henry P. Caulfield, Phillip O. Foss,
Dean E. Mann, Walter A. Rosenbaum, and Norman Wengert
for their intellectual leadership
in the field of environmental politics and policy

Contents

Tables and Figures

Tables

Figures

Preface and Acknowledgments

This book is largely concerned with the political science literature on environmental politics and policy. The impetus for this collection stems from the fact that although much has been written in the area of environmental policy during the period from 1960 to 1988, very little has been done toward synthesizing and evaluating this literature which has matured over the past twenty-eight years and thus it deserves careful consideration as a collective body of research. At the outset, let me also state what this book is *not*. It is not an attempt to provide a comprehensive review of *all* the extant literature on environmental policy, including work by biologists, psychologists, sociologists, economists, lawyers, etc. Rather, the goal is much more modest but nevertheless important, that is, to highlight work by political scientists that bears on environmental politics and policy. This book *does* synthesize and critique a rather large body of research and, in the process, suggests some promising areas for future research.

The audience for the book includes three primary groups. First, this collection is directed to both undergraduate and graduate students of environmental politics and policy. Second, it is addressed to instructors in the area of natural resource politics and administration. Finally, I expect that this compilation of research will provide additional insight for those currently involved in the policy formulation process, including federal, state, and local administrative personnel, as well as other interested public policy professionals.

The analytical approach used stresses the relationships between historical conditions, resource levels, mass political behavior, governmental institutions, and elite perceptions on the one hand, and environmental policy formation on the other hand. It is not intended merely to provide a collection of interesting readings. Rather, my purpose in assembling this material is to explain environmental policy formation and to suggest some promising areas for future research. For the quality of this research and the intellectual effort which has gone into making it accessible and useful, I extend my sincere gratitude to the authors of the individual chapters.

I am also indebted to a number of individuals who, over the past ten years, have encouraged my work in environmental policy. First, Walter A. Rosenbaum initially stimulated my interest in environmental policy when I was a doctoral student, and later as his research associate at the Smithsonian Institution in Washington, D.C. Since that time he has been a steady source of encouragement for my efforts in this (and other) research. In addition, Dean E. Mann has been especially helpful both as a colleague and as a source of ideas through his writings in environmental policy. Others who have been most encouraging are Michael E. Kraft, Paul A. Sabatier, Helen M. Ingram, and Ann Bowman. I am especially indebted to The Martin School of Public Administration (at the University of Kentucky) and The Council of State Governments for their research support during the completion of this project. In addition, my colleagues and students at Colorado State University have always been a source of encouragement and inspiration for my work in this area.

I also wish to thank Richard C. Rowson, Director of Duke University Press, for his continued support. Finally, the book has profited immensely from the advice of Reynolds Smith, who has carefully guided it through several revisions.

James P. Lester

I

Introduction

James P. Lester

Americans . . . have seldom seen environment, as such, as an expression of anything in particular. They have seldom thought of it as a general object of public policy. Their readiness to control environment for particular purposes has not been accompanied by recognition of a need for comprehensive environmental policies. —Lynton K. Caldwell, 1963

Environmental policy has come of age. It is established on the political agenda of the United States, of nearly all advanced industrial nations, and of some developing nations as well. —Dean E. Mann, 1980

In less than twenty years environmental protection policy has moved from being a "non-issue" to one of the most significant issues of our time. Until the late 1960s there had been no clear or explicit formulation of a public responsibility for the state of the environment (Caldwell, 1970:3). However, beginning with the adoption of the National Environmental Policy Act (NEPA) of 1969, "the United States entered the decade of the nineteen seventies committed for the first time as a nation to responsibility for the quality of its environment" (Caldwell, 1970:23).[1]

Moreover, this initial commitment was sustained during the 1970s with the passage of environmental laws which regulated air contaminants such as sulfur oxides and photochemical smog, water pollutants such as dissolved organic chemicals producing lake eutrophication and, most recently, land and groundwater contamination from hazardous wastes (Lester and Bowman, 1983). Table 1.1 provides a list of major environmental legislation from 1948 to 1986.

Given the acceptance, legitimacy, and maturity of environmental policy, it is reasonable to expect that greater attention would also be given to analyzing

Table 1.1 Major Federal Environmental Legislation: A Chronology

1948—Water Pollution Control Act
1956—Water Pollution Control Act (Amendments)
1960—Air Quality Act
1963—Clean Air Act
1965—Solid Waste Disposal Act
1965—Water Quality Act
1966—Clean Water Restoration Act
1967—Air Quality Act
1969—National Environmental Policy Act (NEPA)
1970—Clean Air Act (Amendments)
1970—Water Quality Improvement Act
1970—Resource Recovery Act
1972—Noise Control Act
1972—Federal Water Pollution Control Act (Amendments)
1972—Marine Protection, Research, and Sanctuaries Act
1972—Coastal Zone Management Act
1972—Federal Environmental Pesticide Control Act
1973—Endangered Species Act
1974—Land Use Policy Act
1974—Strip Mining Act
1974—Safe Drinking Water Act
1976—Toxic Substances Control Act
1976—Resource Conservation and Recovery Act
1977—Clean Air Amendments
1977—Clean Water Act
1977—Federal Water Pollution Control Act (Amendments)
1977—Surface Mining Control and Reclamation Act
1978—National Parks and Recreation Act
1978—Environmental Pesticide Control Act (Amendments)
1978—Quiet Communities Act
1980—Comprehensive Environmental Response, Compensation, and Liability Act
1984—Hazardous and Solid Waste Amendments
1986—Superfund Amendments and Reauthorization Act

SOURCE: Council on Environmental Quality, *Annual Report* (1979) and updated by the author.

the process of environmental policy formulation, implementation, and impact. Indeed, the extant literature on environmental politics and policy has evolved from containing "more unanswers than a Dr. Seuss encyclopedia" (Jones, 1972:588) to a major contribution toward our accumulated knowledge of political behavior, the operation of governmental institutions, and the general process of policy formulation and implementation (Sabatier and Wandesforde-Smith, 1979:599). The scholarly literature has increased enormously since the mid 1960s, with contributions from political scientists, economists, and sociologists, among others. However, it was noted that eventually many of these disparate studies will have to be synthesized and related to the broader literature on policy-making (Sabatier and Wandesforde-Smith, 1979:600). In order to make such trans-policy generalizations possible, it is necessary to organize the state of knowledge *within* policy areas.

The purpose of this book is to begin the task of synthesizing and assessing that literature on environmental politics and policy. To do so, I provide an analytical framework for identifying and discussing some of the primary determinants of environmental policy formulation. Using this framework, the contributors identify research gaps which stand in the way of our further understanding of the politics of environmental policy-making.

In beginning the discussion, I first review the historical development of the environmental politics literature before outlining a theoretical framework which guides the analyses in the following chapters. The literature may be divided into roughly two periods of theoretical development: (1) early literature, 1960–1977 and (2) growing maturity, 1978–1988.

Early Literature, 1960–1977

In a 1972 assessment of several environmental politics books, Charles O. Jones asserted that this literature was largely confined to overviews of the issue or of source materials, "how to do it" books, economic analyses, and "the politics of . . ." books (Jones, 1972:589). He also noted that few political scientists were represented, and in general his reaction to this literature was that he was "not encouraged" by what he found (Jones, 1972:595). Jones mentioned that the few political scientists writing in this area at the time included Lynton K. Caldwell, Vincent Ostrom, Grant McConnell, Dean E. Mann, Norman Wengert, James L. Sundquist, and Phillip Foss, among others (Jones, 1972:593).[2]

A major debate during this period examined the proper role of political scientists engaged in the study of environmental problems. According to one line of argument, political scientists should study environmental problems primarily because of the serious threats to global environmental quality. To fulfill that goal, it would be necessary to transcend and to redefine the traditional boundaries of political science as a discipline and to become knowledgeable in many other fields concerned with the environment. Moreover, political scientists should take part in the *political* struggle for a better physical environment by adopting ecological values (Lundqvist, 1978:89).

A second position argued that students of environmental policy should take every necessary precaution to avoid blurring the boundaries of their discipline. The main objective to studying environmental politics should be to enhance our knowledge of political phenomena. Political scientists should thus *not* spend fruitless efforts in trying to become expert environmental engineers or ecologists; rather they should study environmental politics to draw conclusions and generalizations that would extend the discipline of political science. In doing so, political scientists should utilize *scientific* and *professional* goals and standards when studying environmental policies (Lundqvist, 1978:89). This debate characterized much of the literature during this time and continues to color much of the environmental politics and policy research.[3]

Other analysts noted that by 1973 "more political scientists [were] giving serious attention to problems arising from the spreading and worsening environmental crises" (Sprout and Sprout, 1973:192). Those who became involved at this time included Harold and Margaret Sprout, Walter Rosenbaum, Stuart Nagel, Geoffrey Wandesforde-Smith, Michael Kraft, and Lester Milbrath. However, those few political scientists concerned with environmental policy-making largely focused their attention on the federal government (Sabatier, 1973:218). In addition, a number of political scientists used environmental problems to illustrate long-standing theoretical issues within the profession. These included Lettie Wenner, Charles O. Jones, Matthew Holden, and Matthew Crenson. Much of the work at this time, however, was of little explanatory import, being either largely descriptive in nature or failing to depart from and build upon the knowledge—albeit limited—of the American political system accumulated by the profession over the last few decades (Sabatier, 1973:223).

Additional commentary on the state of the literature at this time (i.e., 1974) suggested that "it is an enormously diverse assortment of popular polemics, investigative journalism, and scholarly inquiry of varying purpose, scope, and quality" (Kraft, 1974:140). Specifically, this literature did not address the question regarding whether present institutional structures and political processes are inherently incapable of producing a satisfactory response to the accelerating deterioration of the environment (Kraft, 1974:147). Instead, the literature is too much directed toward "trivial descriptions of routine issues in contemporary environmental politics and administration, micro-analyses of largely inconsequential environmental behavior, and the development of methodological sophistication in policy analysis that seems greatly to exceed the marginal payoffs of the final product" (Kraft, 1974:148).

By 1975 critics still lamented the fact that "very little research had been done by political scientists on environmental policy" (Mann, Wandesforde-Smith, and Lundqvist, 1975:83). During the period of 1965 to 1975, some of the best work was done by people who may best be styled political economists. These included Allen Kneese, Myrick Freeman, Marc Roberts, Edwin Haefele, and Robert Haveman (Mann, Wandesforde-Smith, and Lundqvist, 1975:84). With regard to specific policy sectors within environmental policy, one finds that water resources were the most studied of all resources. Scholars in this area included Arthur Maass, William H. Stewart, Charles McKinley, Henry Hart, Norman Wengert, Ernest Englebert, Hubert Marshall, Albert Lepawsky, Dean Mann, Helen Ingram, and Henry Caulfield.

A number of areas were identified as deserving more attention at this time. For example, analysts suggested that studies of the administration of the environment at the state level were seldom found (Sabatier, 1974; Mann, Wandesforde-Smith, and Lundqvist, 1975). Moreover, "the concepts of the environmental movement [were] little investigated by political scientists in terms of relating them to broader political thought" (Mann, Wandesforde-Smith, and Lundqvist, 1975:88).

In sum, this early literature was still quite underdeveloped, especially as regards the contribution of political scientists. Yet, there were signs of emerging maturity and expansion by the end of 1977.

Growing Maturity, 1978–1988

Analysts noted that by 1978 the studies on environmental politics represented "an advance over the lofty philosophical treatments of the 'enthusiastic' era, and they present a long and interesting agenda for future research" (Lundqvist, 1978:96). By this time a number of political scientists had "begun to apply and contribute to our accumulated knowledge of political behavior, the operation of governmental institutions, and the general process of policy formulation and implementation, at least in the United States" (Sabatier and Wandesforde-Smith, 1979:599). The scope of environmental concern broadened from water and air pollution and pesticide regulation to the management and control of solid wastes, ocean dumping, toxic substances, and land use planning (Mann, 1980:323). It was as if a consensus had been reached that detailed analyses of specific topics, rather than cursory overviews, were needed (Sabatier and Wandesforde-Smith, 1979:600). A new generation of political scientists became involved during this period in the study of environmental politics. These included William Ophuls, Richard Tobin, James Lester, Paul Culhane, Lennart Lundqvist, Jeanne Nienaber, David Orr, Richard N. L. Andrews, John Dryzek, Paul Sabatier, and Daniel Mazmanian, among others. Much attention was now directed toward developing a greater understanding of federal institutional processes of environmental policy-making and implementation problems, and to the normative implications of institutional failures in environmental policy-making.

At present, much more attention still needs to be directed toward the adequacy of subnational institutions in environmental policy-making and implementation as well as an evaluation of alternative institutional designs for resolving environmental disputes. The former suggestion is particularly important given the devolution of federal environmental programs to the states (Lester, 1986). The latter suggestion is important since so many environmental problems involve scientific and technological controversies in which the "experts" are equally divided in their opinions with respect to the environmental risks presented by such problems as ocean pollution, acid rain, and toxic wastes (Lowrance, 1976; Barke, 1986).[4]

Purpose and Method

In view of the growing maturity of the environmental politics and policy literature, our purpose in this book is to synthesize and assess the extant political science literature as well as to suggest some promising propositions for further testing. In this way, we hope to contribute toward the further intellectual growth and development of this literature. Specifically, the goals of the book are to: (1) aggregate, synthesize, and critique the available political science research that has emerged over the past twenty-five years or so, (2) describe the state of the art vis-à-vis this literature on environmental politics and policy, and (3) show that this research can be organized as a cumulative body of knowledge for use in teaching and research purposes.

The empirical evidence around which the chapters revolve is an examination of the contextual, stuctural, and perceptual factors that shape environmental policy formation. For example, the following questions guide the analyses presented in the following chapters:

(1) What has been done in the area each author is writing about? What is the state of the art vis-à-vis this particular body of literature?

(2) How have important findings been changed or modified as new knowledge has developed? Can any new information be provided on the subject at hand either through a synthesis and assessment of the research or through original research?

(3) How does this body of literature contribute to theory development? What are some problems in this body of research?

(4) What is the current research agenda in this area? What are some promising areas of future research? What issues need to be addressed?

This study is not, however, concerned with purely descriptive accounts of this important topic. As students of the public policy process, we are committed to the systematic accumulation of knowledge. Thus, in the following chapters, evidence is oriented around an explicit conceptual framework which guides the inquiry. The model for analyzing the determinants of environmental policy formation is based on the conceptualization advanced by Richard Hofferbert (1974:228). Figure 1.1 represents his conceptualization and it details the factors believed to promote (or inhibit) policy formation. The first sector of the model (a) is intended to show that "history and geography are intricately woven into the actions of contemporary policy-makers" (Hofferbert, 1974:228–29). In chapter 2, attention is given to the history of the environmental movement as a conditioning influence on eventual policy formation. Henry Caulfield details the history of the conservation and environmental movements and illustrates how these movements shaped contemporary environmental policy.

Although history and geography help to condition socioeconomic structures, the latter also promote or inhibit environmental policy. For example, "neighboring states, with almost similar backgrounds and resources, have developed measurably different social and economic climates that may have inde-

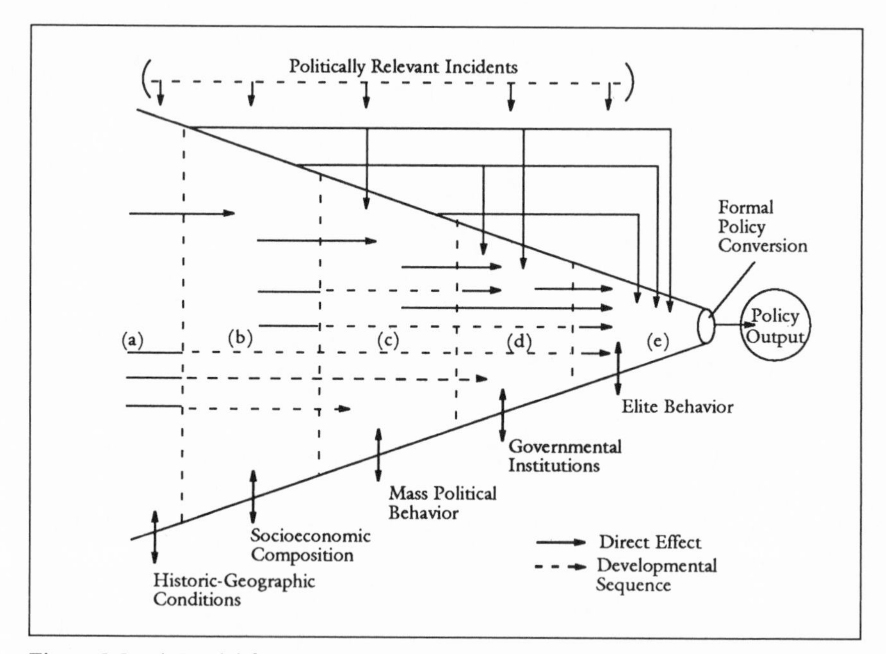

Figure 1.1 A Model for Comparative Study of Policy Formation. SOURCE: Hofferbert (1974).

pendent determinative effects upon the manner in which particular issues are raised and resolved within the policy-making milieu" (Hofferbert, 1974:229). In chapter 3, the issue of different socioeconomic contexts (b) is discussed in terms of federal-state relations. Specifically, Charles Davis and James Lester discuss how reduced federal environmental aid and limited internal state resources are likely to inhibit protection of the environment by the American states.

Mass political behavior (c) may influence elite decisions or governmental institutions independently from socioeconomic determination (Hofferbert, 1974:230). For example, public opinion, interest groups, and political parties may (or may not) exert pressure upon elites or institutions which causes them to respond in ways that promote (or inhibit) environmental policy. In chapters 4 through 6 attention is directed toward an analysis of the role and influence of each of these factors on environmental policy. For example, Riley Dunlap discusses the evolution of public support for environmental protection over time and the correlates of that support. Next, in chapter 5, Helen Ingram and Dean Mann discuss the role and influence of environmental interest groups on environmental policy. Then, in chapter 6, Jerry Calvert discusses the role and impact of political parties on environmental policy at national and state levels.

The role of governmental institutions (d) is the focus for chapters 7 through 9. For example, Michael Kraft discusses the impact of Congress on support for environmental policy while Walter Rosenbaum and Lettie Wenner analyze the role and impact of the bureaucracy (especially the federal level) and the courts, respectively, upon environmental policy.

The last sector (e) of the model prior to formal policy conversion is "elite behavior" (Hofferbert, 1974:231). Most definitions of policy formation—which include nonperception or rejection of proposed alternatives—"encompass some type of action connoting formal legality that must be attached to a policy output by the behavior of relevant elites" (Hofferbert, 1974:231). The point is that any combination of "pre-elite" factors may be operative on a given policy proposal, but elite response in some formal manner is a sine qua non of policy formation (Hofferbert, 1974:231). Attention is thus given to this set of factors by Mark Rushefsky in chapter 10.

Chapter 11, by Dimitris Stevis, Valerie Assetto, and Stephen Mumme, discusses the literature on international environmental politics and policy. As such, it suggests the role of international politics on environmental policy. This chapter thus complements the preceding literature on domestic environmental policy.

Finally, chapter 12, by John Dryzek and James Lester, discusses the normative or prescriptive literature on environmental policy. Much of the extant literature on environmental policy is evaluative in nature with regard to the adequacy of our existing institutions. The purpose of this concluding chapter is to categorize this literature in terms of policy prescriptions using a typology that is based on the locus of decision-making and the type of reform suggested. As such, this concluding chapter contains a review and assessment of reforms that have been discussed in the literature on environmental policy. This chapter also includes some predictions for the future of environmental policy-making. These predictions should help to stimulate thinking about where environmental politics is (or could be) headed in the future.

Part One

The Context of Environmental Policy

2

The Conservation and Environmental Movements: An Historical Analysis

Henry P. Caulfield

The first objective of this chapter is to utilize a version of elite theory to explain the evolution of political movements and resulting public policy outputs. The second objective is to provide a brief historical analysis of the conservation and environmental movements in order to probe the plausibility of the model. In this regard, the basic historical elements of ideology, basic values, and symbolic words are utilized to explain federal public policy developments related to the two movements. The final objective is to draw some conclusions from the analysis with respect to elite theory, and to suggest further research in this area that might prove intellectually useful. Chapter 10 gives additional attention to the role of elites in public policy formation.

An Explanatory Model

Elite theory emphasizes the critical role of political leaders operating as policy entrepreneurs in a situation which is compatible with the exercise of political leadership (McGregor, 1960; Burns, 1978). The situation is ripe for such an exercise when there are perceived policy problems and frustrated policy proposals during preceding years. Leadership by various political actors (e.g., executive officials or legislators as well as nongovernmental leaders) is conceived as critical to the development of political movements and in the utilization of political power conferred by them in the legitimation of specific public policy outputs. Essentially, these relationships constitute the model utilized here. The explanation in the following pages reflects the author's personal experience as a participant/observer in the development of environmental policy during the Kennedy and Johnson administrations (1961–1968).

It should be pointed out, however, that the argument presented here may be contrasted with other authors who have written about the primary determinants of the environmental movement. For example, James L. Sundquist argues in *Politics and Policy: The Eisenhower, Kennedy, and Johnson Years* (1968) that public awareness (and later alarm) about environmental degradation stimulated Congress and Presidents Kennedy and Johnson to propose far-reaching environmental initiatives. In another interpretation, J. Clarence Davies III in *The Politics of Pollution* (1975) stresses the roles of city lobbies in pushing for federal environmental initiatives in environmental policy. Merril Eisenbud in *Environment, Technology, and Health: Human Ecology in Historical Perspective* (1978) argues that the environmental movement has been a serious and weakening distraction from the historical progress of public health. Finally, Samuel P. Hays in *Beauty, Health, and Permanence: Environmental Politics in the United States, 1955–1985* (1987) argues that the conservation movement was an effort on the part of leaders in science, technology, and government to bring about more efficient development of physical resources, while the environmental movement was a product of a fundamental change in public values in the United States that stressed the quality of the human environment. Whereas this chapter presents an alternative interpretation of environmental policy formulation, the serious student should also consult the works cited above.

As noted above, the interpretation presented here stresses the role of elites (especially presidential leadership) in bringing about significant change in environmental initiatives from 1910 to 1988. It is assumed that the role of leaders is: to identify political problems (i.e., incongruities between ideologically inspired values and perceived facts); to formulate general ideas and utilize symbolic terms to which specific problems may be related; and to persuade other elites and the public at large of their importance and the efficacy of proposed solutions. If leaders relate ideology, proposals, and actions to a subject area of potential widespread public concern, then those persuaded will tend to identify themselves with a resulting political movement. That movement will then motivate officials of the executive and legislative branches and cause them to provide appropriate policy responses.

Political movements can be distinctively recognized by their ideology or symbolic sets of basic values and beliefs that are taken to have significance in public policy agenda-setting, formulation, and implementation. Often these movements are bipartisan in nature and hence they are able to attract large numbers of followers. Only a small proportion of these followers may be members of related organized public interest groups. Such groups may be most concerned with only a segment of the total concern, but in a coalition with other groups they generally support the goals of the movement, as well as specific policy initiatives proposed in accord with its symbols (Zeigler and Peak, 1972:73–75).

The rise and decline of the labor movement is illustrative of this point. Although labor unions as organized interest groups existed prior to the 1930s and enjoyed some measure of success, the labor movement may be seen as arising in the 1930s as a result of leadership provided by New Deal political elites. Later, middle-class liberals, with no connection to unions, took up the cause of labor. The National Labor Relations Act of 1935 and other legislation favorable to labor was the result. Middle-class liberals continued their support after World War II. Today, much middle-class support would appear to have vanished. However, labor unions as interest groups survive, but without as much clout.

Of three methods of political decision-making conceived by political scientists, ideological adherence is treated most explicitly in this chapter; however, bargaining and distributive politics also are taken to be present. The involvement of all three methods is made explicit in one case, discussed later, that of the Land and Water Conservation Fund Act of 1964. Another such case is that of the Wild and Scenic Rivers Act of 1968 (Cogan, 1982). Other cases relating to the Wilderness Act of 1964, Water Resources Planning Act of 1965, the Endangered Species Act of 1973, and the Clean Water Act of 1972 could be similarly analyzed, but space in this chapter does not permit such an analysis. In all cases involving natural resources and the environment in which the author has been a participant/observer, all three methods have been involved. This view is contrary to that of Lowi, who identifies one type of decision-making with each statute (Lowi, 1971).

A Prelude to Historical Analysis

Both the conservation movement and the environmental movement have been identified by the press and popular literature, as well as by historians and political scientists, as political realities of this century (Bates, 1957; McConnell, 1954; Hays, 1959; Rosenbaum, 1973). The conservation movement can be said to have begun during the presidency of Theodore Roosevelt and lasted until its basic tenets were enlarged or disputed by the environmental movement, or what President Lyndon B. Johnson called the "New Conservation."

Both the conservation movement and the environmental movement, as political forces, were preceded by perceived policy problems, as well as public policy proposals and developments that failed immediately to crystallize into the unifying ideas and symbols of political movements. Leadership which could capitalize upon this prior situation was not then available or adequate to the task.

Fermenting in the nineteenth century was the idea of management of forests, a natural resource policy field featured by the conservation movement in this century. Early reports of the American Association for the Advancement of Science in the 1860s discussed the need for "sustained yield forestry." Later, in the 1870s, when Carl Schurz, a German immigrant, was Secretary of the Interior, "sustained yield forestry" was further promoted, as it was in the 1880s by Bernard Fernow, also a German immigrant, when he was chief of the division of forestry in the Department of Agriculture. Elites were influenced by this early advocacy. They perceived that private stripping of the forests of Michigan, Wisconsin, and Minnesota for timber, without provision for reseeding and other management, was a major public problem. But this early policy ferment then failed to bring about basic policy change. Nevertheless, concern about dwindling forests did achieve political action to set aside "forest reserves" in 1891 within the federal public domain and to authorize in 1897 selective cutting and marketing of its timber.

Other natural resource fields provided similar influence upon efforts to generalize national concern and action in this century. By 1890 the development of navigation facilities by the Army Corps of Engineers was losing the political support that had been strongly given by the then new Republican party in the 1860s (Caulfield, 1984). Re-creation of support for the Corps' program, along with maintenance of support for the new national irrigation program, as well as watershed management in forested areas were professional goals needing translation into widespread political support. In this connection, hydroelectric power was of particular concern. Not only was utilization of recently achieved technical capacity to develop large-scale hydroelectric power facilities of concern, but concern was also developing that this opportunity should not become the monopoly of unconstrained private utilities. Professional concern for the probability of dwindling supplies of high-quality minerals was also increasing. This concern inspired the idea of publicly supported research on the beneficiation of ores. And, finally, professional interest was developing in biological surveys and research and in sustained-yield management of fish and game.

Likewise, perceived problems and various actions which led to the environmental movement began in the nineteenth century. The symbolic word for these concerns and actions was "preservation" of natural resources, as opposed to the more pragmatic "conservation," which meant mainly controlled *use*. Preservationist concerns led to the transfer of Yosemite Valley to California in the 1860s for a state park (and its retrocession to federal jurisdiction in 1890), to establishment of Yellowstone National Park in 1872, to authorization by the Congress of Rock Creek Park, as a wild-land park, in Washington, D.C., in 1890, and to enactment of the Antiquities Act of 1906. Under this act many national monuments were established by executive order by President Theodore Roosevelt and subsequent presidents. All these actions attest to the influence of a social and political elite which had important access and influence in the nation's capital in specific cases, but not the political power of a political movement.

Despite his close personal and political association with Gifford Pinchot, who became the principal leader of the conservation movement, Theodore Roosevelt was also responsive to preservationist concerns. Some other important political figures, such as William Kent (1864–1928), a wealthy congressman from California, found no difficulty in favoring both conservation policies and preservation. He donated Muir Woods in Marin County, California, to the Department of the Interior to be a national monument. He also was on the side of the conservationists in the Hetch Hetchy controversy. This controversy involved the proposed construction of a water and power dam on the border of the recently enlarged Yosemite National Park, with the reservoir occupying much park land.

The 1913 defeat in the Hetch Hetchy controversy of the preservationists led by John Muir, president of the Sierra Club (founded in 1892), by conservationist forces including Gifford Pinchot is testimony to their relative impotence in the face of the then potent conservation movement. Indicative also is acceptance by preservationists of legislation establishing Rocky Mountain National Park in 1915 and Grand Canyon National Park in 1919, to the effect that nothing in the acts shall preclude Congress from authorizing the construction of a dam in either park.

The only early successful preservationist actions, over the objections of the conservationists, were the establishment of the National Park Service in 1916 and subsequent transfer of public land, piece by piece, particularly that of the Forest Service, to the National Park Service (Ise, 1961; Albright, 1985). It was not until preservationists in the 1950s, led by David Brower, the executive head of the Sierra Club, were able to remove the proposed Echo Park Dam in Dinosaur National Monument from the Colorado Water Storage Project bill (enacted in 1956) that preservationists had their first truly national victory over conservationists (Stratton and Sirotkin, 1959).

This victory led to nationalization of, and greatly increased membership in, the Sierra Club. Prior to the enlargement of the geographic scope and membership of the Sierra Club beyond the confines of California, the National Parks Association, founded in 1919 at the initiative of the director of the National Park Service, was the principal national interest group in support of the Service. Its membership, largely drawn from economic, social, and educational elites, exerted effective, but largely unobtrusive, influence upon the executive branch and the Congress.

In the 1940s and 1950s there were indications (which can now be identified) that a broader political concern was afoot in the land. In 1946 during the Truman administration and in 1956 during the Eisenhower administration, the Congress overrode presidential vetoes of the first federal water pollution acts since the Refuse Act of 1899 and an act of 1924 (repealed in 1970) relating to oil pollution of coastal waters. In 1956, at the initiative of the professional director of the National Park Service, Conrad Wirth, the Eisenhower administration and the Congress, through substantially increased appropriations, supported Mission 66, a badly needed program of maintenance, reconstruction, and development of park roads and facilities which had been neglected since the beginning of World War II. At the initiative of an assistant director of the Bureau of Sports Fishing and Wildlife, James McBroom, the Eisenhower administration supported and the Congress enacted the Fish and Wildlife Coordination Act of 1958, which authorized for the first time the inclusion of fish and wildlife enhancement features in water resource development projects; previously, in 1934 and 1946, the Congress had authorized the inclusion of measures to mitigate damage (e.g., fish ladders for migratory fish). Also in 1958, at the initiative of the conservation director of the Izaak Walton League, Joe Penfold, the Congress provided for the establishment, with the concurrence of the Eisenhower administration, of the Outdoor Recreation Resources Review Commission (ORRRC), which reported in 1962 (ORRRC Report, 1962). In March 1961 Governor Gaylord Nelson of Wisconsin proposed "Wisconsin's Ten Year Resource Development and Outdoor Recreation Program," which included purchase of park lands and wetlands, to be paid for by a one-cent tax on a package of cigarettes. California, New York, and Hawaii were also moving in the same direction (Jordahl, 1986). In January 1961 the Senate Select Committee on National Water Resources, in the context of recommending a revitalized water resources development program, recommended flood plain regulation as an alternative to flood control dams (Senate Select Committee, January 1961).

Attributed to President Taft is the statement: "A great many people are in favor of conservation, no matter what it means" (Mason, 1958:160). Today many environmental groups symbolize their policy views by the term *conservation*. However, in the first half of this century the water resources development programs of the U.S. Bureau of Reclamation and the Army Corps of Engineers, which are an anathema for most environmentalists today, came under the rubric of conservation (Caulfield, 1984). In fact, the first use of the term in the United States related to the damming of spring run-off to provide irrigation water in the summer and early fall (Hays, 1959). There appears to be no interest on the part of political actors to correct this semantic confusion. For purposes of this analysis, the term *conservation* will be used only in reference to the ideology and basic values of the conservation movement as that ideology and those values were understood until the 1960s.

A basic idea that both the conservation movement and the environmental movement can be said to have in common is a concern with achieving and maintaining a long-term sustainable relationship between man and his environment on this Earth. According to Dr. Nicholas Georgescu-Roegen, the law of entropy decrees that Earth will become a dead planet (Georgescu-Roegen, 1971). Few, if any, adherents of either movement are preoccupied with such demise because it is thought to be too far into the future to be of practical concern. And, when former secretary of the interior James Watt suggested that "running out of resources" need not be a concern because the biblical Armageddon (i.e., the end of human history) will come soon enough to make such concern irrelevant, few people, if any, would appear to have taken him seriously.

Now that we have briefly discussed the early context for the conservation and environmental movements, the actual creation of these movements and their resulting policy outputs will be analyzed.

The Conservation Movement, 1910–1963

The philosophical ideas of W. J. McGee, a man of wide learning in the employ of the U.S. Geological Survey, are said to be the ideological foundation of the conservation movement. McGee believed that: "The American Revolution was fought for liberty; the American Constitution was framed for Equality; yet that third of the trinity without which Union is not made perfect—Fraternity—has not been established: full brotherhood among men and generations has not yet come." The mission of conservation, as he saw it, was to bring about "Fraternity" (McGee, 1911). Constraint in the use of natural resources was to be the means to this common good. Liberty he equated apparently with private economic development. His own progressivist spirit he equated apparently with equality. These three elements can be viewed as the three principal policy thrusts of the conservation movement (Caulfield, 1959).

McGee, Gifford Pinchot, John Wesley Powell, Frederick Newell, and others were part of the scientific elite who came into the federal government in the late nineteenth century and were concerned about natural resources. Several were on the staff of the U.S. Geological Survey, which was founded in 1879. They were early members of the Cosmos Club in Washington, D.C., which was founded in 1878. They can be said to have formulated four basic doctrines for what was to become the conservation movement:

(1) *Conservation is not the locking up of resources; it is their development and wise use.* By asserting that conservation favored "development," and not "locking up" of resources, the founders distinguished themselves politically from John Muir and other preservationists who sought to preserve resources in their natural state. The founders wanted to align themselves with the nation's great preoccupation with economic development. Guided by the criterion of "wise use," development should be constrained by the scientific management concept of "sustained yield" of renewable resources (i.e., forest, fish, wildlife, hydroelectric power, and water generally) and by avoidance of "waste" of nonrenewable resources (i.e., oil, natural gas, coal, and other minerals).

(2) *Conservation is the greatest good, for the greatest number, for the longest time.* The object of all legislation should be the "greatest happiness of the greatest number," according to Jeremy Bentham, the well-known English

utilitarian philosopher. The founders of the conservation movement apparently reformulated Bentham's statement and then added "for the longest time." By this addition, intergenerational concerns were asserted consistent with the old agricultural concept of "husbandry" and the biblical concept of "stewardship." The possibilities of the nation's "running-out" of resources in the future was a major concern.

The promotion of egalitarianism was apparently meant to be conveyed by "the greatest number." Although Bentham was brought up as a Tory, his intellect and experience made him a democrat. The founders of the conservation movement were anti-monopolists, as evidenced by President Theodore Roosevelt's veto of legislation passed by the Congress to "give away" valuable hydroelectric development rights to private interest (King, 1959). Doctrinal egalitarianism was a response to the progressive/populist political forces that were strong in the first half of this century with respect to natural resources policy. Policies included in the Water Power Act of 1920, which regulated private and nonfederal public development of hydroelectric power, reflected the strong influence of progressive/populist views. The founding fathers of the conservation movement also supported the concept of the "family farm" via the 160-acre rule of the Reclamation Act of 1902, which stemmed from the Homestead Act of 1862 and Jefferson's idealization of the yeoman farmer. They also supported restriction of the size and numbers of leases per state that any leasee of federal public land could have under the Mineral Leasing Act of 1920.

(3) *The federal public lands belong to all the people.* Conservationists and environmentalists have utilized this doctrinal statement to justify federal regulation, management, and control as against contrary assertions on behalf of the western states, like that around 1980 by the Sagebrush Rebellion (Cawley, 1981). "All the people" has been interpreted by many secretaries of the interior and agriculture to mean that easterners have, in effect, a property right in the western public lands such that western forests, wildlife, beauty, recreational values, etc. should be protected and available to all the nation's people. Thus most federal officials have long seen themselves as national protectors of this right.

(4) *Comprehensive, multiple-purpose river basin planning and development should be utilized with respect to the nation's water resources.* During Lincoln's administration the federal government assumed unequivocal authority (later confirmed by the Supreme Court) to finance, plan, construct, operate, and

maintain inland navigation projects (Caulfield, 1984). These projects carried out by the Army Corps of Engineers received increasing appropriations through the years, but by the 1890s they were seen by political opponents as "pork barrel." In other words, they were not seen as a means for providing inland water transportation and the promotion of economic development of the West as argued by their proponents. In the latter half of the nineteenth century and during much of this century the proponents of inland navigation projects viewed them as competition to the railroads and thus would force freight rates downward.

John Wesley Powell in his *Report on the Lands of the Arid Regions of the United States* (1879) proposed federal planning and development of irrigation projects in the arid and semi-arid West as a means toward its further settlement and economic development. But he also saw, as did Frederick Newell and other colleagues in what became the U.S. Geological Survey, the need for careful technical study, selection, and development of projects by scientists and engineers. Federal financial support would be needed. The Reclamation Act of 1902, signed by Theodore Roosevelt soon after he became president, was the result of their activist professional support in coalition with political forces favoring irrigation as a basic means of economic development and settlement of the arid West and of extension of the "family farm" policy further west.

In contrast to these "single purpose" approaches (i.e., navigation and irrigation) to water resources development, the founders of the conservation movement formulated the doctrine of comprehensive, multiple-purpose river basin planning development (Caulfield, 1984). The first comprehensive river basin plan was undertaken on the Colorado River by E. C. LaRue of the U.S. Geological Survey and completed in 1918. But it was not until 1927 that the Army Corps of Engineers was authorized to prepare comprehensive multiple-purpose river basin plans for all the major river basins of the nation. This planning authorization led to most of the great river basin development authorizations of the 1930s to the 1960s.

Apparently political preoccupation with water resources (evidenced in the vetoes of private hydroelectric power development legislation, Roosevelt's celebrated trip down the Mississippi River publicizing the need for restoration of political support for waterways transportation, and the ongoing promotion of western irrigation development) led to the first major document setting forth the concerns and doctrines of the founders of the conservation movement—the Inland Waterways Report of 1907. The White House Governor's Conference on Natural Resources and its report of 1908, together with the report in 1909 of the National Conservation Commission with Pinchot as chairman, followed.

The preparation of these documents enabled the founders of the conservation movement to identify and publicize public policy problems (e.g., the need for public and private forest management, comprehensive multiple-purpose river basin development, etc.) and to propose bold executive and legislative solutions with which the president became identified. Pinchot and his colleagues participated in the deliberations and provided professional documentation and report drafts.

Gifford Pinchot, a graduate of Yale University who studied forestry at Nancy in France and a member of the social and political elite of the Republican party, was a link between the intellectual and scientific founders of the conservation movement and President Theodore Roosevelt. He was a member of the president's "Kitchen Cabinet" despite his subordinate position in the Department of Agriculture (Fausold, 1961). Pinchot, like the other founders of the movement, was interested not only in development of doctrine and writing reports identifying public policy problems and recommending action, but in taking action, too.

He became head of the U.S. Forest Service within the Department of Agriculture when jurisdiction over the forest reserves of the federal public domain were transferred from Interior to Agriculture in 1905. His intellectual leadership firmly established the professional character, administrative approach, and operating techniques of the Service until his departure in 1910.

Pinchot became chairman of the National Conservation Commission in 1908, in addition to being chief of the U.S. Forest Service. This commission initiated studies and documentation of concerns for the "running-out" of nonrenewable resources. Of particular concern was what was perceived to be the inevitable, eventual "running-out" of nonrenewable energy supplies—petroleum, natural gas, and coal. This farseeing scientific perception led the early conservationists to place great emphasis upon development of hydroelectric power, the only alternative energy resource, so far as they knew, to nonrenewable energy resources. And this perception, in coalition with political forces favoring development per se and progressive/populist concerns, led to the great emphasis upon regulated hydroelectric power development via the Water Power Act of 1920. Later U.S. Senator George Norris, who viewed himself as a conservationist but not a "regulationist," promoted egalitarianism through "cheap power" via the Tennessee Valley Authority, other federal public power developments, and cooperative rural electrification (Caulfield, 1959).

The fight between Pinchot and Secretary of the Interior Ballinger over the acquisition by several corporations of Alaskan coal lands, together with the Hetch Hetchy controversy and other issues, gave the conservation ethic prominence and increasing public support. When Pinchot was dismissed from the Taft administration in 1910, he perceived that Taft was abandoning the principles of conservation. He then became president of the National Conservation Association, seeking to promote conservation policies. Both prior to and after his departure from the Forest Service, Pinchot and his professional colleagues were active in promoting their ideology and specific policy proposals in irrigation congresses, conservation congresses, the American Forestry Association, and through any other means of enhancing elite and popular support (Hays, 1959). In 1909, at the suggestion of Pinchot, Roosevelt was host at the White House to a North American Conservation Conference. A World Conservation Conference was to be held at The Hague, but President Taft vetoed the idea (Smith, 1966).

Public support of conservation was furthered too by the creation of state conservation commissions. This idea was a recommendation of the governor's conference in 1908 and many states created such commissions.

Later Gifford Pinchot was the head of forestry in Pennsylvania and a Republican governor for two terms. As governor he sponsored a report on "giant power," promoting mine-mouth electric power production for interstate transmission. Other conservationists, such as Leland Olds, envisioned a comprehensive, integrated national power grid. Until Pinchot died in 1946 he was very active in promoting conservation causes (Pinchot, 1947). More than any other leader he was the symbolic and principal leader of the conservation movement. Nevertheless, President Roosevelt, as well as Secretary of the Interior James R. Garfield (1907–1909), and his immediate predecessor Ethan Allen Hitchcock, and others, provided important political leadership.

In seeking converts, conservation leaders published books and articles to further their cause. For example: *The Fight for Conservation* (Pinchot, 1910), "Water as a Resource" (McGee, 1909), "The Conservation of Natural Resources" (McGee, 1911), and *The Conservation of Natural Resources in the United States* (Van Hise, 1910).

Public confrontation and controversy assured that the public generally (not just the professionals) became aware of natural resource problems and began taking sides on issues involved in their solution. Vetoes by President Roosevelt of congressional actions granting authority to private interests to construct hydroelectric facilities, as mentioned previously, gave early public notice that something new was under way. U.S. Forest Service policies aroused antagonism among western interests (Richardson, 1958). The celebrated Hetch Hetchy controversy pitting Muir against Pinchot gave Pinchot a clear victory. In the Ballinger-Pinchot controversy Pinchot was able to wear the "white hat" and put the "black hat" on Secretary of the Interior Ballinger, who was appointed by President Taft to succeed Secretary Garfield. These and other confrontations and controversies apparently helped to develop widespread elite and popular acclaim for conservation doctrines and policies.

It is difficult to pinpoint when the conservation movement had become a politically powerful reality. Most historians and other political scientists suggest that this occurred undoubtedly before 1920 and possibly before 1910 (Bates, 1957; Hays, 1959; McConnell, 1954).

Policy outputs through 1920 were of two types. Executive branch policies deemed to have congressional authorization were supported often (but not always) by congressional appropriations, for example, policy development in the U.S. Forest Service under Pinchot's leadership. New legislative authorizations were the second type. The Forest Transfer Act of 1905 as well as early legislation dealing with fish and wildlife and creation of the Bureau of Mines are examples. But major legislative outputs that clearly reflect the ideology of the conservative movement did not occur until after World War I, in 1920: the Water Power Act and the Mineral Leasing Act. These acts clearly reflect McGee's political philosophy and the ideology of the conservation movement. Both presuppose a strong interest in private economic development. But also they provided policy constraints aimed at long-term effective and efficient resource use and protection of the public against monopoly.

From 1920 until the early 1960s the basic policy paradigm of the conservation movement was dominant. This was manifest in the thinking of the professionals in the resources agencies (except the National Park Service), in the statements and speeches of political officials, and in the basic justifications for legislated policy outputs and appropriations. Nevertheless, resources concerns had their ups and downs; and, in a few instances, new doctrine was grafted onto the old.

In the 1930s the economic depression provided added strength to the undertaking of conservation measures. The Tennessee Valley Authority, which had been vetoed twice in the 1920s, was authorized early in the administration of President Franklin D. Roosevelt (King, 1959; Smith, 1966). With broad acceptance of conservation doctrine, the major political problem during the Depression was obtaining large appropriations for water resource developments of the Army Corps of Engineers in the Bureau of Reclamation and for forest management improvements, etc. In 1935 a new conservation program stemming from advances in soil science was authorized with creation of the Soil Conservation Service in the Department of Agriculture (Morgan, 1965). The most widely and favorably remembered program for the 1930s is the Civil Conservation Corps, the CCC. The early expectation of a depression after World War II also gave strong support for conservation programs.

The Eisenhower administration upheld conservation doctrine; but like Pinchot earlier, it was ideologically against federal public power. It favored licensing and regulation of nonfederal projects under the Water Power Act of 1920 (Blue Book, 1955). Nevertheless, possibly because of the nearness of his reelection campaign, President Eisenhower signed on April 11, 1956, the Colorado River Storage Project Act, which authorized not only substantial additional federal public power but also irrigation development subsidized by electric power revenues. Both Republicans and Democrats in the West have supported strongly this tie between irrigation and power since 1906.

The Environmental Movement, 1964 to the Present

President Kennedy followed up on his State of the Union message in January 1961 with some twenty special messages; one of the first was his "Special Message to the Congress on Natural Resources," February 23, 1961. From the first days of the Kennedy administration, Secretary of the Interior Stewart L. Udall was given the lead role in the development of natural resources policy. He, together with Secretary of Agriculture Orville Freeman, Elmer Staats (the career deputy director of the Bureau of the Budget who long had had a major role in natural resources policy), and their staffs (including the author)[1] made substantial input into preparation of the message by Theodore Sorenson, the president's chief of staff and major speech writer.

In contrast to the founding fathers of the conservation movement, those who initiated policies which led to the environmental movement were largely total strangers when they began to work together in January 1961. They were not members of a professional group or "shadow cabinet" that possessed a common intellectual perspective and common policy positions to implement when opportunity was afforded. Secretary Udall had a general vision of where he wanted to go. He contributed general direction to his staff as well as language embodying specific proposals. Udall relished the opportunity for leadership and his staff was generally supportive of his view.[2]

In the special message great stress was put upon the "conservation and development" of natural resources. United States population was estimated to be 300 million by the year 2000–a doubling in forty years. Great supplies of "farm products, timber, water, fuels, energy and opportunities for outdoor recreation" were projected to be needed. Although "running out" of resources was not predicted, the harvesting of supplies of "high-grade timber more rapidly than the development of new growth, the loss of fertile topsoil, and exhaustion of our minerals at increasing rates" was projected. The president also noted in the introductory paragraphs that "the Nation's remaining undeveloped areas of great natural beauty [were] being rapidly preempted for other uses." Nevertheless, the special message at the outset clearly emphasized that "wise investments in a resource program today will return vast dividends tomorrow" and that "we cannot now ignore [the country's] needs for future development." The introductory paragraphs were concluded by tying the administration's resource program to "the progressive principles of national leadership first forged by Pinchot and Theodore Roosevelt."

Among all the particular natural resources, water resources were discussed first because of their political importance among Democrats. The "no new starts policy" which the Democrats in the 1950s had pinned upon the Eisenhower administration was rejected. Kennedy strongly supported federal hydroelectric power development and said the administration would be guided by four "basic principles" of federal public power marketing traditionally supported by Democrats. In response to the bipartisan report of a Senate select committee on national water resources of January 1961, the president accepted the goal to develop a new set of comprehensive river basin plans by 1970 for all the major rivers of the nation; he urged Congress to authorize the establishment of river basin planning commissions; and he strongly endorsed research on saline and brackish water conversion.

The message then urged specific measures for strengthening federal involvement in water pollution control and noted the need for a "Federal air pollution program now." Pinchot and his followers had not perceived water and air pollution as problems. Both Presidents Truman and Eisenhower, as noted above, had vetoed federal water pollution control legislation, which was passed over their vetoes. Here, President Kennedy was breaking new ground for the executive branch.

With respect to public forests and lands, his recommendations were within the traditional ideology of the conservation movement. With respect to ocean resources, he urged development of offshore crude oil, natural gas, and mineral deposits and conservation of fishery resources. And he said he would send to the Congress a "national program of oceanography."

Finally, he came to "recreation," the section which most clearly indicated initial policy thrusts consistent with the concerns of what became the environmental movement. Here, he:

(1) *Urged the Congress to enact a wilderness bill.* The Wilderness Society had been pushing strongly for wilderness legislation in the 1950s. But the Eisenhower administration, together with the U.S. Forest Service and the National Park Service, had been opposed.

(2) *Urged the Congress to establish seashore and shoreline areas such as Cape Cod, Padre Island, and Point Reyes to improve both the quality and quantity of public recreation opportunities.* Since World War II no new national parks had been established except the Grand Teton and Virgin Islands National Parks in the 1950s. These were made possible only because of gifts from the Rockefeller family.

(3) *Instructed the secretary of the interior to take the lead in:* (a) *formulating a comprehensive federal recreation lands program;* (b) *surveying where additional national parks, forest, and seashores should be proposed;* (c) *ensuring that sufficient land be acquired around federally financed reservoirs for recreation purposes;* and (d) *establishing a long-range program for planning and providing open spaces for recreational facilities in urban areas.* This instruction to the secretary of the interior, as will be made clear below, was the most important part of the special message, leading to transformation of preservationism into environmentalism and to enactment of much legislation in the 1960s and 1970s. The report of the Outdoor Recreation Resources Review Commission (ORRRC), chaired by Laurence Rockefeller, became public in 1962 and gave great visibility to, and support for, the substance of this part of the special message.

(4) *Directed the secretary of the interior to take the lead in ending interagency conflicts and in developing a long-range wildlife conservation program.* The presi-

dent hoped, he said, that fish and wildlife opportunities could be expanded by overcoming such conflicts as: federally supported drainage of wetlands for agricultural purposes while elsewhere purchasing lands for water fowl refuges; encouraging use of chemical pesticides that may harm the songbirds and game fowl whose preservation is encouraged by another agency; and settlement of responsibility for watershed and antipollution programs vital to fish and wildlife opportunities. The reference here to pesticides and other pollution, of course, anticipated the problems so vividly portrayed in *Silent Spring,* by Rachel Carson, published in 1962.

Obviously, President Kennedy's first message in this field did not make a clear ideological break with the doctrines of the conservation movement. In the early parts, which drew the most important, immediate, political attention, the message was a reaffirmation of traditional, largely bipartisan conservation ideas; but the Democratic party's traditional adherence to federal public power policy was made clear. Particularly toward the end, however, preservationist values became manifest and were translated into marching orders, particularly to the secretary of the interior (Schlesinger, 1965).

Secretary Udall lost no time in carrying out these orders. Even before the message was delivered he began a series of night meetings with staff to develop what he took to be, strategically, the most significant part of his instructions: to initiate the creation of new national parks and seashores. Despite the many politically significant policy areas with which he had to be concerned at the outset of his tenure in office, only two areas involved regular night meetings with staff to which he devoted his undivided attention: Indian affairs and national parks/seashores. Early in these meetings, he stated that his objective was to double the acreage of the National Park Service in eight years! Clearly he sought to build upon the long preservationist tradition.

The main problem in achieving his objective, particularly if parks and seashores in the East were to be established, was to obtain an adequate and secure source of public funds to buy the necessary lands. He recognized that America's men of wealth could no longer be expected to provide the necessary funds, as they had in the past. He had no doubt that many high-quality areas could be identified by the National Park Service to fulfill his objective. Having been in the Congress when the trust fund for interstate highways was authorized, he proposed a land conservation fund act. His first idea for dedicated revenues was revenue from the sale of "bumper stickers" entitling the car and its occupants to visit all national park areas. A meeting with Wisconsin's

Governor Nelson suggested the possibility of a national cigarette tax with proceeds dedicated to the fund (Stoddard, 1985). But this idea was quickly dismissed as politically impracticable at the national level because of opposition from tobacco production interests. A national tax on "soft drinks" was also considered and rejected. Other suggested sources were: proceeds from the sale of federal surplus real property, tax receipts from the sale of gas and oil used by recreational motor boats, and a tax on new recreational boats—all of which, together with the bumper sticker proposal, were included in the first bill sent to the Congress for consideration.

Foreseeing great political difficulties if the U.S. Forest Service were left out of his proposal, he invited the Forest Service to become a beneficiary of the proposed legislation. Thus he avoided the need for bargaining in subsequent policy processes within the executive branch. The fund would be utilized to purchase private "inholdings" within national forest boundaries for recreational purposes.

By this time the ORRRC report had been published with its heavy emphasis upon the need for state and local parks in contrast to its lesser emphasis upon the need for more federal areas. Nevertheless, Secretary Udall obtained White House clearance to submit to Congress his proposed land conservation fund act with provision only for federal land acquisition.

Congressional hearings made clear that the title of the bill had to be changed to Land and Water Conservation Fund Act; a legislator had wondered why the taxes related to recreational boats if the bill was just for "land acquisition." Also, it was made clear that the boat builders' lobby would be too tough to deal with and that state and local park land acquisition had to be added. With these and other bargains struck, plus proposed dedication of a portion of revenues from offshore oil and gas development to the fund, the proposal became technically ready within the executive branch for further congressional consideration. But the proposal was not politically ripe for congressional action. To be sure, the Sierra Club, the Izaak Walton League, the National Parks Association, and the National Wildlife Federation (with the most members of all) were strongly behind the revised proposal in public statements and, indirectly, through lobbying. However, more public understanding and popular support was believed to be needed.

Beginning with the year 1964, Secretary Udall converted the traditional, stodgy annual report of the Department of the Interior into a "new type of 'annual report' which combined eloquent graphics, i.e., color photography, a consistent and dynamic conservation philosophy and details of the advance of the Department" (Udall, 1968a). By popular demand, widespread distribution was achieved. He gave speeches almost every week throughout the country developing support. With the fund act proposal now broadened to include state and local parks, public open space, and greenbelt lands, he often emphasized urgency for action by the headline-making statement: "We have only fifteen more years before the bulldozers will destroy all the Nation's unspoiled lands!" In addition, he wrote *The Quiet Crisis,* which was published in 1963.

The object of the book, he said, was "to tell the land story of the American earth" and the changing attitudes of those who have used it—from American Indians to devotees of the metropolis. In it he revealed his own reverence for the land, for the beauty of natural areas, and for the ethical importance of respect for the land. Although his ideology and values are in the tradition of Thoreau, Muir, Aldo Leopold, Olmsted Sr. and Jr., and other preservationists, he sought a preservation-of-the-environment program that could somehow be reconciled with realities of the latter half of the twentieth century. The book also reflects understanding of ecology as in *Man and Nature* by George Perkins Marsh, and his admiration of the earlier aggressive leadership of Gifford Pinchot.

The Quiet Crisis, very favorably reviewed, was on the *New York Times* best-seller list for a good many weeks. Not only the *New York Times* and the *Washington Post,* but other papers throughout the country began writing very favorable editorials. Udall's mail indicated that a broad public groundswell in sympathy with his basic values and ideas was developing. Noticeably absent, however, was sufficient activity and enthusiasm on behalf of the proposed Land and Water Conservation Fund Act by the directors of state and local parks. In 1963 the Committee to Enact the ORRRC Report (a private activity financed by Laurence Rockefeller) was formed, with Frank Gregg who resigned from the secretary's staff to become staff director. The committee's mission was to stimulate political interest and the support of state and local park officials for passage of the act, which it did.

On September 4, 1964, President Johnson signed both the Land and Water Conservation Fund Act and the Wilderness Act into law. Thus two initial building blocks of environmental action, in response to a developing environmental movement, were in place.[3] The Eighty-eighth Congress, from January 9, 1963, to October 3, 1964, was labeled the "conservation Congress" (Baker, 1985).

Much, but not all, energy was devoted to the formulation and politics of passage of these basic policy and instrumental acts. Cape Cod National Seashore, which President Kennedy had promoted as a senator, was established in 1961; and strengthening amendments to the Water Pollution Control Act were enacted, as was legislation authorizing the purchase of wetlands in advance of the accumulation of duck stamp receipts. Administratively, in the early 1960s the membership of the National Advisory Board Council and of the state boards, which advised on management of public domain lands, was broadened to better reflect multiple interests. As recommended by ORRRC, the Bureau of Outdoor Recreation (which would administer the fund when established) was created by Secretary Udall within the Department of the Interior in 1962. Also Udall early saw the need to nationalize the clientele of the Department of the Interior by taking on the difficult political task in 1961 of reconciling federal and state interests with respect to the terms of the Federal-State Delaware River Basin Compact. This was politically necessary, he felt, to obtain authorization of a national recreation area to be administered by the National Park Service in the area of the Delaware Water Gap.

Government-wide multiobjective planning standards and procedures for water and related land resources were established in 1962. Preservation of wild rivers, open space, and greenbelts were officially recognized for the first time as legitimate objectives of water resources planning and use. Also reservoir recreation was officially recognized for the first time as a legitimate purpose of water resources development (U.S. Water Resources Council, ad hoc, 1962). An early water resource dilemma (February 1964) for Secretary Udall was contained in the Pacific Southwest Water Plan prepared by the Bureau of Reclamation. It involved a choice between, on the one hand, the proposed Marble and Bridge Canyon dams on the Colorado River as "cash registers" for power revenues necessary to subsidize the Central Arizona Project (to which he had long been committed as a politician from Arizona) and, on the other hand, keeping the Colorado wild between Lake Powell and Lake Meade, with Grand Canyon National Park in the middle. This difficult choice was resolved finally by a later plan to help finance the Mohave steam-electric power plant with federal investment to provide the necessary subsidizing power revenues.

Planning was initiated, and the political strategy and tactics were developed, in the early 1960s, for what would become the Wild and Scenic Rivers Act of 1968 (Craighead, 1963). Political acceptability was tested by proposal of an Ozark National Scenic River which was authorized in 1964. This authorization stemmed, interestingly, from wild river proposals in the interdepartmental comprehensive plan for the Arkansas, White, and Red River basins completed in the early 1950s. Earlier, the concept of wild rivers was promoted and realized by Aldo Leopold in Wisconsin (Cogan, 1982). During the 1950s the National Park Service had quietly cultivated substantial support within Missouri and Arkansas for such an authorization.

In 1961 Secretary Udall instructed the Fish and Wildlife Service to draft an endangered species act. Udall had become a friend of Rachel Carson, who was then a civil servant on the public affairs staff of the Service; and he had learned of her ecological thinking involving the destructive effects of DDT and other pesticides on both humans and wildlife. His instruction to the Service was consistent with President Kennedy's instructions in his special message of February 1961 (Udall, 1985). Within the Service, however, his instruction presented a constitutional and political problem with respect to federal authority vis-à-vis the states. Resident fish and game, it had long been accepted, were the property and under the management of the states. Many resident populations might be determined to be endangered. Only the treaty and commerce powers provided a clear constitutional base for the assertion of federal authority, as in the cases of migratory birds and anadromous fish, respectively. Accordingly, the Endangered Species Act of 1966 and 1969 authorized only limited federal roles in accord with these two powers. It was not until 1973, when the environmental movement was at its peak in terms of public support, that much greater federal authority was asserted in proposed legislation. The Endangered Species Act of 1973 was found later to be constitutional by the Supreme Court.

A draft ecological research and survey act was drafted and considered in 1964 within the Department of the Interior. It was dropped from what was becoming a very crowded legislative agenda because there was information that the Ecological Society of America would not support such a bill. The top officers of the society indicated that the society was only interested in basic scientific research, not research and surveys aimed at applied problems.

President Kennedy and then President Johnson sent messages to Congress each year during the 1960s increasingly highlighting values and concerns which were to become identified in the press as those of the environmental movement. These messages also contained, of course, specific recommendations to the Congress for legislative measures consistent with those values and concerns. Less and less did the messages feature the more traditional concepts and values of the conservation movement (Caulfield, 1964).

President Johnson on February 8, 1965, after his election to the presidency in his own name, sent a special message to the Congress on conservation and natural beauty.[4] This message clearly indicates the transformation in philosophy and practical political concerns which had occurred since 1961. Consider the opening sentences: "For centuries Americans have drawn strength and inspiration from the beauty of our country. It would be a neglectful generation indeed, indifferent alike to the judgment of history and the command of principle, which failed to preserve and extend such a heritage for its descendants." The president then went on to observe that "a growing population is swallowing up areas of natural beauty with the demands for living space" and that "modern technology which has added much to our lives can also have a darker side. Its uncontrolled waste products are menacing the world we live in, our enjoyment and our health. The air we breathe, our water, our soil and wildlife are being blighted by . . . poisons and chemicals. . . . The skeletons of discarded cars litter the countryside. The same society which receives the rewards of technology, must, as a cooperating whole, take responsibility for control." He then called for a new conservation: "Our conservation must not be the classic conservation of protection and development, but a creative conservation of restoration and innovation. Its concern is not with nature alone, but with the total relation between man and the world around him. Its object is not just man's welfare but the dignity of man's spirit."

Consistent with this general philosophy Johnson recommended many specific proposals to the Congress. Included were proposed authorization of twelve specific national seashore, lakeshore, and recreation areas; highway beautification proposals banning billboards and screening unsightly, beauty-destroying junkyards; bills to establish a national wild rivers system and eventually a national system of trails; strong air, water, and solid waste pollution legislation and legislation to strengthen controls on pesticides and toxic chemicals. Finally, he announced planning for a national center for environmental health and a White House conference on natural beauty to be chaired by Laurence Rockefeller.

The White House Conference on Natural Beauty was held in May 1965, attended largely by members of the nation's political, social, aesthetic, architectural, and intellectual elites. Although identified as relating to "natural" beauty, the conference actually included many "unnatural" topics: landscape reclamation, urban waterfront renewal, highway beautification, etc. Papers were given and the proceedings published (White House Conference, 1965).

Greater popular attention was given to Mrs. Johnson's identification with and promotion of beauty, natural and otherwise. The president made clear that highway beautification, including screening of junkyards, was her idea. Mrs. Johnson traveled all over the country giving talks and dedicating urban flower gardens, developed often with the financial support of Mrs. Albert D. Lasker of New York City. The flower gardens of Washington, D.C., itself took on a new character and abundance. Secretary Udall was highly supportive of Mrs. Johnson's activities, which were helping to develop a popular, widespread environmental movement; specifically, he lent professional and other staff to help her. Also, Mrs. Johnson and Secretary Udall took well-publicized trips to national parks and Indian reservations, including rubber rafting trips in Grand Teton and Big Bend national parks, which provided important "photo opportunities."

On the legislative front, the many prior significant actions were to be outdone in 1965 and later years. The Water Quality Act of 1965 established the Federal Water Pollution Control Administration (FWPCA), separate from the U.S. Public Health Service. The strong legislative initiatives and leadership of Senator Muskie of Maine and Congressman Blatnik of Minnesota gave the federal government for the first time supervisory control of the water pollution control activities of state and local governments. The secretary of health, education, and welfare had made it clear privately within the administration that he didn't believe in strengthening the role of the federal government relating to water pollution. Several bureaucratic layers down in the U.S. Public Health Service, however, activist civil servants and public health officers strongly believed in a more dominant role. They fed information unofficially to congressional staff that enabled informed leadership to arise in Congress.

With the support of the National Wildlife Federation and other environmental interest groups, the FWPCA was transferred in early 1966 to the supervision of the secretary of the interior to reinforce the idea that water pollution control was not just to protect human health, but also to protect the environment, particularly fish and wildlife. With passage of the Clean Water Restoration Act of 1966, funds authorized for grants to municipalities for sewerage cleanup were substantially increased. Also, restrictions were removed on the size of cities that could receive grants. Not just small towns and cities, but large cities, too, could qualify for grants.

The Clean Air Act of 1965 and the Air Quality Act of 1967 reflected the changing perception of the air quality problem from a local problem toward a comprehensive national problem. They provided a stronger federal statutory basis for cleaning the air. Also initial endangered species acts, as noted above, were passed in 1966 and 1969.

Many of the national park, seashore, lakeshore, and recreation-area proposals of the executive branch were authorized by the Congress in the 1960s. With the Land and Water Conservation Fund Act in operation, and with strong support to increase its funds from offshore oil revenues, the principal concerns of the Congress were the worthiness of an area for inclusion in the national park system and the accommodation of boundaries, if feasible, to local-interest concerns. In this context it also should be noted that the Forest Service was receiving some $30 million per year or more from the fund to purchase private inholdings within the borders of national forests for recreation purposes. Previous to the fund, the Forest Service had only some $200,000 per year for all land purchases. No longer would federal provision of park, forest, and recreation lands be confined to largely western public land areas. All parts of the nation could and did benefit. Moreover, state and local park and recreation areas expanded nationally, with 60 percent of the annually available funds.

In July 1965 the Water Resources Planning Act was enacted. This act, which had been proposed initially by President Kennedy in July 1961, provided for a statutory cabinet committee called the Water Resources Council to develop policies and review comprehensive water resource plans, for federal-state river basin commissions to develop plans, and for federal grants to states to encourage them to participate in comprehensive water and related land resource planning. These institutional arrangements had the potential to enforce planning vis-à-vis the traditional construction agencies—the Army Corps of Engineers and the Bureau of Reclamation—that would give greater emphasis to fish and wildlife mitigation and enhancement, water-related reservoir recreation, provision for wild and scenic rivers, and upstream watershed projects of the Soil Conservation Service. The act was strongly supported by the Department of the Interior (despite opposition within the Bureau of Reclamation) and by the Department of Agriculture. The League of Women Voters, the National Wildlife Federation, the Izaak Walton League, and other environmental advocacy groups supported the legislation. The Army Corps of Engineers was not opposed to the legislation because the Corps saw the act's formal institutional arrangements as a defense against any future proposals to reorganize the "civil works program" out of the Army Corps of Engineers. The long delay in enactment was due to state ideological insistence upon unprecedented federal-state institutional arrangements and to the crowded agenda of the House and Senate interior committees.

In his last special message to the Congress on conservation on March 8, 1968, President Johnson said:

> Three years ago, I said to the Congress: ". . . beauty must not be just a holiday treat, but a part of our daily life." I return to that theme in this message, which concerns the air we breathe, the water we drink and use, the oceans that surround us, the land on which we live. These are the elements of beauty. They are the forces that shape the lives of all of us—housewife and farmer, worker and executive, whatever our income and wherever we are. They are the substance of the New Conservation. Today, the crisis of conservation is no longer quiet. Relentless and insistent, it has surged into a crisis of choice. Man—who has lived so long in harmony with nature—is now struggling to preserve its bounty. Man—who developed technology to serve him—is now racing to prevent its wastes from endangering his very existence. Our environment can sustain our growth and nourish our future. Or it can overwhelm us. History will say that in the 1960's the Nation began to take action so long delayed.

Subsequently, on October 2, 1968, in the last months of his administration, President Johnson signed into law five acts which had been long in the making, but were ready to become law: the Wild and Scenic Rivers Act, the National Trails System Act, and the acts to establish the North Cascades National Park (involving transference of Forest Service land) and the Redwood National Park (involving purchase of private timberlands at great expense).

When President-Elect Nixon indicated that Walter Hickel was to be the next secretary of the interior, Secretary Udall got hold of some of Hickel's speeches as governor of Alaska and was shocked to find that they gave great emphasis to development of natural resources and showed little, if any, concern for environmental quality. He exclaimed: "Don't they know that the name of the game has changed in these last eight years?" Governor Hickel was soon to find out in his confirmation hearings that the name of the game had truly changed. Hickel was almost crucified by members of the Senate Interior Committee. To save its nominee, the Nixon administration quickly made known that it would appoint Russell Train, the president of the Conservation Foundation and a highly regarded environmentalist, as under secretary of the interior.

The "name of the game" had changed in the eight years of the Kennedy-Johnson administration. No doctrinal concepts like "multiple-use sustained yield forestry" had been propounded. But, building largely upon the latent political force of the John Muir preservationist tradition with its ideological ties to Thoreau, Emerson, Wordsworth, and Rousseau, a political movement was created which overwhelmed traditional natural resource thinking and values (Strong, 1970). Concerns about water and air pollution and hazardous and toxic wastes threatening human survival had been expressed by Presidents Kennedy and Johnson. However, the dominant themes of the 1960s related to aesthetic and ethical values with overtones of nineteenth-century natural theology and what were taken to be the normative implications of modern ecological science. All this was summarized by the political symbol which emerged: environmental quality.

On the level of basic environmentalist values and practical policy proposals, the Nixon administration generally carried forward the programs of the 1960s and added to them. In response to the proposed National Environmental Policy Act, which had been pushed since 1967 under the leadership of Senators Jackson and Muskie upon the initiative of Professor Lynton Caldwell of Indiana University, President Nixon tried to make this legislation appear unnecessary. In May 1969 he created by executive order a council on environmental quality, as well as a citizens committee on environmental quality to be chaired by Laurance Rockefeller. Nevertheless, upon passage by Congress later in 1969 of the National Environmental Policy Act, he signed and implemented the act. Russell Train became its first chairman. After the Santa Barbara offshore oil pollution episode in 1969, Secretary Hickel himself became more and more identified with environmental values and acted accordingly (Hickel, 1972; Quarles, 1976).

In July 1969, President Nixon sent a special message to the Congress on population growth, which called for the establishment of a statutory commission, including members from the House and Senate, to study implications of such growth. Earlier, via Senate committee hearings, Senator Gruening of Alaska had identified population growth as an important environmental issue.

Secretary Udall did also in the Interior's annual report for 1965 and in a book, *1976: Agenda for Tomorrow,* which he published in 1968. Population growth was very much on the public's mind in the late 1960s as a result of documentary TV broadcasts and other media emphasis. The U.S. fertility rate substantially declined in conjunction with pro-environment public policies (*Statistical Abstract of the United States,* 1985). Officially, no domestic population policies were ever seriously considered.

In February 1970 President Nixon sent a special message to the Congress on environmental quality, the first such presidential message utilizing those symbolic words. At the outset he strongly dealt with water pollution, air pollution, and solid waste disposal—and the need for action. The message then dealt with park and recreation area proposals as well as the need for overall natural resource/environment reorganization within the executive branch. Subsequently, he sent a reorganization plan to the Congress that would create the Environmental Protection Agency to deal with water and air pollution, solid waste, and related environmental matters.

In April 1970 he established a national industrial pollution control council within the Department of Commerce, with membership drawn from the leading industrialists of the nation. About this time, also, a quality of life committee was established in the Office of Management and Budget. The committee's function was to review proposed environmental regulations to see that they gave balanced consideration to environmental quality and economic needs. The concepts "quality of life" and "environmental quality" are clearly related but have different practical implications. The former was taken by government officials to refer to both economic and environmental needs. The latter could be, and was, taken by environmentalists to imply that environmental quality was preeminent. Some "balancing" is clearly necessary, of course, and the committee was continued through the Carter administration.

The first Earth Day was celebrated on April 22, 1970, largely focusing on university campuses around the country. It was organized by Senator Gaylord Nelson of Wisconsin. He was concerned that environmental issues were not of great enough popular, social, and political concern. He had observed that in the 1968 presidential election, environmental issues were not involved (Nelson, 1985). Support of Earth Day by some environmentalists possibly was motivated by a belief that the Nixon administration would not aggressively pursue an environmental agenda. Clearly many environmentalists, young and old, believed that transformation of the environmental movement into a popular-social movement, featuring new aggressive leaders outside government, was necessary and desirable. For several years after leaving his position as secretary of the interior, Stewart Udall was in great demand as a speaker on campuses across the nation. He emphasized the importance of new ideas and encouraged a new generation of leaders to arise.

An environmental handbook, prepared for the first environmental teach-in on the first Earth Day, was widely available (DeBell, 1970). Many students and professors seemed to be thinking that they were creating the environmental movement at that time, notwithstanding the efforts that had been going on for a decade or more. To those who had been involved in earlier stages it was noticeable that the Sierra Club and other traditional environmental groups were not out front. Student concern seemed to be more with environmental protection, security, and survival than with the previous issues of environmental quality—parks, wilderness areas, etc.

Professors around the country were offering dire predictions, the most dire of which was that we might have only fifteen more years to live before the whole biosphere would collapse from pollution. Others discovered ozone pollution and condemned the proposed SST aircraft as adding to this form of pollution plus noise pollution. Poisonous methyl mercury was discovered in swordfish about the same time. Charles Reich of Yale University published *The Greening of America* (1970). Barry Commoner, a biologist at Washington University, St. Louis, published *The Closing Circle—Man, Nature, and Technology* (1971), which gave conceptual structure to the environmental problem. The counterattack by John Maddox in *The Doomsday Syndrome* (1972) gained few adherents.

If books could enlarge the numbers of adherents and supporters of the environmental movement, the many published undoubtedly did. Only a few of the more directly focused need be identified:

Paul R. Ehrlich, *The Population Bomb: Population Control or Race to Oblivion* (New York: Ballantine, 1968), followed by nineteen printings through May 1970.

Phillip O. Foss, ed., *Politics of Ecology* (Belmont, Calif.: Duxbury Press, 1972).

Huey D. Johnson, ed., *No Deposit–No Return—Man and His Environment: A View Toward Survival* (Reading, Mass.: Addison-Wesley, 1970).

John G. Mitchell and Constance L. Stallings, eds., *Ecotactics: The Sierra*

Club Handbook for Environmental Activists, with an introduction by Ralph Nader (New York: Pocket Books, April 1970).

Leslie L. Roos, Jr., ed., *The Politics of Ecosuicide* (New York: Holt, Rinehart & Winston, 1971).

James Ridgeway, *The Politics of Ecology: A Nationwide Handbook for Survival—Your Survival* (New York: E. P. Dutton, 1971).

Walt Anderson, ed., *Politics and Environment: A Reader in Ecological Crisis* (Pacific Palisades, Calif.: Goodyear, 1970).

Paul Shepard and Daniel McKinley, eds., *The Subversive Science: Essays Toward an Ecology of Man* (Boston: Houghton Mifflin, 1969).

Concern for the environment became so prominent, not only in the United States but around the world, that in 1972 a United Nation's conference on the human environment was held at Stockholm, Sweden. Russell Train was the leader of the American delegation. As a result, the UN environmental program, with headquarters in Nairobi, Kenya, with substantial financial support from the United States, was created.

From the perspective of the late 1980s, the peak in popular political power of the environmental movement would appear to have been in the early 1970s, before the "energy crisis" starting in 1973. Several political scientists and others have identified the late 1960s or the early 1970s as the beginning of the environmental movement. However, the historian Samuel P. Hays has also indicated that Earth Day was a phenomenon of the peak, not the beginning of the environmental movement: "Earth Day was as much a result as a cause. It came after a decade or more of underlying evolution in attitudes and action without which it would not have been possible" (Hays, 1982). Thus, in this author's judgment, it began around 1964.

Strong leadership in the Congress responded to the environmental movement at its peak. In the early 1970s Senator Muskie, aided by capable staff, was the national leader in air and water pollution legislation. In 1970 a clean air act was passed that did away with any vestiges of air pollution being just a local problem. Air pollution was made a matter of strong, overall, national concern. Muskie also led the Congress in passage of the Clean Water Act of 1977, which President Nixon vetoed. It passed over his veto.

The Clean Water Act is particularly important because it brought to the level of politics the ecological ideology that achievement of clean water could and should reduce the decline in species of flora and fauna. According to the then-prevailing scientific ecological theory, projected instability in the biosphere would be forestalled. To do this, the act aimed to achieve continuous enhancement of water quality and no degradation. Benefit-cost analyses were not permitted to inhibit this process, although short-run consideration of excessive cost was permitted.

Similarly, the Endangered Species Act of 1973 was premised upon ecological theory and its normative counterpart. In its passage, utilitarian arguments concerning the loss of germ plasm for possible human use in the future were emphasized by its more pragmatic proponents. But the principle underlying the legislation, as the Supreme Court recognized when it found the act constitutional, was its consistency with ecological science and related normative concern (U.S. Supreme Court, 1978).

Proposals of the Nixon administration to the Congress led to authorization of specific additional wilderness areas, national lakeshores and seashores, wild and scenic rivers, national parks, and wildlife refuges. Those involving the purchase of land were made financially feasible by an enlarged land and water conservation fund.

After much struggle to influence the Water Resources Council by representatives of water resource development interests and by environmentalists, the council adopted in September 1973 principles and standards for water resources planning. Two diverse planning objectives of equal standing were adopted: national economic development and environmental quality. Alternative plans representing each of these objectives and compromises between them were to be prepared for decision-makers.

The Nixon administration considered various reorganization schemes, for example, one which would create a department of natural resources and the environment. Two administration proposals accepted by the Congress in 1970 established the Environmental Protection Agency (EPA), and the National Oceanographic and Atmospheric Administration (NOAA). All further proposals eventually became infeasible as a result of Watergate.

The Ford administration, aiming primarily to reestablish integrity in government, took no major steps forward with respect to environmental matters. Following up, however, on initial concerns and actions of the Nixon administration, it actively dealt with energy matters stemming from the Arab oil boycott of 1973. Leaders in Congress were preoccupied with energy policy proposals that stressed energy conservation and research—solar, wind, and biomass energy, etc. They also sought development of demonstration projects with respect to oilshale, coal gasification, etc.

Intellectual thinking among many environmentalists of this period was reflected in E. F. Schumacker's book *Small Is Beautiful: Economics as if People Really Mattered* (1973). Also, the "soft energy" proposals by Amory and Hunter Lovins received widespread approval among environmentalists (Lovins, 1977).

During this politically awkward period congressional leaders took the initiative on two major pieces of legislation of great environmental concern. In 1974 the Forest Planning Act was passed to help assure that the Forest Service developed long-range forest management plans and that funds would be provided to carry them out. Later a court decision shut down timber cutting on much Forest Service land because it found that the Service only had authority for very selective cutting and then marketing of the trees so cut. Involved in this issue of general authority was the issue of "clear cutting" on national forest lands, an anathema to environmentalists. Formulation and passage of the Forest Management Act of 1976 involved a great struggle—lasting, however, only fourteen months—between environmentalist values and professional forestry values in the tradition of Gifford Pinchot. Senator Jennings Randolph, upholding environmental values, was pitted against Senators Humphrey and Talmadge. The goals of both sides were legitimized. Administrative regulation and discretion was to determine the balance to be struck.

Seeking the Democratic nomination for president in 1976 were three candidates with established environmental records—Senator Henry Jackson of Washington, Congressman Morris Udall of Arizona (brother of former secretary Stewart Udall), and Governor Jimmy Carter of Georgia. Although Senator Jackson was responsible for initiating congressional consideration of what became the National Environmental Policy Act of 1969, and was a strong supporter of environmental legislation throughout the 1960s, he was also an anti-Soviet hard-liner and a strong advocate of increasing energy supplies as the most direct and feasible strategy for overcoming the energy crisis. Congressman Morris Udall, as a member and then chairman of the House Committee on Interior and Insular Affairs, had long been identified with environmental values and concerns, and he attracted many environmentalists to his campaign. Jimmy Carter, as governor of Georgia, had studied and rejected a major proposed water project of the Army Corps of Engineers, as well as a

Carter

channelization project of the Soil Conservation Service. His environmental and anti-Washington-establishment views became known and he attracted a new generation of environmentalists to his campaign.

The contest between Ford and Carter did not focus upon environmental issues, much to the apparent consternation of Carter's environmental followers. But many of them got their satisfaction from participating on the transition team and later in junior political appointments in pertinent offices, departments, and agencies. In a kind of reverse "pork barrel" process, they compiled a list of water projects they hated and listed them in the transition team report. Later, after some official scrutiny and revision, the list constituted the famous Carter "hit list."

That President Carter was indeed an environmentalist was made fully evident in his special message to the Congress on the environment on May 23, 1977. Also in 1977, a task force report, sponsored by the Rockefeller Brothers Fund, *The Unfinished Agenda: The Citizen's Policy Guide to Environmental Issues* (Barney, 1977) was published. The members of the task force, plus the many others consulted for the publication, represented a wide array of old- and new-generation environmentalists, and the guide contained many provocative environmental policy ideas.

At the outset of his special message President Carter stated his concern for the preservation of wilderness, wildlife, and related elements of America's national heritage. Also he highlighted concern for the effects of pollution, toxic chemicals, and the "damage caused by the demand for energy." "Each of these concerns, in its own way," he said, "affects the environment; and together they underscore the importance of environmental protection in all of our lives." He especially noted the disproportional risks to industrial workers from toxic substances. And he emphasized that environmental measures created new jobs. "I believe," he said, "that environmental protection is consistent with a sound economy"—a theme he would repeat later on several occasions. In the introductory paragraphs of the message he said that "intelligent stewardship of the environment on behalf of all Americans is a prime responsibility of government." The remainder of the message detailed an action program: control pollution and protect health; assure environmentally sound energy production; improve the urban environment; protect our natural resources; preserve our national heritage; protect wildlife; affirm our concerns for the global environment; and improve implementation of environmental laws (e.g., reducing paperwork in environmental impact statements).

Among these actions, and recognizing the earliest elements of environmental concern, Carter proposed what came to be the Alaska National Interest Lands Conservation Act of 1980. Further, he proposed enlargement of park and wilderness areas and new wilderness areas as well as authorization of eight wild and scenic rivers and studies of twenty more. He recommended additions to the National Trail System. And he noted particularly the need to encourage the states to protect nongame wildlife and for federal agencies to take leadership in their areas of responsibility to protect wetlands.

Much of what President Carter proposed was not, by then, outside the bounds of political practicality; but of course it still was somewhat controversial. In the area of water resources planning and development, though, he got into real trouble and failed to gain congressional support. But in so doing the Carter administration developed policy concepts which were novel at the political level, although consistent with ideas within the environmental movement (e.g., energy conservation as opposed to increased supply). Its Water Policy Task Force no longer defined "water conservation" to mean the storage of water in reservoirs in the spring for release in the late summer to irrigate crops, as had long been its definition in the West. Instead, the task force defined water conservation in terms of demand management via proper pricing of water, installation of water meters in urban areas, and improved efficiency in agricultural water use. Its official definition explicitly ruled out water storage as conservation. Moreover, the administration so tightened the principles, standards, and procedures of the Water Resources Council that few, if any, water projects could pass a careful review. Then it proposed that the council staff conduct reviews of all proposed projects. Finally, it proposed up-front sharing by states in financing water projects as well as greater cost-sharing by nonfederal interests.

The negative symbol of the water project "hit list" never died. Over the Carter years congressional antipathy for his water policy initiatives was so intense that when a draft bill on up-front financing and increased cost sharing was ready for introduction, no congressman or senator would lend his name to the bill. The proposed bill was never considered by the Congress. However, increased grants to states for water resource planning were authorized.

In other resource and environmental policy areas the Carter administration had substantial political success: the Marine Sanctuaries Act, the Fish and Wildlife Conservation Act (nongame wildlife), the Surface Mining Control and Reclamation Act, the Nuclear Waste Storage Act, the Comprehensive

Environmental Response, Compensation, and Liability Act (Superfund), and the Alaska National Interest Lands Conservation Act.

Administratively, the Carter administration took great pains to enforce its environmentalist choices in various areas. It issued executive orders with respect to restriction of the import or export of exotic organisms, promotion of flood plain management over structural measures for flood protection, prohibition of off-road vehicles where environmental damage would be created, and protection of wetlands.

In a message to Congress in August 1979, President Carter especially emphasized a balanced multiple-use policy in the administration of the Federal Land Policy and Management Act of 1976 (i.e., the Bureau of Land Management Organic Act). He issued specific instructions to the secretary of the interior in this regard.

Despite his apparent dedication to environmental values, President Carter was confronted with steeply rising energy prices and the apparent necessity of greatly increasing the domestic energy supply. His address to the nation in July 1979 on energy and national goals reflected his difficulties. He reminded his listeners that two years earlier he had called the energy crisis "the moral equivalent of war." However, many environmentalists in and out of the administration were turned off by much of his energy development program.

Despite its strong dedication to environmental values, the Carter administration very carefully abstained from any statements or actions that might be seen as a "no-growth" policy.[5] Governor Jerry Brown of California and others had spoken publicly about "limits of growth" and gotten nowhere politically on the national scene. But among academics, interest groups, and others, a "steady-state" or no-growth economy was conceivable and for some highly desirable (Daly, 1973; Olson and Landsberg, 1973; Ophuls, 1977). Interest groups such as Zero Population Growth (which in its fine print advocates no economic growth) and Negative Population Growth (which sees the necessity for substantial decline in population and economic activity worldwide) continue to attract advocates and members.

During 1981–1983 the Reagan administration sought to reverse what had been a more or less consistent support by past presidents of both political parties for an increasing array of measures to enhance environmental quality and environmental protection. Both Secretary of the Interior James Watt and Anne Burford as head of the Environmental Protection Agency were "point persons" for the administration in such a reversal. The most favorable interpretation that can be put on the objectives of Secretary Watt is that he tried to restore the dominant role of conservation policies, as in the years prior to the 1960s, over those of preservationists (Arnold, 1982).

In June 1981 former senator Gaylord Nelson, the national leader of the first Earth Day who had become chairman of the Wilderness Society, made a broad-scale and scathing attack on the Reagan administration reversal. He noted too that Nathaniel Reed, a former assistant secretary of the interior under Presidents Nixon and Ford, had also attacked the administration. The speech received widespread publicity. This attack and others took their toll. Thus, for a year before the election in 1984, President Reagan sought to repair the political damage he had wrought—clear testimony to the environmental movement's continued widespread political vitality. His appointment of William Ruckelshaus as EPA administrator (the man whose personal and environmental credibility was publicly established in the Nixon administration as the first EPA administrator and as deputy attorney general who resigned over the firing of Special Prosecutor Archibald Cox in the Watergate scandal) was obviously designed to provide a symbolic signal that policy change could be expected. His appointment of Secretary of the Interior Clark as a replacement for Secretary Watt was also intended to appease environmentalists.

The 1984 presidential election campaign did not involve the candidates in a debate over environmental issues. Other issues, as in previous presidential campaigns, formed the debate between the candidates. However, environmentalists were very active in support of former vice-president Mondale. To show its opposition to President Reagan, the Sierra Club (some members of which are Republicans) took the unprecedented action of officially supporting Mr. Mondale.

With the focus of domestic political attention by the Reagan administration upon budget balancing, cutting domestic spending, tax reform, and private market allocation of values, environmentalists have been put largely on the defensive. Much lobbying effort has been put into protection of environmental programs and expenditures, particularly those of the Environmental Protection Agency. The Land and Water Conservation Fund, very regrettably to environmentalists, has almost ceased to exist; and apparently it would have ceased operation except for insistence by the Congress via appropriation acts. Congressional leaders of both political parties have been seeking reauthorization of the Clean Water Act and other major environmental legislation but have had little success, except in preserving the legal status quo.

The heads of the Department of the Interior and the Environmental Protection Agency have apparently been given orders not to rock the boat either negatively or positively, from the perspective of an environmentalist. From the perspective of New Deal–Fair Deal conservationists, however, the proposal to sell the Bonneville Power Administration and the other federal power marketing agencies to decrease the national debt is an abomination. But public and cooperative electric power progressives are now fewer and less effective than in the past. The National Rural Electrical Cooperative Association and the American Public Power Association still exist, but they face major defensive battles.

Political scientists, notably Norman Vig and Michael Kraft, have analyzed environmental policy in the Reagan administration (Vig and Kraft, 1984). That analysis need not be repeated here. The result of that record, however, has been to increase positive popular identification with environmental issues (Dunlap, chapter 4). The Congress has responded by holding the policy line on authorizations and to a great extent on appropriations. Few legislative advances of great importance have been made since 1980, with the exceptions of HSWA and SARA (see table 1.1).

The only governmental arena in which environmentalists continue to be generally successful is in the federal courts. This success is due not only to the favorable terms of the many environmental statutes, but also no doubt to sympathetic judges, most notably on the Court of Appeals in Washington, D.C. Chapter 9 documents this success. Since the 1970s environmentalists have increasingly tried to get court sanction for their interpretation of the law and to obtain court orders to force administrative action. The Environmental Defense Fund, the National Resource Defense Council, and the litigation arms of the National Wildlife Federation and the Sierra Club have become, currently, the most successful instruments of the environmental movement. To support these efforts the organizations appear to be able to obtain substantial private financial support and excellent legal talent.

Divergence and Consensus

The third objective of this chapter, as stated at its outset, is to distinguish the conservation and environmental movements in terms of their ideology, basic ideas, and symbols by indicating divergence and consensus. Both movements, as noted earlier, appear to agree on the main objective of policy: a sustainable relationship between man and the environment. Nevertheless, these movements have marked areas of divergence and few areas of consensus.

1. Object of concern

The object of concern is an area of substantial divergence. The conservation movement focused its concerns upon natural resources, that is, those things in the environment which are of material, economic concern to man. Constraint in their use should be only that degree necessary to assure their long-term availability for material use.

The environmental movement has, as an object of its ideological concern, the whole geosphere and biosphere including man himself. The continued long-term integrity of this whole object of concern is its central value. The earlier preservationist manifestation of its concern, of course, persists in the support of wilderness areas, parks, etc., for aesthetic and other traditional reasons.

Now the conservationists are on the defensive against the environmentalists. Symbolically, Muir now has the upper hand, not Pinchot.

2. Economic growth

No national administration, the Carter administration included, has questioned the desirability of continuous economic growth indefinitely into the future. Faith is expressed that economic growth and environmental values can be reconciled.

Zero Population Growth (ZPG), a private educational and lobbying organization (former Governor Richard Lamm of Colorado was once a national president), not only believes in no growth in population, but also no growth in the use of material resources. Negative Population Growth, a more elite, intellectual environmentalist group, seeks policies throughout the world that will bring about a substantial decline in human population as well as a decline in the rate of use of material resources. A small group of economists, in response to their perception of the long-term environmental situation, has explored the concept of a "steady-state" or no-growth economy in terms of the use of resources.

The early conservation movement was concerned with the "running out of resources," but it did not contemplate a response in terms of consciously curtailing economic growth. Moreover, the ideology of economists, as indicated in a report of the President's Material Policy Commission (1952), saw no need for concern over continuous economic growth. Economic signs in terms of rising real costs of a resource would signal a switch to an alternative resource as well as the need for research to find new and cheaper resources. Faith in technology was the ultimate answer, not curtailment of economic growth.

3. Multiple-use sustained yield of renewable resources

The conservation movement established multiple-use sustained yield of renewable resources as one of its prime doctrines. But in federal public land management, including that by the Forest Service, timber cutting and cattle/sheep grazing have been historically the principal uses in practice. The Forest Service struggled to implement the multiple-use doctrine by regulation. Beginning as early as 1924 it singled out certain lands as primitive areas and wild areas to be managed accordingly. By 1960, however, the Forest Service sought and obtained from the Congress the Multiple-Use Sustained Yield Act to help it honor and implement this conservation doctrine.

The environmental movement has promoted additions to the national park system as well as wilderness designation and management of areas on both national park and Forest Service lands. It does not deny multiple-use sustained yield for other Forest Service lands, but it strongly insists that multiple-use means respect for wildlife and recreation uses, buffer strips of forest to hide timbered areas, and denial of timbering where leaving trees in place would be more economical than cutting. Thus there is some consensus, but also divergence.

4. Federal public lands belong to all the people

Both movements adhere to this doctrine. Neither supported the Sagebrush Rebellion that argued that federal public lands belonged to the states in which they were and that jurisdiction should be transferred to them.

Environmentalists, in addition, favor greater governmental control of private land and the purchase of private land, where necessary, to achieve environmental values. Some conservationists supported federal regulation of private forests earlier in this century, but their views were never accepted.

5. Egalitarianism

The conservation movement supported the "family farm" concept and was anti-monopoly, particularly with regard to private electrical utilities. Some like Gifford Pinchot favored federal regulation of private electrical utilities while others like George Norris favored federal public power and rural electrical cooperatives—all with a view toward achieving greater equality among Americans.

The environmental movement per se does not appear to be concerned with the issue of equality. It has some connections with the consumer movement, spearheaded by Ralph Nader, but apparently not much concern. The civil rights movement appears to embody most twentieth-century egalitarian concerns.

6. Supply development versus demand management

The conservation movement strongly fostered supply development, most notably multiple-purpose water resources development: navigation, irrigation, hydroelectric power, flood control, watershed management, recreation, and fish and wildlife enhancement. Water is a renewable resource via the hydrologic cycle, with finite limits manifest each year. The problem of the changing uses of water as a civilization advances was not anticipated.

The emphasis of the environmental movement, most pointedly, has been its support of the designation of wild and scenic rivers, thus precluding the construction of dams or reservoirs. Also, "nonstructural alternatives" to flood control storage via local flood plain zoning, flood proofing, etc., in trade for the federal subsidized flood insurance program, have been strongly supported.

With respect to demand management, environmentalists and economists have supported strict benefit-cost analysis, and pricing of water at its full cost at least. Both urban and rural water conservation practices have also been supported. Urban measures include metering, water-saving household fixtures, and less water-intensive landscape gardening practices. Agricultural measures include lining of canals and ditches and other "water-saving" practices including the growing of crops requiring less water.

Also, by supporting a "free market" in water under western water laws, environmentalists and economists have supported the transfer of use from agriculture to urban use. They have supported, in effect, the Colorado doctrine that "water moves up hill to money." This policy also discourages further water resources development. The "free market" policy, however, affects the maintenance of a minimum low flow as fish habitat. Where all water is already appropriated, and a state has not reserved the right to regulate appropriated water use in the public interest, the policy requires a state to buy water rights to provide the low flow.

7. Pollution and chemical poisons

The conservation movement did not have to face the problems of air and water pollution, toxic and hazardous wastes, and chemical poisoning. Until the late 1960s these problems largely were not perceived by professionals or the public as general problems.

The environmental movement has reacted strongly against pollution in all of its many forms. Many public policy outputs can be attributed to its political power. Surveys of public opinion indicate that environmentalists strongly favor solutions to pollution problems even if higher taxes are required. Many favor such solutions to assure human protection, security, and survival. Some, who have ecological understanding, seek to prevent the decline of species of the flora and fauna generally. The motive of personal survival is no doubt a strong political component of the environmental movement. This motive is stronger, presumably, than the aesthetic, ethical, and intellectual ecology-related values and concerns that are also involved in the environmental movement. With continued, uncontrolled development of many new chemicals, and new knowledge of the harmful effects of older chemicals, this area of environmental concern will no doubt persist for a long time to come. As a policy issue in the late 1970s and 1980s, this concern focuses on risk. How much risk is too much risk? To people? To fish and wildlife? To the biosphere generally?

The divergences between the ideology, ideas, and basic values of the conservative movement and the environmental movement, as summarized above, can be viewed as animating the politics of growth and the environment. During the peak of the conservation movement such politics involved the political dominance of Pinchot's doctrine over that of Muir. No such dominance, however, has occurred during the heyday of the environmental movement. Under the symbol of "quality of life," involving both economic and environmental considerations, "balance" became the central consideration of official policy through the Carter administration. Faith that economic development and environmental consideration could be reconciled is official doctrine. To take the position that environmental considerations should be dominant over economic development apparently is viewed by sympathetic politicians as courting political suicide.

But more is involved than fears of political suicide. Specific political considerations outside the framework of the natural resources/environmental debate are involved. The necessity President Carter felt to meet the "energy crisis" head on, by fostering increased supplies of oil, gas, and other mineral-fuels, illustrates a more general point. To be sure, he and others responsive to the environmental movement promoted energy-saving policies and research aimed at saving energy. But he, Senator Jackson, and others also promoted increased domestic supply. They did so primarily for national security considerations. More generally, political considerations outside the framework of natural resources/environmental debate will often be involved: not only national security, but also curbing of an international cartel, promoting domestic full employment, controlling inflation, etc.

Conclusions and Suggestions for Further Research

The historical analyses of the conservation movement and the environmental movement appear to support the framework set forth at the outset of this chapter. In each case the political ferment and the few political proposals and actions existing prior to the advent of new aggressive leadership were shown to be present. Thus the situation within which leaders as political entrepreneurs could work was manifest. New, aggressive leadership was identified which sought to develop recognition of specific public problems and proposed policy outputs by developing an ideology, a set of basic policy ideas, and assertions of values that obtained public adherence. Leadership by both public officials and by persons outside government who became nationally prominent was involved. The media, as well as academic and other authors, helped to provide a bandwagon effect. None of this effort, of course, could have created a lasting political movement if the ideology, basic ideas, and values did not have credibility and fundamental human appeal within American society in the twentieth century. New ideas, plus indications of relative weights among values, provided necessary and desirable feedback to leaders. That feedback also enabled them to judge, in the context of other political factors, the political power of the movement to bring about major new public policy outputs consistent with the ideology, basic ideas, and values. The historical analyses indicated that such outputs did result.

A future era of clear resolution of environmental issues is not foreseen at this time. No clear resolution seems likely despite the probability that human insecurities due to continuation and increase of major toxic and other pollutant effects will increase in the future. Such insecurities could provide a major source of political support for the environmental movement in the future. But will such insecurities motivate sufficient political power to resolve substantially the apparent conflict between economic growth and the environment? Will positive and normative ecology provide the data-base to support political action toward substantial resolution?

Is there new positive national leadership arising that possesses the vision that will attempt to provide an era of clear resolution? The present political context within which a new positive leader would be called upon to work is very wide. For example, the environmentalists have an extremist faction called Earth First which espouses a doctrine of "deep ecology." It rebels at the thought of compromise and has adopted the political tactics of the Monkey Wrench Gang (Hooker, 1986). Neither do the two alternatives of the radical right, the libertarians and the moralist conservatives, offer the prospect of new, positive leadership in this field.

At this juncture there are many unanswered questions and much work to be done. What suggestions for research are implied in the foregoing discussion? Much has been included in the chapter that political scientists may wish to question, verify, or rebut. Particular historical matters certainly could be probed more deeply. An obvious area for further research is the validity of the elite model as a set of propositions to be tested. The author has made a case for its validity based upon his own perceptions of fact and their interconnectedness. Possibly fruitful research could be directed toward refuting part or all of this hypothesis in the natural resources/environmental field.

But what about the concept of political movements more generally? Does the elite model fit the historical data of the civil rights movement, the women's movement, the anti-Vietnam, anti-nuclear, and peace movements? What differences can be identified? The civil rights movement and the anti-Vietnam movement had clearly identifiable public policy outputs. What about the other movements with respect to this dependent variable? What about the variable of identifiable national leadership? Do leaders generate movements, or vice versa? Or do both phenomena occur in different situations? What connections, if any, can be identified between the environmental movement and those other movements?

Highlighting political movements as an important concept for political science suggests that research could focus usefully upon comparison of movements and political parties. Political movements, such as the conservation and environmental movements, tend to be bipartisan. Parties, as symbols of ideological commitment and promoters of related policy ideas, have been observed by political scientists to have declined in this country. Political movements apparently have increased in political importance. What, if anything, is the connection between these two phenomena? In this connection, also, what precisely are the relationships between interest groups, political parties, political movements, and public policy outputs?

In previous literature, Norman Wengert and others have stressed that American policy-making has been characterized by pragmatism. They mean by this concept that American policy-making, by and large, has not been a response to widely held ideological commitments (Wengert, 1962). In this essay more weight has been given to ideology. Ideologies, of course, are expressions of political philosophy. Does the political philosophy that apparently inspired W. J. McGee offer a normative beginning for intellectual-political reconciliation between the conservation and environmental movements? As of yet no normative political theory/philosophy closely in tune with the emerging science of human ecology (i.e., man in the geosphere/biosphere) has been developed to help guide the evolution of political reality, except in a vague and inchoate form. The abortive political campaign for the presidency in 1980 of the former governor of California, Jerry Brown, espousing an ideology of "limits" of economic growth, was an heroic attempt by an active politician to forge such a theory/philosophy. William Ophuls, Charles Stoddard, and possibly others have made beginning attempts (Ophuls, 1977; Stoddard, 1982). Clearly, a rigorously developed and sound intellectual foundation is needed to inspire future practical political action.

Another topic for research is suggested by the work of Neustadt (1980) and others who in writing on the presidency imply that there is not much room for political entrepreneurship by a cabinet officer. Yet cabinet-level entrepreneurship does occur. Frank E. Smith, a former journalist, legislator, and TVA director, has stated with respect to Stewart Udall's appointment by President Kennedy as secretary of the interior that "no Secretary since Garfield (1907–1909) has been more personally dedicated to the conservation ideal." He went on to say that "his efforts and achievements may eventually rank him above all others who have held the office" (Smith, 1966). Is Udall unique? Or have cabinet officers (consider Harold Ickes, 1933–1945) played a more important role as policy entrepreneurs, with the express or implied approval of presidents, than political science literature suggests?

Earlier in this chapter it was asserted, on the basis of the author's experience as a participant/observer of the policy process in the natural resource/environmental field, that all three of Lowi's methods of political decision-making are involved, not just one method as asserted by Lowi. Given the prominence in the literature of political science of these three methods of decision-making (with the prevalence of distributive politics particularly emphasized), research on this topic relating to other fields of public policy output should be undertaken. With few exceptions, the prevalence of all three methods of decision-making may be confined to cases where strong political movements are involved in the public-policy-making process.

Finally, do the phenomena of political movements, based upon common ideology, basic ideas, and values, represent a new societal effort to express and realize in public policy outputs a more general public interest? In this regard, political parties have not been found adequate. Movements tend to be bipartisan and overcome party limitations. Moreover, movements may be viewed as bringing about larger increments of policy change, as compared to those achieved by subgovernmental processes. Are they not, therefore, phenomena having a normative and practical significance that students of politics should applaud?

3

Federalism and Environmental Policy

Charles E. Davis and James P. Lester

The proposed transfer of federal environmental program management responsibilities to state and local administrators has received considerable presidential support over the past fifteen years, especially within the Reagan administration. Greater state decision-making authority is typically justified at an ideological level as a means of redressing an historic imbalance in the focus of decision-making responsibility and in promoting greater programmatic independence, responsiveness to constituent needs, and accessibility to citizen input. Proponents of the newest "New Federalism" argue that it is time for state political authorities to reduce their dependency on Washington-based funding and policy direction and to increasingly turn inward for solutions to social and economic problems within their boundaries (Wright, 1982; Glendening and Reeves, 1984).

Even if public officials tend to agree upon the desirability of program decentralization as a policy objective, there are three constraining factors worth considering. One is the scope of the policy problem. Some policies are less amenable to an effective switch in jurisdictional authority than others because of "spillover effects" or "negative externalities" which inhibit the development of a policy approach that is geographically self-contained. To some extent these problems can be addressed through the utilization of regional approaches ranging from informal contact between state officials to the adoption of an interstate compact.

A second factor is the relative degree of state dependency on federal support for the implementation of environmental programs. States vary in terms of willingness or ability to commit political, economic, and administrative resources for conservation or pollution abatement purposes. Moreover, the magnitude of differences between states carries implications for the decision to maintain or delegate policy-making authority. If discrepancies in states' allocations of resources for the administration of federal environmental programs are substantial, prospects for the expeditious decentralization of management responsibilities are less encouraging.

Third, the ability of state policy-makers to implement environmental programs is occasionally restricted by political opposition from local governmental actors. In some cases resistance can be attributed to the perception that state regulatory actions will effectively narrow the range of policy options available to community decision-makers; for example, wetlands preservation statutes in eastern states are resented by developers and municipal officials who see geographic expansion and economic growth as inexorably intertwined. Another example is a set of decisions that provides statewide benefits but imposes concentrated costs on a particular community, such as the siting of a nuclear power plant or a hazardous waste disposal facility. Often the most likely source of opposition is an ad hoc citizens' organization consisting of local residents who see undesirable consequences ranging from risk to public health and the environment to declining real estate values.

Thus the task for students of environmental policy and politics is to specify when, where, and under what conditions states are able to successfully implement environmental programs. Some states may find it easier or more difficult to assume policy-making responsibilities than others because of differing propensities to enter into interstate agreements or to deal with recalcitrant local officials. However, we contend that a state's ability to implement these programs is a function of two different but complementary dimensions: (1) the degree of state institutional capacity to absorb decentralized programs and (2) the degree of state dependence upon federal grants designed to support environmental programs. The chief objective of this paper is to demonstrate the analytic utility of a classification scheme based upon these two dimensions. This scheme will permit us to subsequently examine the degree of correspondence between the conceptual underpinnings of President Reagan's "New Federalism" and to provide an empirical assessment of state preparedness to take over the management of environmental programs.

State Actions within the Federal System

Prior to the 1970s, the role of the states within the federal system was routinely described by academic observers as a "middleman" position (Wright, 1982) or, in more condescending fashion, as an appropriate administrative subunit of the federal government (Riker, 1964; Beer, 1973). General inattention to problems spanning such areas as civil rights, consumer rights, and environmental protection led to large-scale federal initiatives in policy functions formerly reserved for (or left up to) subnational governments. At the same time, urban officials were clamoring for greater economic and managerial assistance from both the federal government and the states to deal with service demands, social unrest, and fiscal stress. States were thus relegated to a secondary and facilitative role, acting in response to Washington-based priorities on the one hand while receiving potent political pressures from local officials on the other (Willbern, 1959).

Proponents of a more active federal policy presence have argued against the decentralization of federal programs on several counts. One of the more compelling points concerns the scope of certain policy problems. Troublesome issues such as poverty or child abuse are widespread; however, each received relatively little attention from subnational political decision-makers until the federal government took action (Beer, 1973). Interstate disputes over water rights or the emission of airborne pollutants represent a problem of negative externalities which must often be resolved by a higher (or different) governmental authority (Kneese and Schultze, 1975). A third advantage pertains to the stimulative (in an economic or policy innovation sense) effects of grants allocated on a competitive basis to local governments. Federal officials contend that they have the necessary expertise and experience to determine where a prospective pilot project or research activity will do the most good (Elazar, 1984; Break, 1979). Finally, a uniform national policy approach is defended as a more efficient means of attacking large-scale problems. A hazardous waste generator will presumably have less incentive to "dump" his illicit cargo across state lines if the probabilities of detection and punishment are the same in either jurisdiction (Getz and Walter, 1980).

Decentralized political systems, on the other hand, are more likely to promote citizen participation, access, and responsiveness (Fesler, 1965; Elazar, 1984). To the extent that state policy-makers have control or influence in a given policy area, it becomes easier to tailor programs to fit local or regional needs. Efforts by citizens and political organizations to influence policy decisions are also perceived to be within the realm of the possible at this level of governance. Available survey evidence indicates that voters are considerably more confident about their ability to affect state policies than proposals under consideration within the national or international arena (Advisory Commission on Intergovernmental Relations, 1980). Retention of programmatic autonomy by state officials not only serves to ensure that occasionally idiosyncratic concerns are addressed but allegedly contributes to greater experimentation and innovation in policy design as well.

A brief review of intergovernmental relations over time reveals considerable fluctuation between periods of federal dominance within functional policy areas and greater state involvement (Wright, 1982). It is evident that the pendulum has now swung to the subnational end of the intergovernmental continuum. Most recently, policy initiatives within the Reagan administration strengthened the role of state governments through the consolidation of numerous categorical programs into nine bloc grants and the issuance of Executive Order 12372 which replaced the A-95 grant review process with state mandated procedures (Conlan and Walker, 1983; Nathan and Doolittle, 1985). While the question of centralization versus decentralization is ultimately dependent upon value preferences of key political actors, the decision may also be affected by the ability and willingness of contending jurisdictions to assume program management responsibilities.

In general, federalism within the environmental policy arena has tended to resemble the larger pattern of relationships. Reagan administration officials, for example, remained committed to the decentralization of federal programs, but the pace of change was slowed by a combination of political and institutional forces. The availability of federal funding for state planning or policy development was one such factor. Insistence that states "share" a larger proportion of water project development costs was actively pursued by Interior Secretary Watt prior to his resignation but was temporarily shelved—at least during the 1984 presidential campaign.

One area of intergovernmental relations that can be pursued at relatively low cost is the development of cordial working relationships between federal and state administrators on the basis of shared policy beliefs and a willingness to cooperate on program management objectives. There is conflicting evidence for the proposition that public officials at differing levels of government tend to agree on substantive policy issues. A study by Davis (1985) found substantial consensus between federal and state administrators across a broad spectrum of hazardous waste concerns. More recently, Gormley (1987) has focused on the degree of attitudinal correspondence between state and EPA officials in region five (encompassing the Great Lakes states of the upper Midwest) on a variety of air, water, and waste management issues. Conflict, according to the author, was found on policy goals and priorities as well as the means by which such objectives might be attained. Disagreement, of course, is not inherently worrisome and may actually contribute useful feedback to federal officials concerned about the identification of potential stumbling blocks to the implementation of environmental programs. However, Gormley does suggest that jurisdictional differences can be especially problematic under the following circumstances: "The policies being disputed are relatively clear and established; the disputes encompass both ends and means; states lack economic or political incentives to protect the environment; states can readily export their problems to other states; and federal funding constitutes a relatively small percentage of total funding."

A good working relationship can be facilitated not only by consensus over policy goals but agreement over the intergovernmental division of labor for program management activities, the perception of crisis or a sense of urgency, the provision of technical and financial support, political pressure for problem resolution generated by community organizations or interest groups, and an open communication process between differing levels of government (Kamieniecki, O'Brien, and Clarke, 1986). The Reagan administration has attempted to promote reciprocity in the administration of environmental programs by balancing a transfer of more decision-making authority to the states with a corresponding decrease in federal funding for program operations.

Ideally, the decentralization of program authority should have been accompanied by improved cooperation between federal and state administrators. However, a study of state environmental administrators in the Great Lakes region indicated that few are inclined to agree that EPA has granted them an equal role in the decision-making process. An especially sore point was the failure of EPA officials to give any weight to the issues of concern to state program managers. This holds true even when states have received a delegation of policy-making responsibility from the federal government (Kraft, Clary, and Tobin, 1985).

The nature of federal-state environmental policy relationships is similarly affected by an "issue attention" cycle among the citizenry which is lengthier and more intense than is evident for low-risk policy matters. This is exemplified by the shift in negotiating strategy within the EPA for handling the cleanup of abandoned hazardous waste dumpsites. Federal officials initially adopted a cooperative bargaining stance vis-à-vis industry and state administrators in an effort to avoid the prospect of litigation and attendant delays in problem resolution (Rickleen, 1982–83; Bowman, 1985). Subsequent media attention to the contamination of Times Beach, Missouri, and allegations of political favoritism in the implementation of Superfund during the turbulent Gorsuch (Burford)/Lavelle era at EPA necessitated a shift in administrative tactics. The continuation of a nonadversarial style of negotiation by incoming EPA administrator William Ruckelshaus became politically impractical. The strategy chosen by Ruckelshaus and his successor, Lee Thomas, includes a greater willingness to initiate lawsuits and to publicly condemn violations by polluting firms in order to enhance the agency's regulatory credibility.

At the state level the chief political barrier to an administrative takeover of federal environmental programs is the perception that such policies may conflict with other objectives, such as economic and energy development (Rosenbaum, 1981). Both Harrigan (1980) and Jones (1976) discuss the historic lack of attention and occasional resistance to natural resource and pollution control programs shown by state officials. Statutory provisions requiring cooperation in the enforcement of relatively weak federal air and water pollution control laws in the 1960s met with efforts by subnational political authorities to postpone abatement actions through the use of hearings, formal requests to study the problem, and other tactics (Jones, 1975; Advisory Commission on Intergovernmental Relations, 1981). In short, much state inaction is attributable to a fear that industries operating within a state's borders will be placed at a competitive disadvantage with firms located in neighboring states if restrictive regulator statutes are passed and implemented (Rowland and Marz, 1982; Bowman, 1985).

An institutional factor which has served to restrict the number of states able or willing to assume greater management responsibilities is the emergence of "primacy" or "preemptive federalism" as a feature of policy design (Advisory Commission on Intergovernmental Relations, 1984). Under this approach minimum federal standards are established for program administration purposes. If federal officials are persuaded that state administrators can effectively manage these programs, either partial or full authorization can be granted. Failure to comply may result in the federal takeover of administrative responsibilities until state officials have either developed a program sufficiently compatible with federal performance standards or have corrected the problems which led to the revocation of program management authority.

A recent study of primacy and the implementation of environmental policy points to a number of unintended consequences for the exercise of political influence. According to Crotty (1987), governors with less formal decision-making authority can use primacy as a political lever to increase their bargaining position within the state. Since the governor is the contact person used by the EPA to monitor compliance with federal policy standards, a functional connection is established which minimizes the role of other state institutions such as the legislature and the courts. Under primacy, the key relationships involve federal and state administrators. Yet another effect is felt in relation to the budget; that is, primacy states are more likely than non-primacy states to replace federal monies lost through declining grant outlays with own-source revenues (Davis and Lester, 1987).

Interstate Relationships

It is evident that numerous environmental policy issues transcend state boundaries. One class of problems can be attributed to the negative effects of actions taken within a state on natural resource availability or environmental quality in a neighboring state (Price, 1982). The inability or unwillingness of Colorado officials to release a sufficient amount of water into rivers to irrigate farms in western Kansas is one such example; another is the interstate migration of air pollutants. Competition between states or regions for resources or economic development can also create friction; for example, midwestern state officials clearly resent paying what they believe to be excessive severance tax on low-sulfur coal imported from Montana or Wyoming (Lopach, 1984). In short, there are a number of bistate or multistate controversies ranging from minor administrative disputes to competing policy priorities, and policy-makers must decide upon the most appropriate approach for resolving such disputes.

Minor problems between states can often be settled informally without resorting to federal involvement (Glendening and Reeves, 1984). Administrators heading natural resource or environmental protection agencies are often acquainted with their counterparts in neighboring states and can handle a given dispute with a phone call or a memorandum of agreement. Such contacts have been facilitated by an increase in the number of organizations or associations representing state officials and the use of these groups as a forum for the exchange of information or policy developments. This holds true for more specialized issue areas as well; for instance, membership on the Western States Water Council can result in contacts between professionals from differing states who share similar concerns and a desire to resolve problems outside the courts.

More complex issues may well require a more formal means of securing agreement between state policy actors. Regional approaches to problems affecting two or more states include the adoption of an interstate compact or the creation of a regional organization. Interstate compacts are formal agreements between states which require ratification from the respective legislatures and eventually from Congress (Glendening and Reeves, 1984). Following the attainment of congressional approval, an interstate agency is established with the responsibility of implementing the compact. The agency consists of individuals representing each of the affected states and, in some cases, the federal government.

Of the 123 interstate compacts currently in existence, a substantial percentage of these deal with natural resource or environmental issues (Bowman and Kearney, 1986). Many of these are associated with the apportionment of water while a lesser number of compacts address conservation and the environment, parks and recreation, flood control, water pollution control, and nuclear energy. A recent study of state participation in interstate compacts by Nice (1987) concluded that such environmental agreements are most likely entered into by states having less educated populations and greater population densities.

Regional organizations, by contrast, have received less attention as a means of handling bistate or multistate policy matters. This type of decision-making body may be distinguished from interstate compact agencies in its focus on multipurpose management functions and by an occasional tendency to deal with regulatory matters as well as planning and coordination (Derthick, 1974). Ongoing examples of regional organizations within the realm of natural resource policy include the Delaware River Basin Commission and the Tennessee Valley Authority, organizations which have managed to survive politically because of a careful cultivation of grassroots support (Walker, 1981) or the cooperation of well-established and influential constituency groups within the policy-making structure (Selznick, 1949). Other attempts to encourage the development of regional organizations, notably the seven river basin commissions established under Title II of the Water Resources Planning Act of 1965, floundered in the early 1980s after the cutoff of federal aid under the Reagan administration.

The usefulness of regional decision-making bodies within the overall context of environmental federalism is subject to debate. Advocates tend to emphasize the flexibility of such arrangements in handling multijurisdictional disputes or the coordination of resource use. Other advantages are more pragmatic from the vantage point of those favoring program decentralization; they observe that additional federal funding is made available for programs of interest to state participants, and the influence of the governor in subsequent negotiations with the federal government is likely to be strengthened. A more skeptical evaluation of regional organizations is centered upon the concern that such organizations might emerge as a fourth level of government without a constitutional foundation. In a related vein, decisions made by interstate organizations cannot easily be attributed to any single individual or jurisdiction; hence the question of policy responsiveness or accountability to the voters is difficult to resolve.

State-Local Relations

For many environmental programs the question of coordination between state and local government officials is moot. Each level has traditionally maintained jurisdiction over selected programs. States bear the major responsibility for the development and management of natural resource programs while municipalities are more inclined to take charge of wastewater treatment, parks and recreation, and water transport (Glendening and Reeves, 1984). A smaller number of governmental programs affecting the environment involve overlapping responsibilities; for example, air pollution programs are occasionally housed in both state-level environmental protection agencies and in the administrative structure of larger urban areas as well.

Within the past two decades a growing number of states have enacted legislation designed to regulate land use in local government (Mushkatel and Judd, 1981). One consequence has been an increase in tension, and in some cases conflict, between states and local units of government over questions of priority uses and decision-making autonomy. Often the debate has pitted environmental groups and state officials against developers, although a different configuration of policy actors will be found with differing policy issues. Two of the most important areas of regulatory concern affecting the environment are natural resource legislation (covering coastal development, wetlands, and critical environmental areas) and siting laws (especially nuclear power plants and hazardous waste treatment, storage, and disposal facilities). In either case, the question of implementation often hinges upon the reservoir of informal power that can be marshaled by local political actors to thwart the exercise of state authority (Morell and Magorian, 1982; Fawcett, 1986).

The ability of governmental or private sector interests to resist compliance with a state program depends upon a number of factors, including the degree of formal authority possessed by state policy-makers, the attitudes of community residents toward the policy, and the intensity of commitment expressed by local public officials. A case in point is the California Coastal Act of 1976 which mandated a planning process involving a state agency, the California Coastal Commission, and sixty-seven local coastal jurisdictions in the preparation of land use plans. Following a complex review process, these plans are certified by the coastal commission. Local governments are then assigned the responsibility of implementing the plans in the form of zoning ordinances (Mazmanian and Sabatier, 1983).

A recent study of local coastal plans was undertaken by Fawcett (1986) to assess the degree of friction between state and local officials and the extent to which the latter set of actors was able to exercise discretionary influence over land use decisions in excess of their constitutionally derived authority. Fawcett found considerable support for his hypothesis that the most intense areas of conflict would be located in the urban fringe, meaning land that is in a state of transition. Local officials representing fringe areas tended to give greater priority to the economic health of the community than to the welfare of prospective coastal resource users, and they were effective in articulating these concerns when negotiating with the state. Preservation of development options was thus seen to be a primary concern. On the other hand, the implementation of the Coastal Act in urban areas was less contentious since choices that would otherwise appeal to the architects of the statute were effectively foreclosed by existing uses (Fawcett, 1986).

A more controversial area of policy affecting state-local relations is the responsibility assigned to the states under the Resource Conservation and Recovery Act of 1976 to develop legislation for the siting of hazardous waste treatment, storage, and disposal (tsd) facilities. Over half the states have adopted siting policies (especially states generating more waste), and the content tends to vary in terms of the relative weight given to state authority versus local control of public participation. Some opt for policies that would effectively preempt local governmental veto powers; Georgia and Arizona, for example, have enacted a policy response which effectively excludes local or citizen participation in the decision-making process (Hadden, Veilette, and Brandt, 1983; Wells, 1982). Often states within this category will assume responsibility for the identification of sites for hazardous waste tsd facilities through the creation of an agency or board. Since the chief arguments for this approach are based on the assumptions that there is a compelling statewide public interest in facility development and that state governments are the best judge of appropriate locations, little effort is made to incorporate citizen representation (Andrews and Pierson, 1985).

Other states have adopted a multimember commission or board to offer siting recommendations but have included ad hoc representation from the affected community. This approach does not call for state mandated selection of a preferred location for tsd facilities but does permit intervention to override local governmental powers that might be used to halt facility construction. A third group of states allows communities to approve or disapprove a decision to site facilities nearby, a position which is sensitive to the notion that local acceptance is a prerequisite for effective program implementation (Morell and Magorian, 1982). Finally, a few states have left primary decision-making authority in the hands of local officials but have included state restrictions on how control is exercised—such as circumscribing the criteria and procedures under which decisions are made (Andrews and Pierson, 1985).

In short, state autonomy in the development and implementation of environmental programs is dependent not only upon federal policy design but upon the degree of cooperation from local public officials as well. State programs affecting the regulation of land use may easily provoke adverse political reaction at the community level since it is difficult to reconcile state powers of eminent domain with provisions for home rule.

State Institutional Capacity

State institutional capacity refers to the ability and willingness of public officials within a given jurisdiction to develop and administer public policies. It encompasses three dimensions—political, fiscal, and managerial. Governmental leaders in states characterized by high political capacity are able to articulate needs, weigh conflicting demands, establish priorities, and allocate resources (Weinberg, 1977). Fiscal capacity is closely linked with the maintenance of a productive and stable revenue base to fund public services. Managerial capacity involves the development of sufficient organizational resources and administrative talent to design and execute governmental programs. A state that is prepared to combine all three within a particular area of policy is indeed well positioned to assume greater decision-making responsibilities (Warren, 1982).

An examination of the literature on intergovernmental relations two decades ago reveals considerable skepticism about the utility of an expanded state role within the federal system. One of the first analysts to suggest that state government was not only the appropriate unit of government to deliver certain kinds of services but was doing a relatively good job was Daniel Elazar. He contended that states have been unfairly charged with fiscal irresponsibility and administrative incompetence in governmental operations (Elazar, 1974).

The allegation that states have done little to shore up sources of revenue since World War II is not supported by empirical evidence. Governmental expenditures have increased at all levels, but the rise is proportionately greater for the states. Own-source revenues expanded from an average of $98.87 per resident in 1957 to $687.93 per capita in 1979, a 597.5 percent increase in current dollars (Walzer and Gove, 1981). Much of this growth is attributable to a decision to bolster state coffers through the imposition of sales and income taxes. The stability of the revenue mix has also improved. By 1979 thirty-seven states had a general sales tax, a corporate income tax, and a personal income tax, in comparison with a total of just nineteen states using all three sources in 1960 (Walker, 1983).

The degree of state financial independence to be found within the realm of environmental policy is less certain. Some critics argue that Reagan administration cutbacks in grant monies for water development, pollution control, and related program areas will result in a decline in environmental quality since many states are hard pressed to make up the difference. A study by the National Governors' Association (NGA) revealed that member states were unenthusiastic about assuming a larger share of financial responsibility for such programs. Over two-thirds of those responding to the NGA survey indicated that a loss in federal funding would not be replaced by state revenues in most environmental program activities (National Governors' Association, 1982).

Moreover, the acquisition of replacement funds today is difficult, given the current mood of fiscal restraint at state and local levels. Revenue-raising capabilities are also limited by the perceived need to compete with governmental jurisdictions for business and the "right kind" of (i.e., more affluent) citizen (Glendening and Reeves, 1984). We hasten to add that there is little empirical work on budgetary outcomes in view of the Reagan administration cutbacks (Lester, 1986), and it is likely that replacement decisions will be tempered by other factors such as the state's own prior commitments to environmental quality, degrees of fiscal well-being, and the strength of liberal or moderate political voices within the policy-making process.

States have made impressive strides in the attainment of management capacity, a process which is largely attributable to structural reforms and the increased professionalization of executive and legislative staffers over the past twenty years. A useful discussion of these developments is offered by Kearney (1983):

> Popular reforms include the short ballot, increased appointment and removal powers, longer terms, larger staffs, enhanced budgetary authority, and the power to reorganize the executive branch. . . . Since 1965, twenty-two states have redesigned their executive branches by consolidating power in the governor's office in efforts to make their bureaucracies function more effectively and to make the governor master of his own house, not just the father figure. Furthermore, many observers agree that the quality of the individual entering the office of the governor has improved substantially in recent years in terms of prior experience, education, aptitude, and other variables.

Federal actions have also played an important part in the modernization of state administrative processes. The grant-in-aid device has been used not only to achieve federal policy objectives but to enhance subnational managerial capabilities as well. Much of the rather sizable increase in state and local government employment during this time period stems from a shift in program management responsibilities from Washington to nonfederal jurisdictions. In corresponding fashion, the number of individuals working directly for the federal government (excluding defense) has remained constant since 1960 (Lee, 1979).

Federal legislation designed to increase managerial effectiveness in state and local operations was passed in 1970. The Intergovernmental Personnel Act (IPA) authorized funds for the provision of technical assistance in personnel administration, one- to two-year intergovernmental mobility assignments for public employees at all levels, training opportunities, and regional centers for the cooperative recruitment and examination of prospective governmental workers. A subsequent evaluation of IPA's impact from FY 1972 through FY 1977 in ten representative states indicates that the program had effectively met its legislative mandate and had further added to a tendency among recipient governments to use intergovernmental communication as a means of handling area-based disputes (Shapek, 1980).

Improvements in both organizational structure and the quality of administrators attracted to the public service are also evident. Within the environmental policy-making arena, states have been quite active in the organization of agencies to better handle new and changing responsibilities. According to the Book of the States, thirty-nine states altered administrative arrangements between 1967 and 1982 to deal with environmental quality control (Council of State Governments, 1984). One of the more popular organizational forms was the creation of state-level EPA's, largely patterned after the federal version. Other commonly used approaches included the formation of environmental super agencies comprised of three or more pollution control agencies (plus an occasional conservation/natural resources department) and the oft-employed health department model (Advisory Commission on Intergovernmental Relations, 1981).

Continuing surveys of state administrators by Professor Deil Wright and his associates at the University of North Carolina provide an optimistic assessment of agency leadership potential (Hebert and Wright, 1982; Wright, 1982). Managers serving within the middle and upper echelons of state government tend to be better educated and more active in professional organizations than their predecessors. A related finding concerns the manner of selection. Individuals with prior experience in another state are increasingly preferred as job candidates by public officials involved in the recruitment process. Finally, an attitudinal analysis of these administrators revealed a willingness to shoulder additional programmatic responsibilities associated with the decentralization of federal programs. To summarize, state administrative capabilities have increased in recent years because of specific federal initiatives designed to upgrade management skills, on-the-job experience with the administration of federal programs, the strengthening of executive authority through a combination of constitutional and structural reforms, and the rise of professionalism among employees within the middle and upper ranks of state bureaucracies.

Another useful indicator of state political capacity is the degree of legislative activity within a given policy area. An upsurge in policy activism at the subnational level can be at least partially explained by changing expectations concerning the appropriate scope of state governmental operations as well as the increased number and quality of legislative proposals developed by legislators, staffers, and functional policy specialists. States have been at the forefront in a number of policy areas such as land-use planning, personnel reform, mental health policy, sunset legislation, nuclear waste management, and energy resources, among others (Kearney, 1983). Bilateral and regional solutions to area-based policy problems have also been attempted with greater frequency because of a rise in the number of national organizations representing the interests of both policy and management specialists, which have, in turn, stimulated the use of informal contacts among state officials with similar concerns (Nice, 1984).

Policy actions at the state level have also been prompted by less salutary motivations. Federal-state conflict over water resources (Caulfield, 1984; Schooler and Ingram, 1982), energy development (Dye and Davidson, 1981; Hall, White, and Ballard, 1978), public lands (Francis and Ganzel, 1984; Culhane, 1984), and reclamation (Menzel, 1983; Hedge and Menzel, 1985; Mitnick, 1980) have provided ample incentives for state officials to initiate legislation, often for the express purpose of minimizing or preventing federal involvement. Whatever the reason, some states have increasingly demonstrated a willingness to independently seek policy solutions for problems created within their borders.

Findings

Whether an increase in state environmental policy developments augurs well for the decentralization of program management responsibilities depends on the extent to which states vary on measures of institutional capacity. If states are relatively equal in terms of their support for natural resource and environmental protection policies and uniformly commit both funding and administrative personnel to these activities, the prospects for a successful transfer of program authority are more encouraging.

To examine these questions more fully, we sought to develop an index of overall institutional capacity among the fifty American states. Institutional capability is defined as follows: $C = f$ (political support + financial support + administrative support) where C refers to state institutional capability and political support refers to the enactment of several environmental protection policies; financial support refers to the amount of expenditures contributed to various environmental programs; and administrative support refers to the type of institutional structure and personnel available to administer federal environmental programs (for sources, see Appendix B).

Table 3.1 provides a summary of state policy responses to environmental policy. The data reveal considerable between-state variation on this dimension of institutional capacity. To some extent, these differences reflect differing policy priorities. Some states are more inclined than others to adopt legislation patterned after federal environmental programs because of the variety and abundance of natural resources within their borders. For others, the spectra of air, water, and land-based pollution poses a more difficult policy problem. Lawmakers placed in the uncomfortable position of considering tradeoffs between economic growth and public health may find it politically prudent to place such issues on the legislative back-burner, barring a well-publicized environmental disaster, such as an air pollution alert (Goetze and Rowland, 1985). Within the hazardous waste policy arena, states with severe pollution problems are more likely to develop corrective policies than states with fewer (or less visible) problems (Lester et al., 1983). It may be useful to integrate a problem-severity component within our classification of state policy responses. Table 3.2 combines a measure of pollution potential with the response index. States range from a low of −44 (Alabama) to a high of +9 (Minnesota).

Closely related to an independent policy-making stance is the degree of state fiscal dependence upon federal grants in general as well as aid to support environmental programs. States that have become more reliant upon the continuing flow of funds from the Washington pipeline to finance governmental operations are not likely to exempt specific policy areas to gain greater management autonomy. An examination of federal spending over the past twenty years suggests that state dependency, overall, has become more pronounced. Intergovernmental aid from Washington to state and local governments in the form of grant monies increased sharply in the 1960s with the passage of numerous social and economic programs sponsored by President Johnson and continued to rise until the latter stages of the Carter administration. Federal outlays rose from $7.1 billion in FY 1961 to $88.9 billion in FY 1980, while the number of grants passed the five hundred mark (Walker, 1981). As Walker indicates, the expansion of aid reflected gradual federal involvement in a variety of assisted activities formerly within the jurisdictional purview of state governments.

The impacts have been far-reaching and multifaceted. Federal aid as a percentage of state-local revenues grew steadily between 1960 and 1978 despite the rather substantial efforts made by these governments to improve the productivity and diversification of revenue sources (Wright, 1982). It has also resulted in the creation of new bureaucracies at the state level to implement federal policies; in other cases state reorganizations have been undertaken to facilitate intergovernmental program ties. Unintentional political conflict has been generated as a consequence of regional disparities in the allocation of federal funds (Arnold, 1980; Price, 1982). Moreover, Levine and Posner (1981) argue that subnational governments are particularly vulnerable to the distortion of programmatic preferences during a period of fiscal austerity since the temptation to use scarce state or local dollars to match federal grants is often overwhelming.

Table 3.3 presents the degree of dependency upon federal environmental aid among the fifty states. This varies from a high of 80.8 percent (Rhode Island) to a low of 24.0 percent (California). High levels of dependency imply, of course, that state governments are exceedingly vulnerable to changes in federal policies regarding expenditures for services provided at the state level. Newly mandated environmental responsibilities, on the one hand, and federal budget cutbacks, on the other, threaten to produce crisis at the state level.

Thus it is incorrect to assume state equivalency in terms of either internal environmental capabilities or external fiscal dependence. Rather, we view the contemporary intergovernmental system as one in which the impacts of Reagan's New Federalism will differ depending upon the states' capacity to absorb the potential adverse impacts. This system is essentially a decentralized one based upon the willingness and capacity of each state to assume control over its environmental programs. An understanding of the basic dynamics of this federal-state organization, then, entails the determination of when states will successfully assume control of environmental programs and when they will not; when the arrangements will concern simply the coordination of unilateral (i.e., state-centric) behavior; when cooperation is required (i.e., a federal-state partnership); when federal intervention is necessary (i.e., state dependency upon federal assistance); or when regional (i.e., state-state) cooperation is more appropriate.

Table 3.1 States' Commitment to Environmental Protection (State-by-State Breakdown by Indicator)

	Ranking Indicators									
	1	2	3	4	5	6	7	8	9	10
	Congressional voting record	State EI process	Priority envir. protection	Wildlife tax checkoff	$ for envir. quality control	Hazardous waste program	Umbrella envir. agency	Solar energy tax breaks	Protection of rivers	$ for noise pollution
Score Range	0–4	0–4	0–4	0–1	0–6	0–2	0–1	0–2	0–2	0–2
Alabama	1	0	0	1	0	1	0	0	1	0
Alaska	0	0	—	1	6	0	1	2	0	—
Arizona	1	2	1	0	1	1	1	2	0	2
Arkansas	1	0	1	1	1	2	1	0	2	0
California	2	4	4	0	3	1	0	1	2	2
Colorado	2	0	2	1	2	0	1	2	0	—
Connecticut	3	4	2	0	2	1	1	1	0	1
Delaware	3	2	3	1	5	1	1	0	1	0
Florida	2	0	3	0	0	1	1	2	1	2
Georgia	2	2	3	0	1	2	1	0	2	1
Hawaii	3	4	—	0	2	0	1	2	0	2
Idaho	0	0	1	1	2	0	1	0	0	—
Illinois	2	0	1	1	4	1	1	0	0	2
Indiana	3	4	3	1	1	1	1	2	2	1
Iowa	3	0	3	1	1	1	1	0	2	0
Kansas	1	0	2	1	1	0	1	2	0	—
Kentucky	2	2	2	1	1	1	1	0	2	2
Louisiana	2	0	1	1	0	1	0	0	2	0
Maine	3	0	3	0	4	1	1	2	1	0
Maryland	3	4	1	0	4	1	0	0	2	1
Massachusetts	4	4	2	1	5	1	1	2	2	2
Michigan	3	4	1	0	2	0	0	2	2	2
Minnesota	2	4	4	1	6	0	1	1	2	0
Mississippi	1	2	0	0	1	2	0	0	0	0
Missouri	2	0	1	0	1	0	1	0	0	0
Montana	2	4	2	1	3	1	1	2	1	1

Ranking Indicators

11 Endangered species, wetlands	12 $ for state parks	13 Power plant siting law	14 Comprehensive land-use planning	15 Envir. is stated goal	16 Surface mine reclamation	17 Flood plain protection	18 Dillard study	19 Aesthetics and zoning	20 $ for natural resources	21 Solid waste program	22 Agricultural preservation	23 Historic preservation	Total
0–2	0–2	0–3	0–4	0–2	0–3	0–2	0–6	0–2	0–2	0–2	0–3	0–2	0–63
1	1	0	0	0	1	0	1	0	0	2	0	0	10
1	2	0	2	2	2	0	2	0	1	0	0	0	23
0	0	3	3	0	0	2	1	0	0	2	1	1	24
0	2	2	0	0	3	2	2	1	2	2	0	2	27
2	2	3	4	2	0	1	4	2	1	2	2	2	46
1	1	0	0	2	1	1	5	2	0	1	1	1	26
2	0	3	0	0	0	1	5	1	0	2	1	2	32
2	1	1	1	0	0	0	4	2	1	0	0	0	29
2	1	2	4	0	1	0	5	2	0	2	0	0	31
2	1	1	0	0	1	0	2	1	0	2	0	1	25
2	2	1	3	0	0	2	3	2	2	0	2	1	34
0	1	0	3	0	0	0	3	0	1	1	2	0	16
1	2	0	0	0	2	2	3	0	0	2	2	2	28
1	1	1	2	0	1	2	3	1	0	2	1	2	36
1	0	3	1	0	2	2	1	1	0	2	2	2	29
1	1	2	1	0	2	2	2	1	0	1	1	1	23
1	2	3	2	0	1	1	4	1	1	2	1	1	34
0	2	0	0	2	2	0	3	1	2	2	0	0	21
2	1	0	2	0	1	2	3	1	1	1	1	2	32
2	1	3	1	0	2	1	6	0	0	0	3	2	37
1	1	3	1	2	0	1	5	2	0	2	1	1	44
1	1	0	0	2	0	2	2	2	0	2	1	1	30
2	1	3	3	2	0	2	5	1	1	2	2	2	47
0	2	0	0	0	2	0	2	0	1	2	0	0	15
1	1	0	0	0	2	0	2	1	0	1	0	1	14
1	2	3	1	0	2	0	3	2	2	1	0	2	37

Table 3.1 *Continued*

	Ranking Indicators									
	1	2	3	4	5	6	7	8	9	10
	Congressional voting record	State EI process	Priority envir. protection	Wildlife tax checkoff	$ for envir. quality control	Hazardous waste program	Umbrella envir. agency	Solar energy tax breaks	Protection of rivers	$ for noise pollution
Score Range	0–4	0–4	0–4	0–1	0–6	0–2	0–1	0–2	0–2	0–2
Nebraska	1	2	1	0	1	1	1	2	0	0
Nevada	1	2	3	0	1	0	0	0	0	0
New Hampshire	3	0	0	0	4	1	0	0	0	1
New Jersey	3	4	2	1	6	0	1	2	2	1
New Mexico	0	0	0	1	1	0	1	0	1	0
New York	3	4	1	1	3	0	1	1	2	1
North Carolina	1	4	1	1	2	2	1	2	2	0
North Dakota	3	0	1	0	1	1	1	2	1	0
Ohio	2	0	2	1	6	0	1	2	2	0
Oklahoma	2	0	2	1	1	2	0	0	2	0
Oregon	3	0	2	1	4	1	1	2	2	2
Pennsylvania	2	0	2	1	2	1	1	0	2	—
Rhode Island	4	2	2	0	4	1	1	2	0	0
South Carolina	1	0	4	1	1	2	1	0	2	1
South Dakota	1	4	3	0	1	0	1	1	2	—
Tennessee	2	0	2	0	1	1	1	1	2	0
Texas	1	2	2	0	0	2	0	2	0	0
Utah	0	2	1	1	1	1	1	0	0	0
Vermont	3	0	2	0	5	1	1	0	0	0
Virginia	0	4	2	1	1	1	0	0	2	0
Washington	3	4	2	0	2	0	1	1	2	1
West Virginia	1	0	4	1	1	0	0	0	2	—
Wisconsin	3	4	2	1	2	1	1	1	2	0
Wyoming	2	0	4	0	2	0	1	0	0	—

SOURCE: Christopher J. Duerksen, *Environmental Regulation of Industrial Plant Siting* (Washington, D.C.: The Conservation Foundation, 1983), pp. 224–25.

Ranking Indicators

11	12	13	14	15	16	17	18	19	20	21	22	23	
Endangered species, wetlands	$ for state parks	Power plant siting law	Comprehensive land-use planning	Envir. is stated goal	Surface mine reclamation	Flood plain protection	Dillard study	Aesthetics and zoning	$ for natural resources	Solid waste program	Agricultural preservation	Historic preservation	Total
0–2	0–2	0–3	0–4	0–2	0–3	0–2	0–6	0–2	0–2	0–2	0–3	0–2	0–63
1	2	1	1	2	0	1	2	0	1	1	1	0	22
1	2	3	2	2	0	0	3	0	1	0	0	1	22
1	2	2	0	0	0	0	2	1	1	1	1	1	21
2	2	1	1	2	0	2	5	2	1	0	3	2	45
1	1	2	1	2	1	0	2	2	1	0	0	1	18
2	2	3	0	2	1	2	2	2	0	0	2	2	37
1	0	1	1	0	0	1	2	0	0	2	0	1	25
0	1	3	0	0	1	0	2	1	1	1	1	1	22
1	1	3	0	0	2	0	2	2	1	1	1	0	30
1	2	0	0	2	1	0	1	0	0	2	0	0	19
2	2	3	3	2	0	0	5	2	1	2	1	1	42
1	2	0	0	0	2	1	3	1	0	2	3	2	28
2	0	0	1	0	0	0	4	0	0	1	1	1	26
2	2	2	0	2	0	0	3	0	0	0	0	1	25
1	1	3	2	0	1	0	5	0	1	1	1	1	30
1	2	0	0	2	1	0	3	0	0	2	0	2	23
2	1	1	1	0	2	0	4	0	0	1	0	1	22
0	2	0	1	0	3	0	5	2	1	0	1	1	23
2	2	3	0	2	0	2	5	0	1	1	0	2	32
2	0	3	3	0	2	0	4	0	0	0	1	2	28
2	2	3	0	2	0	2	5	1	1	1	3	1	39
0	2	0	1	2	2	0	2	1	1	0	1	2	23
2	1	3	0	2	0	2	3	2	0	2	1	2	37
0	2	2	1	2	2	0	2	0	2	0	1	0	23

Table 3.2 States' Commitment to Environmental Quality

State	Ranking by Pollution Potential (1)	Ranking from Survey (2)	Need-Response Index (1)–(2)
Michigan	1	18	−17
Ohio	1	18	−17
Pennsylvania	1	23	−22
California	2	2	0
Illinois	3	23	−20
Texas	3	39	−36
Indiana	4	11	− 7
New York	4	7	− 3
New Jersey	5	3	2
Alabama	6	50	−44
North Carolina	7	29	−22
Florida	7	17	−10
Massachusetts	7	4	3
Virginia	7	23	−16
Louisiana	8	43	−35
West Virginia	8	33	−25
Arizona	9	32	−23
Colorado	9	27	−18
Kansas	9	33	−24
Kentucky	9	12	− 3
Maine	9	14	− 5
Montana	9	7	2
Nevada	9	39	−30
New Mexico	9	46	−37
Oregon	9	5	4
Utah	9	33	−24
Washington	9	6	3
Wisconsin	9	7	2
Wyoming	9	33	−24
Alaska	10	33	−23
Arkansas	10	26	−16
Connecticut	10	14	− 4
Delaware	10	21	−11
Georgia	10	29	−19
Hawaii	10	12	− 2

Table 3.2 *Continued*

State	Ranking by Pollution Potential (1)	Ranking from Survey (2)	Need-Response Index (1)–(2)
Idaho	10	47	−37
Iowa	10	21	−11
Maryland	10	7	3
Minnesota	10	1	9
Mississippi	10	48	−38
Missouri	10	49	−39
Nebraska	10	39	−29
New Hampshire	10	43	−33
North Dakota	10	39	−29
Oklahoma	10	45	−35
Rhode Island	10	27	−17
South Carolina	10	29	−19
South Dakota	10	18	− 8
Tennessee	10	33	−23
Vermont	10	14	− 4

SOURCES: Charles O. Jones, "Regulating the Environment," in Herbert Jacob and Kenneth N. Vines, eds., *Politics in the American States: A Comparative Analysis* (Little, Brown and Company, 1976), pp. 416–17; and Christopher J. Duerksen, *Environmental Regulation of Industrial Plant Siting* (Washington, D.C.: The Conservation Foundation, 1983), pp. 224–25.

A Typology

If we assume that successful implementation of environmental programs is a function of both state institutional capacity and relative dependence upon federal grants within this area of policy, a fourfold typology can be constructed. This classification scheme should aid us in predicting probable state responses in reaction to federal cutbacks in grant expenditures and in formulating testable hypotheses for future research efforts (see figure 3.1).

Each of the four sets of characteristic state behavior will be discussed in terms of the probable actions taken by state policy-makers and their effects on state environmental quality.

1. Interdependence. In this instance, states form a partnership with the federal government in implementing their environmental programs. Thus, simply to do more, or to do more efficiently what it is already doing, a state

Table 3.3 Federal Support of State Environmental Programs, FY 1982

State	Percent Federal Support	State	Percent Federal Support
1. Rhode Island	80.8	26. New York	56.7
2. Montana	80.0	27. South Dakota	56.5
3. Connecticut	79.6	28. Wyoming	56.0
4. Idaho	79.0	29. North Carolina	55.8
5. Vermont	78.8	30. Massachusetts	53.8
6. Nebraska	74.0	31. Georgia	53.3
7. Arizona	71.8	32. New Mexico	53.0
8. Maine	70.5	33. Michigan	50.8
9. Missouri	69.5	34. Colorado	49.0
10. Alabama	68.3	35. Iowa	48.8
11. New Hampshire	68.3	36. Kentucky	47.8
12. North Dakota	67.3	37. Minnesota	47.8
13. Kansas	66.5	38. Tennessee	47.8
14. Delaware	66.3	39. Texas	46.3
15. Arkansas	64.8	40. Virginia	44.3
16. Utah	63.8	41. South Carolina	44.0
17. Wisconsin	63.5	42. Florida	43.5
18. Hawaii	63.3	43. Alaska	43.3
19. Maryland	63.3	44. Pennsylvania	42.3
20. West Virginia	61.5	45. Indiana	41.0
21. Mississippi	61.3	46. Ohio	40.3
22. Oklahoma	61.3	47. Louisiana	38.8
23. Washington	61.3	48. Oregon	36.8
24. Nevada	61.0	49. New Jersey	36.0
25. Illinois	59.5	50. California	24.0
Median Score	58.1%		

Figures express the average percentage of total program costs in air quality, water quality, hazardous waste, and water supply programs.

SOURCE: U.S. Senate, Committee on Environment and Public Works, *The Impact of the Proposed EPA Budget on State and Local Environmental Programs,* Hearings before the Subcommittee on Toxic Substances and Environmental Oversight, February 16 and March 28, 1983 (Washington, D.C.: Government Printing Office, 1983), p. 173.

State Dependency on Federal Aid	State Institutional Capability: High	State Institutional Capability: Low
High	(1) INTERDEPENDENCE Connecticut Delaware Hawaii Illinois Maine Maryland Massachusetts Michigan MONTANA New York South Dakota Vermont Washington Wisconsin *Total 14*	(2) DEPENDENCE Alabama Arizona Arkansas Georgia Idaho Kansas Mississippi MISSOURI Nebraska Nevada New Hampshire New Mexico North Carolina North Dakota Oklahoma Rhode Island Utah West Virginia Wyoming *Total 19*
Low	(3) INDEPENDENCE CALIFORNIA Florida Indiana Iowa Kentucky Minnesota New Jersey Ohio Oregon Pennsylvania Virginia *Total 11*	(4) PASSIVITY Alaska Colorado LOUISIANA South Carolina Tennessee TEXAS *Total 6*

Figure 3.1 A Typology of State Behavior: Fiscal Dependency and Institutional Capability. SOURCE: Compiled by the authors.

may enter into federal arrangements to facilitate such desires. The purpose of such collaboration is to facilitate or enhance a particular state's capacity—to enlarge the range of what is financially possible for each state in the performance of an environmental task. The federal role is essentially limited to financial assistance for state environmental activities. An example of such behavior is Montana, which exhibits a high level of environmental institutional capability coupled with a high level of fiscal dependency.

Research Expectation: If federal aid for environmental programs is reduced to the states in this category, then we would expect a subsequent reduction in state environmental programs. Environmental programs would be expected to continue, albeit without the same level of funding prior to the federal budgetary reduction. We would expect to see a continuation of some programs but not others, or a slight reduction across all programs. Temporary federal assistance would enable these states to fully restore these programs.

2. Dependence. The second case arises when states are quite dependent upon federal environmental aid and assistance to successfully implement state environmental programs. These states lack any strong internal capability and largely depend upon federal aid to fund state programs. They have not developed strong internal capabilities because they lack adequate fiscal resources of their own and/or because they do not have a strong commitment to environmental protection. Instead, they rely upon the federal government to provide funds, information, and technical assistance for the implementation of state programs. A prominent example found within this category is Missouri. This state exhibits one of the lowest levels of state institutional capacity and it is one of the nine most dependent states in terms of fiscal federalism in the environmental area.

Research Expectation: If federal aid and assistance is reduced to these states, then we expect that state environmental protection activities will be drastically reduced. These states have little choice but to curtail such activities since they lack an internal commitment and/or the fiscal resources necessary to carry out environmental tasks. In this situation we would expect states to exhibit much reduced activity in the environmental sphere due to a reduction of federal presence and assistance. Only a return to federal control and assistance would ensure state program implementation.

3. Independence. The third case is where states have developed strong institutional capabilities and are not heavily dependent upon federal aid for implementing state environmental programs. In this instance, states rely upon their own fiscal resources, political institutions, and state policy formulation in the environmental area. They have established themselves as leaders in the environmental sphere and have often enacted environmental standards that exceed national standards.

California is a good example of states in this category. California has aggressively pursued environmental protection in terms of its resources committed, legislation enacted, and institutions formed. In addition, this state is the least dependent on federal aid.

Research Expectation: Federal aid reductions in this instance will have little or no effect on the implementation of state environmental programs. Rather, these states will continue their high levels of activity in the environmental area since they have long relied upon their own internal resources as opposed to federal aid. Decentralization of environmental programs is likely to be both successful and desirable.

4. Passivity. The fourth and final set of states are those that have neither an internal institutional capability nor a strong dependency upon federal aid. These states are typically the "policy-laggard" states who are not entirely comfortable with environmental protection as a policy goal and who resist federal intervention. They have not developed an internal capability due to a lack of commitment as well as a scarcity of fiscal resources to apply to environmental protection activities. In addition, they resist federal intervention aid into what they consider to be a state policy domain. Louisiana and Texas typify this category of states. Texas, for example, has not exhibited a strong commitment to environmental protection over the years and, in addition, it has a well-known aversion to federal aid and federal intervention into state politics and policy (Lamare, 1981).

Research Expectation: Federal aid reductions in these instances will also have little or no effect on the implementation of state programs. However, unlike the previous category of states, these states will maintain their previously low level of activity in the environmental area. Given their aversion to federal aid and their own inability to implement environmental programs by themselves, regional cooperation may be most appropriate.

This fourfold classification by no means exhausts the range of possibilities, but it does facilitate the explication of some dynamics of contemporary intergovernmental relations, their application to specific cases, and systematic speculation about the likely impacts of New Federalism upon state environmental policy. This research also suggests that some states (e.g., Missouri) may be incapable of successfully implementing environmental policies without federal aid and control, others (e.g., Montana) may need only temporary federal monetary support for state planning and administrative efforts, while still others may need a transitional phase involving greater use of regional organizations and/or interstate compacts (e.g., Louisiana). Finally, for some states (e.g. California), a decentralization approach may be quite successful and even desirable.

Directions for Future Research

The preceding analysis provides a conceptual device for examining the prospective decentralization of federal environmental policies. We have suggested that two critical dimensions are the institutional capacity of a state to administer these programs and the relative degree of dependence upon federal grant monies for both start-up and operating costs. The interaction between these variables, in our view, will aid in explaining why some states are better equipped than others to assume greater responsibility for the management of environmental programs in the 1990s. A remaining task is to assess the empirical validity of this typology, giving particular emphasis to interstate variations in the replacement of declining federal funding with own-source revenues. In the spirit of encouraging additional research along these lines, the following hypotheses are offered:

H1 : The greater the state dependence on federal funding for environmental programs, the less the probability that funding cuts will be replaced with state-generated revenues.

H2 : The greater the institutional capacity of a state, the greater the probability that funding cuts will be replaced with state generated revenues.

H3 : States characterized by high institutional capacity and low dependence on federal funding for environmental programs are more likely to replace funding cuts with state-generated revenues.

H4: States characterized by low institutional capacity and high dependence on federal funding for environmental programs are less likely to replace funding cuts with state-generated revenues.

H5 : States characterized by high institutional capacity and high dependence on federal funding for environmental programs are less likely to replace funding cuts with state-generated revenues.

H6: States characterized by low institutional capacity and low dependence on federal funding for environmental programs are less likely to replace funding cuts with state-generated revenues.

Additional hypotheses on the importance of fiscal pressures, political ideology, and the severity of environmental problems can easily be culled from our work and the writing of other IGR researchers such as Nathan and Doolittle (1983). Subsequent testing should reveal whether decentralization and federal defunding of environmental programs is associated with a decline (or increase) in state environmental management effectiveness.

Part Two

Actors and Institutions in Environmental Policy

4

Public Opinion and Environmental Policy

Riley E. Dunlap

About two decades ago environmental quality began to emerge as a major social problem in our society. Issues such as wilderness protection and air pollution had previously received the attention of relatively small numbers of conservationists and public health officials, but in the mid-sixties a wide range of threats to environmental quality began to attract the attention of the media, policy-makers, and the public (see, e.g., Trop and Roos, 1971). By 1970 "the environment" had clearly become a major national concern, as reflected by the huge scale of Earth Day (April 22, 1970) celebrations across the nation. Path-breaking environmental protection legislation was enacted at all levels of government during the late sixties and early seventies, reflecting the link between public opinion and governmental action widely assumed to exist in democratic societies (e.g., Key, 1961).

While the degree of correspondence between public opinion and policy output is a matter of debate (Pierce et al., 1982:chapter 14), it is generally assumed that the success of efforts to protect or improve "public welfare" (as opposed to efforts to enhance private interests) is significantly dependent upon supportive public opinion. Whether such efforts are spearheaded by political leaders, issue entrepreneurs such as Ralph Nader, or full-fledged social movements, their success or failure is likely to be heavily influenced by the amount of support they receive from the general public. Although contributions (money, time, etc.) and political support (voting, petition signing, letter writing, etc.) are obviously crucial, the mere expression of supportive opinion in a scientific survey or informal poll—as often conducted by local newspapers and politicians—can also be a vital resource. As Mitchell (1984b:52) notes with regard to the environmental movement, "Public support of environmental groups provides them with a key lobbying resource because it lends credibility to the claim that they represent the 'public interest.'" The existence of supportive public opinion is a resource not only when lobbying for new legislation, but when pressing for the effective implementation of existing legislation as well (Sabatier and Mazmanian, 1980:550; also see Lake, 1983:216).

For these reasons the status of public opinion on environmental issues has received a great deal of attention over the past two decades. The degree to which the public supports efforts to protect environmental quality, and whether such support has increased or decreased, has been the subject of considerable debate over the years (see, e.g., Ladd, 1982). The purpose of this paper is to present a comprehensive review of the available evidence on public concern for environmental quality over the past two decades. I will focus in detail on the available longitudinal data in an effort to draw conclusions about trends in public opinion over the past twenty years. The effort will be difficult because there are no data sets which have continuously monitored public opinion on environmental issues over this time period. However, by piecing together several sets of relevant trend data I hope to be able to draw accurate conclusions about the broad contours of trends in public concern. These conclusions will be compared to expectations derived from an influential model of the evolution of public concern with environmental problems in particular, and social problems in general, set forth by Downs (1972) shortly after the emergence of environmental quality as a major social issue.

Before turning to the available trend data I will describe Downs's "issue-attention cycle" in some detail, and also examine the concept of public opinion itself in an effort to develop some conceptual distinctions that may prove useful in evaluating public concern for environmental quality. I shall then review four sets of trend data, covering the late sixties to 1970, the early seventies, the mid- to late seventies, and the eighties. Along the way I will attempt to assess the degree to which the available data conform to expectations derived from the issue-attention cycle, and suggest modifications of Downs's model where appropriate. I will end by offering an assessment of the overall strength of public support for environmental quality in the United States.

A Model of the Evolution of Public Opinion: The Issue-Attention Cycle

A variety of models of the evolution of public opinion have been developed by opinion analysts (e.g., Pierce et al., 1982:151–56), but Downs's (1972) model of the issue-attention cycle has clearly been the most influential among those interested in public opinion on environmental issues. Writing shortly after Earth Day, 1970, when environmental quality had clearly become a major social problem, Downs suggested that environmental problems would likely meet the fate experienced by most social problems—have a brief "moment in the sun" and then fade from public attention as newer problems take center stage on the national agenda. Specifically, he suggested (1972:39–40) that social problems typically proceed through a five-stage cycle: (1) the "pre-problem stage" where the undesirable social condition exists, and may have aroused the interest of experts or interest groups, but has not yet attracted much attention from the public; (2) the "alarmed discovery and euphoric enthusiasm" stage in which one or more dramatic events or crises brings the problem to the public's attention and creates enthusiastic support for "solving" it; (3) a "realization of the cost of significant progress," which dampens public enthusiasm; (4) a gradual "decline in the intense public interest" due to recognition of the costs of a solution, boredom with the issue, and decline in media attention to the problem; and finally (5) the "post-problem stage" in which an issue is replaced at the center of public concern by new problems and moves into "a twilight realm of lesser attention or spasmodic recurrences of interest," typically with little if any improvement in the problematic conditions. Downs went on to say that in 1972 environmental quality was about halfway through the issue-attention cycle, although he was careful to qualify his prediction that it would soon disappear from public attention.

Perhaps the reason Downs's analysis has been so influential is not only that his issue-attention cycle was elegant in its simplicity (and readily accessible to lay persons), but that it also corresponded nicely to a vast amount of social science research—especially by sociologists and political scientists—on societal efforts to solve social problems. Sociologists have posited a "natural history" model of social problems, in which a social movement or interest group organizes on behalf of a perceived problematic condition (environmental degradation, racial prejudice, etc.) and works to obtain the attention of the media, the public, and ultimately policy-makers. While most "social-problem movements" fail to get off the ground, some are successful in getting the larger society to accept their view of certain conditions as "problematic" and to take action designed to ameliorate such conditions—usually in the form of government legislation. The very success of a movement in this regard ironically contributes to its demise, however, as some activists are co-opted by government, others lose interest, and the media and public tend to assume the problem is being solved and turn their attention to more pressing problems. Frequently all of this occurs with little if any improvement in the conditions which gave rise to the movement (see, e.g., Mauss, 1975; Spector and Kitsuse, 1977; and Schoenfeld et al., 1979).

While also paying attention to the important role played by interest groups in getting perceived problems onto the political agenda, political scientists have focused relatively more attention on the latter stages of the problem-solving cycle—specifically, why policies designed to solve problems are frequently ineffective. On the one hand it has been noted that many interest groups achieve only "symbolic" victories, with government passing reassuring but essentially meaningless legislation to placate the groups (Edelman, 1964). On the other hand, even when well-funded agencies are set up to solve a problem, they are likely to fail, typically because they are "captured" by the very interests they are supposed to regulate (e.g., polluting industries). Indeed, the presumed common failure of governmental agencies to achieve their intended results has led to the formulation of the "life-cycle" or "natural decay" model of regulatory agencies (Bernstein, 1955).

Like Downs, then, many social scientists posit a pattern in which social problems are discovered or created by a group of activists who are successful in getting the larger society to accept their definition of the conditions as problematic. Such efforts are nearly always transitory, however, and a major reason seems to be the inevitable decline of public interest in and attention to the problem. Most authors are rather vague about precisely why the public loses interest, but basic "boredom" with the problem and the fact that the media typically turn to newer, more exciting issues are often mentioned (Downs, 1972; Mauss, 1975:64; Sabatier and Mazmanian, 1980:550). What seems particularly probable and important, however, is that a movement's success in stimulating governmental action to solve a problem leads the public to believe that the problem is "being taken care of" and there's no longer any reason to worry about it. In other words, once the government assumes responsibility for a problem, the general citizenry (and the media and activists to lesser degrees) is likely to feel less personal concern for the problem. Ironically, then, the very success of a movement in getting policy-makers to address its grievances (usually dependent upon substantial public support) may tend to undercut its support among the public.

Thus, rather than just assuming that public attention to social problems inevitably progresses through Downs's issue-attention cycle, recognition of the crucial role of governmental action (emphasized in the traditional social science literature on social-problem solving) provides insight into *why* public concern for social problems typically declines—as well as conditions under which the decline is likely to be exacerbated or retarded. In terms of the latter, I would expect that aggressive governmental action to solve a social problem would, somewhat nonintuitively, lead to a decline in public concern for the problem. Given its origins in the natural history of social problems and natural decay of regulatory agency literature, I have elsewhere termed this hypothesized decline in public concern the "natural decline" model of public opinion toward social problems (Dunlap et al., 1979).

Public Opinion: Some Conceptual Issues

Before going further I should acknowledge that the term "public concern for environmental quality" is a rather broad concept. It has the advantage, however, of being applicable to a wide range of available data. Throughout this paper, for example, evidence will be reviewed on the public's perception of environmental problems in general (or air and water pollution in particular) as serious, on its support for governmental efforts to improve and protect environmental quality, on its endorsement of environmental protection relative to other social goals, and on its avowed willingness to pay for pollution abatement. All of these indicators appear to reflect a broad "concern" for protecting and improving the quality of the physical environment (see, e.g., Keeter, 1984), and thus my choice of labels. However, the situation is further complicated by the fact that one can still discern various aspects of this broad concept of environmental concern, a point illustrated in mainstream work on public opinion. Indeed, public opinion theorists have written a great deal about the meaning of both "opinion" and "the public," and some of their distinctions will prove useful in reviewing the data on trends in public opinion toward environmental quality.

Beginning with the concept of opinion, most public opinion analysts distinguish between *individual opinions* and *public opinion,* the latter defined as the aggregate of the former. Many analysts also note the multiple characteristics or aspects of opinions at both the individual and public levels, although there is far from perfect agreement concerning the number and nature of these aspects. The following discussion draws heavily upon Pierce et al. (1982:15–21) and Nimmo and Bonjean (1972:4–6), and to a lesser degree upon earlier sources (Key, 1961; Lane and Sears, 1964).

One can distinguish four important aspects of individual opinions. First is the *direction* of an opinion, whether an individual is pro or con, favorable or unfavorable, toward pollution control, for example. Second is the *degree* (or extremity) of an opinion—whether, for example, an individual is "strongly" or "mildly" in favor of pollution control, or whether he or she views pollution as "very," "moderately," or "slightly" serious. Third is *salience,* or the degree to which an individual is personally interested in an issue. Environmental quality is salient to an individual when it is "on the mind" of that person, and not just something that he or she thinks about when asked for an opinion. Finally, an individual's opinions on different issues vary according to the *intensity* with which they are held, just as individuals vary according to the intensity with which they hold opinions in general. Acknowledging variation in intensity recognizes that two individuals may both "strongly favor" environmental protection, for example, but that one may be far more committed to it than is the other (joining an environmental organization, carefully recycling household wastes, etc.).

Turning to public opinion as the aggregate of individual opinions, one can discern four related but not identical characteristics. First is the *distribution* of opinion on an issue, or the proportion of the public falling into each of the various direction/degree categories on the issue. For example, the distribution of opinion on the issue "Federal funding for water pollution programs should be increased" would be the number (and percentage) of people who "strongly agree," "agree," "disagree," or "strongly disagree" with the statement. Second, given the distribution of opinion on an issue, one can determine the extent of *consensus* in public opinion on the issue—that is, whether a sizable majority of the public expresses agreement (or disagreement) or whether the public is sharply divided or polarized on the issue. Third, mirroring the situation at the individual level, issues may be of interest to smaller or larger proportions of the public and therefore vary in their *saliency* among "the public." In other words, some issues are more likely to be "on the minds" of large segments of the public than are others. Finally, similar to individual opinions, public opinion varies in its *intensity* across issues. Thus, two issues (e.g., inflation and pollution) may evoke similar opinions from equally large proportions of the public, but the opinions may be felt more intensely for one of them.

While the foregoing distinctions are important to keep in mind when examining public opinion on environmental issues, applying them to the existing data will not be easy. The reason is that standard measures of public opinion do not provide unambiguous indicators of all of these aspects. Most items used in public opinion surveys provide adequate measures of the direction and degree of individual opinions, and thus allow one to determine the distribution of opinion and degree of consensus among the public, but this is not the case for salience and intensity. While there appear to be some rough but plausible indicators of the salience of environmental quality for the public, there are no agreed upon indicators for judging the intensity with which the public supports environmental protection. Yet, as we shall see, much of the debate over the degree of public concern with environmental quality, both absolute levels and trends over time, reflects differing interpretations of the salience and intensity of such concern. Consequently, I shall apply these concepts as appropriate when reviewing the data on environmental opinions, with the goals of providing insight into existing debates as well as clarifying as much as possible the state of public concern with environmental quality.

I noted above that the concept of the public has also received a good deal of attention from public opinion analysts. Probably the most widely used distinction is that between the "mass public" and the "attentive public," the latter defined as the segment of the public that is particularly interested in and informed about the policy issues being examined and the former referring to the rest of the public (see, e.g., Pierce et al., 1982:13–14). However, when dealing with a policy area that is intimately related to the activities of a social movement, as is true of environmental quality, it is helpful to make some finer distinctions which specifically recognize the important role played by the movement.

Sociologists who have examined the interrelations between social movements and public opinion have suggested the importance of distinguishing between various layers or "orbits" of the public organized around an issue such as environmental quality (Hornback and Morrison, 1975; Mauss, 1975:47–49). The following seem most pertinent. At the core of the environmental movement are the "activists," individuals intensely concerned about and personally active on behalf of environmental quality (including but not limited to joining an organization such as the Sierra Club). Surrounding the core is a layer comprised of the "attentive public," individuals interested in and informed about environmental issues. These individuals are likely to provide occasional support for environmental causes, signing petitions, voting for pro-environmental issues and candidates and perhaps even contributing time and money to specific environmental campaigns. The third and probably largest layer is the "sympathetic public," individuals who—although not very attentive to environmental issues—express support for efforts to enhance and protect environmental quality (i.e., the goals of the environmental movement). Outside of these pro-environment layers are the "neutrals," persons who have little interest in and typically no opinion concerning environmental issues. And, finally, there are the "opponents," individuals who are opposed to some degree to the goals of the environmental movement and hold opinions that can be characterized as "anti-environmental."[1]

As in the case of the opinion concept, these distinctions among types of publics are important, but applying them will not be easy because of the absence of clearcut indicators of the diffferent orbits. Nonetheless, where appropriate I will use the available data on public opinion toward environmental issues in order to make rough estimates of the proportions of the public falling into each orbit. Doing so may prove useful in summarizing and evaluating trends in public concern for environmental quality.

Lastly, I should point to what appears to be a correspondence, albeit imperfect, between the types of publics and the types of opinions noted above. Thus, it seems likely that environmental issues are not only salient for environmental activists, but that their opinions on such issues are held with considerable intensity. Environmental issues should also be relatively salient for the environmentally attentive segment of the public, while the nonattentive but sympathetic public should respond in a pro-environment direction when queried about environmental matters. Finally, we would expect the neutrals to indicate "no opinion," and the opponents to express varying degrees of anti-environmental opinion, when asked about their views on environmental issues.

Trends in Public Concern for Environmental Quality

Reflecting the relatively recent emergence of environmental quality as a major societal issue is the fact that there are virtually no data on public opinion toward environmental issues prior to the mid-sixties. Public opinion pollsters and academic survey researchers both generally ignored environmental issues until the last half of the sixties (see, e.g., Trop and Roos, 1971; Erskine, 1972a;

1972b). I shall therefore begin the review of trends in public concern with environmental quality by focusing on the emergence of such concern in the sixties and its rapid escalation up to 1970, and then turn to a review of the trends in public concern since 1970. The coverage of the existing data, as well as the nature of the discernible trends, suggests the appropriateness of dividing the latter review into three periods: the early seventies, the middle to late seventies and the eighties.

The sixties to 1970: the emergence of widespread public concern

The fact that environmental issues were virtually ignored by public opinion pollsters in the early sixties indicates the low level of societal attention to such issues at that time, and that environmental quality was still in what Downs (1972) terms the "pre-problem stage" (of interest mainly to conservationists and air and water pollution experts). The situation rapidly changed in the latter half of the decade, however, as several interrelated developments thrust environmental issues onto the public agenda. Traditional conservation organizations such as the Sierra Club were becoming much more visible, both because they were appealing for widespread public support in battles such as the fight to prevent the damming of the Grand Canyon, and because they were increasingly broadening their focus from the preservation of wilderness and scenic areas to a wider range of environmental problems (e.g., air and water pollution and pesticide contamination). These strategies coincided with a rapid increase in outdoor recreational activities among Americans, likely contributing to the significant increase in membership experienced by several conservation organizations during the late sixties (McEvoy, 1972). At the same time, political leaders such as President Johnson and Senators Muskie and Jackson were pushing important environmental legislation through Congress. These measures ranged from those designed to improve air and water quality to those protecting endangered species, and culminated in the landmark National Environmental Policy Act (NEPA) of late 1969. The above activities no doubt helped sensitize the mass media to environmental issues, and by the late sixties environmental problems were receiving tremendous exposure in the media. (On these points see, e.g., Davies, 1977; Fanning, 1975; McEvoy, 1972; Mitchell and Davies, 1978; Schoenfeld et al., 1979; Trop and Roos, 1971).

Underlying and facilitating the above phenomena were two broad societal trends. First, growing affluence led to a decline in materialistic values and an increased concern with quality-of-life issues such as recreation and environmental amenities (Watts and Wandesforde-Smith, 1980). Second, more than a decade of civil rights and antiwar activism created a conducive atmosphere—both a sense that change is possible and a search for a less conflictual issue—for the mobilization of widespread support for environmental protection (Schnaiberg, 1973). The mobilization occurred with preparations for the first Earth Day, an activity spearheaded by Senator Gaylord Nelson and Congressman Mike McCloskey and led by a student-oriented organization that evolved into Environmental Action (a major organization still in existence). The April 22, 1970, celebration of "E-Day" is estimated to have involved twenty million participants, an unprecedented level of environmental activism, and more than any other event before or since, it thrust environmental quality into public prominence (see, e.g., Dunlap and Gale, 1972; Fanning, 1975:chapter 2).

The effect of all of this on public opinion is illustrated by several pieces of trend data summarized in table 4.1. The first set of data, Gallup polls conducted in 1965 and 1970, show that the percentage of the public selecting "reducing pollution of air and water" as a problem that should receive the attention of government more than tripled (from 17 to 53 percent) during those five years. Almost as impressive an increase is documented in a series of Opinion Research Corporation surveys covering the same time period, as the percentages viewing air and water pollution as "very or somewhat serious" in their vicinity more than doubled, from 28 to 69 percent for air pollution and from 35 to 74 percent for water pollution. A bit less impressive was the increase in the percentage responding that there was "a lot" or "some" air pollution in their area, from 56 to 70 percent, in 1967 and 1970 Harris surveys. Yet, note that the Harris and ORC questions focused on perceived levels of pollution in the respondent's vicinity, whereas the Gallup question focused on national priorities. It seems logical that the former would be influenced somewhat more by actual conditions than would the latter, and since there was very little change in actual pollution levels during this period, the increases found by Harris and especially ORC are impressive.

The Harris surveys also asked respondents if they would be willing to pay $15 a year more in taxes for an air pollution control program, perhaps a somewhat more stringent measure of personal commitment to environmental protection. The 1967 to 1970 increase in the percent "willing" rose from 44 to 54, while the percent "unwilling" dropped from 46 to 34 ("not sure" rose from 10 to 12 percent). The last set of Harris data covers only seven months, from

Table 4.1 Trend Studies of Public Concern for Environmental Quality—Mid-Sixties to 1970

National Trend Studies		Percent Response by Year					
		65	66	67	68	69	70
1. Gallup[a]	"Reducing pollution of air and water" selected as one of three national problems that should receive attention of government	17	—	—	—	—	53
2. Opinion Research Corporation[b]	Air/water pollution viewed as "very or somewhat serious" in the area:						
	a. air pollution	28	48	53	55	—	69
	b. water pollution	35	49	52	58	—	74
3. Louis Harris[c]	"A lot or some" air pollution thought to exist in the area			56	—	—	70
4. Louis Harris[d]	Willing to pay $15 a year more in taxes to finance air pollution control program			44	—	—	54
5. Louis Harris[e]	"Pollution control" selected as government spending area "least like to see cut"					38	55

[a]See Mitchell (1980:404) for question wording and complete results.
[b]See Erskine (1972b:121).
[c]See Erskine (1972b:123).
[d]See Erskine (1972b:132).
[e]See Erskine (1972b:129).

August 1969 to March 1970, but reflects the impact of the mobilization for Earth Day on public opinion. Thus, the percentage selecting "pollution control" as one of the three or four government programs (from a list of ten) that they would "least like to see cut" increased by nearly half, from 38 to 55, during that short period of time.

These trend data, especially those covering 1965 to 1970, indicate how substantially public concern with environmental quality rose during the last half of the sixties. Especially notable is the fact that in the Gallup surveys the 17 percent selecting pollution reduction ranked it ninth among the ten problems in 1965, while the 53 percent selecting it in 1970 placed it second only to crime reduction. Such results led Erskine (1972b:120) to conclude that, "A miracle of public opinion has been the unprecedented speed and urgency with which ecological issues have burst into American consciousness. Alarm about the environment sprang from nowhere to major proportions in a few short years." The results also suggest that by 1970 environmental quality had definitely moved from the pre-problem stage to the "alarmed discovery" stage of Downs's issue-attention cycle, the point where the public clearly acknowledges the seriousness of a problem and enthusiastically supports efforts to solve it.

Drawing upon earlier terminology, it seems appropriate to argue that environmental protection had become a *consensual* issue by 1970, as majorities of the public expressed pro-environment opinions and typically only small minorities expressed opinions in the anti-environment direction. Thus two-thirds to three-fourths of the public saw pollution as at least somewhat problematic, and the 55 percent selecting pollution control as one of the areas they would least like to see cut in the 1970 Harris survey overwhelmed the 3 percent who selected it as one they would most like to see cut. Even avowed willingness to pay $15 a year more in taxes to control air pollution quickly moved from a minority position in 1967 (44 percent willing vs. 46 percent unwilling) to a strong majority position in 1970 (54 percent willing vs. 34 percent unwilling). The high and consensual level of concern for environmental quality at the end of the decade is also reflected by a variety of cross-sectional data collected in 1969 or 1970 (see Erskine, 1972b).

Environmental quality had clearly achieved a position of prominence on the public agenda by 1970, and when queried about environmental issues, majorities of the public expressed pro-environment positions. But to what degree had environmental quality become a "salient" issue for Americans—to what extent was it on their minds? This is a difficult matter to judge, but many public opinion analysts have argued that *volunteered* responses to "most important problem" (MIP) questions—that is, open-ended questions that ask respondents what they see as the country's most important problem or problems—provide a good indicator of the salience of an issue (see, e.g., Key, 1961:46; Lane and Sears, 1964:15; Peters and Hogwood, 1985:249). Not surprisingly, there is very little data on the salience of environmental quality in the sixties, and since the two available trend studies beginning in the sixties extend

Table 4.2 Longitudinal Studies of Public Concern for Environmental Quality—Late Sixties to Mid-Seventies

		Percent Response by Year								
		68	69	70	71	72	73	74	75	76
National Trend Studies										
1. Michigan National Election Survey[a]	Pollution, ecology, etc., volunteered as one of the country's "most important problems"	2	—	17	—	10				
2. Louis Harris[b]	Pollution, ecology, etc., volunteered as one of "the two or three biggest problems facing people like yourself"			41	—	13	11	9	6	
State Trend/ Panel Studies										
1. Wisconsin[c]	Environmental problems volunteered as one of two most important facing the state	17	—	40	—	15	—	10		
2. Washington panel[d]	Favor government spending "more money" on:									
	a. pollution control			70	—	—	—	32		
	b. protection of natural resources			52	—	—	—	37		
3. Washington trend[e]	"Reducing air and water pollution" selected as one of two or three most serious problems in:									
	a. state			44	—	—	—	—	—	18
	b. respondent's community			23	—	—	—	—	—	15

[a]See Hornback (1974:87, 233–34) for question wording and response coding.
[b]See Mitchell and Davies (1978:fig. 2) for question wording and complete results.
[c]See Buttel (1975a:83–85; 1975b:58) for question wording and response coding.
[d]See Dunlap and Dillman (1976:383–84) for question wording and complete results.
[e]See Dunlap and Van Liere (1977:110) for question wording and complete results.

past 1970, I have summarized them in table 4.2, along with other longitudinal studies beginning in 1970.

The only trend study of the salience of environmental quality at the national level beginning in the sixties was Hornback's (1974) analysis of MIP data collected in the Michigan National Election Survey (NES), where respondents were encouraged (via probes) to mention up to three problems facing the country. Hornback found that only 2 percent of the public volunteered any type of environmental problem in 1968, an extremely low figure given the survey results we have reported in table 4.1 for other types of indicators of environmental concern. In 1970 the comparable figure was 17 percent, representing a dramatic increase but still only a small proportion of the public. The only other study of MIP trend data beginning in the sixties was limited to the state of Wisconsin. As noted in table 4.2, Buttel (1975a; 1975b) reported that the percentage of Wisconsin residents volunteering environmental problems as one of the two most important facing their state rose considerably, from 17 to 40, between 1968 and 1970. While the pattern of substantial increase in Wisconsin was similar to that found at the national level, the absolute levels in that state were much higher than at the national level both years. Whether the higher figures for Wisconsin reflect a far higher than average level of environmental concern in that state, or differences in survey methodologies (or both), is difficult to determine.

The situation is not helped when the 1970 data from the above two studies are compared to two other sets of MIP data beginning in 1970. First, Harris began reporting the results of an MIP question in late 1970, and as shown in table 4.2 fully 41 percent of a national sample volunteered some type of environmental problem as one of the "two or three biggest problems" facing them in 1970—a figure comparable to the Wisconsin results. In contrast, three 1970 Gallup surveys included a question asking about the *single* MIP facing the country, and the percents mentioning environmental problems ranged from only 2 to 10 (prior to 1970 Gallup did not list environmental problems among MIP results, presumably because the percentages mentioning them were too small to warrant doing so—see Hornback, 1974:220–21). The results of the Gallup surveys, taking into account that they asked for only *one* MIP, thus seem more in line with the results of the Michigan NES reported by Hornback.

The discrepant results obtained on MIP questions, especially those between the results of the Michigan NES and Harris surveys in 1970, are difficult to reconcile. They do not seem attributable, for example, to differences in the wording of the MIP questions. Despite the inconsistency in results, however, two conclusions can be drawn from the available MIP data: first, the salience of environmental problems increased significantly from 1968 to 1970; second, even in 1970 only a minority (albeit a large one in some surveys) volunteered environmental problems when asked what they saw as the most important problems facing the country (or state of Wisconsin). The latter finding contrasts sharply with the results reported in table 4.1 for other indicators of environmental concern, and suggests that even around the time that our nation was celebrating the first Earth Day the salience of environmental problems did not match that of the traditionally dominant worries about war (in this case, Vietnam) and the economy (Erskine, 1972b:120; Hornback, 1974:223).

Overall, then, the available data suggest that public concern for environmental quality escalated rapidly in the sixties, and by 1970 majorities of the public were expressing pro-environmental opinions ranging from acknowledging the seriousness of pollution to supporting governmental efforts to protect and improve the environment. However, despite the relatively strong consensus in support of environmental protection and the increased salience of environmental problems in 1970, the state of the environment was viewed by only a minority of the public as one of the nation's most important problems. From a social movements perspective, it appears that a majority of the public was sympathetic to the environmentalists' goal of protecting the environment and a sizable minority was explicitly attentive to environmental issues.

The early seventies

As the high level of environmental activism stimulated by Earth Day, such as community cleanups and recycling drives, inevitably began to lose momentum, several commentators suggested that public concern for environmental protection would likewise decline. The most influential was Downs (1972), who—as noted earlier—suggested that by 1972 environmental quality had already passed from the stage of alarmed discovery and enthusiastic support into one of somber realization of the costs of environmental protection and improvement—both in terms of lifestyle and of purely economic adjustment.

The situation surrounding the problem of environmental quality certainly seemed conducive to its passing through the issue-attention cycle in the early seventies. As noted previously, at the end of 1969 the National Environmental Policy Act (NEPA), establishing the President's Council on Environmental Quality and requiring the preparation of the now-famous "environmental impact statements" for federal actions, was passed, and in 1970 the U.S. Environmental Protection Agency was established. Congress continued to pass important environmental legislation over the next couple of years (Dunlap and Allen, 1976:388), and most states followed the federal government's lead by passing environmental protection legislation (often including "little NEPAS") and establishing environmental agencies of their own (Haskell and Price, 1973). These governmental efforts on behalf of environmental protection involved the expenditure of large sums of money, and provoked increasing complaints from the private sector that environmental protection was hampering economic growth and contributing to the escalating inflation rate. In addition, it was becoming clearer that solving pollution and other environmental problems was not going to be easy, requiring changes in personal lifestyles as well as industrial and governmental practices (Morrison, 1980; Schnaiberg, 1980:chapter 8). Finally, media attention to environmental issues began to decline significantly after 1970 (Davies, 1977:92; Schoenfeld et al., 1979:48). The setting was ripe for environmental quality to pass through the final stages of Downs's issue-attention cycle, especially when the "energy crisis" of 1973–74 quickly took over center stage on the public agenda.

What, in fact, happened to public concern for environmental quality in the years immediately following 1970 and the first Earth Day? Sadly, the data needed for providing anything approximating a definitive answer to this question are not available. Not only did pollsters often stop asking questions they had used in the sixties, but surprisingly—given the prominence of environmental issues at the time—they failed to start asking new questions in 1970 to provide a baseline for following changes in environmental concern throughout the seventies. The situation led Erskine (1972b:120) to express consternation over public opinion pollsters' failure to develop good trend data on environmental issues, and it forces us to rely on the very limited body of data shown in table 4.2.

I have already referred to three of the data sets reported in table 4.2: the two national studies and the Wisconsin study. All three employed MIP questions, and they all show a similar pattern: the salience of environmental problems declined substantially by 1972 from its peak in 1970, and even further by 1974–75. The patterns in the national Harris data and the Wisconsin data are especially similar, and indicate that the proportion of the public volunteering environmental problems as among the nation's/state's most serious problems declined from a large minority in 1970 to a small minority (10 percent or less) by mid-decade. A similar pattern was found in Gallup surveys employing an MIP question asking for the *single* most important problem. As noted earlier, the percentage volunteering environmental problems reached a peak of 10 percent in 1970; it then fluctuated between 7 and 2 percent during 1971 and 1972 (Hornback, 1974:221). Unfortunately, in 1973 Gallup began asking respondents to name the *two* MIPs, making comparisons with prior years impossible. Nevertheless, the environment continued to show up low on the list of two MIPs throughout 1973, and it dropped further in 1974—replaced by "energy" (Rosa, 1978). (The percentage mentioning the energy shortage also exceeded the percentage mentioning environmental problems in the Harris surveys beginning in 1974—Mitchell and Davies, 1978:fig. 2.)

I noted earlier that public opinion analysts tend to regard responses to MIP questions as good indicators of the salience of an issue to the public. But it has been suggested that responses to such questions are especially susceptible to media attention to particular problems (Funkhouser, 1973) and that—more broadly—salience as measured by MIP responses "is transitory for all but the most momentous issues such as war or depression" (Mitchell, 1984b:55). Since media attention to environmental problems did decline considerably in the early seventies (Davies, 1977:92; Schoenfeld et al., 1979:48), perhaps these trends reflect little more than the public's susceptibility to the agenda-setting function of the mass media (and, implicitly, to the inadequacy of MIP questions as valid indicators of public concern about social problems). Some analysts of environmental concern have, in fact, suggested that the obvious decline in the salience of environmental problems was *not* matched by decline in strength of commitment to environmental protection (Mitchell, 1984b:54–55).

Amazingly, the only two sets of data available for testing this possibility are limited to the state of Washington, as I have been unable to find a single set of national-trend data using something other than an MIP question. Fortunately, the two Washington studies used very different indicators of concern for environmental quality, but nonetheless produced similar results. In both cases a fairly sharp decline in environmental concern was found by mid-decade, although not quite as great as registered in the MIP indicators. The first set of data are from a panel study which compared the priorities for spending government funds in 1970 and 1974 as indicated by over 1,600

Washington state residents. "Pollution control" and "protection of forests and other natural areas for public enjoyment" were two of fifteen areas on which respondents were asked whether they wanted "more," the "same," or "less" tax money spent. As shown in table 4.2, the percent wanting more spent on pollution control declined by more than half, from 70 to only 32 percent, while the percent wanting more spent on natural resources declined by nearly a third, from 52 to 37 percent, over the four years. In short, the Washington panel study found a substantial decline in public endorsement of support for environmental protection.

The Washington trend study compared different samples of 800+ residents in 1970 and 1976 in terms of their selection of "reducing air and water pollution" as "one of the two or three most serious problems" facing their state and their communities from a list of eleven potential problems (as opposed to volunteering responses to an MIP question). At the state level there was a very large decline in the percent selecting reducing pollution, from 44 to 18 percent, over the six years. At the community level there was a far smaller decline, from 23 to 15 percent, due in part to the fact that respondents were so much less likely to see pollution as a community problem to begin with (a pattern found in other studies—see Murch, 1974).

In short, the two Washington state studies found that public concern for environmental quality, measured both by spending priorities and perceived seriousness of environmental problems, declined substantially between 1970 and mid-decade. Especially noteworthy is the fact that in the 1970–74 panel study not only did the percentage wanting "more" spending on pollution control decline from 70 to 32 percent, but the percentage wanting "less" spending in this area increased from 5 to 21 percent. While great caution is called for in generalizing from a single state to the entire nation, the Washington results suggest a deterioration of the strong consensus on behalf of environmental protection surrounding the first Earth Day in 1970.

The decline in public consensus for environmental protection in the early seventies paralleled the growth of organized opposition to the environmental movement (Albrecht, 1972; Morrison, 1973). Yet, care should be used in attributing declining environmental concern among the general public to the opposition's efforts to blame economic problems and the energy shortage on excessive environmental protection. Indeed, the panel study (which followed the same individuals over time and thus allowed for an examination of predictors of decline in support for environmental protection spending) found little evidence of an "ecological backlash." Whether or not respondents viewed environmental protection as contributing to economic problems and the energy shortage was a poor predictor of declining support for environmental spending; a better predictor was whether or not they viewed environmental problems as less serious in 1974 than in 1970 (Dunlap et al., 1979). These findings suggest that Washingtonians' decline in support for environmental spending over the four years stemmed more from their belief that past spending had been successful in improving environmental conditions (and that *increased* spending was therefore unnecessary) than from their blaming environmental protection for economic and energy problems.

In sum, while the available evidence on trends in environmental concern in the early seventies is admittedly sparse and often based on single states, it consistently indicates a significant decline in public concern for environmental quality in the years immediately following 1970. The evidence thus supports Downs's (1972) contention that by 1972 environmental quality was about halfway through the issue-attention cycle and his prediction that it would shortly move into the fourth stage—the decline of intense public interest. However, whereas Downs emphasized the importance of public recognition of the costs of environmental improvements in leading to decline in public concern, the results of the Washington panel study suggest an alternative explanation: public concern over environmental problems declined because the public thought they were being solved, presumably because laws were passed, agencies were established, and money was spent to solve them. This "natural decline" explanation complements rather than contradicts Downs, for it points to an alternative source of the decline in public concern for environmental quality. As we shall see later, more recent trends in environmental concern appear to have been influenced by public perception of changes in governmental efforts to protect environmental quality.

Middle to late seventies

I now turn to several studies that tracked environmental concern from the early or middle part of the seventies through the end of the decade. Their results will indicate whether environmental concern continued to decline throughout the decade and, if so, whether the rate of decline was as steep as in the early seventies. The data will also be helpful in evaluating whether environmental quality reached the final, "post-problem" stage of the issue-attention cycle. In reviewing these studies, however, it must be kept in mind that they began at least two or three years after Earth Day, at a time when—judging from data reviewed in the prior section—environmental concern had already declined a fair amount. Some analysts of environmental concern have ignored this fact.[2]

Four sets of trend data beginning in 1972 or 1973 and extending through the end of the decade, and one covering 1976 to 1979, are shown in table 4.3 (most extend past 1980, but trends in the eighties will be postponed until the next section). The first set of data include biennial nationwide surveys conducted for Potomac Associates by Gallup from 1972 through 1976, plus a followup survey conducted by Mitchell (1980) for the U.S. Council on Environmental Quality in 1980. The surveys asked respondents how worried or concerned they were with a number of domestic issues, including "cleaning up our waterways and reducing water pollution" and "reducing air pollution." As shown in table 4.3, the Potomac surveys found a noticeable decline in the percentage indicating "a great deal" of concern from 1972 to 1974, but then an upturn two years later that put the 1976 levels of concern only a few percentage points below the 1972 levels (57 versus 61 percent for water pollution and 55 versus 60 percent for air pollution). The 1980 CEQ survey, in contrast, found far lower levels of concern four years later: only 39 percent indicated a great deal of concern about water pollution and only 36 percent the same degree of concern about air pollution.

Whereas the above figures suggest a substantial decline in concern about pollution in the last half of the seventies, Mitchell (1980:412) urges caution in drawing this conclusion. He points out that, in contrast to the Potomac surveys, in the 1980 survey he conducted for CEQ the question containing the two pollution items was immediately preceded by two questions in which respondents were asked to rank pollution relative to other domestic problems. Mitchell suggests that this placement of the Potomac question may have inadvertently dampened the levels of concern expressed about air and water pollution. As evidence he notes that a national Roper survey conducted two months after his CEQ survey found 54 percent expressing a great deal of concern over "cleaning up our waterways and reducing water pollution," only three percent lower than the 1976 figure. Yet, since the Roper survey did not ask about the full range of domestic issues covered in the original Potomac question, it is possible that comparability of responses was again colored somewhat by question context. At any rate, while great caution is obviously called for, the Potomac-CEQ surveys indicate at least a modest and—if one is willing to take the 1980 data at face value—possibly substantial decline in concern about air and water pollution from 1972 to 1980.

The conclusion that there was at least modest decline in environmental concern from the early seventies through 1980 is consistent with the other sets of data in table 4.3. First, in late 1973 (reflecting the emergence of the energy crisis) Roper began asking a trade-off question in which respondents were asked if they were "more on the side of producing adequate energy or more on the side of protecting the environment." For the sake of brevity I have reported only the percentages for these two positions, deleting the sizable percents who either *volunteered* "neither" or "no conflict" or indicated "don't know." In 1973 the two positions received equal levels of support (37 percent each), but after that the percent siding with adequate energy began to exceed that siding with environmental protection (with the exception of 1976). By 1980 the gap had reached a modest 9 percent (45 versus 36), indicating that worries about energy adequacy had clearly exceeded concern about environmental protection—but had not caused an erosion of support for environmental protection as many people expected, as the latter held virtually constant from 1973 to 1980.[3]

Interestingly, the second Roper question, asking respondents whether they think "environmental protection laws and regulations have gone too far, or not far enough, or have struck about the right balance," shows a more substantial decline in environmental concern. Table 4.3 shows the percentages indicating not far enough or too far, with the percentages indicating "about right" or "don't know" deleted for brevity and readability. In 1973 the percentage indicating that environmental protection efforts had not gone far enough sharply exceeded that indicating that such efforts had gone too far (34 versus 13). The gap quickly began to close (with the exception of a temporary growth in 1976) and reached a low point of only 5 percent in 1979 (29 versus 24).

The next set of data in table 4.3 comes from a question used in NORC surveys in which respondents are given a long list of problems facing our nation and asked if we're spending "too much money on it," "too little money," or "about the right amount" on each one. Surprisingly, as late as 1973 the percentage indicating that too little was being spent "on improving and protecting the environment" overwhelmed the percentage indicating that too much was being spent in this area: 61 versus 7 percent (the percentages indicating "about right" or "don't know" are not shown). In subsequent years there was a modest but fairly consistent decline in the percentage indicating "too

Table 4.3 Trend Studies of Public Concern for Environmental Quality—Early Seventies t
Mid-Eighties

National Studies		72	73	74	7
1. Potomac-CEQ[a]	Concerned a great deal about:				
	a. water pollution	61	—	51	–
	b. air pollution	60	—	46	–
2. Roper[b]	More on the side of:				
	a. protecting environment		37	39	3
	b. adequate energy		37	41	4
3. Roper[c]	Environmental protection laws and regulations have gone:				
	a. not far enough		34	25	3
	b. too far		13	17	2
4. NORC[d]	Spending on improving and protecting the environment:				
	a. too little		61	59	5
	b. too much		7	8	1
5. Cambridge[e]	Sacrifice environmental quality or sacrifice economic growth:				
	a. sacrifice economic growth				
	b. sacrifice environmental quality				
6. CBS/*N.Y. Times*[f]	Environmental improvements must be made regardless of cost:				
	a. agree				
	b. disagree				
7. Cambridge[g]	Amount of environmental protection by government:				
	a. too little				
	b. too much				

[a]See Mitchell (1980:413) for question wording and complete results.

[b]Volunteered responses of "neither," "no conflict," or "don't know" are not shown. Also, in some yea
Roper asked this question more than once, but only the results from surveys conducted in September
each year are reported. See Gillroy and Shapiro (1986:275) for question wording and complete results

[c]Percentages responding "struck about right balance" or volunteering "don't know" are not shown. S
Gillroy and Shapiro (1986:273) for question wording and complete results.

[d]Percentages responding "about right" or volunteering "don't know" are not shown. See Gillroy an
Shapiro (1986:273) for question wording and complete results through 1985, but note that they repo
1984 and 1985 results only for subsamples receiving "old" format (see footnote 6 of text). See Nation
Opinion Research Center (1986) for 1986 results.

Percent Response by Year

'6	77	78	79	80	81	82	83	84	85	86
7	—	—	—	39						
5	—	—	—	36						
4	35	—	38	36	40	46				
3	43	—	43	45	39	35				
2	27	—	29	33	31	37	48			
5	20	—	24	25	21	16	14			
5	48	52	—	48	—	50	54	58	58	58
9	11	10	—	15	—	12	8	7	8	6
8	39	37	37	—	41	41	42	42	53	58
1	26	23	32	—	26	31	16	27	23	19
					45	52	58	—	—	66
					42	41	34	—	—	27
						35	44	56	54	59
						11	9	8	10	7

'ercentages volunteering "don't know" are not shown. See Gillroy and Shapiro (1986:277) for question ording and complete results through 1985. See Cambridge Reports, Inc. (1986:9) for 1986 results.
'ercentages volunteering "no opinion" are not shown. See Gillroy and Shapiro (1986:279) for question ording and complete results.
'ercentages responding "about the right amount" or volunteering "don't know" are not shown. See illroy and Shapiro (1986:274) for question wording and complete results through 1985. See Cambridge eports, Inc. (1986:7) for 1986 results.

little," and a small but relatively consistent increase in the percentage indicating "too much," through 1980. The result is that the initial 54 percent difference between these two positions in 1973 (61 versus 7) declined to 33 percent by the end of the decade (48 versus 15).

The fourth item, which Cambridge Reports, Inc., did not use until 1976, poses a trade-off between economic growth and environmental quality. It asks respondents whether we must "sacrifice environmental quality for economic growth," or whether we must "sacrifice economic growth in order to preserve and protect the environment." In 1976 the public was almost twice as likely to prefer sacrificing economic growth for environmental quality as vice versa (38 versus 21 percent). While the percentage choosing to sacrifice economic growth for environmental quality held nearly constant over the next three years, the percentage indicating a willingness to sacrifice environmental quality steadily grew (with a consequent decline in the large proportion of volunteered "don't knows," which are not shown). The result is that by 1979 the pro-environment position ("sacrifice economic growth") had only a 5 percent margin over the pro-growth position, 37 versus 32 percent.

The data covering the seventies in table 4.3 provide a generally consistent view of trends in environmental concern from the early part of the mid-seventies to the end of the decade: modest but continual decline in public support for environmental protection. These results, coupled with those reviewed in the two prior sections, suggest the following evolution of public concern with environmental quality: after growing rapidly in the late sixties, such concern appears to have reached a peak in 1970 following Earth Day; it then experienced a fairly sharp decline in the early part of the seventies, followed by a much more gradual decline through the rest of the decade.

The long-term trend I have just sketched is supported by one final piece of longitudinal data (covering too long a time period to be summarized in the prior tables). The 1980 CEQ survey repeated the question used by Gallup in 1965 and 1970 listed in table 4.1. Recall that respondents were given a list of ten national problems, including "reducing pollution of air and water," and asked to indicate which three they wanted to see government devote most of its attention to in the next year or two. As we noted previously, reducing pollution was selected by only 17 percent in 1965, ranking it ninth out of the ten problems; in 1970 it was selected by 53 percent, sending it to second. A decade later, in the 1980 CEQ survey, reducing pollution was selected by 24 percent, ranking it sixth in the same list of ten problems (Mitchell, 1980:404).

While the Gallup-CEQ results suggest that by 1980 environmental concern had declined from its 1970 peak to a level only moderately above its 1965 "pre-problem" level, care should clearly be used in drawing such a conclusion from a single item. This is particularly the case for three reasons. First, the 1970 Gallup survey was conducted in late April, *immediately* after Earth Day. Second, changing societal conditions no doubt influenced the public's priorities over the course of the seventies. For example, "reducing unemployment" jumped from a tie for seventh to second (25 percent to 48 percent) from 1970 to 1980, reflecting the substantial deterioration of the economy during the decade. Third, the results in table 4.3—especially those for the NORC spending item—as well as a large amount of cross-sectional data (see, e.g., Mitchell, 1980) indicate the existence of a substantial degree of environmental concern in 1980. Thus, the comparison of the 1970 Gallup findings and 1980 CEQ survey likely exaggerates the degree of decline in environmental concern during the seventies. Nonetheless, the overall trend suggested by the Gallup-CEQ results is compatible with the conclusions I drew from the studies summarized in tables 4.1, 4.2, and 4.3: a very sharp rise from 1965 to 1970, followed by a decline (apparently fairly sharp at first, then much more gradual) throughout the rest of the decade, but not down to the "pre-problem" level of the mid-sixties.

In view of the foregoing data, should we conclude that by the end of the "environmental decade" (as the seventies have been termed) public concern for environmental quality had moved into the "post-problem" stage of the issue-attention cycle? This is not an easy question to answer, largely because Downs (1972:40) vaguely defines the final stage as when "an issue that has been replaced at the center of public concern moves into a prolonged limbo—a twilight realm of lesser attention or spasmodic recurrences of interest." Clearly if one were to judge public concern by "salience," as measured by MIP questions, then one should conclude that environmental quality had moved into the post-problem stage—indeed, it apparently did so as early as 1974 when it was supplanted by the energy crisis. However, the fact that the data in table 4.3 indicate at least moderate levels of public concern with environmental quality throughout the decade, long after "environment" had disappeared from the list of most frequent responses to MIP questions,[4] suggests that salience may be a poor indicator of public concern for social problems. Even though it is the aspect of public opinion that best reflects the issue-attention cycle, salience may well be unduly influenced by mass media coverage, as argued by Funkhouser (1973).

Even if one ignores the salience dimension, it is difficult to determine if environmental quality had entered the post-problem stage at the end of the decade.[5] First, note that Downs (1972:41) refers to this stage as a "realm of lesser attention"; second, he later adds that "problems that have gone through the cycle almost always receive a higher average level of attention, public effort, and general concern than those still in the pre-discovery stage." The data reviewed thus far, indicating that environmental concern was lower at the end of the seventies than at the beginning of the decade, but still higher than in the mid-sixties, would thus seem to indicate that environmental quality was at least nearing the post-problem stage by the late seventies (see Anthony, 1982:19).

Regardless of what one concludes about the issue-attention cycle, it is apparent from table 4.3—and a large amount of cross-sectional data collected in the late seventies (see, e.g., Mitchell, 1980)—that while public concern for environmental quality had become less consensual it had by no means disappeared by the end of the seventies. Although the data can clearly be interpreted differently, depending upon whether one emphasizes the decline or the endurance of environmental concern throughout the decade, I would generally agree with Mitchell's (1980:423) assessment of the situation in 1980: "Although the state of the environment is no longer viewed as a crisis issue, strong support for environmental protection continues. . . . [F]ar from being a fad, the enthusiasm for environmental improvement which arose in the early 1970s has become a continuing concern." Indeed, I think that public concern for environmental quality showed impressive staying power in the face of a continuing series of essentially competing concerns: the energy crisis of 1973–74 and continuing concerns about energy supplies throughout the decade, a worsening economic situation, and a "taxpayers' revolt" begun by California's Proposition 13 in 1978 (Mitchell, 1984b).

Besides surviving the challenges of these competing concerns reasonably well, public support for environmental protection also survived the fruits of its own success—namely, the "natural decline" expected from public apathy due to continued governmental efforts to protect and improve environmental quality throughout the decade. Thus, given the growth in governmental expenditures for environmental programs in the seventies, it may be surprising that the percentage indicating that "too much" was being spent in this area in the NORC surveys did not decrease even more. Similarly, given the continuing passage of additional environmental legislation such as the Endangered Species Act, and the publicity received by issues such as the snail darter and Tellico Dam, it may be surprising that an even larger percentage did not indicate that environmental laws and regulations had gone "too far" in the Roper surveys (see, e.g., Conservation Foundation, 1980). Particularly during the Carter administration, which saw the appointment of numerous environmental advocates to prominent governmental positions (Baldwin, 1977), the public had reason to believe that government was "taking care of" environmental problems. Under such conditions some decline in public concern for environmental quality would be expected, even in the absence of competing concerns.

The eighties and the Reagan administration

The federal government's orientation toward environmental protection changed considerably when Ronald Reagan took office in 1980. Environmentalists were wary of President Reagan because of his general emphasis on "deregulating" the economy, and because of his tendency to view environmental regulations in particular as hampering economic growth and as largely unnecessary (Holden, 1980). The Reagan administration quickly fanned the fears of environmentalists, changing course after a decade of generally bipartisan commitment to federal environmental protection. The Council on Environmental Quality was virtually dismantled, the budget of the Environmental Protection Agency was severely cut, and the enforcement of existing environmental regulations was curtailed by administrative review, budgetary restrictions, and staff changes. It was the latter that received the most attention, as the appointment of Anne Gorsuch as director of the EPA and James Watt as secretary of the Department of Interior symbolized the administration's commitment to changing the thrust of environmental policy, with Gorsuch easing the burden of environmental regulations on industry and Watt opening up public lands to increased resource development (Thompson, 1985; Vig and Kraft, 1984).

Not surprisingly, environmentalists were upset by the Reagan administration's environmental policies, and began to vigorously oppose and criticize them. Perhaps most notable was the issuance in 1982 with considerable publicity of a report, *Ronald Reagan and the American Environment,* prepared by ten of the nation's largest environmental organizations and termed an "indictment" of the Reagan administration's environmental policies (Friends of the Earth, 1982). Similarly, opposition to these policies grew in Congress, where efforts were made to restore budget cuts and oversee effective enforcement of regulations. Most significant, of course, was the congressional investigation of the EPA's handling of "superfund," which led to the resignation of Gorsuch and several other EPA administrators (see Szasz, 1986). Similarly, congressional criticism of James Watt led to pressure for his resignation, although the precipitating event was his ethnic slur rather than Interior's policies.

In the face of mounting criticism the Reagan administration defended its environmental initiatives in terms of its "electoral mandate," arguing that President Reagan's landslide victory was evidence of the voters' approval of his efforts to get the economy going again by freeing it from the burdens of governmental (including environmental) regulations (Kraft, 1984). The president was a vigorous spokesman for his policy of deregulation, and made the issue a test of his leadership capability. Since public opinion analysts have long recognized political leaders as a potent force on public opinion (Pierce et al., 1982:30–33), it might be expected that a popular president would succeed in convincing the American public that environmental regulations had gone too far and were hampering the economy. Was President Reagan able to do this?

The last six sets of trend data in table 4.3 clearly indicate that the president was not successful in lowering the American public's commitment to environmental protection vis-à-vis the economy. Indeed, quite the contrary seems to have occurred. In each case there is a pattern of increasing public commitment to environmental protection during the Reagan administration. In the Roper item asking people whether they are more on the side of environmental protection or adequate energy, there was a 10 percent increase in those siding with the environment and a comparable decrease in those siding with energy from 1980 to 1982 (the last year the question was used). The 46 percent siding with environmental protection in 1982 is the highest figure recorded with this item, and the 11 percent margin it enjoyed over energy adequacy matches the previous high point of 1976. These results are especially impressive, even though they extend only to 1982, because a major theme in the Reagan administration's environmental/resource policy had been that environmental regulations must be relaxed in order to allow for the increased energy production needed for a strong economy (Axelrod, 1984).

The second Roper item, asking respondents if "environmental protection laws and regulations have gone too far, or not far enough, or have struck about the right balance," provides an even more direct indicator of the public's evaluation of the Reagan administration's environmental policy agenda. The data indicate a growing rejection of the administration's position that such laws and regulations have gone too far. After having reached a low point in 1979, the margin between those indicating "not far enough" and "too far" increased in the first year of the Reagan administration (1981) and in each subsequent year through 1983 (the last year the question was used). In 1982 the 37 percent saying "not far enough" exceeded the previous high of 34 percent in 1973, while the 21 percent margin by which that position was favored over "too far" equaled the margin for 1973. In 1983 the percent indicating that environmental regulations had not gone far enough jumped to 48 percent, greatly exceeding the previous high in 1973, while the percent indicating that the regulations had gone too far dropped to 14 percent, nearly matching the previous low of 13 percent in 1973.

The next item, the NORC spending item, is also pertinent for judging the impact of the Reagan administration's environmental policy, since budget cuts for environmental protection agencies had been a major factor in that policy (Vig and Kraft, 1984). Although still fairly strong, support for increased spending on environmental protection had reached a low point in 1980, with 33 percent more people indicating that "too little" was being spent on the area than saying that "too much" was being spent on it (48 versus 15 percent). The gap between the two positions had begun to increase by 1982, and in 1984 it reached 51 percent—matching the 1974 level and approximating the previous high of 54 percent in 1973. The gap remained remarkably stable in 1985 and 1986, despite the use of different item wordings for varying subsamples.[6] While not as dramatic as the results for the two prior items, the pattern of increased support for environmental spending on the NORC item also suggests public disagreement with the Reagan administration's environmental agenda.

The next item, from Cambridge Reports, Inc., forces a trade-off between economic growth and environmental quality. By 1979 the percentage preferring that economic growth be sacrificed for environmental quality held only a slim margin over those with the opposite preference (37 versus 32 percent). In the first year of the Reagan administration the percent preferring that economic growth be sacrificed rose to 41, a new high, while the percent opting to sacrifice environmental quality dropped to 26, producing a margin that nearly equaled the 1976 level. Despite surprisingly large fluctuations over the next three years, the 1984 results were nearly identical to those for 1981. The next two years, however, saw a sharp rise in the preference for sacrificing economic growth on behalf of environmental quality and a modest decline in the opposing preference. The result is that in 1986 the public was nearly three times as likely to favor environmental quality over economic growth as the opposite (58 versus 19 percent), a margin that exceeded considerably the 1976 gap. The public's preferences in this regard are clearly at odds with the administration's priorities.

The CBS News/*New York Times* Poll began using the next item in September of 1981, by which time the Reagan administration was under attack from environmentalists (especially for its agency appointments) but before its environmental policies had become the object of intense media attention via the Watt and EPA controversies. This item asks respondents to react to an extreme pro-environmental position, that environmental improvements should be pursued "regardless of cost." The public was almost evenly divided on the issue in 1981, but a year later those agreeing held an 11 percent margin (52 versus 41) over those disagreeing with this extreme position. By 1983 the gap had more than doubled to a 24 percent margin, and in 1986 it reached nearly 40 percent (66 versus 27). That two-thirds of the public gave verbal support to such a staunch pro-environment position indicates strong disagreement with the administration's policy of emphasizing the economic costs of environmental regulations.

The final item was not used by Cambridge Reports, Inc., until March 1982. Like the second Roper item, it provides a good indicator of public reaction to the Reagan administration's overall environmental policy agenda, asking respondents if they think "there is too much, too little, or about the right amount of government regulation and involvement in the area of environmental protection." From the outset the public clearly rejected the administration's contention that environmental regulations were excessive (by a margin of 35 to 11 percent), and this view has become more pronounced over the years. By 1986 the public overwhelmingly indicated that it thought there was "too little" rather than "too much" governmental regulation for environmental protection (59 versus 7 percent). These results, along with those for the NORC spending item discussed above, indicate that in 1986 the public was nearly ten times as likely to see a need for increased governmental efforts and spending on behalf of environmental protection as to take the opposite view. The public's view of the need for environmental regulations appears to be quite different from that of the Reagan administration.

Taken together, the last six sets of data reported in table 4.3 provide a consistent view of recent trends in public support for environmental protection. After having declined moderately from the early to late seventies, public support for environmental protection began to rise shortly after the Reagan administration took office *and has continued to do so.*[7] The recent level of support appears to exceed that found in the early seventies (except in the case of the NORC spending item, where 1986 support for increased environmental spending is comparable to the 1973–74 level), although it likely falls short of the 1970 peak. In general, it appears fair to conclude that after suffering declining public support throughout the seventies, environmental quality has again become a "consensual" issue—as it was at the beginning of the seventies. The data suggest that majorities of the public support increased environmental protection efforts and *huge* majorities oppose weakening current efforts, judging from the small percentages indicating that current efforts should be reduced relative to those supporting increased efforts *or* at least maintaining the status quo (the unreported "neutral" categories for each item).[8]

On the surface it may appear strange that a popular president has been so unsuccessful in swaying public opinion toward his view of environmental protection, particularly when this view was consistent with his overall antigovernment image, which does seem to be popular with the public. From the perspective of the natural decline model discussed previously, however, the rise in public concern for environmental quality under the Reagan administration is more understandable.

Recall that I suggested that a major factor in the decline in environmental concern in the early seventies was the perception by the public (and the media) that the government was "taking care of" environmental problems—a perception reinforced by some degree of success in air and water pollution abatement—and that individuals could therefore afford to become less personally concerned about these problems. Throughout the seventies this perception likely persisted, as there was reasonably strong federal commitment to environmental protection during the Johnson, Nixon, Ford, and Carter administrations. But under the Reagan administration the federal government's commitment to environmental protection appeared to weaken considerably. And, quite importantly, thanks to environmental organizations and the media, and with the unwitting support of James Watt, Anne Gorsuch, et al., this change was quite apparent to the general public. In a March 1983 Harris survey, for example, 74 percent indicated having heard or read about the congressional investigations of the Environmental Protection Agency, and majorities agreed that Democratic allegations against EPA officials were justified. More generally, only 21 percent gave President Reagan a positive ("excellent" or "pretty good") rating on "his handling of environmental cleanup matters," while 74 percent gave him a negative ("only fair" or "poor") rating (Harris, 1983).[9]

At the same time that the Reagan administration was seen as reversing the federal government's long-term commitment to environmental protection, the public was hearing more and more from the media about problems such as toxic wastes in Love Canal, Times Beach, and other communities, groundwater contamination in scores of towns, acid rain in the Northeast, and the possibility of disastrous global climate change due to the buildup of carbon dioxide in the atmosphere. Such problems not only helped offset public perceptions of earlier progress on air and water pollution, but typically posed far more serious threats to human health and welfare than had earlier environmental problems such as wilderness and wildlife preservation, litter and other forms of aesthetic pollution, and even most forms of air and water pollution publicized in the sixties and early seventies. That widespread attention to these newer and more threatening problems by the media coincided with the widely held perception of the Reagan administration as "soft" on environmental protection likely accounts for the resurgence of public concern shown in table 4.3 as well as the significant increase in membership experienced by many environmental organizations in the eighties (Mitchell, 1984a).[10] Yet Reagan's landslide reelection suggests that his administration's poor environmental record had little impact on voters (Stanfield, 1984a), a point to which I will return later.

Rethinking the issue-attention cycle

The resurgence of public concern for environmental quality in the eighties obviously poses an interesting anomaly for Downs's issue-attention cycle, in that, instead of continuing to fade away, environmental quality moved back to a more prominent position on the public agenda under the Reagan administration.[11] This would probably not come as a complete surprise to Downs, as he noted that problems which have passed through the issue-attention cycle may sporadically recapture public attention (1972:41–42). He was also careful to note several characteristics of environmental issues that might serve to retard the decline of public interest in them (46–49). In retrospect, the most important factors he mentioned appear to be that environmental problems are more visible and threatening and affect a larger proportion of the public (virtually everyone) than most social problems, and that the ambiguity of "environmental protection" allows it to encompass a variety of specific causes. Downs could hardly have foreseen how problems such as toxic wastes, acid rain, and climate change would come to be seen as far more threatening to the general population than was air pollution in the early 1970s, nor that a seemingly endless series of ecological problems would be "discovered" with each passing year despite existing environmental protection efforts (also see Mitchell, 1984b:57–58). Environmental quality has become a large umbrella, encompassing a wide and growing range of problems.[12]

Still, Downs viewed the seriousness and ambiguity of environmental problems as merely prolonging the inevitable, rather than reversing the decline in public concern with environmental issues. In this regard I think his preoccupation with the role of the media led him to ignore the crucial roles played by two other key actors—the environmental movement and the government—in affecting public opinion on environmental issues.

It is clear that the environmental movement played a major role in calling public attention to the Reagan administration's environmental record. On the one hand, the major environmental organizations appealed directly to the public (via the media) by condemning the administration's "misdeeds" in reports, press releases, and direct mailings to solicit new members. On the other hand, these organizations also received a good deal of publicity when lobbying against the Reagan policies in Congress or challenging them in the courts (Mitchell, 1984a; 1984b). In addition, the key institutionalized components of the environmental movement, or what Morrison (1973:76) has termed "institutional movement organizations," also played a role in opposing the Reagan administration. First, *career employees* of government agencies such as EPA were active (albeit somewhat covertly) in opposing *and* exposing administration policies and practices (Szasz, 1986). Second, the large number of environmental scientists in academia, government, and nonprofit research centers continued to produce and publicize findings concerning environmental problems (e.g., acid rain) that implicitly and often explicitly challenged the Reagan administration's disregard of such problems.

The commitment and resources that these environmental interest groups were able to bring to bear in the battle for public opinion and congressional and legal action against the Reagan administration's environmental policies were clearly not foreseen by Downs. The success of the "environmental lobby" in stimulating increased public concern for environmental problems in the eighties suggests that a key variable affecting the passage of social problems through the issue-attention cycle is the strength of the interest groups that are committed to solving the problems (including career employees in relevant government agencies). The effect of their efforts in keeping the issues on the political agenda is a fact recognized in recent work on policy implementation (Sabatier and Mazmanian, 1980) but generally ignored by social problems theorists (e.g., Mauss, 1975).

The other major factor in influencing public opinion on environmental issues is "the government," in this case the executive branch, although it is possible that Congress could have a similar effect in some situations. When discussing the "natural decline" phenomena I suggested the rather nonintuitive hypothesis that when the public thinks the government is taking care of a problem it is likely to become less concerned about the problematic conditions. And, as a logical extension of this hypothesis, I suggested that when the public came (with the urging of environmentalists) to perceive the Reagan administration as *not* taking care of environmental problems it began to express greater concern over the problems and stronger support for environmental protection. At this point I want to acknowledge that the plausibility of this explanation of recent trends in public concern with environmental quality rests upon the assumption that the public does in fact view the government as responsible for protecting environmental quality. This seems to be a safe assumption, in that a variety of data indicate that the public believes the government ought to play a major role in environmental protection.[13] In contrast, it is likely that for some social problems, perhaps those involving the regulation of "immoral behavior" such as alcohol and drug use and various sexual acts, the public is more ambivalent about government responsibility for solving the problems.

What I am suggesting is that at least for those problems for which the public clearly attributes to government ameliorative responsibility, the actions (or, more accurately, perceived actions) of government can have a significant effect on public opinion. Ironically, the more diligently the government appears to be attacking the problem, the more probable the public's attention to the problem will wane; conversely, obvious government inaction or backsliding on the problem is likely to stimulate renewed public concern with the problem.[14] Regardless of which effect it produces, my point is that the government, like the environmental movement, is a key actor in influencing public opinion toward environmental issues.

In short, while the issue-attention cycle described by Downs may apply to the typical social problem, and while it is very compatible with mainstream social science thinking on social problems, it should definitely not be viewed as a set of stages through which all problems will inexorably progress and thus eventually pass out of existence. Several factors in addition to the actual seriousness of the problem are likely to influence a problem's progression through the cycle. The foregoing analysis of trends in public concern with environmental quality suggests that the strength and resolve of the interest groups committed to solving the problem and the perceived actions of the governmental entities responsible for solving it are two particularly important factors affecting public opinion. Under the right circumstances, they may keep public concern with a problem sufficiently high to prevent the problem from passing through the issue-attention cycle and disappearing from the political agenda.

Assessing the Strength of Environmental Concern

As early as 1970 commentators were calling the growing awareness of environmental problems an "attitude revolution" (Odum, 1970), and this perspective has become more common over the years. Shabecoff (1985:2), for example, has recently written that: "The burst of environmental activism that began in the late 1960s and sparked a series of landmark laws is likely to be recalled by future generations as a significant turning point in the history of the twentieth century. It was a revolution of sorts . . . [and] . . . it changed, probably forever, the way people look at the world." Such comments imply that environmentalism has brought about a fundamental shift in our beliefs and values, and there is evidence to this effect. Thus, whereas Americans have historically tended to view their resources as abundant and their prospects for growth and progress as virtually unlimited (e.g., Whisenhunt, 1974), the last fifteen years have seen widespread questioning of these assumptions. While not very knowledgeable about ecological problems (Mitchell, 1980:416–18), and ambivalent if not confused about issues such as energy supplies (Farhar et al., 1980), the public has nonetheless begun to give credence to the ideas that natural resources are finite and that there are also limits to nature's ability to absorb the waste products of industrial societies (see, e.g., Yankelovich and Lefkowitz, 1980). For example, in a 1982 national survey by Research and Forecasts, 76 percent of the public agreed that "the earth is like a spaceship with only limited room and resources" and 84 percent agreed that "the balance of nature is very delicate and easily upset by human activities" (Bloomgarden, 1983).

Similarly, whereas the natural environment has traditionally been valued primarily as a resource, something to be used in the production of goods, profit, and growth, it is increasingly seen as valuable in its own right. In other words, more and more Americans seem to view a good environment as desirable, some would say as a basic entitlement (Ladd, 1982), turning environmental quality into an important social value (Milbrath, 1984). In the Research and Forecasts survey, for example, respondents were asked to rate each of twelve national goals, and "protecting nature" was rated a "high priority" by 77 percent of the public, making it the sixth most highly rated goal on the list (Bloomgarden, 1983:49).

The emerging belief in ecological limits and the increasing value placed on environmental quality are widely interpreted as constituting a change in our society's basic "worldview" or social paradigm (e.g., Dunlap and Van Liere, 1978; Milbrath, 1984), as they call into question the way in which Americans have traditionally viewed their relationship to the natural environment.[15] Most Americans certainly have not fully embraced this emerging "ecological worldview," especially its lifestyle implications, nor clearly comprehended the contradictions between it and traditional values such as economic growth, free enterprise, and private property rights (e.g., Van Liere and Dunlap, 1983). Yet even the partial endorsement of this new worldview represents a potentially momentous change from the past (e.g., Milbrath, 1984).

Acknowledging that environmentalism has in fact modified our society's basic beliefs and values helps account for the fact that public concern for environmental quality has proven to be an enduring concern. While public opinion is an indirect and imperfect function of underlying beliefs and values, the more opinions are rooted in underlying cognitions the less likely they are to prove transitory and ephemeral (Pierce et al., 1982:chapter 6). Still, recognizing that public opinion on environmental issues is increasingly rooted in basic beliefs and values does not provide an adequate answer to the question of just how strong is public support for environmental quality. To provide a better assessment of this question I will summarize the evidence on trends in environmental concern employing the various conceptual distinctions introduced previously.

Direction and degree of opinion: environmental quality as a consensual issue

The most basic concepts in this kind of study are the direction and degree of opinion, whether the public responds in a pro- or anti-environmental manner and whether they do so "strongly," "mildly," and so forth. When queried specifically about environmental issues, and not forced to choose between environmental quality and some other value such as energy adequacy, the public consistently favors the pro-environmental over the anti-environmental position. In fact, the pro-environment position often received *majority* support in the early seventies and has regained it in the eighties (recall the last four items in table 4.3). In those cases where the public is also given a chance to express *degrees* of environmental concern, even larger majorities of pro-environment opinion often emerge. For example, on the 1980 CEQ items shown in table 4.3, the 39 percent expressing a "great deal" of concern about water pollution are joined by 44 percent expressing a "fair amount" of concern, while the comparable figures for air pollution are 36 and 40 percent (Mitchell, 1980:413). When combined, these two pro-environment responses overwhelm what can be considered the two anti-environment responses, "not very much" or "not at all" levels of concern about these problems (Mitchell, 1980:413). Similar patterns have been found in a wide range of cross-sectional data over the past fifteen years (e.g., Erskine, 1972a; 1972b; Mitchell, 1980; 1984b).

Even when forced to choose between environmental quality and other desired goals, typically involving jobs and economic growth, a larger proportion of the public generally chooses the former (except where energy needs are an alternative—recall the first Roper item in table 4.3). While use of such "trade-off" items has become popular among environmental analysts (e.g., Bloomgarden, 1983; Mitchell, 1979; 1980), their use has been criticized severely for forcing the public to choose between goals—e.g., environmental protection and economic growth—that are *both* deemed worthy (Ladd, 1982). In fact, evidence shows that when given the option of choosing between environmental quality and economic welfare *or* supporting both, the public is most likely to choose the latter (Keeter, 1984; Roper Center, 1983:27–32). Nonetheless, regardless of their form, trade-off items nearly always show only ***minority opposition*** to the goal of environmental protection.

In sum, despite a decline in the seventies, somewhat offset by a rise in the eighties, public support for environmental quality has consistently outweighed public opposition. Indeed, when asked directly about environmental protection, and not forced to choose between it and other goals, solid majorities of the public typically express support for protecting the environment. Such results suggest that environmental quality has remained a relatively consensual issue. Earlier I suggested that individuals expressing pro-environment opinions could be considered to be "sympathetic" to the environmental movement, and this pattern of consensus in reinforced by more direct data on public sympathy toward the movement. Between 1978 and 1983 four national surveys asked respondents whether they think of themselves as "an active participant in the environmental movement, sympathetic towards the movement but not active, neutral, or unsympathetic." The percents indicating that they are active in or at least sympathetic toward the movement range from 60 to 66 percent, while the percents indicating that they are unsympathetic toward the movement range from only 4 to 8 percent (Mitchell, 1984b:62). These results reinforce the conclusion that the environmental movement's goals of protecting and improving the quality of the environment have not polarized the nation, and continue to receive broad, consensual support.

Salience and intensity: an ambiguous situation

The remaining two aspects of public opinion, salience and intensity, are the crucial factors for judging the "strength" of public concern for environmental quality. Unfortunately, they are also the most difficult to assess. Not only do public opinion analysts often use the terms interchangeably (e.g., Roper Center, 1983:4), but those who carefully distinguish between them have relied upon empirical indicators that seem inappropriate, in the case of salience, or inadequate, in the case of intensity (Dunlap, 1985; Mitchell, 1984b). Let me begin with the concept of salience.

Earlier I defined a salient issue as one that is "on the minds" of individuals, something that is important to them, and not just something they think of when asked for an opinion. I also indicated that public opinion analysts have typically treated volunteered responses to "most important problem" questions as good indicators of an issue's salience. After reviewing the available trend data on environmental concern, however, I am forced to question the appropriateness of MIP data for judging an issue's salience. Even though analysts have suggested that "mass salience is transitory for all but the most momentous issues such as war or depression" (Mitchell, 1984b:55), the MIP data on environmental problems suggest to me that such questions are poor indicators of an issue's salience.

Consider the following points emerging from the prior review of trend data on the salience of environmental problems. First, around the time of Earth Day, when support for environmental quality was exceptionally high, only a minority (and a small minority in some surveys) of the public volunteered environmental problems on MIP questions. Second, by 1974 so few people were mentioning environmental problems on MIP questions that environment no longer showed up on MIP lists. Yet, other data show that while environmental concern had definitely declined by then, it had certainly not come close to disappearing. Third, even during the early eighties, when there was great unease over the Reagan administration's environmental policies and a consequent resurgence of environmental concern, environmental problems did not reemerge on MIP lists. Finally, I suggested that environmental issues ought to be salient for the "attentive" public, the broad segment between the environmental activists and the vast "sympathetic" segment of the public. It is from the attentive public, for example, that organizations such as the Sierra Club were able to draw so many new members by capitalizing on the Reagan administration's anti-environmental orientation. Yet, the MIP data imply that by the mid-seventies and continuing up to the present no more than a couple percent of the public are attentive to environmental issues, since environmental problems do not show up on MIP lists, whereas the surveys just cited found that nearly 10 percent of the public claim to be active participants in the environmental movement and nearly that many claim to belong to local or national environmental organizations (Mitchell, 1979:19; 1984b:63). In other words, reliance on MIP data would suggest that far more people are active in the environmental movement than are attentive to environmental issues—a nonsensical conclusion, I think.

What would prove to be a more reliable indicator of an issue's salience, if MIP responses are too stringent? It seems to me that an option that would be compatible with the standard meaning of salience as "prominent or conspicuous" would be various *ranking* procedures, where an issue such as environment is evaluated relative to other issues. Either an explicit ranking, where respondents are given a list of problems or goals and asked to rank them, or a more implicit ranking procedure, where respondents are given a list of problems or goals and asked to indicate which two or three they think are most important, could be used. Both procedures force respondents to evaluate environmental issues relative to other issues, and they would seem to indicate the degree to which environmental problems and/or goals are in fact salient to them.[16]

Of the longitudinal data reviewed in this paper, only the Gallup data in table 4.1 are based on even an implicit ranking of issues. Recall that respondents were given a list of ten national problems and asked to indicate the three that they felt should receive the attention of government. Also recall that I noted that after rising from 17 to 53 percent from 1965 to 1970, "reducing pollution of air and water" was selected by only 24 percent in the 1980 CEQ survey (Mitchell, 1980:404). Although the 1980 figure is lower than expected, given the other trend data, the overall pattern is generally consistent with the long-term trends pieced together from the other sets of data. And, unlike the MIP data, the Gallup-CEQ data suggest that environmental problems were still of moderate salience in 1980.

A similar measure of salience was used in a cross-sectional survey conducted in fall 1981 for the Democratic National Committee (see Anthony, 1982:33). The respondents were asked to select from among 26 issues the "three or four they felt were the most important facing the country," and the 15 percent choosing "protecting the environment" meant that it placed twelfth. Economic issues were well represented among the top issues, with joblessness placing first with 33 percent, inflation fifth with 22 percent, and high interest rates eighth with 19 percent.

Also relevant to the proposed conceptualization of salience is a set of trend data collected by Roper since 1974, and not previously discussed in this paper. Shown in table 4.4, the data are based on a question that is fairly similar to that used in the Gallup-CEQ surveys, except that respondents are asked to indicate the issues they are "personally most concerned about" rather than those which they think should receive the attention of government. In looking at the responses over time, it is apparent that they are sensitive to changing social conditions. For example, the percent expressing concern about "inflation and high prices" peaked at 63 percent in 1979 but declined to only 27 percent in 1986, following the actual trend in inflation rates rather closely. Similarly, concern about "the fuel and energy crisis" stood at 46 percent in

Table 4.4 Trends in Personal Concern about Air and Water Pollution Relative to Other Personal Concerns, 1974–1986[a]

Concerns[b]	Percent Response by Year											
	74	75	76	77	79	81	82	83	84	85	86	Change from 74 to 86
Our relations with foreign countries	18	10	13	9	15	19	21	17	29	28	37	+19
Crime and lawlessness	30	34	40	40	31	35	37	33	34	42	34	+4
Drug abuse	23	20	24	21	14	16	17	17	21	24	28	+5
Inflation and high prices	56	58	44	48	63	56	53	46	33	33	27	−29
The way the courts are run	20	22	30	27	23	24	25	27	30	26	26	+6
Money enough to live right and pay the bills	25	30	26	28	33	31	29	27	27	28	26	+1
Getting into another war	7	11	10	8	9	18	16	14	26	18	24	+17
A recession and rising unemployment	15	33	20	19	20	24	34	50	22	20	17	+2
Wrongdoing by elected government officials	40	26	32	22	24	18	17	17	21	15	16	−24
The way young people think and act	10	14	15	17	14	14	12	11	14	16	15	+5
Pollution of air and water	12	11	11	13	10	10	7	8	12	14	13	+1
Alcoholism	c	c	6	7	6	7	7	6	10	10	12	+6
The fuel and energy crisis	46	27	22	31	25	30	17	13	8	7	7	−39

[a]Data provided by the Roper Center. Question wording: "Here is a list of things people have told us they are concerned about today. Would you read over that list and then tell me which 2 or 3 *you personally* are most concerned about today?" [b]Concerns are listed in order of the percentage selecting them in 1986. [c] = not asked.

1974 but has gradually declined to only 7 percent in recent years as the "energy crisis" has turned into an "energy glut" (at least in the eyes of the typical consumer).

In view of the substantial fluctuations experienced by some of the items, the relatively stable and low levels of concern (from 7 to 14 percent) expressed for "pollution of air and water" may be surprising. However, keep in mind that these data begin in 1974, when environmental concern had already declined considerably. It seems likely—judging from trend data beginning in 1970—that a pattern somewhat closer to that for energy would have been observed for pollution had the item been used as early as 1970. Also, the fact that the question asked respondents to indicate which problems they were *personally* most concerned about, as opposed to which ones they felt should receive the attention of government as in the Gallup-CEQ question, likely had a dampening effect. Just as people are more likely to view environmental problems as serious at the national level than at the local level (Murch, 1974), they are probably more likely to see pollution as a problem facing the nation rather than one that is bothering them personally. In the 1982 Research and Forecasts survey, for example, 60 percent agreed that "pollution is one of the most serious problems facing the nation today" but only 35 percent said that "pollution is affecting [their] life" (Bloomgarden, 1983). Nonetheless, the striking features of table 4.4 are that pollution ranked near the bottom of the list of personal concerns from 1974 through 1986, and that the belated upturn beginning in 1984 (two years *after* the EPA and Watt controversies) has only brought it back up to the modest levels of the mid-seventies.

The foregoing three sets of data, employing various forms of the proposed ranking technique to measure salience, provide results that seem more sensible than do those obtained with *volunteered* MIP questions. While all three indicate that by the mid-seventies environmental problems were of low to at best moderate salience compared to other problems, they nonetheless suggest that a significant minority of the public (at least as many as claim to be active environmentalists) continue to view environmental problems as among our nation's most serious problems. Hopefully future research will examine the relative utility and logic of such ranking items with MIP questions as empirical indicators of issue salience.

Until now virtually all analysts of environmental concern have employed MIP items to indicate salience, and thus it has been common for us to argue that while environmental quality is no longer a salient issue, public support for environmental protection remains surprisingly strong (e.g., Anthony, 1982; Dunlap, 1985; Lake, 1983; Mitchell, 1984b). What is being implied, sometimes quite explicitly (Mitchell, 1984b:54–57), is that the "strength" dimension of environmental concern remains impressive. However, we have been very lax in judging strength of public concern for environmental quality, relying upon direction and at best degree of opinion to indicate strength. Yet, the concept of intensity appears to be the appropriate indicator of opinion strength, for it represents the strength with which people hold their opinions (e.g., Nimmo and Bonjean, 1972:5). And while students of public opinion in general and of environmental opinions in particular have sometimes treated the "degree" of opinion—"strongly" versus "moderately," for example—as indicating intensity (e.g., Anthony, 1982:32–33; Mitchell, 1984b:55), as far back as Key (1961: chapter 9) public opinion analysts recognized the inadequacy of this approach.

While it has often been ignored, there is a body of work which suggests that in order to measure the *strength* of an opinion adequately, researchers should first ask people to express their opinion and then follow by asking them to indicate how strongly they hold the opinion (Key, 1961:chapter 9). The best recent work on this topic has been conducted by Schuman and Presser (1981:chapters 9 and 10), who followed standard pro-con questions on gun permits and abortion with questions designed to measure the strength of the expressed opinions—including subjective evaluation of importance, perceived importance in evaluating political candidates, and reported political behavior on the issues. They found that the combination of opinion direction *and* strength provided insight into the relative strength and commitment of the opposing "camps" on these two controversial issues, as well as the stability of opinions on these issues over time.

Unfortunately, to my knowledge no research has been conducted to evaluate carefully the strength of public opinion on environmental issues along these lines. There are, however, limited data on the potential impact of environmental issues on voting behavior, one of Schuman and Presser's indicators of opinion strength. The first set of data, or at least the inferences drawn from them, have proved to be controversial.

In a February 1982 survey Louis Harris (1982) found 15 percent indicating that they probably would not vote for a congressional candidate whose views on "controlling air and water pollution" disagreed with their own, even if they mostly agreed with the candidate on other issues. Further, since 13 percent held pro-environment views and only 2 percent held anti-environment views, Harris concluded that environmental issues represented a potential swing vote of 11 percent—ranking it third among nine issues examined. Harris's assertions subsequently attracted a good deal of criticism, including a scathing attack by the political scientist Everett Carl Ladd (1982). Ladd's major point was that the 15 percent indicating that a candidate's stand on pollution control would probably influence their vote ranked environment eighth out of the nine issues (well below abortion, with 32 percent, and barely above affirmative action programs, with 14 percent), suggesting—contrary to Harris—the limited electoral impact of environmental issues.[17]

Additional evidence on the voting impact of environmental issues would seem to support Ladd. In September 1982 the CBS News/*New York Times* Poll asked a sample of registered voters, "Is there any *one* issue that is so important to you that you would *change* your vote because you disagreed with a candidate's position on that single issue?" The 48 percent who replied "yes" were then asked to name the issue, and environment was one of several issues cited by only one percent, well below the 16 percent mentioning economic issues and the seven percent citing abortion (reported in Goodman, 1983:12). CBS News/*New York Times* also conducted an exit poll after the November 1982 election, asking voters, "Which of these issues were most important in deciding how you voted for the U.S. House?" Although voters were allowed to check two of the nine issues listed, only three percent checked "the environment," ranking it last on the list (reported in Roper Center, 1983:21–22).

Although it would be unwise to draw sweeping conclusions from such limited data, these results do suggest that the intensity or strength of public concern for environmental quality—as reflected in electoral impact—may not be as high as it is for economic well-being (Goodman, 1983). The results may also provide insight into the anomaly that even though the Reagan administration's environmental policies failed to win public support and even helped produce a resurgence of environmental concern and activism, the policies nonetheless failed to prevent his landslide reelection. I therefore turn to a more detailed examination of the possible electoral impact of environmental issues.

Concern for environmental quality as a political issue

In democracies, the "bottom line" for judging the strength of public opinion is the impact of that opinion on the electoral process. The 1984 presidential election is therefore useful for drawing conclusions about the strength of public concern for environmental quality. In discussing the trend data in the eighties earlier I noted that large majorities of the public were aware of the EPA "scandal" and also gave President Reagan negative ratings on his environmental policies (Harris, 1983). Even more pertinent is the fact that "protecting the environment" was one of the issues on which Walter Mondale consistently received a better rating than did Ronald Reagan. From late 1983 through late 1984, the percents indicating that Mondale "could do a better job" on protecting the environment ranged from 50 to 59, while the comparable figures for

Reagan ranged from 30 to 39 (Harris, 1984). Finally, shortly after the 1984 election, a Harris (1985) survey found two-thirds of the respondents believing that in his second term Reagan's "handling of environmental cleanup matters" would be about the same (60 percent) or worse (7 percent) than in his first four years, while only 30 percent felt it would be better. Apparently the president's poor record on environmental protection had little effect on voters (Stanfield, 1984a).

While it would be asking a great deal to have public support for environmental protection turn into a powerful single-issue voting lobby that could block the reelection of a popular president who was riding the crest of an economic upturn (Goodman, 1983), the failure of Reagan's environmental policies to cost him at the ballot box must surely give pause to environmental advocates. The fact that the president's record on environmental issues was unpopular enough to have apparently stimulated a significant increase in the memberships of national environmental organizations as well as the significant upturn in public support for environmental protection noted in table 4.3, yet had little if any effect at the ballot box suggests again that public concern for environmental quality may not be an intensely held opinion.[18]

All of this leads me, albeit somewhat reluctantly, to agree with the conclusion reached (apparently by Ladd) in a Roper Center (1983:39) review of the data on public opinion on environmental issues: "A value may be clear and consensual, without dominating life in the way that mass unemployment did during the Depression or runaway inflation did in the 1970s. The value of a clean environment is nearly consensually held. The public when asked directly if environmental problems are serious will reply that they are. Yet, the environmental issue is not a particularly 'salient' [or 'intensely held'] one." The existence of consensual but at best moderately intense public support for environmental quality appears to reflect what public opinion analysts term a "permissive consensus" (Pierce et al., 1982:19). In such situations of widespread but not terribly intense public support for a goal, government has considerable flexibility in pursuing the goal and is not carefully monitored by the public—unlike the situation surrounding core economic goals such as low inflation and unemployment rates (Goodman, 1983). It is only when government policy becomes obviously out of tune with the public consensus that the government risks political reprisals. This is precisely what occurred during the first two years of the Reagan administration, as Watt's outspokenness and the EPA scandal attracted enough attention to highlight the discrepancy between

Reagan's environmental policies and the public's goal of environmental quality.

Organized environmentalists, already opposed to Reagan's policies, certainly led the charge against the administration. However, it is clear that they were able to mobilize people who were previously inactive on environmental issues to join their organizations, sign petitions, write and call officials, etc. to protest the administration's efforts to weaken environmental regulations (Mitchell, 1984b).[19] In light of this active opposition, as well as opinion polls showing widespread displeasure with Reagan's environmental record, the administration apparently began to fear political damage. It therefore jettisoned Watt and top EPA officials and undertook public relations efforts to signal that it was changing course on the environment (Alter et al., 1984; Stanfield, 1984b). Had it *not* done so (e.g., had Watt and Burford et al. been retained) it is *possible* that the president would have suffered political damage. The pro-environmental consensus may be "permissive," but it might not tolerate such a blatant rejection of its goal of environmental protection.

In addition to prompting some degree of change within the administration (Stanfield, 1984b), the public outcry against Reagan's environmental policies likely strengthened the hand of Congress in its efforts to combat the administration on environmental issues. In fact, the consensual support for environmental protection revealed in the polls (and Lou Harris's predictions about the political costs of ignoring that consensus) was prominently used in congressional hearings on the Clean Water Act and the Clean Air Act (Kenski and Kenski, 1984:108). And, as Anthony (1982:19) points out, public support for environmental protection is crucial when it helps convince policy-makers such as congressmen "that relaxing environmental safeguards is politically dangerous."

Still, we should not lose sight of the fact that—despite the departures of James Watt and Ann Gorsuch et al.—the Reagan administration was relatively successful in halting or at least hampering the enactment and enforcement of strong environmental legislation. Through budgetary review by the Office of Management and Budget, policy and personnel changes within agencies such as EPA, and lobbying with Congress, the Reagan administration has managed to hamper if not halt federal programs to control pollution (e.g., acid rain and ozone) while easing restrictions on access to public lands by oil, timber, and mining interests (see, e.g., Vig and Kraft, 1984; Thompson, 1985). In short, the administration may have failed to win public support for its environmental policies, but it has nonetheless managed to make considerable progress in implementing such policies—and has done so without suffering noticeable harm at the ballot box. I doubt that the administration's performance on economic matters could have been as discrepant with public preferences without having provoked a far more negative reaction at the polls.

Conclusion

Having questioned the strength of public concern for environmental quality, let me reiterate the earlier point that the environmental movement has nonetheless been remarkably successful compared to most social-problem movements. Indeed, it seems fair to argue that, along with a handful of other major movements such as the civil rights, antiwar, and feminist movements, the environmental movement has changed the character of our society.

Throughout its history the environmental movement has received strong support from the public in pursuit of its goal of improving and protecting the nation's physical environment. This support was exceptionally strong in the early seventies, and although it waned somewhat in the ensuing years it never came close to disappearing and has recently experienced a resurgence. Thus environmental quality appears to have become an enduring concern in our society, reflecting the fact that it has achieved the status of an important value among Americans.

With the help of supportive public opinion environmentalists have been able to institutionalize their goals in the form of government regulations and agencies, scientific research endeavors, university curricula, and media positions (e.g., "environmental reporters"). This "infrastructure," along with the major environmental organizations, provides a vital resource for continuing to lobby for environmental protection, including arousing public support. As suggested earlier, for example, the increase in public concern for environmental quality in the eighties likely reflects the success of environmental interest groups in mobilizing public opinion against the Reagan administration's challenge.

The fact that public support for environmental protection increased in the eighties also suggests that Downs's issue-attention cycle is not an inexorable process, and that once a social-problem movement has had its moment in the sun it is possible for it to rekindle public support rather than fade into the sunset. In other words, I believe that public opinion analysts need to give more attention to the role of social movements and interest groups (which successful movements become) in affecting public opinion, particularly in mobilizing it in order to defend past accomplishments.

Yet, while mindful of the environmental movement's success in maintaining public support, I cannot help but question the fundamental strength of that support in view of the Reagan administration's relatively successful challenge to environmentalists' goals. Even though the public appears to be increasingly concerned about toxic wastes and other environmental hazards, environmental problems often lack a sense of immediacy for the vast majority of us whose water supplies have not yet been found to be contaminated, for example. As the threat to human health and well-being posed by toxic wastes, acid rain, ozone depletion, and so on becomes increasingly apparent to the general public, it is possible that the situation will change and that voters will consistently weigh environmental factors along with economic ones when evaluating candidates. In the meantime, I suspect decisions in the ballot booth will be influenced more by economic than by environmental conditions—survey responses to environment-economy trade-off items notwithstanding!

5

Interest Groups and Environmental Policy

Helen M. Ingram and Dean E. Mann

The rise of the environmental movement in the 1970s and its staying power through the 1980s is one of the major alterations in the landscape of American politics. The movement has become one of the major forces in the political system, capable of altering the political agenda and winning significant victories against the dominant industrial and commercial interests of the United States.

The success of the environmental movement has been described in terms of "the institutionalization of environmental concern" (Langton, 1984:3). Evidence for this institutionalization is found in the passage of legislation but also in the professionalization of educational programs in environmental engineering, environmental economics, yes, even environmental politics. It is also found in the creation of professional associations specializing in environmental matters, the creation of numerous public agencies dedicated to the preservation of the environment, and the proliferation and strengthening of environmental interest groups (Langton, 1984:5). The environmental movement has grown from a cause to an accepted set of institutionalized American values.

The obvious importance of the environmental movement has spawned an enormous amount of research about public opinion and the environment, the effectiveness of environmental laws, and the growth and development of environmental interest groups. While quantitatively the research is substantial, much of it carries a tenor of advocacy, aiming to build up or tear down perceptions of public commitment, extol or criticize the effectiveness of environmental laws, or to exaggerate or minimize the influence of environmental groups. This chapter focuses particularly upon environmental interest groups and adopts a straightforward political science perspective. Our thesis is that environmental interest groups can best be understood with reference to pluralist thought which envisions group membership as motivated by ideological appeals, concerns over public policy, and successful sales approaches by leadership. Influencing policy is dependent upon effective leadership, the employment of appropriate strategies, and the forging of coalitions. The problems faced by environmental interest groups are those to be expected of groups whose development has reached maturity.

The evidence presented in this chapter sharply contradicts two other interpretations of environmental interest groups that take issue with the pluralist perspective. First, the ideological and policy appeal of environmental interest groups defies Mancur Olson's thesis about the origin and persistence of interest groups. He argued that groups are likely to form and to maintain themselves in direct proportion to their ability to offer selective benefits to their members (Olson, 1965). Otherwise they run afoul of the free-rider problem: the lack of incentives for individuals to join large membership organizations that may provide benefits to all individuals regardless of membership. A second ecological approach that our study determines to be too narrow has its origins in a longing for political decision-making which will reflect a "holistic" understanding of the environment. Encouraged by the success of movements in West Germany, these analysts foresee the transformation of fragmented, narrow, particularistic lobbies into a broad-scale social movement that would change the nature of American politics (Gottlieb and FitzSimmons, 1986). Whatever the merits, we judge it far more likely that decision-making will continue to be piecemeal, incremental, halting, and only approximating desired environmental solutions. This pluralist perspective undergirds an assessment of future problems that concludes the chapter.

Growth of Number and Size of Environmental Interest Groups

The substantial increase in the number of environmental organizations attests to the dominance of interest group pluralism as an explanatory framework. The vast increase in the number of interest groups during the past two decades, a substantial number of which were membership organizations, were precisely these kinds of organizations Olson suggested would be difficult to form and to maintain. While exploring a variety of explanations, including the growth of government programs and improved methods of communication and fund raising, Walker argued that the principal explanation was found in the sponsorship of external funding agencies. These agencies provided a substantial part—often as much as half—of the funding of a broad range of membership organizations. Hansen (1985) identifies environmental groups as particular beneficiaries of the patronage of external funding sources, both private and public.

Organizations concerned with protection of the environment have played important roles in American politics at least since the foundation of the Sierra Club in 1892. (For an excellent discussion of the histories of the major environmental groups, see Mitchell, 1985.) With the National Audubon Society formed in 1905 and the National Parks and Conservation Association in 1919, these organizations constituted the core of the "first wave" of groups concerned about conservation of natural resources, with particular emphasis on land resources, protection of specific sites against despoliation, and specific species of wildlife. Ensuing decades saw the formation of two additional important organizations, the Izaak Walton League in 1922 and the National Wildlife Federation in 1935. While organized in a variety of ways and having different policy concerns and geographic concentrations of membership, all of these were strong membership organizations that relied on member support and involvement for their survival. They of course have survived and remain among the most influential groups in the environmental movement.

A second generation of environmental groups entered the scene during the period of the 1960s and 1970s as public attention shifted to environmental pollution. At the same time the traditional groups expanded their vision of the environment to adopt the "ecological" approach to the natural environment, that is, to recognize the complex integrated interrelationships of living things, to use science as a tool for understanding and protecting the environment, and to promote an awareness of the cumulative and potentially disastrous impact of imprudent use of resources on all forms of life. In terms of organized group life, this new orientation brought forth new organizations committed to combatting pollution. The first was the Environmental Defense Fund in 1967, followed by the Natural Resources Defense Council in 1970. Both benefited from substantial external funding, particularly from the Ford Foundation. Both had a focus on litigation as the instrument of reform and both eventually ended up being membership organizations with their own topical emphases: EDF on toxics, water quality, and power generation and NRDC on air pollution, nuclear power, and solid waste. Still another set of groups originated during this period, some like Friends of the Earth as a schismatic from the

Sierra Club or the Environmental Policy Institute as a further schism from Friends of the Earth. Environmental Action was created as a result of the enthusiasms generated by Earth Day in 1970. Whereas FOE and Environmental Action contributed to the membership organizations (but with difficulty in the case of FOE), the Environmental Policy Institute is an organization dependent on wealthy patrons for support. Each group has its specialization, and FOE and Environmental Action tend to emphasize radical opposition to the existing system and technological developments.

While external funding unquestionably facilitated the creation of environmental organizations in the 1970s, it does not explain either the persistence of the more traditional conservation organizations into the environmental era or the persistence of these as well as the newer environmental organizations into the late 1980s. Those organizations that began with the support of a financial patron now have developed their sources of income, particularly relying on membership dues to provide a major proportion of their budgeting needs.

Recent evidence from survey research suggests strongly that two elements are crucial in maintaining membership in environmental organizations: the perceived existence of threats either to one's own environment or to the general environment of the nation and the appeal of an ideology that corresponds with the concerns of the individuals to whom appeals for membership are made. Selective benefits, in the forms of books, sponsored outings, even credit cards, provide substantial income to an organization like the Sierra Club, but they do not account for growth and maintenance of membership strength.

Robert Mitchell argues (Mitchell, 1984a) that membership in social movement organizations like environmental groups reflects a demand that exists among people for collective goods. This demand, he argues, depends upon the existence of the perception of a right or entitlement as a reference point. The reference point for the public with respect to the environment was established in the 1970s with the perception of rights to a clean environment, protection from the effects of such ills as toxic wastes and air pollution, and the right, perhaps only a proxy right but nevertheless real, to the preservation of scenic wonders or unique species. The existence of this reference point, then, translates into a demand for action to secure these rights and entitlements, action that can be stimulated only through collective action.

Mitchell, citing persuasive evidence comparing the views of committed environmentalists with less committed environmentalists, argues that the existence of a threat, the possible denial of collective rights to which they believe they are entitled, is the principal motivation for joining voluntary collective enterprises. A 1978 survey by the Sierra Club of its membership suggests that reasons for joining had little relationship to either attaining selective benefits or expressing ideological views quite distinct from that of the American public as a whole. The top three responses were: (1) If we don't act now to preserve the environment, things will get much worse (64 percent), (2) If the Club achieves its goals, my life and my children's lives will benefit (56 percent), (3) My contribution to the Sierra Club is helping to influence government action on environmental/conservation problems (42 percent) (Utrup, 1979:14–15).

Smith (1984a), citing survey research evidence, argued that expressive values are highly correlated with environmental group membership. While members may join and maintain their membership for certain selective benefits, as in a club, the members also value highly the more expressive benefits that may come from the public interest activities of the organization. He notes, for example, that the extent of additional voluntary contributions, above that necessary for sheer membership, is quite high in environmental organizations, coming from 17 to 49 percent of individuals who join such organizations. Similarly, Milbrath (1984:73) concludes that two motives tend to lead to group membership: perception of environmental threat and a desire to be out in nature with others with similar interests. In his judgment, perceptions of dire threats are the principal agents mobilizing individuals into membership and more overt activity.

The pattern of *growth of membership* in some environmental groups would seem to closely parallel perceived threats to the environment. For instance, growth of the Sierra Club relates to political cycles. In the 1960s the Sierra Club was a small California-based club of 35,000 members. A spurt of growth occurred in the 1970s, slowing toward the end of the decade (see figure 5.1). Only incremental growth took place during the Carter years; perceived threat declined when the administration was friendly. The Sierra Club had a membership of 180,000 by 1980. Another great spurt of new members came during the Watt/Gorsuch tenure. By the beginning of 1983, Sierra Club membership had climbed to 346,000. The National Audubon Society (not shown in figure 5.1) was up 70 percent in the same period. That patterns of growth vary as shown in figure 5.1 suggests that some groups were able to profit from perceived threats much more effectively than others. It should be noted that

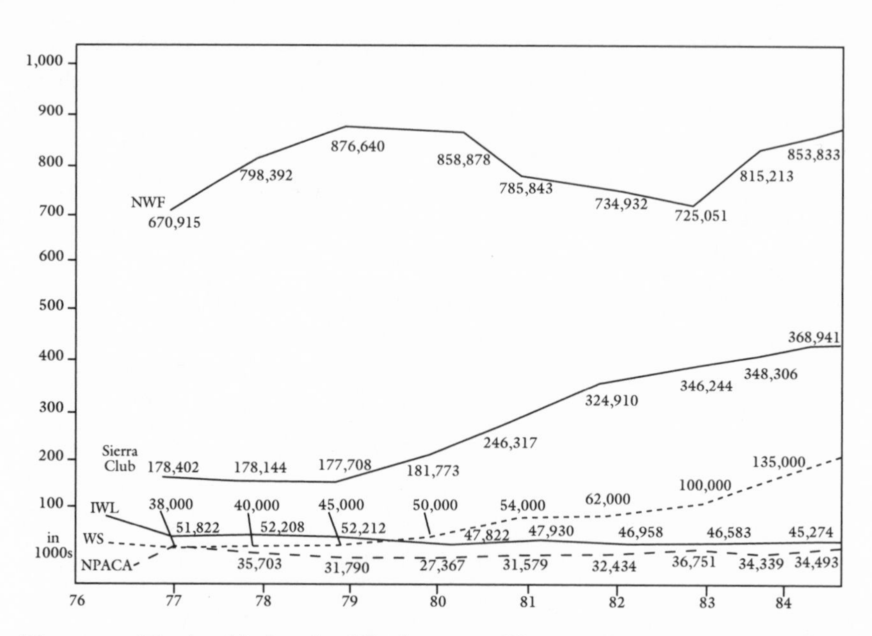

Figure 5.1 Membership Levels of Environmental Interest Groups 1977–85. (National Wildlife Federation, Sierra Club, Izaak Walton League, Wilderness Society, and National Parks and Conservation Association)

membership increases have fallen again for all groups now that noncontroversial figures hold top administrative posts.

Turning to an analysis of the kinds of persons who join environmental groups, there is little to suggest the emergence of a broad, revolutionary social movement. The people who join environmental groups differ most strongly from the public as a whole in the extent of higher education received. It is noteworthy that they are not especially distinguishable from the general population in terms of income or occupational prestige. They may be an elite of a compositional sort, but mostly in the sense that activists in almost any social movement reflect higher socioeconomic status (Morrison and Dunlap, 1986). The evidence suggests that environmentalists may in some instances seek goals that merely reflect self-interest, but the increasing concern for pollution may demonstrate that the arguable elite actually work in the interest of the poor (Andrews, 1980).

Environmental group members also tend to identify themselves more strongly as independents. There are other ideological differences. Members are somewhat more liberal than the population as a whole (Mitchell, 1978). But there is nothing like the ideological coherence necessary for a "Green movement" such as in Europe. When asked about such a possibility, Michael McCloskey, former executive director of the Sierra Club, responded: "We are trying to kindle a sense of political identity for the environmental movement in the United States, to encourage activists to understand the requirements for success and the need to mobilize behind candidates committed to our cause, However, because of basic differences in the political systems of the United States and Europe, I doubt there will be any need to think in terms of a separate political party concerned with the environment" (Gendlin, 1983:127).

Surveys of members of environmental groups suggest no real polarization against industry as the root cause for environmental problems. "Members were no quicker to blame industry (97 percent) than the general carelessness of people (96 percent)" when asked to rate the importance of a list of possible causes of environmental problems. "Nor do members feel environmentalists should adopt a totally adversary approach in their relations with industry. Ninety-five percent agreed that 'it is a good idea for environmental leaders to engage in dialogue with industry to break down stereotypes and see if there is any common ground for the solution to specific conflicts'" (Utrup, 1979:15–16).

Environmental interest groups, at least the largest and most well known among them, tend to be membership rather than nonmembership groups. Some groups, like the Environmental Defense Fund and originally the Natural Resources Defense Council, were originally tightly held and led organizations, consisting principally of the officers who were supported by contributions of foundations. Subsequently, they developed sizable memberships, in each case around 50,000 in 1983. Alone among major environmentalist groups with no membership is the Environmental Policy Institute. On the other hand, the Sierra Club has all along been fundamentally a democratic organization with regular elections and occasionally real contests over leadership positions. This distinction presumably makes a significant difference in the extent to which organizations are free to take or not take stands on controversial issues or issues that may be of marginal interest to factions within the organization. As a grass-roots organization with multiple interests and lots of participation by individual members, the Sierra Club has been described as "a sort of flight of bumble bees flying along stinging everything it runs into" (Stanfield, 1985: 1351).

It is of course true that nonmembership organizations or organizations in which membership involvement in policy choices is not strong are not entirely free of external influences, dependent as they are on external sponsors. Nevertheless, their day-by-day and issue-by-issue decisions are made by staff and are measurably less subject to scrutiny than those in which members have the opportunity for oversight of their leadership. Indeed, there are those who argue that the prevalence of such groups does not augur well for a pluralist institutional arrangement, given their lack of responsiveness to larger elements in society (Hayes, 1983).

Private interests, such as the private foundations, have been crucial to the founding and maintenance of environmental as well as other citizen interest groups. But the role of government in facilitating the growth and maintenance of such organizations should also be recognized. Indeed, it may be argued that government itself is the principal agent in fostering interest group activity, especially as a supplement to elective representative institutions (Anderson, 1977). Government creates by legislation institutional arrangements by which it balances the influence of various group interests, perceiving that the market economy does not in itself foster such a balance. Of particular importance have been such general legislation as the National Environmental Policy Act and other specific legislation such as the Clean Air Act and Toxic Substances Control Act. Each required involvement of public groups through public notice, hearings, the creation of advisory groups, the holding of workshops, and in some instances the direct funding of interest groups that were incapable of sustaining the prolonged activity that attention to environmental matters required (see Daneke et al., 1983; Lester and Bowman, 1983; and O'Hare et al., 1983). Funding for such activities has been drastically reduced by the Reagan administration and not entirely compensated for by support at the state level so that the extent to which environmental groups can depend upon government as an aid to group maintenance is problematic (Lester and Bowman, 1983:184–93).

Strategies of Environmental Groups

The environmental movement is not homogeneous in the goals and values it seeks to maximize. Some groups have concentrated on certain environmental problems such as air quality or wilderness protection while others have sought to involve themselves in a broad range of issues. It would hardly be surprising, then, to find that there are differences in the strategies and tactics pursued by the various groups and shifting coalitions among them as they perceive their group advantages and their priorities in allocating their scarce resources.

Strategies of environmental groups can best be understood as attempts to gain access to governmental decision-making rather than attempts to differentiate themselves in order to have relatively better positions in competition for members and contributions, or to build support and a rationale for a more radical solution to the nation's environmental problems.

The differences among environmental groups may be very significant indeed. At the one extreme one finds such an organization as the Sea Shepherd Conservation Society, members of which are alternately described as "environmental guerrillas" or modern-day pirates. While espousing Ghandi-like tactics, the organization has utilized violence in ramming and sinking whaling vessels of various nations (*Los Angeles Times,* 1987). Clearly, adopting nonviolence is the Greenpeace Society and its efforts to thwart environmental damage by placing its members in locations designed to thwart environmentally damaging practices.

At the other extreme are the organizations that engage in standard American political practices of lobbying, public information campaigns, electioneering, litigation, and coalition building. Their success in utilizing those tactics and approaches of course depends on the resonance their appeals find in the American public's thinking, the standing of the organizations in the public's mind, the nature of the times, and the specific threats that exist to American ideals and values.

Two of the basic distinctions among the environmental groups is their orientation toward science versus activism and their willingness to engage in negotiations with those whom they consider to be the adversary. Some environmentalist organizations tend to eschew science and believe their principal role is that of advocacy and publicity. The Sierra Club is a notable example of the latter, with its spectacular public relations programs that blocked dams in Dinosaur National Monument in 1956 and Grand Canyon National Park in 1968. Other groups such as the Natural Resources Defense Council and the EDF embrace science and seek to demonstrate through technical mastery the prescience of their positions on toxic substances and air quality.

On the question of cooperation, the Environmental Defense Fund has maintained a constant record of negotiating "deals" with the perpetrators of environmental harms to achieve workable solutions. Thus EDF worked with the staffs of the California Public Utilities Commission and the Pacific Gas and Electric Company to achieve conservative solutions to the utility's problems in meeting future demands for energy, thus avoiding the construction of several nuclear power plants that were on the utility's agenda (Roe, 1984). Similarly, EDF has developed working plans with the Westlands Water District in central California to resolve the problems associated with high levels of selenium in the Kesterson Wildlife Refuge.

There is no question that prior to the 1970s conservation/preservation groups oriented their appeals more to the public than to government. Some interpret this as a carry-over from the isolation of John Muir from the utilitarian conservationists who dominated the Roosevelt administration at the turn of the century. Energy was spent articulating and popularizing preservationist perspectives, but not in regularly influencing specific legislative and administrative actions. Specific battles were waged in Congress, such as those to defeat dams in Dinosaur National Monument or the Grand Canyon, but a continuous lobbying capability did not exist.

Influencing policy

Changes began to take place after 1969. According to Michael McCloskey, a former executive director of the Sierra Club whose staff career spanned a longer period than most, the transformation was deliberate and related to policy goals. "What I have emphasized has been a serious approach toward achieving our ends. I thought that we were not here just to bear witness or to pledge allegiance to the faith, but in fact we were here to bring that faith into reality. . . . That means we could not rest content with having said the right things, or with having made our convictions known, but we also had to plan to achieve them. We had to know how the political system worked, how to identify the decision makers and how their minds worked. We had to have people concerned with all the practical details of getting our programs accomplished" (Gendlin, 1982:41).

The Carter administration initiated an era during which environmental groups were not only increasingly political, but also one in which they became comfortable with inside strategies. The six-year tenure of Russell W. Peterson as president of the National Audubon Society began in the Carter era. Upon his retirement in 1985 he reminisced, "My most important contribution within Audubon was to make it more of an activist group" (Esch, 1985:D–12). The appointment of a number of environmentalists in the Environmental Protection Agency, the Department of Interior, and the Justice Department provided groups with built-in access. According to Brock Evans, former director of the Sierra Club Washington Office, "some of the fiercest attacks on Carter have been mounted by the oil, timber, and mining industries because the President appointed so many environmentalists to key policy posts—something that had never happened before" (Evans, 1980:22). As Evans wrote in 1980:

> They frequently criticize Carter's appointments of such leaders as James Moorman, former executive director of the Sierra Club Legal Defense Fund, as Assistant Attorney General for public lands. Moorman's job is to enforce environmental laws on public lands and to defend the government against such lawsuits as the one filed by Anaconda Copper Company in Alaska challenging the validity of the President's landmark designation of 56 million acres of public lands as national monuments. Moorman argued and won the case—but another administration could have chosen not to defend it at all, or to settle out of court.
>
> The appointment of Robert Herbst, former executive director of the Izaak Walton League, as Assistant Secretary of the Interior for parks and wildlife, also had important consequences for the protection of Alaska's public lands. (Evans, 1980:23)

Environmentalists behaved as might be expected toward friends. One commented, "Before, we filed lawsuits and held press conferences. Now we have lunch with the assistant secretary to discuss a program" (quoted in Mosher, 1980:212).

The shift to more confrontational strategies during the Reagan administration can be explained by the loss of inside access. As McCloskey perceived the challenge:

> Normally one's ability to lobby government depends on there being a sufficient number of people who have not made up their minds on all subjects, or who don't have a dogma covering every question that gives them the answer automatically. But we find there are almost no such people who are open to persuasion in this administration, at least among the people dealing with environmental policy. So our traditional techniques just won't work with them. We may find some limited opportunities in Congress, but less so there too.

> As a result, we are turning more to two other techniques. One of them is to go to the grassroots and to use techniques of direct action. Our petition campaign was an example of obtaining a large manifestation of sentiment from the grassroots. It was one of the largest public petition campaigns in history. Also, our people locally have been picketing James Watt at almost every one of his appearances around the country. We've done very little picketing in the past. That's a way of making our protest manifest both to him and to the local press corps. We are also trying to carry our case to the public much more through the media.
>
> The Club has not had an appetite, in the past, for direct action. One reason is that the techniques are not as effective as lobbying when the figures in public office are open to persuasion. But we're forced to these techniques because we don't enjoy such a receptive situation today. (Gendlin, 1982:38)

Coalition building

Collaboration among environmental groups has improved. Since 1980 a group of ten environmental groups has met regularly to plot strategy. Prior to that time, cooperation was more ad hoc. In the view of McCloskey, coalitions among environmentalists are becoming easier because groups have become more alike, drawing their members from mailing lists of persons with the same characteristics (Gendlin, 1982:37).

The terms of cooperation and the strategies adopted are matters that require assessment by interest groups and their leadership. Zeckhauser describes several strategies that might be selected when there is a very real possibility that preferred policies might be adopted: (1) linking the proposals imposing costs with other legislation that provides benefits to the constituencies that might be harmed, (2) phasing the implementation of programs so that effects are delayed, and (3) purposely introducing uncertainty that makes it difficult for the organized interest groups to determine whether their constituents will be more likely to incur costs than benefits (Zeckhauser, 1981).

Attempts at linking environmental groups with other interest groups are also taking place and show promise. This strategy worked when the environmentalists supported the Clean Water Act in 1972 in alliance with the major urban interests that wanted money for construction of municipal waste treatment plants (Mann, 1975). The National Wildlife Federation has established a Corporate Conservation Council to encourage communication between environmentalists and business (Hassler and O'Conner, 1986). Environmentalists are working with agriculturists to facilitate research by the EPA on pesticides (Stanfield, 1985:1352). They can take similar action in cooperation with industry with respect to the disposal of toxic wastes. They have already cooperated with conservatives to defeat costly and unnecessary water development projects. There are important opportunities for cooperation with farmers with respect to soil erosion.

Participation in elections

Participation in the electoral process, including the endorsement of the Mondale/Ferraro ticket, is best interpreted as an attempt to obtain access rather than to establish a separate "green party" preserve. Activity has evolved slowly and haltingly, beginning with voting ratings rather than candidate endorsements. In 1970 a newborn environmental lobby group, Environmental Action, mated two concepts, the group rating and the wanted poster, to create an environmental hit list christened the "dirty dozen." Environmental Action selected "key" votes, picked twelve powerful members of Congress with low scores, and campaigned for their defeat. In the course of five elections, fifty-two incumbents made the dirty dozen list and twenty-four were defeated the same year (Keller, 1981). The League of Conservation Voters, also established in 1970, evaluates and publishes the environmental record of public officials and supports those with outstanding environmental records, mainly when elections appear to be close. In 1984, forty of the congressional candidates it endorsed won their contests while twenty-one lost.

Large membership environmental groups have been slower to make electoral endorsements. In 1980 the Sierra Club endorsed a few California legislative candidates on a trial basis. In February 1982 the Sierra Club made its first ever federal endorsement of Congressman Sidney Yates (D-Illinois). By November 1982 it had backed 153 candidates for the House and 15 for the Senate in addition to 10 gubernatorial candidates. Its overall success rate was an encouraging 80 percent. The vehicle for electoral involvement is the Sierra Club Committee on Political Education (SCCOPE), an eight-person national committee, appointed by the club's executive committee, which is responsible for endorsing federal candidates, overseeing compliance with election laws, and mapping electoral strategy. The 1982 success at the polls, in addition to the "abysmal record" of the incumbent president, led the board of directors of the Sierra Club along with other groups to take the unprecedented step of endorsing Mondale. A number of signals may have misled the groups to exaggerate their possible influence on voters: rapid growth of membership and contributions, and the very favorable responses of the electorate to opinion polls on environmental issues (Mitchell, 1984).

In assessing their electoral experience, environmentalists are uncertain whether they will again endorse a presidential candidate, but do not regret having done so. In their view the Reagan environmental record was so poor as to give them little choice. Further, little was sacrificed and a few gains were made. A Sierra Club representative reported that there was little sign of disaffection among Republican members. Contributions may have suffered slightly. This loss was more than offset by valuable electoral experience. Environmental leaders envision greater future participation in recruitment of candidates, in primaries, and in political party conventions. They see their greatest potential in areas where the influence of numbers of grass-roots workers is important.

Litigation

Another option often followed by environmental groups since the 1970s is the litigation of environmental disputes. A successful litigation strategy depends on numerous factors in the political environment; success is certainly not preordained (Wasby, 1983). These conditions range from (1) accessibility of the courts to the environmental groups as reflected in the issue of standing to sue or the availability of fee awards to litigants, (2) estimates of the costs and benefits to the organization of a litigation strategy or alternative courses of action—the extent to which members of the organization will be supportive of given litigation, (3) the existence of a favorable distribution of opinions among the general public or attentive publics, and (4) the complexity of the legal and constitutional issues themselves. Wasby (1983) stresses, however, that intraorganizational and interorganizational factors may be paramount. These factors include control over timing and sequence of cases, the identification of legal issues, the extent to which the strategy is flexible in response to changes in litigational conditions, and perhaps most importantly, whether the organizations are membership-based or essentially nonmembership groups.

That the litigational strategy is highly variable in its utility to the environmental movement is demonstrated by the evidence for the decade 1970–1980, arguably the decade of the environmental movement (Wenner, 1982). The environmental groups tended to win about as often as economic interest groups, but governmental agencies, when they took the initiative, tended to be the most successful of all. When environmental groups are challenged by conservative legal foundations in court, the evidence suggests that the environmental groups are likely to come out on top (Hassler and O'Conner, 1986). Economic interests tended to be particularly successful at the level of the Supreme Court.

For some time environmental groups were severely threatened in their litigation efforts by decisions by the Supreme Court that limited their standing (the organization or its members could not demonstrate direct injury owing to a governmental agency's action) and the limitation on litigation and lobbying owing to possible loss of tax-exempt status for public interest law firms and public foundations. In a series of cases beginning in 1966 with *Scenic Hudson Preservation Conference v. FPC* (354 F. 2d 50F, 2d Cir. 1965, cert. denied 384 U.S. 941, 1966) and *Sierra Club v. Morton* (405 U.S. at 737, 1972), the Supreme Court relaxed the standards for standing so that environmental groups could in effect represent those whose interests were threatened. Similarly, the Internal Revenue Service reviewed its standards and granted tax-exempt status to environmental law groups.

Entrepreneurship and organization building

As indicated above, initial public choice theory, such as that of Mancur Olson, attributed little weight to the entrepreneurial function in group activities except where economic interests are highly concentrated and provide selective benefits. Subsequent research and analysis have demonstrated that leadership is indeed a powerful independent factor in private organizational development and maintenance. Individuals with appropriate skills, experience, and contacts have sufficient incentives to direct their energies toward securing funding, soliciting membership, and developing programs that justify their input of energy and time. The vast increase in the number of interest groups during the last two decades attests to this entrepreneurial spirit in that most of these membership organizations required exceptional inputs of energy by individuals who were able to secure the external funding, communicate with the appropriate attentive public, and publicize the public advocacy functions so as to incite group membership (Frohlich et al., 1971). Moreover, that same leadership had to maintain these organizations through skillful efforts to ensure continued membership support as the external sources of funding declined (Walker, 1983).

The technology for creating mass membership and thus more financial security vastly improved over the past two decades. Direct mailings to individuals on lists of people who are deemed likely to be sympathetic to the environmentalist cause have proven to be a provident source of financial and mass support for environmentalist organizations, as they have to other organizations. Using appeals based on impending environmental crises and offering such benefits as a monthly publication, books, and other benefits, the environmental organizations have been able to tap sources of support which are quite capable of paying the rather modest annual membership fee.

Leadership in many environmental organizations arguably has concentrated on the dramatization of issues—particularly in combatting the enemy or the devil that has created the threat or the unsavory condition to which the group objects (Berry, 1984). The evidence is strong that these expressive appeals have a powerful impact on attentive publics. Even though they know they are unable to capture exclusively the public benefits that may come through the lobbying and litigational activity in which the organization engages, they are prepared to support this activity with their money and even their energy (Smith, 1984b).

It is at least arguable that in many cases, as the organization develops and matures, it enhances its survival power by emphasizing selective benefits available to members that are not available to nonmembers. Thus, all members of the public enjoy the benefits that may come from the passage of legislation controlling the flow of toxic substances into the environment but not all members of the public have the benefits of publications, discounts on group activities, channels to information, insurance programs, and solidary benefits that come from group interaction. The groups founded for the public purposes may find it advantageous to *add* these selective benefits in order to maximize membership support.

This suggests, then, that the context of the activity in which environmental groups engage may alter and that the groups themselves—the leadership and its relationship to the membership—may have to change as well. The issues may become more complex, the devils less obvious, the necessary alliances more difficult to form, the sources of funding more heterogeneous and subject to competition, and the ideological fervor more difficult to arouse.

Langton calls this the "fourth wave" of the environmental movement, in which the issues may be largely new and the movement itself more diverse and decentralized. Environmental values will be more completely ingrained in the public thinking but probably more integrated with thinking about economic and social values. The emphasis, therefore, will be on "leaders capable of managing and leading environmental organizations with efficiency and effectiveness" (Langton, 1984:11).

Except perhaps for David Brower and his leadership of the Sierra Club during the 1950s and 1960s, it is difficult to argue that the modern environmental movement or its organizations have had much in the way of charismatic leadership. Nevertheless, there has been a charismatic sense about environmentalism—a dedication to its values as superior to all others, an emotional commitment that transcended the rational, a sense of solidarity within environmental organizations—that partook of the relationship that individuals feel toward charismatic leaders. The question we are addressing is whether institutionalization has changed the spirit of the movement and thereby changed the relationships between leaders and followers and therefore the skills required for environmental leadership. Some argue that it has. Langton, for example, contends the "environmental movement is being transformed from a relatively charismatic movement to a more institutionalized movement. It is a movement dominated less and less by charismatic leaders, protest, and dramatic causes as it becomes characterized by day-to-day efforts of education, research, and rule making. . . . It is a movement less marked by inspirational leaders and more dominated by leaders who manage" (Langton, 1984:4).

This transformation was predictable by sociological theory. Weber argued that charismatic leadership is really a phenomenon of the early phase of social and economic organization. To survive, social organizations had to transform themselves into rationally organized and led institutions with established routines and specialization of functions in order to cope with an economic and social environment in which their existence was no longer at stake and in which there was an expectation that they would play certain roles in the social processes of the community (Weber, 1966). More specifically, leadership would be transformed in such ways that they would become managers, conservers, negotiators—in effect, institutionalized leaders rather than those who inspired their members to leap up on the barricades (see Selznick, 1957).

What needs to be done in terms of leadership of the environmental movement? Langton contends that environmental leaders and organizations must develop new skills of institutional leadership if they are to be effective. They must develop a dual consciousness: "There should be as much concern for the institutional capability of environmental organizations as there is for the substance of specific environmental issues. In the future, environmentalists need to be as concerned about the state of leadership of the environmental movement as about the state of the environment" (Langton, 1984:5).

Langton defines the new competencies of environmental leadership in the following terms: (1) professional administration, which includes such skills as planning, fund raising, financial management, program evaluation, effective personnel management, and information systems, (2) ability to foster collaboration, as in cooperating with governmental organizations and other groups disposed toward similar values; the formation of coalitions, sharing of resources, joint planning and execution of plans, etc., (3) the development of political action skills, such as the ability to lobby effectively, to draft legislation, and to mobilize citizens behind given environmental programs, (4) the ability to develop and to assess technical information, including influencing research agendas and collaborating with others in such technical assessments, and (5) development of a new educational orientation, particularly toward the public and with respect to the public concern for economic as well as environmental values (Langton, 1984:5–11).

A good deal of evidence has already been provided to illustrate that the development of the political action skills Langton prescribed is taking place. Involvement in elections has been noted. Evidence suggests that environmental groups are changing toward managerial-type leaders. At the end of 1985 half a dozen or so environmental groups were in the process of changing leaders. While different circumstances explained the exodus—one informant suggested general burnout from the long and intense struggles of the Gorsuch/Watt era—"a common thread ties the organizations' search for new executives—an emphasis on managerial skills and a pragmatic approach to environmental advocacy" (Stanfield, 1985:1350). That this transition is not altogether easy is evidenced by the serious conflict between the Friends of the Earth and its founder, David Brower. The struggle appears to have been so damaging that Friends of the Earth has been referred to as "brain dead" among professional environmentalists (McComb, 1986).

Some see this change in leadership as a symbol of the "third wave" of the environmental movement. The third wave, it is argued, is marked by a shift from confrontational tactics—litigation and highly publicized media contests—to an era of bargaining and deal making. The third wave reflects both the technical character of the problems being faced and the fact that the cooperation of industry is necessary to make the laws already on the books effective (*Los Angeles Times,* December 22, 1986; *Wall Street Journal,* November 20, 1986).

Thus the new leadership tends to be highly professional rather than coming from the ranks of backpackers or local protest groups. The new leadership must be not only committed to environmental values but also skilled in organization maintenance. As one representative of the Wilderness Society put it, "The question is whether the organization will be run by well-paid, skillful professionals or whether we will cling to the bleeding heart concept. If we continue with the latter, I believe we are doomed" (*Los Angeles Times,* December 27, 1984). With budgets as high as $50 million and staff that run into the hundreds, many of whom are highly trained scientists, lawyers, and other professionals, management becomes a significant element in the operation. Michael McClosky of the Sierra Club stated, in looking for his successor, "We're looking for a person who's very strong in finance and budgets, who has a track record in management, who can offer entrepreneurial leadership, who is alert to changes in the market place" (*Los Angeles Times,* December 27, 1984).

Mitchell (1985) describes the transformation of the Wilderness Society in the late 1970s and 1980s. With expanding budgets, staff, and membership, the organization hired a top lobbyist from the Sierra Club and a professional economist to head an economic policy department funded by a major foundation grant. Its forest management department had a staff of professional foresters, ecologists, and policy analysts. The society had twenty Washington lobbyists and eight regional offices and a dozen specialists to review forest plans.

Such choices are not without peril for an organization with an activist bent. The Sierra Club hired a professional in 1985 and had to find a new head in early 1987 because the professional did not fit the activist orientation of the club. Its new director noted that the Sierra Club is "an aggressive, gutsy, grass-roots organization" that works with lots of people, mostly volunteers. Making deals requires professionals but "that's not the club, that's not the club's strength" (*Los Angeles Times,* April 23, 1987).

Maintaining cohesion

Pluralist theory has identified as critical to the success of political movements the maintenance of cohesion, or allegiance to shared, common interests, in the face of centrifugal forces of diverse, separate claims. There is no question that the strategies and organizational changes identified above have increased the effectiveness of environmental groups in the national political arena, but these strategies have also put stress on the movement's cohesion. The moderate and accommodating decision-making style of contemporary managerial leaders is perceived by some as sacrifice of principle. The increased sophistication in the labyrinth of Washington policy-making appears to critics within the movement as co-optation. The attention of national groups upon Congress and federal legislation has diverted attention from the grass roots and some rapidly emerging changes in local priorities (Rheem, 1978).

An important segment of the environmental community has taken issue with environmental groups' becoming just another lobby. Inside negotiations conducted in closed forums, the use of computerized mail technology in large-scale membership and fund-raising campaigns, and the passive role of the membership of groups in changing environmentally damaging behavior has alienated those who hoped environmental groups to be different. Some of these critics are attracted to relatively more extreme groups such as Earth First and Greenpeace whose members engage in direct action as preferable to indirect political bargaining. While such groups are small and outside the mainstream, their significance should not be discounted. Through their actions difficult issues may get placed on the environmental agenda that would be otherwise ignored. Further, their vocal criticisms of compromise probably restrain the leaders of mainline groups from the appearance of excessive moderation.

Another issue with which some judge contemporary national environmental groups to be dealing poorly is the cleavage between traditional conservation concern and more recently emergent fears about toxic wastes. Preserving nature is a good deal less urgent than protecting human health for groups like the Citizens Clearing House on Hazardous Waste, whose executive director, Lois Gibbs, characterized the members as "not environmentalists" but ordinary people frightened about dangers in their neighborhoods (Rheem, 1987). Such fears have spawned hundreds of local groups, many of which target state capitals and city halls rather than Congress. National groups have responded slowly and uncertainly to groundswells of activism. Some groups, such as the Sierra Club, have fashioned programs like "Hunt the Dump" that aid members in identifying potential neighborhood hazards. Whether such efforts foster environmental consciousness or shortsighted "not in my back yard" attitudes is a matter of some dispute. Fearing that excessive localism may thwart rational natural source planning, some groups have remained aloof from what they regard as essentially local land use questions. Yet staying out of localized public health issues removes national groups from a fast-growing area of public concern. The explosion of neighborhood organizations built around health and quality-of-life matters diffuses the attention of the environmental movement at the same time it provides opportunities for further growth and influence. Finding simple strategies to maintain cohesion, such as combining around the common enemy James Watt, are not likely to be easy.

Prospects for the Future

The American political system is notable for its fragmented, pluralistic structure. Decisions in the public sector are predominantly the result of a process of group interaction within a framework of accepted capitalist values. Authoritative writers on its present and future character are in general agreement that there are few signs or forces on the horizon that indicate a substantial alteration in that structure. The perspective of this chapter has been that environmental groups are best understood in the context of pluralist politics. There is little evidence to suggest that environmentalism will spawn a social movement that will basically challenge the foundations of pluralist politics. In fact environmental groups provide little evidence of any public-choice challenge to pluralism. The evidence is quite clear that the growth in the number and size of environmental interest groups has responded to numerous factors, such as ideological appeals and concerns over public policy, as well as the entrepreneurial talents of individuals who realize substantial psychological as well as material rewards for such activity.

The problems faced by contemporary environmental interest groups are those of mature institutions that must be concerned with maintaining capability including:

1. *Maintaining membership without the confrontation of the Watt/Gorsuch years.* Data suggests a large turnover in members, although few groups are losing members. There are associated problems of building esprit de corps and common identity. Groups such as the Sierra Club have experimented with such devices as an annual assembly to draw together its large and diverse membership (Gendlin, 1983:126).

2. *Maintaining adequate funding.* Financial problems in environmental groups have been practically endemic, although few have such serious prob-

lems as does Friends of the Earth, which recently shifted offices to Washington and cut back on staff. Aspirations and ambitions outreach capability, and trimming agendas to resources will be difficult, especially without a rapidly expanding financial base. Money promises to be a special problem as contributions toward buying television time appear to outstrip the value of campaign workers for candidates.

3. *Choosing appropriate priorities*. The environmental movement can maximize its influence by building coalitions with groups holding shared or similar goals. Endorsing some issue positions, however, threatens to spread resources thin and to cross-pressure members. For instance, there are clear problems with associations with groups against nuclear weapons, against defense spending, and pro-choice groups. Such issues have become conflictual within organizations such as Friends of the Earth and the Sierra Club. There are also considerable challenges for environmental groups as they prepare to address what they term second-generation environmental issues. In the words of McCloskey:

> After the original problem is dealt with, you are no longer working with an issue that appears fresh. You aren't just reacting to a grievance. Addressing a first-generation problem generates enthusiasm, because you can point primarily to a clear and present evil. But once you have a curative program and perhaps find it's not working well, the dialogue becomes cast much more in terms of how the program needs to be improved. It gets a bureaucratic or highly technical cast to it. These stages of development are not easily publicized, and they certainly are not the stuff that stirs people's souls. (Gendlin, 1982:40)

Prospects for Research

The challenge to future researchers of the environmental movement is nearly as exacting as that for the movement itself. In the past researchers have often served as advocates and apologists for the movement. This orientation is not surprising at early stages of the issue-attention cycle when there is a common interest of everyone involved in the subject matter to gain widespread governmental and public recognition that a problem exists. Early research in poverty, welfare, civil rights, and women's issues has tended to be more advocacy than analysis. However, future research must be more critical and balanced if it is to contribute to understanding and to have scholarly credibility.

The pluralist nature of American politics is reflected in the considerable differentiation within the environmental movement. More research is needed on the particular groups and interests that make up the whole, especially those groups at the fringes of the mainstream. How are the more radical national groups who believe that broad social change is essential reacting to the "technocrats" who are becoming the leadership of mainstream groups? Are environmental leaders serving a gatekeeping function in keeping such issues as abortion, gay rights, disarmament, and nuclear power off the active agenda of mainstream groups? Grass-roots organizations growing up around local toxic pollution and growth control issues have different motivations and different sorts of leadership than national organizations. What is the relation of such groups to national organizations? Are they co-opted by groups at the national level, and if so on what terms?

As environmental policy becomes decentralized to state and local levels, environmental groups will need to refocus their efforts outside Washington to be effective. What is the relative strength of environmentalists at state capitols and city halls? What strategies are being used, and are strategies appropriate?

The particular questions future research on the environmental movement addresses are probably less important than how the researchers go about their job. In past writings about the environment much of the theoretical and conceptual insights of interest group and public policy theory has been ignored. The consequences have been unfortunate in that environmental research has continued to be regarded as esoteric and atheoretical by disciplines as a whole. Further, general theory has remained uninformed about the variations offered in the environmental case. It is time for environmental politics researchers to attend more carefully to the theoretical relevance of their work.

6

Party Politics and Environmental Policy

Jerry W. Calvert

The 1970s will rightly be labeled as the "environmental decade." During those years the national and state governments began to assume a responsibility for protecting the nation's environmental quality, adding to government's already established role in managing the public lands for economic, recreational, and wildlife uses. At the federal level several important pieces of landmark legislation were enacted. Among these were the National Environmental Policy Act, the Clean Air Act, the Endangered Species Act, the Water Pollution Control Act, the Federal Land Policy Management Act, the Surface Mining Control and Reclamation Act, and the Alaska National Lands Conservation Act. All in all, twenty important environmental bills were enacted into law, and a regulatory mechanism, the Environmental Protection Agency (EPA), was created to enforce the nation's new commitment to environmental quality (Vig and Kraft, 1980).

But if the 1970s may be viewed as a decade of innovation and relatively minimal partisan conflict in the field of environmental policy, the 1980s have been one of retrenchment and heightened partisanship triggered by the emergence of a new and quite different environmental agenda under the administration of President Ronald Reagan. The Reagan agenda represented a sharp break with the immediate past. Committed to a policy of rapid development of the nation's natural resources and sensitive to the cries of industry for "regulatory relief," the administration's approach appeared to be an assault on a broad front that was directed toward minimizing a governmental role in the preservation of environmental quality. Agencies charged with enforcing the nation's environmental laws had their budgets slashed and their staffs cut. New men and women who were often free market ideologues and overtly pro-industry were appointed to head these agencies (such as James Watt at Interior, Ann Gorsuch at EPA), while the promised regulatory relief was to be implemented by the application of something called "cost-benefit analysis" in the making of regulatory decisions (Kenski and Kenski, 1984; Vig, 1984; Kraft, 1984).

The purpose of this study is to first examine the influence of political party affiliation as a factor in the legislative choices made during the 1970s and during the first half of the 1980s. And secondly, the study will conclude with suggestions for future research on the role of political parties in the determination of environmental policy. It is assumed, in the tradition of Schattschneider (1960), that the major raison d'etre of political parties in a democracy is to provide voters with alternative conceptions of the "public good" so that citizens can make informed choices about the kind of government and the kind of government policies they want. To be sure, America's major political parties have been seen as not fulfilling this democratic responsibility very well in a variety of policy areas. Nonetheless, substantial differences between the Republican and Democratic parties are readily apparent to the moderately informed observer. These differences are manifest in national party platforms (Engelbert, 1961; Monroe, 1983) and in the endemic legislative conflict concerning the role and scope of government, especially in the area of regulating economic activity. Such differences statistically appear in legislative voting. From one-third to almost one-half of the roll call votes in Congress will be partisan votes in which a majority of one party voted in opposition to the majority of the other party (Keefe and Ogul, 1985).

Given that partisan conflict is often triggered by governmental intervention in the economy and given the fact that environmental degradation is often the end product of private economic activity, it is not surprising to find that a partisan political identification is a significant variable in policy-making, even at the local level (Crenson, 1971), and that it significantly conditions executive and legislative performance depending upon which party is in control of the institutional levers of power (Engelbert, 1961).

As stated above, this essay will confine itself to one aspect of political party influence in environmental decision-making—the party affiliation of elected congressional and state representatives. This is not meant to imply that party is not a significant factor in executive, administrative, or judicial arenas as well, for there is little doubt that where environmental policy is made, party will play a role. Nonetheless, chief executives, administrative agency heads, and judges are obliged to operate within a policy environment whose parameters have been marked out by prior legislative action. Legislators have mandated that clean air and clean water are a governmental responsibility. In acting thus they have provided the basis for executive actions, regulatory mechanisms, and judicial interpretations. The engine that drives the legislative process is the political party organization of Congress and the state legislatures and in many institutions of local government. It is in this process that parties "deliver" on the promises made to the voting public and to organized interests, and it is here that the parties face each other in public combat over the allocation of values.

Studies of congressional behavior during the 1970s demonstrate that legislative choices in the area of environmental policy were more conflictual than consensual, with Democrats generally supporting a governmental responsibility to protect the environment and Republicans generally opposing (Ritt and Ostheimer, 1974; Dunlap and Allen, 1976; Kenski and Kenski, 1981). Significant partisanship was also apparent in state legislative choices as well (Dunlap and Gale, 1974; Calvert, 1979, 1982; Lester, 1980; Francis, 1984). Speaking of Congress, Ritt and Ostheimer concluded (1974:469–70): "Contrary to early expectations of environmentalists, this issue [environmental quality] has not been 'above politics.' It involves federal government expenditures of sizeable proportions and has consequently given rise to those same antagonisms which have separated Democrats and Republicans over the last forty years. The hope that there could be non-partisan solutions to the environmental crisis would seem to be most unrealistic." Thus in both the national and state legislative arena party affiliation is an important variable in legislative choice, in fact more important than such factors as district characteristics, primary nonlegislative occupation, and seniority (Dunlap and Gale, 1974; Ritt and Ostheimer, 1974; Dunlap and Allen, 1976; Calvert, 1979).

Nonetheless, some of the studies on the relationship between party affiliation and legislative choices in environmental policy suggest that party affiliation is not the most important factor in these choices. Rather, the factor that is most strongly associated with legislative choice is a legislator's ideology as defined by his or her placement on the conservative-to-liberal continuum (Ritt and Ostheimer, 1974; Kenski and Kenski, 1981; Mazmanian and Sabatier, 1981). For example, using congressional ratings on environmental policy prepared by the League of Conservation Voters (LCV) and comparing those scores to other interest group ratings on the conservative-to-liberal dimension, Ritt and Ostheimer (1974:469) concluded: "Political liberals in both parties, but liberal Democrats in particular, were the strongest supporters of environmental legislation." In a more comprehensive examination of congressional behavior (1973–1978) the Kenskis (1981) arrived at the same conclusion. Using also the generally reliable annual ratings prepared by the LCV, they reported that party affiliation was a major factor in legislative decision-making in environmental policy. For example, House Democrats during the 1973–1978 period had a mean LCV score of 57.7 percent while Republicans had a mean score of 33.9 percent on the LCV scale (0 meaning that the member never voted with the LCV on the issues; 100 percent meaning the member always voted with the LCV). In the Senate the Democrats' mean was 58.0 percent, the Republicans 33.9 percent. (A summary of the Kenskis' data is reproduced here in table 6.1.)

The Kenskis also reported significant regional differences in congressional support for environmental legislation. For example, eastern Republicans were the most pro-environmental group among all Republicans (as measured by regional LCV scores) while southern Democrats proved to be not unexpectedly the least supportive within the Democratic ranks. But party affiliation was overshadowed by ideology as a predictor on environmental voting. Using congressional support for the "conservative coalition" (a coalition of southern Democrats and Republicans that regularly appears in congressional roll call voting) as their measure of ideology, the Kenskis' data revealed a stronger association between ideology and environmental support (gamma=.95) compared to the relationship between party affiliation and pro-environmental voting (gamma=.68) in the House of Representatives during the 1973–1978 period (similar results were reported for the Senate). The Kenskis' data is reprinted here in table 6.2.

Kenski and Kenski warn, however, that it is hard to clearly separate ideology from partisan affiliation given the recognized policy differences between Democrats and Republicans, and they assert (1981:98): "Political ideology is causally prior to party and pro-environmental voting. Representatives rarely take on an ideology *after* being elected under a particular party label. Instead, they self-recruit or are recruited to run under a given party label because of their ideological inclinations." Given the close linkage between ideology and party affiliation (in this particular instance the fact that Democrats are generally more pro-environmental than Republicans), the important public fact is that party affiliation makes a difference! A legislative assembly in which

Table 6.1 National and Regional Support for Environmental Legislation (LCV) by Party in the U.S. House and Senate, 1973–1978

Area	Congress	Democrats	Republicans
House:			
Nation	93rd	57.9%	39.4%
	94th	58.0	32.0
	95th	57.2	30.3
East	93rd	72.3	45.8
	94th	71.7	49.8
	95th	70.7	49.9
South	93rd	32.4	20.9
	94th	32.1	22.6
	95th	35.0	18.8
Midwest	93rd	70.6	27.5
	94th	69.3	28.8
	95th	67.9	30.0
West	93rd	69.4	28.0
	94th	66.2	23.6
	95th	61.0	17.6
Senate:			
Nation	93rd	57.2	41.2
	94th	53.1	28.6
	95th	63.6	31.9
East	93rd	74.9	67.2
	94th	69.6	61.9
	95th	78.6	66.5
South	93rd	26.7	19.8
	94th	29.0	10.2
	95th	40.2	11.1
Midwest	93rd	74.9	40.4
	94th	64.6	17.2
	95th	77.8	26.4
West	93rd	58.0	30.4
	94th	55.5	16.9
	95th	64.4	20.0

SOURCE: Kenski and Kenski (1981).

Table 6.2 Relationship Between Party and Environmental Support (LCV) and Between Ideology (CCSR) and Environmental Support in the U.S. House, 1973–1978

Environmental Support	Party		Ideology		
	Dem.	Rep.	Lib.	Mod.	Cons.
Nation					
High	40.3%	8.1%	72.8%	16.2%	0.2%
Medium	39.4	32.2	27.2	71.0	22.2
Low	20.3	59.7	0.0	12.8	77.6
	Gamma = .68		Gamma = .95		
East					
High	58.1	26.0	74.4	29.8	0.0
Medium	39.6	43.9	25.6	64.5	38.6
Low	2.2	30.1	0.0	5.8	61.4
	Gamma = .65		Gamma = .87		
South					
High	9.5	0.0	73.9	8.3	0.0
Medium	35.4	15.2	26.1	69.0	17.3
Low	55.1	84.8	0.0	22.6	82.7
	Gamma = .65		Gamma = .92		
Midwest					
High	54.5	2.3	73.9	10.1	0.0
Medium	41.9	38.4	26.1	78.7	29.3
Low	3.7	59.3	0.0	11.2	70.7
	Gamma = .94		Gamma = .96		
West					
High	49.7	3.5	68.3	7.8	1.3
Medium	43.4	22.4	31.7	76.5	13.2
Low	7.0	74.1	0.0	15.7	85.5
	Gamma = .92		Gamma = .96		

SOURCE: Kenski and Kenski (1981).

Democrats are the majority is likely to react differently to environmental initiatives than one controlled by Republicans. Bearing in mind the regional peculiarities of many southern Democrats and eastern Republicans, a voter for whom environmental quality is important need only understand that Democrats have a well-established record of support for environmental protection through governmental action while Republicans do not. Lest there be any doubt on that score, the election of Ronald Reagan and a Republican majority in the U.S. Senate clarified the issue.

In the 1980 electoral campaign both Reagan and the Republican National Platform stressed the need for economic growth and industrial revitalization. This agenda was made perfectly clear by Reagan in his speech accepting the GOP nomination (quoted by Kraft, 1984:34–35):

> America must get to work producing more energy. The Republican program for solving economic problems is based on growth and productivity. . . . [Energy development] must not be thwarted by a tiny minority opposed to economic growth which often finds friendly ears in regulatory agencies for its obstructionist campaigns.
>
> Make no mistake. We will not permit the safety of our people or our environmental heritage to be jeopardized, but we are going to reaffirm that the economic prosperity of our people is a fundamental part of our environment.

Once elected, Reagan immediately began to get his new agenda in motion. First, the Reagan team was heavily larded with men and women who were committed to rapid economic growth and natural resource exploitation and who were perceived as hostile to the environment and the organizations that represented it (Brownstein and Easton, 1982; Jonathan Lash et al., 1984). Secondly, the administration proceeded on a well-articulated strategy to implement a new environmental agenda. Perhaps recognizing that public support for environmental quality remained strong, the administration chose not to make a frontal assault through proposing major changes in the nation's environmental laws. Rather, it tried to fulfill its pro-development policy goals by less visible, but potentially equally effective means.

Pro-development ideologues were appointed to manage the agencies charged with the enforcement of environmental laws. Secondly, the staffs of key agencies such as the EPA and the Office of Surface Mining (OSM) were sharply reduced. Simultaneously, such agencies were subjected to drastic cuts in funding under the Reagan budget proposed and accepted by Congress in 1981. Fourthly, all agencies were ordered to use cost-benefit analysis in assessing the regulatory impact of all proposed rules and regulations. Finally, spokespersons for environmental organizations who had been treated as legitimate and important participants in the policy process under previous administrations found their ideas denigrated or ignored, and their loyalty questioned by the new Reaganite captains in the affected agencies (Vig, 1984). And all of these changes were pursued in the absence of an electoral mandate for doing so, as public opinion polls consistently showed (Mitchell, 1984).

A singular example of the new regime's attitude toward environmental policy was personified in the administrative actions taken by Interior Secretary James Watt. Repeatedly Watt demonstrated a personal antipathy toward environmental organizations. He tried to accelerate the leasing of federal offshore oil and gas and federally owned coal in the Powder River Basin of Wyoming and Montana. He tried to open up federal wilderness areas to mineral exploration. He cut back drastically acquisition of new lands for national parks while simultaneously proposing to sell off "surplus" public lands (*The Battle for Natural Resources,* 1983; Culhane, 1984). Actions like these stiffened the resistance of environmental advocates and heightened conflict between Congress and the White House.

Looking at congressional reaction to the new initiatives of the Reagan administration in 1981 and 1982, Kenski and Kenski (1984) concluded that Congress basically adopted the role as defender of the status quo (the exception being its acceptance of the previously mentioned sharp budget cuts in 1981). Again, in these battles party affiliation proved to be the most significant visible factor in legislative choice. The Kenskis reported mean LCV scores for House and Senate Democrats of 67 and 60 percent respectively while House Republicans manifested a mean score of 33 percent and Senate Republicans of 29 percent. But ideology, as measured by members' support for the conservative coalition, was even more significant (p. 112): "The single most important variable in explaining environmental support is ideology, and it is equally important for both the House and the Senate. A member's philosophical orientation on a range of policy issues . . . best explains his or her floor vote, with liberals most supportive of environmental legislation, conservatives least supportive, and moderates in between."

In this chapter we will replicate and expand upon the studies of Kenski and Kenski (1981, 1984) by examining once more environmental voting in the 97th Congress (1981–1982) and the 98th Congress (1983–1984). The dependent variable is the measure of environmental support revealed in the annual ratings of Congress compiled by the League of Conservation Voters. The LCV used 123 roll call votes during this period, 76 in the House and 42 in the Senate. Reflective of the Reagan administration's policy goals, many of the votes used

Table 6.3 National and Regional Support for Environmental Legislation (LCV) by Party in the U.S. House; Mean Scores 1981–1984

Area	Year	Democrats	Republicans
Nation	1981	63.2%	31.5%
	1982	71.0	34.2
	1983	68.5	31.6
	1984	68.5	36.4
East	1981	76.8	44.4
	1982	82.0	55.0
	1983	75.8	55.5
	1984	76.8	60.6
South	1981	36.4	22.2
	1982	49.8	21.6
	1983	51.6	18.6
	1984	50.2	26.1
Midwest	1981	76.5	34.3
	1982	82.2	35.9
	1983	77.9	37.3
	1984	78.8	37.6
West	1981	76.3	20.3
	1982	78.9	17.8
	1983	77.7	13.8
	1984	78.0	22.1
Without the South	1981	76.6	34.1
	1982	81.4	37.7
	1983	77.0	35.5
	1984	77.8	39.6

SOURCE: 1981–1984 annual ratings of Congress published by the League of Conservation Voters.

by the LCV involved roll calls on budget cuts for environmental protection and energy conservation programs and continued funding (opposed by environmental groups) for nuclear power projects (i.e., the Clinch River Breeder Reactor). Other important votes included the toxic cleanup "Superfund," limiting the leasing of federally owned coal, providing regulatory relief for polluters, and preventing oil and gas exploration in wilderness areas. Given the large number of votes used by the LCV, it is fair to assume that the scores

Table 6.4 National and Regional Support for Environmental Legislation (LCV) in the U.S. House; Mean Scores 1973–1978 and 1981–1984

	All Members		Democrats		Republicans	
Years	73–78	81–84	73–78	81–84	73–78	81–84
Area						
Nation	47.9%	53.6%	57.7%	67.8%	33.9%	33.4%
East	63.4	68.2	71.6	77.9	48.5	53.9
South	29.8	39.0	33.2	47.0	20.8	22.1
Midwest	50.0	58.1	69.3	78.9	28.8	36.3
West	49.7	49.4	65.5	77.7	23.1	18.5

SOURCE: Derived from Kenski and Kenski (1981) and 1981–1984 rating reports by the League of Conservation Voters.

are good indicators of each congressperson's degree of concern for environmental quality.

In order to examine the influence of party affiliation, the mean LCV scores for House Democrats and Republicans for 1981–1984 were compiled and are reproduced in table 6.3 for the Congress as a whole and by region. Table 6.4 summarizes the data in the previous table and compares the mean scores for 1981–1984 with the mean scores derived from the study of Congress in 1973–1978 by Kenski and Kenski.

If we examine table 6.1 (scores for 1973–1978) and tables 6.3 and 6.4 (1981–1984), it is apparent that congressional support for environmental quality did not decline during Reagan's first term, but actually increased modestly for Congress as a whole and in the East, South, and Midwest. Only in the West were mean House LCV scores lower in the present period compared to the 1970s. Secondly, it can readily be seen that during the Reagan administration environmental issues have become more partisan compared to the decade immediately preceding it. This is particularly evident in the behavior of House Democrats, whose mean LCV score was 10 percentage points higher than it was in 1973–1978. In contrast, House Republican scores declined slightly from a mean value of 33.9 percent to 33.4 percent. Indeed, in all four regions the House Democrats' mean environmental scores were higher in the present period, with the most dramatic change occurring among the southern Democrats.

Table 6.5 Support for Environmental Legislation (LCV) in the U.S. Senate; Mean Scores 1981–1984

Area	Year	Democrats	Republicans
Nation	1981	59.4%	28.4%
	1982	61.4	29.7
	1983–1984*	71.1	36.5
East	1981	84.8	48.6
	1982	78.3	49.3
	1983–1984	87.3	61.3
South	1981	34.0	13.2
	1982	42.6	14.6
	1983–1984	55.1	25.5
Midwest	1981	62.5	30.6
	1982	67.4	35.9
	1983–1984	74.9	50.1
West	1981	58.8	23.2
	1982	61.4	20.4
	1983–1984	67.9	18.0
Without the South	1981	70.5	32.4
	1982	69.9	33.5
	1983–1984	78.3	33.5

SOURCE: 1982 and 1984 rating reports by the League of Conservation Voters.

*The League of Conservation Voters rated the Senate for 1983–1984 with a two-year average score.

The behavior of House Republicans was more complex. In the East and Midwest the mean LCV scores were higher; the western Republicans manifested a slight decline; and the southern Republicans' mean score was slightly higher in comparison to 1973–1978.

Turning to the Senate (tables 6.5 and 6.6), we find that support for environmental quality showed a marginal decline in the latest period and in three out of the four regional groupings. Senate Democrats as a whole were slightly more supportive in the latest period compared to 1973–1978 while Senate Republicans were slightly less so. Looking at the regions, the mean Senate Democrats' score for 1981–1984 was higher in the East, South, and West

Table 6.6 National and Regional Support for Environmental Legislation (LCV) in the U.S. Senate; Mean Scores 1973–1978 and 1981–1984

	All Members		Democrats		Republicans	
Years	73–78	81–84	73–78	81–84	73–78	81–84
Area						
Nation	48.6%	46.3%	58.0%	64.0%	33.9%	31.5%
East	70.2	69.2	74.4	83.5	65.2	53.1
South	26.5	32.2	32.0	43.9	13.7	17.8
Midwest	57.6	51.1	72.4	68.3	28.0	38.9
West	42.6	34.5	59.3	62.7	22.4	20.5

SOURCE: Derived from Kenski and Kenski and 1982 and 1984 ratings by the League of Conservation Voters

and lower in the Midwest, while Senate Republicans were lower in the East and West and higher in the South and Midwest compared to the 1970s.

In summation, the data suggest that congressional support for the environment held up overall despite determined lobbying by the Reagan administration. To be sure, no new policy initiatives in environmental legislation were enacted, but Congress did hold the line, with the exception of the "honeymoon" period of 1981 when it accepted drastic budget cuts for a variety of agencies charged with the enforcement of the nation's environmental laws. It is also clear that the partisan affiliation of House and Senate members remained a potent and visible factor in congressional decision-making. This is especially evident if we take into consideration the peculiar regional politics of the South, where Democrats have historically acted as a quasi–third party in their voting behavior. To illustrate the peculiarities of southern Democrats, recall that the mean LCV scores for House and Senate Democrats were 67.8 percent and 64.0 percent respectively. But if we consider only non-southern Democrats, those mean scores increase to 78.2 percent for House Democrats and 72.9 percent for Senate Democrats.

What of the role of ideology in the 1981–1984 period? Data for this period suggest that ideology was a less potent factor. In assessing the role of party and ideology in legislative choices House and Senate members have been classified here as high (mean LCV score 71 to 100 percent), medium (mean score 31 to 70 percent), and low (mean score 0 to 30 percent) in their recorded support for environmental quality. In order to test for the influence of ideology each member was also given a mean conservative coalition support ratio score (CCSR), which is obtained by dividing each member's conservative coalition support score by the sum of his or her opposition and support scores (Kenski and Kenski, 1981). The mean CCSR scores for the 97th and 98th congresses were then used to classify members as conservative (71 to 100 percent), moderate (31 to 70 percent), and liberal (0 to 30 percent).

Table 6.7 presents the results: the association between ideology and pro-environmental voting remained quite strong (gamma=.92) in comparison to the association of the former with party affiliation in the U.S. House of Representatives (gamma=.82) in the 1981–1984 period. But it is also interesting to note that the relative influence of ideology was not uniform across regions. Indeed, only in the East does it appear that ideology is clearly the stronger factor associated with pro-environmental voting. This seems to be a function of the behavior of eastern Republicans, where 28.5 percent scored high on the LCV scale, a significant deviation from the behavior of other House Republicans. Note also that southern Democrats remained the deviant case among Democrats, although much less so in comparison to their behavior in the 1970s. Indeed, if we look only at the voting behavior of House members outside the South, the relative strength of ideology virtually disappears, producing a gamma of .92 between pro-environmental voting and party affiliation and a gamma of .90 between ideology and support for environmental policy.

Perhaps the most interesting finding in the data, however, is the evidence of increased partisanship. The change appears to have come primarily from a change in behavior among House Democrats. In 1973–1978 40.3 percent of House Democrats scored high, 39.4 percent medium, and 20.3 percent low on the LCV scale (table 6.2). But during the first Reagan administration a majority of House Democrats (53.2 percent) scored high, 39.2 percent were medium, and only 7.6 percent scored low on the LCV scale (table 6.7). Thus in this more recent period there appears to have been a rather significant shift toward a more pro-environmental stance among House Democrats, especially among the southern Democrats who manifested the most dramatic shift of all. In contrast, the behavior of House Republicans remained similar to that of Republicans in the 1970s. As a consequence of the Democratic shift in the House there was generated a stronger association between partisan affiliation and pro-environmental voting (gamma=.82) in 1981–1984 in comparison to the 1973–1978 period (gamma=.68) studied by Kenski and Kenski.

Table 6.7 Relationship Between Party and Environmental Support (LCV) and Between Ideology (CCSR) and Environmental Support in the U.S. House, 1981–1984

Environmental Support	Party		Ideology		
	Dem.	Rep.	Lib.	Mod.	Cons.
Nation					
High	53.2%	8.7%	85.6%	36.4%	2.1%
Medium	39.2	37.5	14.4	61.0	42.0
Low	7.6	53.8	0.0	2.6	55.9
	Gamma = .82		Gamma = .92		
East					
High	70.7	28.5	85.2	40.5	5.3
Medium	28.6	53.9	14.8	57.1	59.6
Low	0.7	17.6	0.0	2.4	35.1
	Gamma = .73		Gamma = .89		
South					
High	15.2	0.0	64.6	24.3	2.0
Medium	62.5	23.4	35.4	68.9	45.0
Low	22.3	76.6	0.0	6.8	53.0
	Gamma = .81		Gamma = .87		
Midwest					
High	72.3	5.8	92.9	34.5	2.6
Medium	27.7	50.0	7.1	64.4	46.4
Low	0.0	44.2	0.0	1.1	51.0
	Gamma = .96		Gamma = .96		
West					
High	73.8	0.7	81.6	46.2	0.0
Medium	26.2	15.0	18.4	53.8	12.7
Low	0.0	84.3	0.0	0.0	87.3
	Gamma = .99		Gamma = .93		

SOURCE: Derived from annual ratings by the League of Conservation Voters and members' support scores for the conservative coalition compiled by Congressional Quarterly, Inc.

Table 6.8 Relationship Between Party and Environmental Support (LCV) and Between Ideology (CCSR) and Environmental Support in the U.S. Senate, 1981–1984

Environmental Support	Party		Ideology		
	Dem.	Rep.	Lib.	Mod.	Cons.
High	46.4%	4.9%	84.0%	21.6%	2.3%
Medium	44.1	43.8	14.4	75.7	40.7
Low	9.5	51.8	1.6	2.7	57.0
	Gamma = .82		Gamma = .92		

SOURCE: Derived from annual rating by the League of Conservation Voters and 1981–1984 members' scores in support of the conservative coalition compiled by Congressional Quarterly, Inc.

In the Senate (table 6.8) a shift also has taken place in the first half of the 1980s, although the movement was less dramatic (data for the Senate could not be disaggregated by region due to the small number in each region, the small numbers making use of gamma inappropriate). As can be seen, Senate Democrats' support for environmental quality remained virtually unchanged in comparison to the 1970s, but this was parallel to a marginal downward shift among Senate Republicans. These two trends (no change among Democrats; modest shift among Republicans) produced an association between partisanship and environmental voting that was stronger (gamma=.82) than in the earlier period examined by the Kenskis (gamma=.58), while the association between pro-environmental voting and ideology remained virtually unchanged (see Kenski and Kenski, 1981:98).

The data strongly suggest that the Reagan administration's policies have increased the partisan cohesiveness of the Democrats in distancing themselves from administration policy and bringing themselves closer to perceived voter preferences. Further, the data presented here simply reinforce observations made in previous studies. Democrats and Republicans sharply differ on issues involving environmental quality, and these sharp differences manifest themselves in the state legislatures as well.

In order to investigate the role of party affiliation on environmental issues at the state level, inquiries were directed toward approximately two dozen environmental organizations in states who might be expected to publish annual or biennial voting analyses of their state legislatures. The names of these organizations were derived primarily from the most recent Conservation

Directory published by the National Wildlife Federation. As a result of these inquiries, usable information was provided for ten states for the 1980–1985 period. The results are summarized in table 6.9, which reports the mean support scores for Democrats and Republicans as derived from roll call reports compiled on an annual or biennial basis by state environmental organizations (see the Appendix). These mean scores are based on 153 state senate and 151 state house roll call votes in the states in the 1980–1985 era. As can be seen, in all of these states there were significant differences between the two parties in their responses to environmental legislation, with Democrats in all states achieving higher mean support scores in comparison to Republicans.

In order to more closely describe the degree of partisanship at the state legislative level we will use a simple measure called *partisan difference* (Calvert, 1979, 1982). Partisan difference expresses the degree of disagreement between legislators in percentage point terms using the mean scores as the basis for the comparison. For example, if the mean environmental scores for Democrats and Republicans in a legislative assembly had been 55 percent and 49 percent respectively, the mean partisan difference would be six percentage points, a small difference indeed. In contrast, had the mean score for Democrats been 90 percent and the Republicans 10 percent, the partisan difference would be a massive one, 80 percentage points.

Turning to the data, there was little variation between types of states in the level of partisanship manifested on environmental issues. For example, in rural, sparsely populated states like Alaska, Idaho, Montana, and Wyoming the mean difference between Democratic and Republican house members was 38.7 percentage points; in heavily urbanized, industrialized, and heavily populated states (California, Illinois, New York) the mean partisan distance between members of the two parties was 33.9 percentage points. The data suggest the possibility that there is little difference between the parties despite the vast differences between the states in the level of economic development, urbanization, etc. A Wyoming Democratic legislator may have much more in common with a Democratic counterpart in California in his or her orientation to environmental legislation than with the Republican just across the aisle.

Secondly, the level of partisan difference on environmental issues at the state level is similar to that found in Congress. Looking at partisan differences in the state legislatures as a whole, we find that the mean difference between Democrats and Republicans in the lower houses was 39.9 percentage points. In the U.S. House of Representatives for 1981–1984 the mean difference

Table 6.9 Environmental Support in Selected State Legislatures, Both Houses, 1980–1985

		Mean Support Scores*			
		Senate		House	
State	Year	Dem.	Rep.	Dem.	Rep.
Alaska	1983–84	60.0%	46.0%	68.0%	30.0%
California	1980	64.1	41.1	74.8	38.8
	1981	40.5	20.6	69.8	51.8
	1982	51.5	32.6	76.7	40.0
	1983	57.3	30.9	77.8	32.7
	1984	75.1	41.1	84.4	40.2
Idaho	1980	81.1	28.0	78.7	30.6
	1981	95.5	35.3	81.6	45.0
	1982	71.2	27.3	72.8	34.1
	1983	80.6	32.9	65.0	35.1
	1984	71.7	50.9	87.7	38.8
	1985	77.6	42.7	78.8	53.3
Illinois[a]	1981	83.6	47.4	62.4	40.8
Montana	1981	59.3	17.9	76.5	29.4
	1983	75.0	21.3	77.8	38.5
	1985	82.4	33.4	83.1	27.9
Oregon	1981	76.7	23.4	69.9	38.8
	1983	80.2	41.5	78.2	40.1
New York	1981	51.0	33.9	56.6	33.2
	1982	73.0	22.0	84.6	38.1
Washington	1981–82	60.8	17.9	66.7	16.0
	1983–84	71.3	30.3	84.3	17.9
Wisconsin	1981–82	79.1	34.8	78.2	19.5
	1983–84	69.5	36.1	77.4	37.7
Wyoming	1981–82	83.1	47.4	84.4	45.4
	1983	75.7	30.3	62.4	38.2

*Mean support scores derived from roll call analyses by state-level environmental organizations.
[a]In 1983 party leaders in the Illinois Legislature started the practice of presenting bills in "packages" that insured strict party-line voting and many unanimous votes. As a consequence of this practice, the Illinois Environmental Council ended the practice of rating individual legislators on roll call votes on environmental bills beginning in the 1983 session.

between the two parties was 34.4 percentage points (if southern Democrats are excluded from the analysis, the mean difference climbs to 41.6 percentage points).

In summation, partisan affiliation is a critically important determinant of legislative choices in environmental policy at the state level. It defines an essential difference between Democrats and Republicans and this essential difference transcends differences between types of legislative assemblies (whether they are professional, full-time bodies or amateur, part-time ones) and types of states, that is, whether they are urban or rural, rich or poor, etc. Whether partisan affiliation is also an important factor in choices made by elected officials in the counties and cities cannot be answered at this time, and the answers must be found in future research.

Why should partisan affiliation be such a strong factor in legislative choice in environmental policy? Probably the principal reason can be found in the historic policy differences between the two major parties. Since the Great Depression Democrats have been generally committed to seeing government as a positive agency of social progress while Republicans have not. These differences are revealed in a comprehensive examination of congressional voting behavior in 1981–1983 by the *National Journal*. Compiling annual ratings employed by several interest associations in which an aggregate score on a liberal-to-conservative continuum was derived, the *National Journal* reports showed Democrats to be consistently more liberal than Republicans in three policy dimensions—economic, social, and foreign policy (Cohen, 1982; Schneider, 1983; Schneider, 1984). With regard to heightened conflict in the environmental policy area, Walter Rosenbaum has written (1985:11):

> Leaders of both parties attempted in the early 1970s to create a tradition of bipartisan support reaching from Congress to the White House for environmental policy. Bipartisanship endured throughout the 1970s but largely evaporated with the advent of the Reagan presidency and the appearance of the first Republican majority in the Senate since 1955. The president's promised regulatory reforms were seen by critics as a sharp reversal of almost all federal environmental programs enacted since 1970. Congressional debate over the proposals was strident and partisan; congressional Democrats, considering themselves the guardians of the imperiled programs, regarded the president's regulatory agenda as an assault upon their legislative record. Environmentalists saw "regulatory

relief" as the cutting edge of a massive administrative assault on the legislative foundations of the Environmental Era. They almost unanimously considered the Reagan administration as the most environmentally hostile presidency in half a century and rallied behind his Democratic critics.

It is not surprising that the heightened interparty conflict manifested itself in a more general way during the first Reagan term. From 1981 through 1984 an average of 44 percent of the congressional roll call votes were "party unity" votes, a situation in which a majority of one party votes in opposition to a majority of the other. (An operational definition used by Congressional Quarterly, Inc., the "party unity" vote is a standard and often-used indicator of party cohesion.) The strongest indication of increased partisanship in Congress under Reagan occurred in 1983, where 56 percent of the roll call votes in the House of Representatives were party unity votes, the highest percentage of such votes since 1954 (*Congressional Quarterly Weekly Report* 42, October 27, 1984).

Concurrent with the rise in partisan conflict (and hence intraparty cohesion), the percentage of roll calls in which the "conservative coalition" made an appearance declined in the 1981–1984 period. Bearing in mind that a congressperson's support for the conservative coalition is the measure of ideology used in this study, it is worth noting that the coalition appeared on 17.5 percent of the roll calls during the Reagan first term in comparison to a mean appearance rate of 21 percent under the Carter administration (*Congressional Quarterly Weekly Report* 42, October 27, 1984). Increasing levels of party unity are associated with declining support for the conservative coalition. The presence of both these factors in the congressional arena reinforces the picture developed with regard to environmental policy. Partisanship was stronger in the 1981–1984 years, and while ideology as a variable was still important, it was less of a factor in comparison to the 1970s.

"Progressive politicizing of environmental quality" (to use Rosenbaum's expression) aptly describes the trend during the first four years of Reagan, and this partisanship is reinforced by the competing and antagonistic interest constituencies that are attached to each party. Industries seeking "regulatory relief" know that, based on past experience, they will find a sympathetic audience in the ranks of the Republicans; environmentalists have learned the same thing with regard to Democrats. One symptom of this bipolar interest-group/party linkage is found in campaign giving. Since enactment of the Federal Election Campaign Act in 1974 the number of interest group political action committees has grown enormously, from 608 in 1974 to 3,371 in 1982, the greatest growth being among corporate and trade association PACs. Not unexpectedly business tends to favor Republican candidates. In 1982, 66 percent of corporate PAC contributions ($18 million) went to Republicans (Alexander, 1984). Given the historic policy differences between the two parties and given the reinforcement of those differences by powerful interest group constituencies, it is hard to imagine that the issue of environmental quality could ever be "above politics."

At the same time the role of ideology in environmental voting has probably been exaggerated. While it is true that "liberals" of both parties tend to be the strongest supporters of environmental laws and "conservatives" the least supportive, it is also true that most Democrats, excepting the South, are liberals, and most Republicans, excepting the East, are conservatives. "Party regularity" rather than ideological deviation describes the behavior of most Democrats and Republicans. Schneider (1983) in examining congressional voting behavior across three dimensions (economic, social, and foreign policy) found only twenty-four members of the House to be ideologically inconsistent (and therefore deviating from party regularity) while in the Senate eleven members were found to be ideologically inconsistent.

There are many more general and important questions concerning the role of parties in environmental policy-making that need to be addressed in future research. First, what is the linkage between party platforms and legislative performance in the area of environmental protection and natural resource conservation? As Monroe (1983) has demonstrated, national party platforms are not mere campaign gimmickry. Platform planks do follow, that is catch up with, public opinion on important policy questions; they link the party to and ensure the support of important interests to the party; and occasionally, planks shape public opinion, bringing the voters themselves into a condition of support for where a party wants to go. To what extent do these observations apply to environmental issues specifically? To what extent do they apply to state party platforms, state party organizations, and state legislators? Secondly, if ideology is an important factor in legislative decision-making, how is it conceptually and behaviorally separate from party platforms and party policy? Is it necessarily true that ideology is prior to party affiliation and candidacy for elective office? Might not a person once elected to public office become socialized in a particular ideological orientation that for most legislators translates into "party regularity" more often than not? Further, are there particular dimensions of ideology, that is, economic, foreign policy, moral questions, that particularly correlate to a legislator's voting behavior on environmental issues? Is the role of ideology enhanced in officially nonpartisan and appointive policy-making positions in government as Mazmanian and Sabatier (1981) suggest?

Finally, it is clear that research is needed to determine the influence of party in nonlegislative settings, in particular regulatory agencies and the courts. With regard to the behavior of regulatory agencies, it is clear that the election of Ronald Reagan did change agency enforcement and regulatory behavior and a strong bet can be made that the president's opportunity to appoint a large corps of judges to the federal bench will have continuing significant policy implications in the interpretation of national environmental laws long after his administration has become history. Environmental policy determination has been a partisan issue during the 1980s. Given the strong interface between environmental policies, government regulation, and income redistribution issues, it is likely to remain so for some time to come in the national and state legislative arena.

7

Congress and Environmental Policy

Michael E. Kraft

The late 1980s is an appropriate time to take stock of achievements and identify future opportunities for scholarship in the subfield of environmental politics and policy. More than twenty years have passed since the time usually assumed to represent the beginning of the modern environmental movement. During that period a vast range of environmental policies have been enacted, implemented, and, particularly in the Reagan administration, subjected to intense scrutiny and reappraisal (Portney, 1984; Vig and Kraft, 1984a). The scholarly literature has also undergone exceptional growth and has matured markedly, as Lester notes in Chapter 1. Fifteen years ago commentators typically complained about how little political scientists had contributed to understanding political processes affecting the environment (Jones, 1972; Kraft, 1973b; Nagel, 1974). But by the early 1980s one could point to an impressive body of literature in political science, public administration, and policy studies and to increasing concern for addressing important theoretical and methodological issues largely ignored in the first generation of scholarship (e.g., Mann, 1981 and 1982; Ingram and Mann, 1983; Ingram and Godwin, 1985). These trends are as evident in studies of the legislative process as they are elsewhere. Hence it is time to inquire broadly into the nature of the contributions made and to ask about future research priorities in the area of Congress and environmental policy.

There are many ways one might try to answer those questions. Although there are advantages in categorizing this literature in terms of the usual subdivisions of American politics (e.g., political parties, legislatures, bureaucracies, the courts), and assessing the contributions made in terms of the usual disciplinary expectations, there are also some disadvantages in doing so. For example, studies of environmental policy-making and implementation often cut across institutional boundaries, with analysis directed at functional activities in the policy process rather than institutions and their actors. Also, interdisciplinary environmental studies, including policy studies, and legal and economic analyses, may make important contributions, both theoretically and substantively, to our knowledge of how government addresses environmental problems, but these works cannot be assessed adequately using chiefly disciplinary criteria. The task at hand is to focus on one component of this developing scholarly literature within political science, namely that dealing with the United States Congress and its role in the policy process. The limitations of such an approach should be borne in mind, and will be noted below where useful.

Four major questions guide this enterprise: How can the wide-ranging literature on Congress and environmental politics best be organized to highlight the most significant characteristics of the institution, its actors, and the most important scholarship? What have been some of the most important findings and perspectives offered in this literature over the last fifteen to twenty years? What have been the major contributions of the literature, especially to theory building, and what major problems have arisen in efforts to describe and explain the congressional role in environmental politics? What are some of the most promising areas for future research? These are imposing questions that can be answered only partially and tentatively.

I make no claims for comprehensiveness in what follows. Rather, the purpose is to try to cast some light on one sector of environmental scholarship and see what even a partial review and assessment might suggest about how far we have come and what interesting paths may lie ahead for students of environmental politics and policy. For present purposes I include in the category "environmental politics and policy" the political activities and policy processes associated with environmental, resource, energy, and population problems facing American society and government. Appropriate distinctions will be made below where useful.

Congressional Scholarship and Environmental Politics

How can one best organize the literature on Congress to identify significant characteristics of that institution and its policy actors and simultaneously to review major scholarship on environmental politics and policy? I begin with the assumption that Congress is an important institution notwithstanding a considerable body of literature that questions the capacity of American government to deal effectively with environmental problems short of a paradigm change (e.g., Ophuls, 1977, esp. chap. 6). Indeed, Congress has played a vigorous role in environmental agenda setting and policy formation historically; in particular, its role in formulating the key environmental policies adopted in the 1970s has been well documented (Davies and Davies, 1975; Jones, 1975). I will return later to the question of congressional policy-making capacity.

I argue further that the study of Congress and environmental policy cannot and should not be entirely separated from the more general study of Congress and public policy. The reasons are simple. There has been relatively little systematic research on environmental politics within Congress, but there is a vast and sophisticated body of scholarship on the institutional structure of Congress, on congressional decision-making, and on Congress and public policy. At least some of that broader literature on Congress provides a rich source of hypotheses that might be studied in relation to the particular questions raised by environmental politics and policy. Thus perusal of several of the better review essays on Congress (e.g., Peabody, 1981; Rieselbach, 1983) should bring measurable dividends to students of environmental politics. However, at least two points of caution must be made. The first is that despite several decades of extensive and increasingly systematic congressional scholarship, "no single theoretical viewpoint has yet emerged" (Peabody, 1981); one sees instead a variety of conceptual frameworks, from systems theories and role analyses prominent in the 1960s and early 1970s to purposive behavior and policy-making emphases more recently.

The second limitation is that the literature on Congress has been notably deficient in relating internal structures and decision-making processes to policy outputs. With the growth of the policy studies field over the past two decades, this oversight has been corrected to some extent. For example, Ripley and Franklin (1984) use the familiar Lowi typology to distinguish congressional-executive relations in four policy areas (distributive, protective regulatory, redistributive, and foreign and defense), and a recent collection by Wright, Rieselbach, and Dodd (1986) examines Congress and policy change. Yet most research on Congress continues to give only limited attention to policy implications of congressional politics.

Given the pluralism and eclecticism that characterizes congressional scholarship, the present review adopts a fairly conventional organizational framework. Such an approach facilitates a broad review of the institution and imposes the least restrictive boundaries on what constitutes significant or legitimate research. However, I try to identify theoretical frameworks and substantive topics that are especially noteworthy for understanding the congressional role in environmental politics.

Following the pattern of most surveys of Congress, I consider selective congressional and environmental politics scholarship, its contributions, problems in theory and methods, and some promising areas for future research in three broad categories: membership characteristics and behavior, institutional structure, and policy-making processes. A concluding section on congressional performance and environmental policy considers critical evaluations of the various congressional roles and prescriptions for reform. Given the purpose of this review and the substantive policy discussions in several of the other chapters in this volume, I will refer to particular environmental policies only to illustrate the broad patterns of congressional behavior on these issues.

Membership Characteristics and Behavior

A common observation in contemporary work on Congress is that the institution has undergone major changes in the last twenty years, and especially since the early 1970s (Ornstein, 1981; Davidson, 1981; Davidson and Oleszek, 1981). Certainly among the greatest changes is the membership of Congress itself: the kinds of individuals attracted to a congressional career, their attitudes and goals, their willingness to challenge the established norms of behavior, their use of the powers of incumbency to solidify their standing with constituents, their sources of funding for reelection contests, their use of media and staff, and their behavior on matters of public policy—from actions intended to shape the congressional agenda to the oversight of policy implementation. It would be surprising if such changes did not have major implications for the way members respond to environmental policy issues. Thus there is the possibility that some long-standing generalizations about congressional behavior will need to be revised in light of the emergence of a "new Congress."

Congressional scholars have proposed several modest theoretical frameworks for understanding the behavior of members. The two most prominent in recent years postulate purposive behavior, that is, members as rational actors seeking certain goals. For Mayhew (1974) members are "single-minded seekers of reelection" who engage primarily in the three activities likely to enhance their prospects of reelection: personal publicity or advertising, credit-claiming, and position-taking. For Fenno (1973) member goals include not only reelection, but gaining influence within Congress and making good public policy (policy influence). Such models suggest certain patterns of congressional behavior with respect to environmental policy that might be tested against the historical record and contemporary behavior. For example, when environmental issues are highly salient for constituents, as they were in the early 1970s—and for a time during the controversy over Anne Burford's handling of the Environmental Protection Agency's toxic waste programs in 1983—incentives exist for members to pay attention to the issues, participate in agenda building and policy formulation, and engage in oversight of administrative actions. Clearly, however, the position-taking value of environmental issues does not explain very fully the policy entrepreneurship of some leading members in the 1960s (e.g., Henry Jackson, Edmund Muskie, Gaylord Nelson, Paul Rogers, John Saylor, Morris Udall, John Blatnik, and John Dingell). Nor does it explain why some members continue to work on issues like energy policy or population growth in the 1980s where there is little apparent political incentive to do so, other than the continual search by some members and their staffs for new issues that might be used to build a congressional career (Malbin, 1981; Davidson, 1981; Kingdon, 1984). Thus interesting questions meriting further research are the factors that motivate members have to work on environmental policy issues, the way in which various incentives shape legislative activities, and the conditions under which one might expect a greater or lesser congressional role in various policy actions.

One of the major lines of congressional scholarship has been to differentiate members not only by personal characteristics (e.g., education, age, occupational background) but by legislative roles adopted, the nature of the constituency represented, electoral vulnerability (marginal versus safe districts), and seniority. Most commentary on congressional behavior and the environment ignores such variance among the membership and thus it has been relatively insensitive to variables that often play an important role in determining member interest, level of activity, and decision-making behavior. The insightful research by Fenno (1978) on members' "home style" and the innovative study by Kingdon (1981) of congressional voting behavior suggest the value of a fuller exploration.

In one early study of my own, based on focused interviews in 1970 with the membership of five House subcommittees (Kraft, 1973a), member attitudes toward environmental issues and their degree of involvement in this issue area were shown to be related chiefly to the nature of the district represented and to personal characteristics. Those in the sample for whom environmental issues were most salient and those whose conceptualization of the issues could be described as ecologically oriented tended to represent areas either environmentally attractive or threatened areas of the country and urban rather than rural districts, and to have had a long-standing personal concern for environmental quality. They were also found to be more liberal, more nationally oriented, and more concerned with the legislative aspects of their jobs than others in the sample. Relationships between demographic attributes (age, education, prior occupation) and both the member's level of attention and orientation to the issues proved to be very weak or nonexistent. Factors such as seniority, perceived constituency interest, and electoral vulnerability were also related to the extent of agenda-setting activity (e.g., the number and variety of bills introduced and the number and kind of speeches made on environmental issues), although in general these relationships proved to be weak. There is some reason to believe that electoral security and seniority may be important variables affecting member willingness to devote substantial time and resources to environmental issues not deemed to be attractive to a mass constituency. A fuller understanding of such relationships may be especially pertinent if one is seeking to describe the conditions for congressional leadership on long-term ecological problems (e.g., see Milbrath, 1984). The more general scholarship on policy entrepreneurship and policy innovation would be a good place to begin for insightful propositions and methodological guidance (Kingdon, 1984; Polsby, 1984).

The dominant form of empirical work on congressional behavior and the environment has been roll call analysis. Much of this work is covered in Calvert's chapter in this volume and thus I will discuss the subject here only briefly. Early work by Dunlap and Allen (1976) and Ritt and Ostheimer (1974), and more recent studies by Kenski and Kenski (1981), confirm propositions commonly found in the congressional literature, namely, that voting on issues like environmental quality is related to party affiliation, ideology, region, and constituency characteristics. Pro-environmental voting, as judged by the League of Conservation Voters (LCV) scores, for example, is more likely among liberals, Democrats, and members from urban and suburban districts and districts in the East than among conservatives, Republicans, and members from rural districts and the South. In both the House and the Senate ideology appears to be the most important factor (Kenski and Kenski, 1984). But roll call studies have not been consistent in methodology, and hence the findings are not always comparable or cumulative. LCV scores are commonly used as a measure of pro-environmental voting, but like other organizational scorecards, they may conceal several issue dimensions and may not differentiate as much as desirable between qualitatively different votes (e.g., their policy significance).

Studies of energy policy voting yield similar conclusions, with ideology and party emerging as the best predictors of the vote (Bernstein and Horn, 1981; Riddlesperger and King, 1982). But energy issues involve a large number of cross-cutting cleavages—regional, partisan, ideological, and constituency—and once again the studies do not adequately isolate the issue dimensions and sort out the effect of variables such as party, ideology, and constituency.

Constituency influence on legislative voting is exceedingly difficult to measure even when one seeks only to show a correspondence between constituency policy preferences and member voting. Perhaps the most elaborate and methodologically interesting study is that of Ingram, Laney, and McCain (1980; see also Laney and Ingram, 1981), which focuses on state-level representation of constituency views on environmental and energy issues in four southwestern states in 1975. They find that legislators have great difficulty representing their constituencies in part because of the disparate and conflicting attitudes among voters. Thus if representation is taken to mean "the ability to construe voters' wishes and act in a manner responsive to them," there are major obstacles to developing comprehensive policies that are designed to resolve conflicts between environmental protection and energy development. Laney and Ingram suggest that legislators have little incentive to risk provoking special interests and the public at large by making such explicit policy choices.

One particular aspect of representation in Congress concerns the influence of environmentalists within the district. Here the evidence is mixed; Kau and Rubin (1978) report a moderate statistical relationship between the number of Sierra Club members in a state and roll call votes in the House, but Fowler and Shaiko (1983), using a data base generated by Robert Mitchell on the opinions of environmentalists in the states, conclude that there is not much impact of pro-environmental opinion on Senate roll call voting. Of greater importance is Fowler and Shaiko's conclusion that a broader perspective than that afforded by roll call analysis is needed to test the validity of propositions about the impact environmental groups have on congressional decision-making. In short, roll call analysis has helped to confirm some relationships, but this approach is necessarily limited by its focus on floor voting as the sole measure of congressional policy activity and by the narrowness of the propositions that can be tested by comparing member characteristics and voting.

The better work on congressional voting behavior (e.g., Kingdon, 1981) relies on interviews with members and a more sophisticated theoretical framework than typically found in studies of environmental voting behavior. For example, Kingdon asked members "How did you go about making up your mind?" and he was able to rank order the factors determining House voting on some of the major votes at that time (1969) and to explore probable causal mechanisms in some detail; in general the order is fellow members of Congress, the constituency, interest groups, the administration, and party leadership, with personal reading and staff in close competition as the least important factors. Given the changes in the membership and operation of Congress over the last twenty years, one might expect to see some shifts in that order today. But the more important point here is that roll call studies of environmental voting in Congress have been far too limited to answer the more challenging questions of member behavior.

Constituency opinion is clearly an important variable affecting member voting, as are perceptions of the electoral environment. The general literature on congressional campaigns and elections (Jacobson, 1987; Goldenberg and Traugott, 1984) tells us that the electoral process itself is equally important and can significantly influence members' calculations about public preferences on policy issues and the salience of those issues. There is some discussion of the role of environmental groups in congressional elections in the chapters in this volume by Ingram and Mann and Dunlap and in a few other recent articles (e.g., Mitchell, 1984; Dunlap, 1987). But there is a paucity of systematic research on the role of environmental issues in congressional election campaigns. Such an omission is striking in light of the increasingly active role in elections played by environmental groups in the 1980s. Particularly in the 1982 midterm elections, environmentalists formed new political action committees (PACs) and funneled significant sums of money into congressional campaigns. Seemingly, the "green vote" is a force to be reckoned with for the future, as candidates in both major parties increasingly believe it necessary to take positions on environmental issues, but the evidence is mixed. In a number of campaigns, environmental quality has emerged as one of the most important issues, particularly when state and local environmental issues are highly salient. Nevertheless, it would be difficult to characterize environmental issues as playing a major role in presidential elections or in most congressional elections; other issues typically dominate in the campaign, and numerous surveys indicate that voters show little inclination to change their vote based on a candidate's environmental policy positions (Dunlap, 1987; Kraft, 1984).

Aside from anecdotal material and postelection reports by environmental groups, however, we have little evidence on the extent of involvement of environmentalists in congressional elections, the impact they have had on campaigns and the issues raised, and the subsequent effect, if any, on both voter behavior and congressional decision-making. What might be said of these relationships? Are they much the same or different from what is found for other groups, including public interest groups (Schlozman and Tierney, 1986)? There are at least some important characteristics of environmental issues that must be considered in evaluating the role and impact of environmental and conservation groups on Congress. For example, there is considerable evidence that the salience of the issues and public knowledge of environmental problems are fairly low despite the generally positive public attitudes toward environmental protection policies (see Dunlap's chapter). Studies of the role of environmental issues in congressional elections need to pay special attention to the effect of such low salience, and perhaps in particular explore why these issues have become so salient in some congressional elections in the last several years.

Another possibly useful line of inquiry into members' behavior would focus on the quality of representation aside from roll call voting and electoral activities per se. Borrowing from Fenno's (1978) illuminating study of House members in their districts, we might ask how members present themselves back in the district. How accurately do they perceive constituency opinion on environmental issues? What relationship do they have with state and local environmental organizations? In what ways, both symbolically and substantively, do they attempt to represent district views? While any comprehensive study of such questions would be quite difficult, carefully selected case studies might shed light on the subtleties of congressional representation.

Congressional Structure and Environmental Politics

Congressional action on environmental issues cannot be understood without an appreciation of the impact of institutional structure. Like member characteristics and behavior, institutional aspects of Congress have undergone significant changes in the last two decades, and some earlier observations must be revised in light of these changes in the structure and the distribution of power in Congress. Given the limited work focusing directly on environmental politics and policy issues, I make considerable use once again of the more general literature on Congress to illustrate how broader theoretical frameworks and findings might inform the study of environmental politics. The particular features meriting comment here include the committee system, party leadership, staffs, informal caucuses and groups, and professional support offices.

Because policy-making and oversight activities take place almost exclusively within the highly specialized committees and subcommittees of Congress, congressional scholars have long dissected the workings of these bodies. The most prominent scholarship that brings some theoretical coherence to the subject is Fenno's (1973) pioneering comparative committee study, supplemented by the more recent efforts of Smith and Deering (1984) and Price (1985). Fenno argued that committees differ significantly in the nature of their political environments and their members' personal goals, which in turn affect committee politics, operations, and policy outputs. Such an approach proves helpful in distinguishing the various House and Senate committees with jurisdiction over environmental policy.

For example, in their recent review of committees, Smith and Deering apply Fenno's typology of member goals (reelection, power, and policy) and, based upon interviews with members, distinguish among prestige committees, policy committees, and constituency committees. In the Senate, environmental committees are overwhelmingly constituency committees, including Commerce, Science, and Transportation; Energy and Natural Resources (formerly the Interior Committee); Environment and Public Works; and Agriculture, Nutrition, and Forestry. Commerce is described as less policy oriented than its House counterpart, and the Environment and Public Works Committee less policy oriented in the early 1980s than was the case in the early 1970s. In the House the picture is somewhat mixed, with Energy and Commerce classified as a policy committee, and Interior and Insular Affairs, Public Works and Transportation, Merchant Marine and Fisheries, and Science, Space and Technology considered to be chiefly constituency committees. With its jurisdiction over air pollution, health, consumer protection, and energy policy issues, Energy and Commerce is especially attractive to policy-oriented members (those interested in salient national issues, even if complex and conflict ridden). In contrast, the constituency committees are thought to be of greatest interest to those members motivated mainly by constituency-oriented concerns. Such reelection-minded members, it is argued, tend to avoid issues that alienate important segments of the constituency and seek instead to curry favor with constituents by channeling federal funds back to the district, or otherwise providing particularized benefits that impose widely dispersed costs (such as taxes and consumer price increases). As Smith and Deering put it, a committee "with low national salience, high local salience, low conflict, and a narrow jurisdiction is especially attractive to the constituency-oriented member" (1984:86).

While necessarily oversimplifying the diversity and complexity of congressional committee politics, such theoretically informed classification schemes help to differentiate committees along familiar lines. Thus Murphy's (1974) description (among others) of the Public Works Committee provides an explanation for its pronounced tendency to favor distributive (pork-barrel) policies. In an entirely different policy area, the failure of Congress to address population policy issues during the 1970s, other than in the short-lived Select Committee on Population in the House from 1977 to 1978, is explained in part by the absence of a committee with jurisdiction in this area and the lack of incentives to pursue such low salience issues. The one committee that has held hearings on national population policy has been the Subcommittee on Census and Population of the House Post Office and Civil Service Committee, a committee categorized by Smith and Deering as "undesired," that is, one that consistently attracts few members (Kraft, 1983).

If one common theme has been that committees differ and that such differences are to be explained mainly in terms of member goals and the political environment of the committee, another has surely been the observation that the congressional committee system, with twenty-two standing committees and some one hundred and forty subcommittees in the House and sixteen standing committees and some one hundred subcommittees in the Senate, is the embodiment of structural fragmentation and dispersal of influence in American government. Table 7.1 indicates committee jurisdiction in the House and Senate for selected environmental statutes and illustrates the problem of fragmentation of responsibilities. As even this listing of committees makes clear, jurisdiction over environmental policies is sometimes unclear and may complicate policy-making. For example, twelve of the twenty-two standing committees in the House have at least some responsibility for en-

Table 7.1 Committee Jurisdiction over Selected Environmental Statutes

Statute	House Committee	Senate Committee
Appropriations for EPA/Interior Dept.	Appropriations	Appropriations
Clean Air Act	Energy and Commerce	Environment and Public Works
Clean Water Act	Public Works and Transportation	Environment and Public Works
Coastal Zone Management Act	Merchant Marine and Fisheries	Commerce, Science, and Transportation
Endangered Species Act	Merchant Marine and Fisheries	Environment and Public Works
Federal Insecticide, Fungicide, and Rodenticide Act	Agriculture	Agriculture, Nutrition, and Forestry
National Environmental Policy Act	Merchant Marine and Fisheries	Environment and Public Works
Nuclear Waste Policy Act	Energy and Commerce; Science, Space and Technology; Interior and Insular Affairs	Environment and Public Works; Energy and Natural Resources
Ocean Dumping Act	Merchant Marine and Fisheries	Environment and Public Works
Safe Drinking Water Act	Energy and Commerce	Environment and Public Works
Comprehensive Environmental Response, Compensation, and Liability Act (Superfund)	Energy and Commerce	Environment and Public Works
Surface Mining Control and Reclamation Act	Interior and Insular Affairs	Energy and Natural Resources
Toxic Substances Control Act	Energy and Commerce	Environment and Public Works; Commerce, Science, and Transportation
Federal Land Policy and Management Act	Interior and Insular Affairs	Energy and Natural Resources
Wilderness Act	Interior and Insular Affairs	Energy and Natural Resources
Resource Conservation and Recovery Act/Solid Waste Disposal Act	Energy and Commerce	Environment and Public Works

vironmental issues. By one calculation, in 1976 there were twenty-three committees and fifty-one subcommittees in the Congress that dealt with some aspect of energy policy (Jones, 1984:105).

Some of the consequences of divided jurisdiction are illustrated by the protracted congressional effort, especially in 1981 and 1982, to deal with the problem of high-level nuclear waste disposal. Three House committees have primary jurisdiction over nuclear waste legislation, with another four having some influence. Three committees in the Senate were also deeply involved in negotiations over what eventually became the Nuclear Waste Policy Act of 1982. Although a fragile compromise was approved in this case, Congress was forced to consider major repairs only four years later after the Department of Energy encountered massive public resistance to its waste repository siting program. Conceivably, a more coherent committee system might have allowed Congress to anticipate such public reaction and therefore design a more effective policy.

More generally, the consequences of such jurisdictional complexity include delay in addressing some policy needs, piecemeal consideration of related policies handled by different committees, and inconsistencies and lack of coherence in the nation's environmental policy. As Dean Mann has noted in another context, environmental policy in the United States is "rather a jerry-built structure in which innumerable individuals, private groups, bureaucrats, politicians, agencies, courts, political parties, and circumstances have laid down the planks, hammered the nails, plastered over the cracks, made sometimes unsightly additions and deletions, and generally defied 'holistic' or 'ecological' principles of policy design." Certainly the fragmentation of policy formulation in Congress that results in part from the present committee system is a major contributing cause of this state of affairs. Not surprisingly, scholars regularly complain about some of the particular effects of the lack of policy coherence—from inconsistent standards for assessing environmental risks (e.g., Lave, 1981) to continued emphasis on single media (e.g., air pollution or land-based disposal of hazardous wastes) rather than cross-media approaches to pollution control (e.g., dealing with the transport of pollutants across several different media, from air to land and water).

As might be expected, numerous analyses of environmental issues in Congress have addressed the fragmentation question, and most scholars reach similar conclusions. Kenski and Kenski (1984:110) take special note of overlapping committee jurisdiction for a broad range of environmental issues, as have

Jones (1979), Oppenheimer (1980), and Katz (1984, especially chapter 12) with respect to energy issues. I have called attention to the same phenomenon in consideration of population policy issues (Kraft, 1983:635). In these cases the argument has been that such institutional fragmentation makes difficult the formulation and adoption of comprehensive and coordinated national policies dealing with various aspects of environmental quality; the centralizing influence of party leaders and the president is often insufficient to overcome this constraint (see, e.g., Sundquist, 1981). With the further decentralization brought about by the evolution of "subcommittee government" in the 1970s (Davidson, 1981), one might imagine the situation has become far worse.

There is, however, a competing interpretation of the decentralization of influence in Congress. As noted by Davidson (1981), Kingdon (1984), and, in a slightly different context, Ingram and Ullery (1980), decentralization and institutional pluralism allow for greater policy entrepreneurship by individuals who might not otherwise be in a position to shape agenda setting or policy formulation. A related argument is that decentralization requires greater effort to build majority coalitions and helps to promote the legitimacy of the resultant policy. Thus as Kenski and Kenski (1984) note, fragmentation may constrain Congress in its policy initiation and partnership roles, but it could be seen as an opportunity in its defender-of-the-status-quo and overseer roles, where individual members are given a forum to challenge those promoting policy change.

These observations about the political consequences of a decentralized Congress suggest the value of studies that explore the particular effects of decentralization on environmental politics in the House and Senate. The prevailing view in the environmental policy literature is that excessive fragmentation and dispersal of power in American politics frustrates the provision of leadership for long-term policy change, as is evident, for example, in the failure of President Carter's energy policy plan to emerge from the Congress unscathed and the failure of Congress to substitute a coherent plan of its own devising (Kraft, 1981; Katz, 1984). Such critiques were especially common in the early to middle 1970s (e.g., Ophuls, 1977). More recently, with Congress thrown into a defensive posture against the Reagan administration's attempts to reverse environmental policy of the 1970s, one finds more positive evaluation of the contribution made by individuals in that institution. Studies that can sort out conflicting propositions and create some order in our understanding of the impact of congressional structure on environmental policy-making would be valuable. For example, under what conditions and in what way does fragmentation affect policy-making? What effects would result from the changes in congressional structure most often recommended (e.g., committee reorganization or stronger party leadership)?

Turning from the structure of the committee system to its operation, the role and impact of committee staffs, especially on technical issues, should be a fruitful area for study. Several general treatments of committee staff have appeared in recent years (Fox and Hammond, 1977; Malbin, 1980), but we have little knowledge of how committee staff collect and use technical information on environmental quality issues, the way in which they define policy alternatives, the use they make of policy analyses, and their impact on committee decision-making. Comparative committee studies might illuminate the various roles played by staffs and the conditions for effective use of technical information and analyses in this policy area.

In a related vein, one can find little scholarship in political science focused on the activities and impact of the various caucuses, party policy committees, and study groups that have proliferated on the Hill in the last decade. Some of the environmental caucuses and study groups date back at least ten years (e.g., the Environmental and Energy Study Conference, the Solar Coalition, and the Congressional Clearinghouse on the Future), while others (the Renewable Energy Group and the Caucus on Science and Technology) are of more recent origin. The gap in general scholarship on groups is slowly being filled (Loomis, 1981; Hammond, Stevens, and Mulhollan, 1983), but this literature deals with environmental groups only indirectly or for illustrative purposes. For example, Hammond, Mulhollan, and Stevens (1985) analyze how informal caucuses, including the Environmental and Energy Study Conference, shape agenda setting, and conclude that the larger "personal interest" caucuses serve chiefly an informational or educational rather than an advocacy function; they were formed largely to help set the congressional agenda, not to further specific policy goals. The work of the Congressional Clearinghouse on the Future can be similarly categorized; it serves to call attention to long-range policy-making needs that are often neglected on the Hill.

In comparison to other congressional scholarship, however, these topics are still understudied. We might ask more about the contribution made by these informal groups (and the various party groups and caucuses) to environmental policy deliberation in Congress. For example, do they significantly increase Congress's capacity to formulate environmental policy or oversee the executive by providing crucial technical information or mobilizing important constituencies? Do they play a major role in promoting policy innovation or change, or in building advocacy coalitions on specific environmental battles? If so, in what way? If they promote representation of environmental interests by building ties to the multitude of environmental organizations that have opened Washington offices in the last ten years, how successful have they been at doing so? Although most of the caucuses and study groups are fairly small in size and operate with modest budgets, their distinctive role in Congress deserves more attention than has been received to date.

Similarly, there is considerable value in studying the various analytic offices that support environmental policy activities on the Hill. Although the General Accounting Office (GAO), the Office of Technology Assessment (OTA), the Congressional Research Service (CRS), and the Congressional Budget Office (CBO) figure prominently in some case studies of environmental policy-making, there are only a few general descriptions of their origins, structure, and operation. Gibbons and Gwin (1985) provide a very useful review of the reasons for OTA's creation, the forces that led to its approval in 1972, the congressional expectations for the kinds of technology assessment that would be produced, what OTA was able to do in its first decade, and the way its assessment process works—including the relationship between OTA staff and pertinent bodies both within Congress and outside. Similarly, Harvey Brooks (1985) has provided an insightful article on the origin of the idea of technology assessment and the nature of the assessments and related policy analyses conducted by OTA, GAO, CRS, and CBO.

One might conclude from these kinds of descriptive accounts of congressional advisory bodies, and from the voluminous publications they produced on environmental policy implementation, budgetary analyses, and technical assessments, that collectively they are a major influence on environmental policy decisions in Congress. Yet there has been little effort to systematically assess their capabilities and activities. What has been done tends to characterize their contribution as modest. For example, Whiteman (1982 and 1985) studied the use of five OTA projects within congressional committees, with several of the projects involving environmental and energy concerns. Through some fifty-nine interviews with OTA and committee staff as well as review of the documentary record, he found that strategic use of OTA policy analysis was the most common "where analytic information is used in a supportive capacity to reinforce and advocate existing positions." Presumably studies that point to the need for new and controversial positions would be used less. Conceptualizing and measuring utilization of knowledge in policy-making is a challenging enterprise. For that reason, Whiteman's well-developed conceptual scheme for studying the use of technical information in committee decision-making might help guide future efforts to assess the role and impact of analytic offices on the Hill as well as to address the broader question of how knowledge affects congressional decision-making on environmental and resource issues.

One illustration of the potential contribution of empirical research is in the area of Congress and risk management. Some writers, especially legal scholars such as Green (1986), review "the way Congress has gone about establishing criteria for managing risk," and complain that congressional decisions are irrational and the policies that govern regulatory agencies such as the Environmental Protection Agency (EPA), the Occupational Safety and Health Administration (OSHA), and the Food and Drug Administration (FDA) are inconsistent at best. In a similar vein, others (e.g., Rodgers, 1980) argue that Congress should engage in more vigorous oversight of risk management decisions in the agencies, particularly when what they regard as questionable methods of cost-benefit or risk-benefit analysis are being applied. Descriptions and arguments of this kind are not grounded in empirical study of Congress. But such studies might tell us something useful about the actual capabilities, and willingness, of Congress to engage in risk management decisions, and thus assist in devising appropriate remedies.

For example, an exploratory study of my own (Kraft, 1982) found a severely limited congressional capacity for conducting and evaluating risks to public health, safety, and the environment. Professional staff in the support agencies (especially OTA and CRS) believed that in general members fail to understand such technical information and to make effective use of it in policy-making and in overseeing administrative decisions on risk-related policies. One implication is that institutional capacity for risk analysis needs to be improved; another is that sufficient political incentives must be created to encourage members to make use of that capacity. Simple injunctions to engage in more oversight are not likely to produce much change. These findings seemingly support Rosenbaum's (1985) observations that in environmental affairs "Congress is an assembly of scientific amateurs enacting programs of great technical complexity to ameliorate scientifically complicated environmental ills most legislators but dimly understand." But there are ways in which congressional involvement with the technical aspects of environmental decision-making can be improved and perhaps promote consideration of pertinent constituency interests not well represented in environmental risk management at present. Following Whiteman's approach to these difficult questions may help illuminate how effective use of technical information can be increased in the future.

Congressional Policy-making and the Environment

Descriptions of congressional functions or roles typically divide the work of Congress into five categories: representation, constituency service, policy-making, oversight, and public education (e.g., Vogler, 1984). Although all may affect public policy directly or indirectly, our concern here is chiefly with the legislative and oversight functions. In particular, students of environmental politics are interested in the political processes affecting agenda setting, policy formulation, policy legitimation, budgeting, and evaluation of policy impact in a wide range of substantive policy areas, from pollution control to natural resources management. Contributions to our knowledge of such subjects can be reviewed and assessed for selected policy areas and for building a foundation for theory that cuts across substantive policy areas.

Most of the early studies of environmental policy-making in Congress dealt with specific policy topics and were largely descriptive narratives of policy formation. Such work falls into a long-standing tradition of congressional scholarship: case studies. Thus early work by Jennings (1969) on water pollution control, Ripley (1969) on air pollution control, contributions to an edited collection by Cooley and Wandesforde-Smith (1970) focusing largely on natural resource and conservation policies, and more recent work by Katz (1984) and Sanders (1981) on energy policy provide useful accounts of how such policies were shaped by individual legislators, committee staffs, and interest groups, and the effect of the larger political climate of the time. Many such studies go well beyond Congress, of course, and deal as well with the influence of the president, the bureaucracy, and a variety of other actors external to Congress (e.g., Goodwin's [1981] collection on energy policy and Sundquist's [1968] review of policy in the Eisenhower, Kennedy, and Johnson administrations). While most such case studies are stronger on description than analysis, they demonstrate the important role that Congress has played historically in environmental policy formation, and at least hint at the influence of congressional structure, members' political incentives, and leadership in a way that may facilitate theory building. For those with special interest in the particular policy areas, these studies also provide a rich factual history that supplements the even more purely descriptive accounts found, for example, in Congressional Quarterly's annual almanacs and the *Congress and the Nation* collections.

Other studies of environmental policy-making could be characterized as far more analytical, implicitly or explicitly suggesting the utility of one or more theoretical frameworks. One of the most influential studies of this kind is Charles Jones's account of the formation of air pollution control policy, *Clean Air* (1975). Jones's original and amply documented account of the formation and implementation of air quality policy is noteworthy for its careful assessment of the congressional role in the larger policy process, and in particular the eagerness Congress displayed in responding to public demands for a dramatic "escalation" in clean air policy in 1970. His critique of Congress's "speculative augmentation" and his defense of (modified) incrementalism preceded by several years the critical assessments of environmental policy-making of the late 1970s and early 1980s. Two other treatments of the congressional role in air quality, Ackerman and Hassler (1981) and Lundqvist (1980), similarly demonstrated the virtues of analytical approaches, with Lundqvist's also suggesting the rich possibilities of cross-national comparison, in his case the United States and Sweden. Lundqvist's conclusions about the proclivity of Congress to ignore technological and economic feasibility and to press for "technology-forcing" approaches with stringent objectives and deadlines parallel Jones's observations in many respects. Lundqvist argues especially that the difference between the aggressive U.S. response to air pollution and Sweden's tortoise-like response is a function of political structure (weak party system, decentralized influence in Congress) and the highly individualistic politics of the Congress. Additional comparative policy studies should be undertaken to supplement this rather modest literature.

Perhaps the limitation of even the more analytical case studies is apparent in some of these conclusions, for they may reflect the peculiar political environment of the early 1970s that led Congress to favor a number of nonincremental environmental policies despite the usual obstacles to such policy-making. Since that time Congress seems to have returned to the more common incremental policy-making patterns or, for several years in the mid-1980s, to a politics of stalemate over renewal of virtually all the major environmental policies. While one explanation for this deadlock is the sharp disagreement between Congress and the Reagan administration over particular features of environmental policies, there have been broader changes in the political system that have affected congressional policy-making.

Assessing congressional policy-making in the mid-1980s, Cook and Davidson (1985) argue that during much of the early 1980s, Congress was practicing "deferral politics." This assessment was widely echoed in the press in editorial comments, for example in the *New York Times* (1984), about environmental protection being "paralyzed in Congress and mired in the courts." The *Times* went on to report that "Congress failed to agree on important revisions of the acts governing clean air, clean water, drinking water and abandoned toxic dump sites."

As the "motherhood" nature of environmental politics in the early 1970s gave way to more sharply conflictual politics by the 1980s, Congress did indeed find itself unable to resolve major differences between environmentalists and their opponents, with both sides well represented in Washington. In the new political climate of the 1980s, where environmental policies have become low salience (at least most of the time) and high conflict issues, not only are there fewer incentives for policy leadership, but members have been cross-pressured and were unable for several years to reach agreement on even incremental policy amendments to the major acts. Clearly, the 98th Congress (1983–84) was not very successful in resolving these differences, with the major exception of renewing and strengthening the Resource Conservation and Recovery Act.

The 99th Congress (1985–86) was strikingly different, in part because of public and congressional reaction to the Reagan administration's attempts at environmental deregulation. Environmentalists were clearly pleased; the Sierra Club congratulated Congress for its "solid record on environmental quality and public lands issues," and noted that "bipartisan majorities supported the improvement of key laws despite resistance from President Reagan" (Sierra Club, 1987). In May 1986 the Safe Drinking Water Act was renewed for five years and expanded in scope, with Congress adding language requiring stricter enforcement by the EPA; spending was authorized at $170 million for the next fiscal year, up from $91 million in fiscal 1986. In the fall of 1986 the Superfund program for hazardous waste clean-up was reauthorized for five years at a total budget of $8.5 billion, far greater than supported by the Reagan administration. Other notable actions of the 99th Congress included renewal of the Coastal Zone Management Act in April 1986, the enactment of soil conservation measures in a new farm bill, adoption of a wild and scenic rivers bill environmentalists hailed as a major step forward, the adoption of energy efficiency standards for appliances (vetoed by the president, but enacted and signed into law in early 1987), and reauthorization in late 1986 of the Clean Water Act with a price tag over nine years of $18 billion; the water bill was vetoed by President Reagan (after Congress adjourned) as too expensive, but in February 1987 the 100th Congress easily passed the same bill (at $20 billion) and overrode the president's second veto.

Despite that considerable record of productivity, a number of major environmental policy measures were not successful in the 99th Congress. These included renewal of the Federal Insecticide, Fungicide, and Rodenticide Act (FIFRA) and the Clean Air Act, and action on acid rain. The Democrats regained control of the Senate following the 1986 election, but that in itself was not expected to shift committee action greatly; of greater importance was the arrival of newly elected members of both the House and Senate who were thought to be more environmentally oriented than those departing Congress. Thus prospects for action on a number of fronts appeared promising in 1987.

Despite the more recent movement on major environmental acts, the observations made by Cook and Davidson in 1985, among other similar assessments, serve as a useful reminder that the characteristics of environmental politics in Congress vary over time. Since the early 1970s environmental problems have become more complex and technical (e.g., acid rain and hazardous waste), solutions more costly, and agreement on goals—and especially means—often more elusive. As Jones has noted in a more general context (1984:240–45), the ambitious policy-making of the 1970s has shifted to incremental policy-making, with administrative and technical issues now more prominently debated than the broader policy goals themselves. Studies of congressional policy-making are necessarily timebound, but the building of more general theory would be aided by greater attention to such variance.

Other treatments of substantive environmental policies introduce different theoretical issues. Ferejohn (1974), for example, studied rivers and harbors legislation between 1947 and 1968 to examine the allocation of pork barrel projects and its relationship to particular features of Congress. Like many scholars using purposive behavior theories, he finds a congressional bias for divisible or distributive policies that reflects the geographic (state and local) representation of Congress, the rules of decision-making, and the operation of the committee system. Similarly, Mayhew (1974) postulates a distinct congressional preference for particularistic benefits that are highly visible and for which members can claim credit as elections approach. While use of the familiar Lowi typology (distributive, redistributive, and regulatory policies) is now common in texts on Congress and public policy, it is not favored by all. Oppenheimer's (1974) study of the influence of the oil industry in decisions on the oil depletion allowance and water pollution control policy uses Edelman's distinction between symbolic and material policies to characterize the shifting nature of water pollution control (from symbolic to strongly material by the 1970s).

Even this brief survey of selected works on environmental policy-making indicates that there has been little agreement on the most profitable frameworks of analysis and little cumulation of environmental policy scholarship. Beyond the addition of more substantive policy explorations, there would seem to be some value in comparing the findings from previous studies with the goal of identifying the conditions (e.g., public support for environmental policy or the perceived distribution of the benefits and costs of environmental protection) under which one might expect one form of policy-making or another. Are there, in fact, clear patterns in the way Congress has responded to environmental policy issues? Can environmental policies be classified in a manner to facilitate the search for such patterns, for example, using the Lowi scheme or, preferably, one that more clearly differentiates among types of environmental policy? In one instance, James Q. Wilson (1980:367–72) has distinguished four forms of regulatory politics that depend on the distribution of the benefits and costs of regulation: majoritarian politics, interest-group politics, client politics, and entrepreneurial politics. Clearly most of the major environmental policies of the 1970s are regulatory in nature, but to say that is not to say very much. The politics of toxic waste issues in Congress is surely different from the politics of clean air or surface mining control or endangered species protection (for example, in salience, technical complexity, and the organization of interests). It would be helpful to clarify the commonalities and the differences if one goal is indeed comparative analysis across policy areas and across time that will help to explain congressional policy-making behavior.

Environmental policy scholars also should begin paying more attention to some features of congressional policy-making ignored in the past. With most of the basic statutes in place, political interest has shifted from creation of major new programs to appropriations for those that we have and to oversight of administrative activities. The severity of budget cuts under the Reagan administration has prompted some concern for the way Congress considers environmentally related budget requests (e.g., Bartlett, 1984), but the time seems ripe for fuller studies of this process and its policy implications. Studies of the Budget and Appropriation committees would be a good place to start. Similarly, Congress is credited with engaging in vigorous oversight of the Reagan administration during the early 1980s, which may have constrained administration activity to some extent (Kenski and Kenski, 1984). Political conditions in the early 1980s seemed perfectly suited for encouraging congressional oversight, and the evidence indicates the extent to which Congress is capable of oversight when the right incentives are present. Between May 1981 (when she was confirmed as administrator of the EPA) and December of 1982, Anne Burford testified fifteen times before congressional committees. EPA officials appeared more than seventy times between October 1981 and July 1982 (Cook and Davidson, 1985). During the 97th Congress (1981–82) Interior officials appeared at 383 hearings. Cook and Davidson (1985) compared the frequency of oversight hearings between the 96th (1979–80) and the 97th Congress and found that the House Agriculture, Energy and Commerce, and Interior committees all increased their oversight significantly, as did the Senate Environment and Public Works Committee.

The frequency of oversight is clear enough in these figures, but the quality of the process and its impact are more difficult to judge. The general congressional record on oversight suggests that Congress is greatly limited in its capacity to engage in sustained and systematic oversight of technical policy administration and typically lacks sufficient political incentive to do so (Ogul, 1981; Aberbach, 1979). Holding hearings on Anne Burford's activities at the EPA, James Watt's record at Interior, or on the chemical industry's behavior following the Bhopal accident (Davis and Green, 1984) provides political dividends that cannot be expected under more normal circumstances. What are the conditions favoring oversight of environmental policy actions? What is the quality of congressional oversight? Deficiencies in the process? Its impact on administrative decision-making? Its impact on congressional evaluation of environmental policy and policy reformulation?

One way to begin building such generalizations is to review Aberbach's (1979) summary of conditions promoting a greater incidence of oversight (slightly modified here): (1) split partisan control of the presidency and the Congress, giving Congress an incentive to seek out "inappropriate" activities in the agencies and to publicize them; (2) bureaucratic unresponsiveness to constituency casework inquiries on the part of strategically placed members of Congress; (3) congressional efforts to satisfy group interests to which administrative agencies have been insufficiently responsive; (4) a congressional desire to protect favored agencies—the oversight in this case would be largely positive or supportive of the agencies' efforts; (5) decentralization of the committee structure—in which staff and funds are controlled by subcommittee chairpersons; (6) an increase in staff resources; (7) publicity over and evidence of corruption in administrative agencies; and (8) the existence of a "crisis" in regulatory programs, especially one well publicized.

The quality of oversight, as contrasted with its incidence, is likely to be promoted by other conditions: (1) scarcity of monetary resources, which creates a strong interest in ways of determining program effectiveness and in considering alternative policy approaches; (2) an influx of new senators and representatives skeptical about governmental regulation and traditional public policy approaches; (3) the dramatic increase in program evaluation within government agencies, which puts pressure on Congress to review the results; and (4) reforms in the congressional budget process which force consideration of particular spending demands within the larger context of national priorities and budget limitations. To what extent are such hypotheses supported by the record of environmental policy oversight? Investigation of a range of important cases over the last decade should help to fill this notable gap in the scholarly literature.

External Participants in Congressional Policy-making on the Environment

As reference to oversight activities makes clear, Congress does not operate in a vacuum. It responds to other policy actors, particularly in the executive office and in the bureaucracy. Among other participants to whom members of Congress must react are active members of the constituency, a multitude of organized interest groups, and government officials at the state and local level. Space precludes discussing all external policy actors, but some brief references serve to indicate the nature of extant scholarship and future possibilities.

Congressional relations with the president are the most thoroughly studied of these external influences. There is a large and insightful general literature on the subject (e.g., Wayne, 1978; Orfield, 1975; Edwards, 1980; Jones,

1981; King, 1983) as well as a small but significant body of material focusing on environmental and energy issues. The older case study literature cited above underscores Congress's historical dominance in policy formulation or initiation (including agenda setting) on environmental issues, especially during the 1960s and early 1970s, where cooperation with the president was also common. Democratic party control of both houses of Congress encouraged a strong congressional role, as did the salience and public support for environmental issues. Particularly striking was the activity of a number of congressional policy entrepreneurs who engaged in what Polsby (1984) has called policy incubation, keeping issues alive by promoting studies and conducting hearings while public support for action grew (Kraft, 1973a). During the Carter administration, Congress demonstrated its capacity for a quite different role on energy issues, which Jones (1979) has called the "facilitator of interests"; denied effective representation in the executive office, energy industry interests in particular turned to the Congress (especially the Senate) to make their case against Carter's national energy plan. Oppenheimer (1981) has explored that particular "obstructionist" role of Congress on energy issues in some detail. In the first six years of the Reagan presidency, Congress was divided in party control; with Republicans running the Senate and Democrats the House, it would have been difficult for Congress to play a policy initiation role. But those conditions encouraged what Kenski and Kenski (1984) call the defender-of-the-status-quo and the overseer roles. Although Congress did not prevent Reagan from achieving many of the organizational, budgetary, and regulatory changes engineered by James Watt and Anne Burford, it did blunt some of the president's more aggressive efforts to weaken environmental policy (Kraft and Vig, 1984).

One notable battleground concerned the Office of Management and Budget (OMB), which had taken on major new authority under a Reagan executive order on the use of cost-benefit analysis in regulation (see Smith, 1984; Eads and Fix, 1984). Congressional committee chairmen regularly denounced OMB's efforts to intervene in the writing of health, safety, and environmental regulations, and held frequent hearings on the subject. In late June 1985 the chairmen of five House committees submitted a joint brief to the United States Court of Appeals for the District of Columbia challenging the legality of one such intervention, asserting that OMB's efforts represented "systematic usurpation of legislative power" (Burnham, 1985). Further congressional challenges to OMB, including frequent criticism by John Dingell, chairman of the House Energy and Commerce Committee, and threats to cut off funds for the Office of Information and Regulatory Affairs in OMB, led the agency to promise some changes in its behavior.

Cases of this kind suggest that one fruitful area for investigation would be the nature of congressional-executive interaction on environmental policy formulation, budgeting, and oversight. Who initiates contacts, what are the communication patterns, and what difference does it make in legislator attitudes and behavior? What is the relationship between congressional staff and the executive agencies? How well does the White House congressional liaison operation function on environmental issues, and what special arrangements are made to inform members of Congress and their staffs on the more technical aspects of the issues? How influential are agency presentations before committees, both formal testimony and informal communication? The more general literature on agency-congressional interaction can yield useful propositions, but more specific applications to environmental and energy issues would be desirable. For example, Ripley and Franklin (1984) have developed an elaborate conceptual framework to differentiate congressional and executive relationships for six categories of public policy (distributive, protective regulatory, redistributive, structural, strategic, and crisis) and also suggest how the personal characteristics of congressional and bureaucratic policy actors differ in ways that might affect policy-making behavior. How usefully can such frameworks be applied to specific cases of environmental policy-making or oversight to help explain how congressional-bureaucratic relationships affect the policy process?

Another line of investigation would look more to the process of policy legitimation. Without generalizing too much from the Reagan administration experience and the few other case studies available, what can one say about how Congress legitimizes environmental policy? Many scholars (e.g., Jones, 1979) celebrate Congress's role in representing the diversity of interests in American politics, for providing an extended process of inquiry, deliberation, bargaining, and compromise that helps to insure the technical soundness of policy proposals as well as their public acceptability. Yet congressional responsiveness to narrow but well-organized interests (especially on low salience issues)—along with the fragmentation and low visibility nature of much policy-making in the Congress—raises questions about how representative Congress is of major constituency interests. Which interests are represented under varying political conditions? How responsive has Congress been to general public preferences on environmental issues? Detailed case studies of policy-making might shed some light on the character of policy legitimation and thus on congressional performance of this role. For example, are there institutional barriers to more effective processes of legitimation? How might public knowledge of congressional activity (generally poor) be improved, and what difference would that make for environmental decision-making? How much do members of Congress know of public preferences on environmental issues? On the necessary tradeoffs between economic costs and the extent of environmental protection? Between energy policy and environmental quality? If Congress is expected to make critical judgments about acceptable levels of environmental risk (which is done implicitly in setting statutory standards and instructing the EPA on program priorities), how might the process of making such determinations be improved so as to adhere more closely to democratic principles?

Consideration of policy legitimation suggests a related topic that has received quite limited study to date, namely, the impact of organized interest groups on congressional decision-making. The role of industry groups and environmentalists has been much speculated on, and is considered to a modest extent in a number of case studies, but it has not been studied systematically. Indeed, not since some early work on interest group influence on Congress (Bauer, Pool, and Dexter, 1972) has the impact of groups been carefully examined. To judge from the proliferation of interest groups in recent years and the diversity of new techniques of lobbying, the older conclusions of ineffective group activity must be questioned (e.g., see Berry, 1984, and Schlozman and Tierney, 1986). Studies of environmentally related groups active in lobbying Congress should be particularly worthwhile. There are some sixty-five national environmental organizations with offices in the Washington metropolitan area. Moreover, the growth of public interest groups in the 1970s seems to have encouraged a vast expansion of corporate interest groups and trade associations with Washington offices (Berry, 1984:35–41).

For both kinds of groups, we need additional empirical inquiry on their activities and impact on environmental policy formation and implementation. A range of questions can be suggested. What groups are most active on environmental policy issues? What resources do they have at their disposal, what strategies and tactics do they use, and how effective do they seem to be? As noted above, roll call analyses find little evidence of the influence of groups on floor voting, but such a focus is too narrow to gauge the impact of groups on public policy. One must turn to the interaction of groups with committee members and staff, and look at how groups shape the definition of problems and the selection of policy alternatives in the earliest stages of policy formulation. That is, one must go beyond the traditional focus on floor voting. Several studies of public interest groups may suggest fruitful ways to proceed (e.g., Berry, 1977; McFarland, 1976 and 1984). At this stage our knowledge of how both corporate and environmental groups operate is so limited that even a basic description of the major groups, their resources, and activities would be a useful point of departure for more elaborate studies in the future.

A number of scholars have suggested the special role played by the interaction of interest groups (especially "clientele" groups), bureaucrats with program responsibilities, and interested members of the relevant committees and subcommittees. Variously termed subgovernments, subsystems, little "cozy little triangles," and more recently "issue networks," they tend to dominate congressional policy-making within a narrow domain; this is particularly so for low-salience issues where cooperation among the cluster of participants on the distribution of benefits substitutes for the conflict one often finds on regulatory issues such as clean air, clean water, and hazardous waste policy. Some environmental policy issues are clearly distributive (e.g., parks and other public lands issues), but more often the issues are regulatory. Thus one would expect to find differences in the organization of interests from one policy area to another. One finding of special note is that few groups are so intensely committed to regulatory agencies that they testify at appropriation hearings for those agencies in contrast to those held for distributive and redistributive agencies (Meier, 1985:20). Why is this, and what is the significance for appropriation decisions for environmental protection programs? Particularly given recent reassessments of various assertions about subgovernments, Rieselbach's (1983) observations on the phenomenon are worth noting: "Theory has outrun research: much of what we know is anecdotal . . . or contradictory"; we need, he says, clearer lines of demarcation among policy types, more detailed analyses of the contacts among the participants in the subgovernment, the strategy and tactics they employ, the conditions under which they are likely to succeed, and the results they are able to achieve. Such inquiry would be particularly valuable for natural resource policies, including ocean policy, public lands policy, and energy policy. There have been a few such studies in recent years (Temples, 1980; Lester, 1980; Chubb, 1983; see also Davis, 1985). There are also a few in the older natural resources policy literature

(Foss, 1960; McConnell, 1966, chapter 7). But these only begin to scratch the surface of the role of subgovernments in environmental policy decisions.

Congressional Performance and Environmental Policy

Aside from the numerous empirical inquiries summarized or suggested above, a major topic of concern to environmental policy scholars is the extent to which Congress performs its various roles successfully. The general literature on Congress includes a considerable body of evaluative studies and commentaries, both positive and negative, but little of that literature concerns congressional performance on substantive environmental policy issues or more general assessments of congressional capacity for effective representation and policy-making on this range of issues. The major exception is the collection of case studies by Cooley and Wandesforde-Smith (1970), now quite dated. Moreover, what we have reveals no consensus. Thus Jones (1974 and 1975) criticized Congress's performance on the Clean Air Act in 1970, but found its handling of Carter's national energy plan (i.e., its searching criticism of it and its ultimate rejection) more appropriate (1979); at the same time, other students of energy policy (Katz, 1984; Oppenheimer, 1981; Kraft, 1981) found Congress's performance lacking because it failed to enact a policy that could guide the nation's future energy development, particularly in an environmentally benign direction, and also avoid the considerable economic and national security costs of a future energy crisis. Cooley and Wandesforde-Smith (1970), writing just before congressional attention to environmental issues escalated in 1970, were harshly critical of Congress's response to emerging environmental issues: "The major conclusion is inescapable and bitterly disappointing to those aware of the environmental crisis facing the nation. It is that Congress has failed to do more than make halting progress through a series of incremental adjustments. Every chapter in this book points to serious flaws in the response of Congress to the basic moral and political issues posed by the quiet crisis identified by Stewart Udall in 1963" (1970:227).

Presumably, the authors would reach a different conclusion in the late 1980s after the impressive record of major policy enactments in the 1970s (Vig and Kraft, 1984b) and the more recent renewal and strengthening of these same acts. But what would that conclusion be? Following Gary Orfield (1975), one might say that Congress is an active and responsive shaper of public policy when the American public reveals sufficient interest and concern and where there is evident consensus on the desired policy change. Clearly, Congress followed public preferences in the early 1970s when it enacted the Clean Air Act and the Clean Water Act and other dramatic departures from previously modest environmental policies. Indeed, it is often criticized for having been too responsive to an ill-informed public and for enacting ambitious and costly policies in the 1970s that overtaxed administrative capabilities. Congress again demonstrated its independence and activism under the condition of sufficient public support in the 1980s when it blunted the Reagan administration's attack on those policies.

These few comments suggest that clarification of the standards or criteria for assessing institutional performance might help sort out this conflicting body of material. What should one expect from the Congress—in policy-making, oversight, representation, and public education? What evidence is pertinent to rendering some judgments on these matters? If Congress is deemed to be falling short in some area, why is that? That is, what particular features of the institution explain its failures and successes? Insofar as the offering of recommendations for various kinds of institutional reform has been a fixture of congressional scholarship and political commentary for decades, students of environmental policy might consider how particular reforms (e.g., changes in the committee structure to reduce fragmentation of responsibility or public funding of congressional election campaigns to reduce dependence on political action committees) might affect environmental policy-making and the substance of public policy. They might also explore the political feasibility and probable effectiveness of the range of reform proposals commonly offered by environmental policy scholars (including economists). For example, what merit is there in the legislated regulatory calendar proposed by Litan and Nordhaus (1983), expanded reliance on market incentives in pollution control, or various proposals for adopting clearer and more consistent standards of risk acceptability across the full range of environmental and other social regulation policies (Lave, 1981)?

Evaluation of proposals of this kind might be extended to consideration of institutional capabilities for leadership and policy innovation, particularly for long-term environmental problems such as global resource scarcity. One long-standing critique of Congress is that its time horizon is invariably shaped by the electoral cycle, thus providing few incentives to address long-term policy problems (e.g., Rosenbaum, 1985). The ineffective efforts of the Global

Tomorrow Coalition to encourage Congress to follow through on the Carter administration's Global 2000 report by considering "foresight capability" legislation is seemingly a case in point; aside from a few hearings on the issue, there appears to be remarkably little interest. Some regard Congress's neglect of long-term energy policy needs as further evidence of this deficiency. What conditions facilitate leadership and innovation on such issues? What particular reforms (institutional structure, advisory offices, etc.) might provide the requisite capabilities and incentives? Those who look to representative political institutions for policy leadership in a democracy should find such questions worthy of investigation.

Conclusions

As this review of the literature on Congress and environmental policy makes clear, political scientists have contributed a great deal of material since the early 1970s. Congress has been a natural focus of interest, given its leading role in policy formation in the 1970s, its defense of environmental policy against the Reagan administration's assaults of the 1980s, and its reflection of the basic ambivalence of the American public on environmental policy goals and means. As a representative and politically reactive institution, Congress affords students of politics multiple opportunities for studying how a democratic government responds to the challenges posed by environmental problems. Research to date has dealt with a wide range of concerns, from voting behavior to committee decision-making. There remain many significant gaps in this literature, however, and suggestions have been offered throughout the paper for new research. Particular emphasis has been placed on the building of middle-range theory as one way to cumulate the somewhat disparate studies to date and relate their approaches and findings to the more general (and very extensive) literature on Congress.

Despite the centrality and importance of Congress as an institution that shapes environmental policy, there are some major constraints imposed on scholars who study environmental politics in Congress. From a broader perspective, Congress must be studied in relation to other elements in the political system and not as an isolated institution, a flaw which has long characterized congressional scholarship. Political scientists should concern themselves not only with decision-making within each major institution but with the *interaction* of institutions and other policy actors. Only a broader analysis is likely to explain adequately the impact of Congress on environmental politics and policy.

From the even broader perspective of interdisciplinary environmental studies, one must also acknowledge the constraints of disciplinary research. Environmental policy and politics can be studied from the perspective of a single discipline, and clearly that is the predominant approach reflected in the political science research summarized in this book. Political scientists define what are considered to be interesting topics and choose approaches and methods in a way that reflects disciplinary concerns for the most part. Yet there is obviously a significant omission in treating environmental policy and politics in this manner. One can hardly engage in comprehensive analysis of the subject without consideration of the work of economists, legal scholars, planners, policy analysts, sociologists, philosophers, students of public administration, engineers, and natural scientists—especially environmental scientists and ecologists. If the major objective of such study is to build theoretical and substantive knowledge within the discipline, this constraint may seem quite minor. However, if objectives include application of theories and concepts from political science to the study of political processes of concern to a wider audience, other needs should be addressed. In particular, more attention might be paid to the contribution political scientists can make to interdisciplinary environmental studies.

However, to attempt comprehensive analysis of environmental problems and the public policy solutions chosen by governments overtaxes the abilities of any single individual—or single volume such as the present one—to say the least. What else might be suggested for political scientists and others who by professional training and interests are likely to view environmental policy and politics largely through the conceptual lenses of their particular discipline? Interdisciplinary research is one possibility, although it is not easy. For example, the technical and political components of nuclear waste policy-making need to be studied together to understand how Congress tried to resolve the policy issues in this area. That suggests that political scientists could benefit from cooperative research with nuclear or chemical engineers knowledgeable about radioactive wastes. Another possibility is to communicate more effectively with the larger environmental policy audience, from economists to natural scientists; that means giving at least some consideration to their interests when studies are designed and carried out, and the findings and conclusions reported. Finally, we might be more alert to disciplinary shortcomings in selecting topics worthy of study. Thus we might address some of the larger questions of environmental change in the American political system and in other settings that typically receive little attention. One example is the implication for political conflict and regime stability of increasing global resource scarcity (Ophuls, 1977; Gurr, 1985). Another is the relationship of environmental policy questions to the broader set of issues that form a progressive policy agenda in the United States and other developed nations (e.g., see Paehlke, 1989). Such advice is at least as applicable to studies of Congress and environmental policy as it is to the study of other components of the political system.

8

The Bureaucracy and Environmental Policy

Walter A. Rosenbaum

The first Earth Day, that historic April 22, 1970, has become the signature for the environmental era. In fact, the era began six months earlier, when President Nixon signed the National Environmental Policy Act (NEPA), the first of twenty major federal environmental laws intended to alter radically the nation's environmental programs and priorities. Significantly, the era began with legislation intended to force a restructuring of the process by which all federal agencies made decisions affecting the environment.

Administrative reform has been a strategic principle in the environmental movement's politics from the environmental era's inception. Environmental legislation written during the 1970s commonly attempted to promote ecological protection by mandating fundamental changes in administrative behavior that eventually involved three presidential staff agencies, twelve cabinet departments, and two independent agencies. The success of this legislation was predicated upon unusual, sometimes unique, provisions in substantive policy, administrative structure and process directly challenging traditional values, and procedural norms firmly rooted in agency practices.

A large body of literature about these administrative strategies already exists, and of continuing analysis there appears no end. Any informative survey of this research must necessarily be selective. Since the bureaucratic impact of environmental legislation is a fundamental measure of the environmental movement's success, this essay focuses upon what the literature tells us about the consequences of these administrative innovations—good, bad, and otherwise—and, especially, upon the newer environmental agencies and programs. It concludes with a proposed agenda for future research based on important issues raised in the current literature.

The Administrative Style of Environmental Legislation

Environmental legislation since 1970 typically entails several administrative provisions, in different combination, that distinguish it substantively and procedurally from most federal laws outside the domain of the environment and public health and safety.

Imposing scientific norms on administrative determinations

The environmental legislation of the last two decades intends to alter fundamentally the way scientific information and scientific criteria are used in administrative determinations affecting the environment. The laws attempt to compel this reordering of the administrative process in several ways. First, the National Environmental Policy Act (NEPA) mandates that all federal agencies must identify any programs or determinations significantly affecting the environment, define the adverse environmental consequences of such action through the development and use of relevant, interdisciplinary scientific analysis, and then use the impact assessment as distinct and significant criteria for policy evaluation. (Much the same thing was intended in the Federal Land Policy and Management Act of 1976, known as FLPMA, although it has been far less studied.) In effect, as Serge Taylor has observed, NEPA intends to institutionalize scientific analysis committed to ecological values within federal agencies. It means to compel decision-makers to consider the ecological implications of policy thus revealed as a criterion apart from economic and political factors in calculating the acceptable trade-offs in policy choices (Taylor, 1984:chap. 4).

Most environmental regulatory programs, such as the Clean Air Act (1970) or the Toxic Substances Control Act (1976), are also based on what Jurgen Schmandt has called "a new model of scientific regulation" (Schmandt, 1984). Scientific and technological determinations must be one, and sometimes the only, standard by which substantive regulatory decisions affecting environmental quality are reached. This dependence upon scientific criteria in regulatory rule-making is essential because most federal environmental programs since 1970 require the implementing agencies to specify quality standards for ambient air and water effluents, to identify the appropriate control technologies for pollution sources, to define acceptable risk from exposure to toxic or hazardous substances, and to make a multitude of other environmentally relevant technical judgments. In effect, federal statutes thrust upon federal agencies the burden of scientifically defining acceptable levels of pollution, pollution abatement, and risk of exposure to environmental pollutants.

Preventing program "capture"

Environmental partisans created many statutory barriers intended to frustrate "capture" of environmental programs by the regulated interests. One structural technique was deliberate program organization and staffing to assure a strong environmentalist bias at the outset—no gambles with implementation by ideologically neutral professional staffs. The Environmental Protection Agency's (EPA) enabling legislation, as Alfred Marcus observes, was deliberately intended to produce an administrative structure and professional staff "to represent environmentalists" and to institutionalize environmentalism within the federal government to counterbalance other agencies partisan to business and other regulated interests (Marcus, 1980:294–95). "Action-forcing" provisions in environmental laws were a procedural device to thwart capture. For example, EPA's first major regulatory programs, the Clean Air Act (1970) and the Federal Water Pollution Control Act (1972), abounded with strict compliance deadlines and explicit procedural timetables calculated to constrict agency discretion that might be exploited by regulated interests.

To frustrate capture of federal surface mine regulation, drafters of the Surface Mining Control and Reclamation Act (SMCRA) of 1977 added an extraordinary provision to Title II intended to prevent the Office of Surface Mining Reclamation and Enforcement (OSM) from hiring individuals previously associated with "any legal authority, program or function in any Federal agency which has as its purpose the development or use of coal or other mineral resources" (Public Law 95–87 [1977], Sec. 201 (b); Harris, 1984:46). Sometimes agency charters or programs were defined in statutory language calculated to bring them within the jurisdiction of the most environmentally sensitive congressional oversight committees.

Applying the administrative "hammer"

Environmental legislation has commonly included so-called hammer clauses intended to compel strict agency compliance with regulations and programs through mandatory program deadlines, explicit and detailed procedural prescriptions, provisions for citizen participation and citizen standing to sue agencies, and other statutory prescriptions.

Compliance deadlines have become the congressional house style with environmental legislation. Some common examples:

The Clean Air Act (1970): EPA was required to propose national ambient air quality standards within thirty days of the act's passage, to review and approve state implementation plans for the act within a year following proposal of air quality standards, and to develop technology standards to meet congressionally mandated auto emission reductions within five years of the act's passage.

The Toxic Substances Control Act (1976): EPA had to issue labeling and disposal regulations for polychlorinated biphenyls (PCBs) by July 1977, restrict their use to closed systems by January 1978, prohibit production by January 1979, and stop commercial distribution by July 1979 (Council on Environmental Quality, 1977:5–6).

The Comprehensive Environmental Response, Compensation, and Liability Act (1980): Required EPA to provide Congress with a comprehensive report, and several other more detailed reports, on the act's implementation within four years.

Action forcing is not confined to program deadlines. Many laws were intended to induce changes in substantive policy by compelling procedural reordering. One of NEPA's creators clearly had this in mind when describing its requirement for agency environmental impact assessments as an "ends-oriented agency forcing" device (Caldwell, 1984:11).

Almost all federal environmental laws since 1970 have required extensive, and sometimes innovative, forms of public involvement in their implementation and enforcement. More than 75 percent of all the public participation programs in federal statutes originated since 1970 and most of these were associated with environmental legislation (ACIR, 1980:100; Rosenbaum, 1978:81–97). Environmentalists vigorously promoted, and subsequently used, public involvement programs as a means of mobilizing support for environmental regulation and countering the administrative influence of regulated interests (Sabatier, 1975; Caldwell, Hayes, and MacWhirter, 1976; Rosenbaum, 1984).

Most major environmental enactments since 1970, including the Federal Water Pollution Control Act and the Surface Mining Control and Reclamation Act, granted citizens standing to sue the implementing agencies. Environmental groups viewed this "standing" as a potentially potent instrument for applying external pressure upon agencies to implement the law and to discourage "capture." By facilitating judicial review of agency determinations, environmentalists also hoped that liberalized "standing" could force very strict standards of agency compliance with environmental mandates through institutions to which regulated interests did not enjoy far better access. Equally important, as Shep Melnick observes, liberal judicial access was the strategic complement to "action forcing" legislation, the institutional means for enforcing substantive policy goals (Melnick, 1984:127).

Reform in Retrospect: Examining the Results

The history of political reform, like the history of science, often involves the slaying of beautiful hypotheses by ugly facts. Research literature tells us much, albeit not yet enough, about the consequences—intended and unintended—of the environmental era's administrative reforms.

Science and administrative norms

Three kinds of research literature provide a critical perspective on the scientific reforms associated with environmental programs: evaluations of NEPA, evaluations of the scientific basis for standards and emission control technologies required for air and water pollution regulation, and evaluations of the scientific basis for "risk assessment" methodologies used to identify hazardous and toxic substances regulated by federal law, including the Toxic Substances Control Act (TSCA) of 1976, the Resource Conservation and Recovery Act (RCRA) of 1976, and the Federal Pesticides Act of 1978.

NEPA's impact. NEPA's most important action-forcing provisions are contained in Title I, describing the purpose and procedure to be used by federal agencies in preparing environmental impact statements (EISs) "in every recommendation or report on proposals for legislation or other major Federal actions significantly affecting the quality of the human environment" (Section 102 [c]). It is important to emphasize that Section 102 mandates the *quality* of scientific data as well as the *method* of its utilization in administrative policymaking: agencies are required to "utilize a systematic, interdisciplinary approach which will insure the integrated use of the natural and social sciences and the environmental design arts" and to develop arrangements that will "insure that presently unquantified environmental amenities and values may be given appropriate consideration in decisionmaking along with economic and technical considerations" (Section 102 [a] and [b]). NEPA then requires agencies to use these data in addressing five issues in all EISs: the environmental impact of proposed agency actions, the alternatives to the proposed action, the relationship between long-term and short-term impacts from the proposed action, and the irreversible and irretrievable resource commitments for the proposed action.

NEPA's proponents believed this linkage of information quality to procedural decision-making was essential. "NEPA assumes that changing the rules governing the generation and distribution of knowledge will change the political and intellectual content of agency decisionmaking" (Taylor, 1984:8; see also Caldwell, 1984:2). With few exceptions, however, detailed summaries or case studies about the quality of information in EISs and its relationship to substantive policy decisions are scarce. Instead, evaluations tend to rely upon box scores for the number of EISs prepared and for federal actions or projects halted and altered by EISs (CEQ, 1985:162–75; Environmental Law Institute, 1981; Wichelman, 1976); or they rely upon analysis of court decisions concerning the adequacy of EISs, the procedural obligations imposed on agencies by the EIS process, and the courts' impact on agency consideration of EISs (Liroff, 1980; Liroff, 1981; Anderson, 1973; Wenner, 1982).

These approaches probably lead to underestimating the impact of the EIS procedure on agency decision-making by ignoring the important influence the process of EIS preparation may have upon relevant agency policies and, more importantly, by ignoring the ongoing relationship between EIS specialists within agencies and other policy-makers. Additionally, the relationship between EIS formulation and substantive agency decisions may often be subtle and elude easy quantification.

Still, much is clear about the impact of the EIS process. First, most of the undesirable impacts predicted at NEPA's inception—especially huge agency workloads imposed by EIS preparation and delay of major development projects through EIS-related litigation—have not materialized. After an initial floodtide of two thousand EISs in 1971, volume has abated until, by 1985, less than 550 were produced by all federal agencies (CEQ, 1971 through 1985). The process has not incited a large volume of litigation delaying administrative determinations and obstructing federal projects (Liroff, 1981; Wenner, 1982; CEQ, 1985:162–65). Serge Taylor's meticulous summary of EIS-related litigation from 1970 to 1981 suggests that about 10 percent of all EISs ended in litigation and about 11 percent resulted in court injunctions that rarely caused serious delay in major projects, like nuclear power plants (Taylor, 1984:359). While assertions of unreasonably high cost have sometimes been made about EIS preparation (Bardach and Pugliaiesi, 1977; Lave, 1981), this has not been a finding common to most studies of the process.

Second, evidence that the EIS process has caused significant, environmentally benign changes in the development policies and projects of federal agencies is fragmentary, at best, and confined mostly to recent research during NEPA's second decade. Most researchers have been hard pressed to discover convincing evidence that EISs have had a major impact upon substantive agency decisions (Anderson, 1973; Dreyfus and Ingram, 1976; Hill and Ortolano, 1976; Liroff, 1978; Ozawa, 1982). Information is most often described as "fragmentary," "anecdotal," and "scattered." The few studies attributing importance to the EIS process also admit, almost routinely, its tenuousness within agencies. Thus, Mazmanian and Nienaber observed in 1979 that despite the Army Corps of Engineers' "serious effort to cope with environmental considerations" in project development "it is yet to be seen whether the Corps will want or be able to continue incorporating environmental considerations into its construction activities" (Mazmanian and Nienaber, 1979:3 and 183). Lynton Caldwell, one of NEPA's authors, seemed to be writing an epitaph for his own creation in 1978: "Virtually nobody seems to read and make use of environmental impact statements, (*particularly*) the decision-makers who must act on the projects for which the statements are prepared" (Caldwell, 1978:55).

By 1984, however, Caldwell had concluded (at least in respect to the Bureau of Land Management, the Corps of Engineers, and the U.S. Forest Service where his more recent research occurred) that "multidisciplinary science is generally being integrated into the planning processes of the major resource management agencies," so that the environment is "better managed" and "the case for [NEPA's] effectiveness is stronger" (Caldwell, 1984:87 and 73). A NEPA co-author might be suspected of bias, but Serge Taylor's recent study of NEPA's impact upon the Forest Service and Corps of Engineers reaches much the same conclusion: "By a rough but telling standard of judging outcomes, the EIS process (in the two agencies described at least) not only tends to produce environmentally better outcomes but does so in some socially efficient sense by making (again roughly but significantly) the right kinds of distinctions among situations" (Taylor, 1984:150; see also Cohen, 1979).

Third, the EIS process has altered the structural relationships between organized interests and agencies by creating new means of access and new political strategies that seem most to benefit environmental groups. Regulated interests have, with some success, exploited the requirements for public review and comment on draft EISs and the related "environmental assessments" together with opportunities to appeal to judicial review of agency EIS preparation. But environmental interests and their allies have, it appears, done it best and with the greatest net gain in political advantage. Thus, Shep Melnick counts NEPA among the major reasons for "a new era in administrative law" characterized by the rapidly expanding participation of environmental and other nontraditional groups in administrative decision-making (Melnick, 1983). Significantly, many commentators have suggested that the enhanced administrative influence derived from NEPA can be generalized to many agency activities unrelated to the EIS process itself (Liroff, 1980; Taylor, 1984:260–61; Magat, 1982).

Finally, the EIS process has opened agency preparation of impact assessment to close judicial scrutiny and, in the opinion of most observers, the courts have become a major external influence strongly encouraging strict compliance with the procedural requirements of Section 102. But there is no agreement upon the consequences. One common assertion is that agencies, anxious to make their EISs a fortress against judicial criticism, pack the documents with technical data of uncertain policy relevance or write "telephone book" statements bloated with too many issues and details undifferentiated in importance (Bardach and Pugliaiesi, 1977). Equally pessimistic is the very common observation that the courts have interpreted NEPA in a manner that compels strict procedural compliance with Section 102 but imposes no substantive agency obligation to make policy decisions responsive to issues raised in relevant EISs (Rosenbaum, 1974; Henderson and Pearson, 1978; Mandelker, 1981; Wenner, 1982). A few scholars, including Serge Taylor and Lynton Caldwell, believe close judicial scrutiny has compelled agencies to make substantive policy changes based in EIS documents. At best, one concludes that the administrative effect from judicial review of EIS procedures is uncertain.

One might also ponder the disciplinary factionalism of NEPA evaluations. Economists, with few exceptions, seldom find NEPA a constructive innovation. Most lawyers would agree, at least to the extent that NEPA is failed legislation in light of its intentions. It is the academic social scientists, primarily in political science, public administration, and sociology, who claim to discover more constructive aspects to NEPA. At times evaluations of NEPA have been so strident and unqualified that academic sociology rather than scholarly rigor would seem responsible. Consider, for instance, a leading economic scholar's dismissal of NEPA: "The principal effect has been to slow passage of new legislation, the enactment of agency decisions, and the commencement of private sector projects. . . . Generally, the resulting impact statements are so voluminous that no one considers or even reads them, much less attempts to modify decisions on the basis of their findings" (Lave, 1981:126–27).

Setting standards and assessing risk. Most environmental legislation passed, or amended, since 1970 requires federal agencies to protect individuals from adverse health effects associated with exposure to hazardous or toxic substances, particularly carcinogens. The mandates commonly impose upon the implementing agencies—usually the EPA, the Occupational Safety and Health Administration (OSHA), the Food and Drug Administration (FDA), the Department of Agriculture, or the Consumer Product Safety Commission (CPSC)—responsibility for utilizing scientific research in two related ways: to identify levels of risk associated with varying human exposure to suspected hazardous or toxic materials ("risk assessment") and to specify permissible levels of human exposure according to statutory criteria ("acceptable risk").

Three problems inherent to risk assessment by public agencies were evident from the environmental era's beginning. The scientific data upon which agencies were expected to rely in defining "dose-response" parameters and other variables essential to risk assessment were incomplete and often inadequate. "The basic problem in risk assessment," the National Research Council has concluded, "is the spareness and uncertainty of the scientific knowledge of the health hazards addressed, and this problem has no ready solution" (National Research Council, 1983:6). Also, political values and ideological bias often appeared to influence the opinion of scientific experts, as well as administrators, in resolving technical problems and controversies associated with risk assessment and definitions of acceptable risk (Nelkin, 1984:preface; Mazur, 1981; Crandell and Lave, 1981; Conservation Foundation, 1984:261–318). The National Research Council identified at least fifty phases in the risk assessment process where uncertainty required scientists to make "inferential bridges" to continue the process (National Research Council, 1983:29–33; see also House and Schull, 1985:127ff.). The choice among the alternative "bridges" can apparently be influenced, as later discussion will illustrate, by political or economic bias.

Finally, the statutory criteria intended to guide agency identification of substances to regulate and acceptable risks of exposure are frequently vague and inconsistent, making discretionary judgments inevitable and obscuring how scientific and nonscientific criteria are actually related in the decision-making process. Chris Schroeder, for instance, has identified fifteen different environmental laws passed by Congress since 1969 involving at least three substantially different statutory formulae for defining acceptable risk. Even within single categories, the laws require different weighing of criteria and, sometimes, leave relative weights unspecified (Schroeder, 1984:13–17). The statutory language, in any case, is commonly vague:

The Clean Air Act: Regulates any "air pollutant . . . which . . . may cause, or contribute to, an increase in mortality or an increase in serious irreversible, or incapacitating reversible, illnesses" and requires a standard with "an ample margin of safety to protect the public . . . health" (Secs. 112[a][1] and 112[b][1][b]).

The Resource Conservation and Recovery Act: Regulates substances that "may cause, or significantly contribute to an increase in serious irreversible, or incapacitating reversible illness; or, pose a . . . hazard to human health or the environment" to a standard "necessary to protect human health and the environment" (Secs. 1004(5)(a)(b) and 3002–04).

Legislative histories often contribute little in clarifying legislative intent. Chronic obscurity of intent is one more reason why blaming Congress has become almost ritualistic among explanations for deficiencies in implementing environmental legislation.

Initial research on the implementation of risk-assessment procedures was conducted primarily by economists, lawyers, and natural scientists. This bespeaks the general lack of major theorizing and comprehensive studies of environmental decision-making processes among political scientists which Paul Sabatier and Geoffrey Wandesforde-Smith noted as late as the 1970s (Sabatier and Wandesforde-Smith, 1979). Like most social scientists, political scientists were slow to recognize that risk assessment constituted a new genre of public policy process to which many traditional concerns of policy analysis were relevant. However, by the end of the 1970s, a growing number of political scientists were examining at least three fundamental political issues involved in risk assessment: (1) in what ways is scientific data obtained and used by agencies in the risk-assessment process? (2) how important is scientific and technical data in comparison to economic or political considerations in risk assessment? and (3) how do varying procedural and structural arrangements for risk assessment affect the way technical information is used and conclusions are reached? (A useful survey of such studies may be found in Hadden, 1984:170–78.)

From this newer research have emerged some significant conclusions about the impact of scientific data and norms on agency decision-making. First, the deficiencies of scientific data and the difficulties in utilizing available data appropriately in risk assessment are fundamental reasons why agencies have had great difficulty in meeting the statutory deadlines for standard setting and enforcement in most recent environmental legislation, including, especially, the Clean Air Act, the Federal Water Pollution Control Act, and the Toxic Substances Control Act (Doniger, 1978; Lave and Omenn, 1981; Dorfman, 1982). Second, legislation containing a multiplicity of different, often inconsistent statutory criteria for determining acceptable risk in regulation—the norm for most environmental legislation, as illustrated by the Toxic Substances Control Act—forces administrators to adopt balancing formulas among scientific, economic, and political criteria in which scientific considerations are often subordinate or the relative weight of differing criteria is obscured (McGarity, 1979; Crandall and Lave, 1981:intro.).

Third, even statutory provisions requiring exclusively scientific criteria for administrative determinations of acceptable risk often do not prevent consideration of political and economic factors in the actual decision-making. This intrusion of presumably proscribed considerations has been found to affect risk assessment associated with standard setting under the Clean Air Act, the Federal Water Pollution Control Act, and the Safe Drinking Water Act, among others (Crandall, 1984; Crandall, 1981). Robert Crandall's blunt conclusion after studying risk-assessment procedures in five federal regulatory agencies in the latter 1970s depicts a situation frequently described by other researchers: "Regulators do not seek scientific contributions in a way that is likely to elicit the most helpful analysis and are not able to utilize the material they do receive. Both problems stem partially from the inability of agency heads to interpret inconclusive information. The problems are exacerbated by scientists' alienation from the chaotic, pressured world of the regulator" (Crandall and Lave, 1981:17).

Fourth, a small but developing set of studies suggests that political and economic bias may influence the methodologies preferred by scientists in assessing risk under conditions of uncertainty (McCray, 1983; Whitmore, 1983; Lynn, 1986). Frank Lynn's survey of research scientists involved in OSHA's risk assessment of carcinogens found, for instance, that the more politically and socially conservative scientists working for industry "chose scientific assumptions that decreased the likelihood that a substance would be deemed a risk to human health" while more politically liberal government and university scientists tended to favor assumptions increasing the probability that a substance would be deemed to require regulation (Lynn, 1983:41). Perhaps the most administratively significant implication of these findings is the debate raised about the efficacy in using a purely organizational arrangement to separate procedures for "risk assessment" from those for "risk management" in an attempt to free technical decision-making of "contamination" by political and economic bias.

A few studies suggest, more optimistically, that agencies improve their science base for regulatory decisions and their capacity to evaluate technical data when they have enough time to learn (Greenwood, 1984). These writings often assert that the uniqueness of the regulatory and scientific procedures mandated by environmental legislation in the 1970s did, in fact, force administrative innovation in which the quality of scientific data and its utilization improved as the decade progressed. But this more hopeful perspective remains a minority opinion.

Finally, research generally attributes to the federal courts a major influence in biasing agency decision-makers toward the most risk-averse definitions of acceptable risk when setting regulatory standards. This administrative "tilt" in the characteristic situation of scientific uncertainty attending agency risk assessment is presumed to benefit environmental interests and to amplify their influence in administrative risk assessment—as if to confirm their wisdom in promoting enhanced citizen access to the courts with environmental statutes and regulations (Melnick, 1983: chap. 10).

Is "uncaptured" better?

Only a few years into the environmental era researchers became less concerned about capture of environmental agencies and more troubled about the social and economic cost of achieving uncaptured agencies. And so things have remained. Few researchers, even after the early Reagan "regulatory reform," believe the EPA, the Office of Surface Mining (OSM), the National Oceanic and Atmospheric Administration (NOAA), or most other agencies with major new environmental responsibilities have been "captured" in the traditional way, or even in the more moderated manner of the current Nuclear Regulatory Commission where leadership and staff are unabashedly pro-nuclear but not always accommodating to specific utilities.

The (real or alleged) costs of capture. Most researchers, especially when discussing EPA's legislative mandate and its implementation, appear to accept the notion that the innovations intended to prevent "capture" have often entailed high costs: frequent inflexibility in implementation; at least some economic inefficiencies; program delays; and diminished agency credibility. The harshest criticism usually falls upon program deadlines and technological innovation mandated through "action forcing," and upon strict, risk-averse regulatory health criteria. Political scientist Charles Jones, early characterizing the Clean Air Act as "speculative policy," adopted a definition implicitly accepted by many other scholars for later environmental laws like TSCA, RCRA, and Superfund: "policy beyond capability . . . a response to estimates of what [Congress believes] will satisfy the public" (Jones, 1974:273).

Few researchers, environmentalist or otherwise, have a good word for the early administrative style of EPA and OSM, where environmentalist values were the most thoroughly institutionalized. Writers have commented on EPA's "legalistic," "confrontational," and "politicized" style, its legalistic approach to regulation, and its "rigidities" in interpreting its legislative mandate (Daneke, 1984; Vogel, 1986:178; Marcus, 1980:163). The OSM emerges from most descriptions of its first years under the Carter administration even more aggressive and uncompromising than EPA (Edgcomb, 1983:318; Harris, 1984: chap. 3). Some scholars have attributed this early zeal to staff and leadership inexperience, or a desire by agency managers to establish strong constituency bonds with environmental groups, or to other factors which time and experience might mitigate with better results.

But a significant number of critics (including many admittedly hostile to most environmental legislation of the 1970s) assert that the administrative style of 1970s environmental legislation renders agencies like EPA and OSM inherently incapable of learning from experience in ways that promote more administrative and economic efficiency. "The political constituencies that created most of [the new environmental agencies] . . . were largely unaware of and uninterested in the problems of potentially rigid and non-adaptive regulation," asserts a version of this argument. "Indeed . . . these are the very traits that were meant to ward off the evils of capture" (Bardach and Kagan, 1982:184; see also the collection of articles in Baden and Stroup, 1981). While researchers more sympathetic to environmental regulation customarily deny an inherent EPA incapacity to implement its regulatory responsibilities, they have often acknowledged that policy implementation depended less upon EPA initiative than upon the weight of pressure generated by environmentalist litigation and congressional oversight (Conservation Foundation, 1984b:432–42; Bartlett, 1984; Davies, 1984; GAO, 1981; GAO, 1983; GAO, 1984).

David Vogel has argued that the economic and administrative inefficiencies designed into the newer environmental agencies are unnecessary, in any case, because American interest-group politics has become too pluralistically competitive to permit business capture of new regulatory agencies. It is the very success of new nonbusiness groups like environmentalists, he asserts, that makes the "capture" they fear now improbable. "The significant increase in the number of non-business interest groups since the mid-1960s has made the making of public policies affecting business more public—and their outcomes more problematic" (Vogel, 1986:278).

The Office of Surface Mining Reclamation and Enforcement has been the most consistently criticized among all the new environmental agencies. It is hard to find a good word for the design of OSM's statutory mandate, its administrative structure, or its implementation of SMCRA even among scholars normally sympathetic to environmental regulation. Critics have been quick to assert that OSM's deliberate staffing with environmental partisans resulted in excessive zeal in enforcing program deadlines and regulation writing. Critics often cite OSM's alleged intransigence in requiring technology standards rather than performance standards for regulations affecting "restoration" of mined land to epitomize what they consider the worst "command and control" regulation. (Harris, 1985: chapters 7 and 8; Leone, 1979). OSM's brief but turbulent history and the resulting disruption in implementing SMCRA were, partially, the result of Ronald Reagan's early "regulatory reform" and not wholly the product of badly drafted and implemented legislation. Nonetheless, OSM's apparent rigidness in writing and enforcing regulations had become a problem even for President Carter, a strong proponent of surface mining regulation. The virtual silence of scholars in defense of OSM's performance during 1978–1987 suggests that it may become the "worst case" example of environmental innovation gone awry in the federal bureaucracy.

Backdoor capture and regulatory reform. The Reagan administration's early "regulatory relief" seemed to environmentalists the gravest threat of "capture" for federal agencies and programs they had sought to protect since the environmental era's beginning. This danger, moreover, was "capture" in a politically potent and untraditional style: through presidential administrative authority and staff agencies—primarily the Office of Management and Budget—with an intent to alter program objectives rapidly through budgeting and personnel change. "Regulatory relief" involved four related strategies: (1) reducing program budgets and priorities; (2) reducing and redistributing agency personnel; (3) requiring, when possible, that agencies adopt benefit/cost analysis when writing or revising regulations; and (4) requiring OMB review and approval of agency regulatory proposals when possible.

The first two strategies created the greatest public controversy and most immediate disruption at EPA, OSM, NOAA, and other agencies with environmental programs. These tactics also mired the Reagan administration in protracted, politically costly struggles with Congress and environmental groups that convinced the White House by 1984 to rely more on other means to achieve its purposes. The most drastic use of budget and personnel reductions to achieve "regulatory relief" occurred during the first three years of the Reagan administration. Between FY 1981 and FY 1984, for example, EPA's water quality program budget had been reduced by 59 percent, its air quality program by 31 percent, and its hazardous waste and toxic substances expenditures by 34 and 40 percent respectively (Crandall and Portney, 1984:67–68). During this period, EPA personnel declined by about 23 percent. Studies from the mid-1980s commonly assert that these techniques produced a major decrease in EPA's regulatory enforcement, in new regulations, and in the implementation of program deadlines (Vig and Kraft, 1984; Crandall and Portney, 1984).

Even greater disruption occurred in OSM, where during this period personnel were reduced by almost a third. The rate of ticket writing and other indicators of enforcement declined sharply between 1981 and 1983; OSM's technical assistance programs to the states almost ended; and judicial fines against violators of the law were largely uncollected (Menzel, 1983; Hendge and Menzel, 1985; Harris, 1985: chapter 8).

These swift changes were achieved without legislative amendment to the major laws enforced by the agencies or White House directives inconsistent with the laws' substantive intent. Nonetheless, the effect was to delay the laws' implementation, to constrict the administrative resources essential to carrying out the intent of the law, and otherwise to blunt the impact of the law. However, by the end of Reagan's first term Congress had restored a substantial portion of the reduced agency budgets. Agency reductions in work force and other personnel changes were largely curtailed or reversed. The most ideologically zealous "regulatory reformers" were eliminated from middle- and upper-level management at EPA, NOAA, and OSM. Nevertheless, most observers agree that budget and personnel policies of 1981 through 1984 significantly delayed implementation of most major programs at EPA and OSM, impaired enforcement of existing programs, and slowed essential research activities in major programs throughout most of Reagan's first term. The long-term consequences have yet to be calculated.

The new requirement that agencies prepare "regulatory impact analyses" (RIAs) when creating and revising environmental regulations, was issued as Executive Order 12291 in February 1981. It was the first White House directive requiring that a benefit-cost (b/c) test be applied and met in all cases where it was not expressly excluded by law. It also invested OMB with unprecedented authority to oversee agency compliance with the order "off" the public record in regulation writing or revision (Smith, 1984; Andrews, 1984). Environmentalists, convinced that b/c analysis was inappropriate and prejudicial to environmental regulation, feared its principal impact would be to subvert the goals of existing environmental legislation (Kasper, 1977; Green, 1977; Swartzman, Liroff, and Croke, 1982).

But subsequent studies suggest RIAs have had a very limited impact on environmental policy-making. Many environmental statutes, including the Clean Air Act and Clean Water Act, prohibit b/c analysis as a criterion for regulatory decision-making. Many regulations do not meet the $100 million impact criterion required for review under EO 12291. Thus, OMB deemed only 62 of 2,802 regulations appropriate for its review in the president's first year of office (GAO, 1984). OMB's tardy guidelines for preparation of RIAs and agency inexperience with the process produced many RIAs too technically deficient and confusing to be useful. Many agency officials have been reluctant to justify regulatory decisions on the basis of RIAs whose inherent limitations may not withstand rigorous judicial review. And RIAs quite often fail to identify the costs and benefits most important to decision-makers. EPA's experience is instructive. EPA's analyses are considered to be among "the most ambitious and detailed," yet they are rarely reported to have influenced regulatory decisions (Grubb, Whittington, and Humphries, 1984; see also Whittington and Grubb, 1984). Thomas McGarity's 1986 review of RIAs at EPA concluded that the documents were seldom influential in decision-making:

> The Agency's RIA Guidelines . . . acknowledge that cost-benefit analysis is of limited usefulness to real-world decisionmaking because determining which regulatory options are best in terms of economic efficiency often is made difficult by uncertainties in data, by inadequacies in analytical techniques, and by the presence of benefits and costs that can be quantified but not monetized or that can only be qualitatively assessed. . . . In actual practice the regulatory analysis documents are even less useful to the lead offices and the Work Groups. . . . Under the agency's typically tight schedules, the members of the Work Group must make decisions without awaiting the completed document. (McGarity, 1986:111–316).

Have RIAs then become a ritual? Some observers think the RIA process has made agency decision-makers more sensitive to regulatory costs and, sometimes, willing to propose alternatives that would not be considered on purely political grounds. The most costly policy alternatives can sometimes be identified and removed from agency consideration by using RIA procedures. Few researchers are willing to say much more.

The most significant impact of EO 12291 upon environmental programs appears to be the least overt. By vesting in OMB the authority to consult with environmental agencies "off the record" during the preparation of RIAs, the president's order armed OMB with enormous influence upon agencies during regulation drafting, review, and revision prior to formal proposal "on the record." During the first Reagan administration, notes Martin Belsky, OMB exerted this influence with considerable effect. "Some regulations were suspended or postponed because of direct requests by OMB . In other cases, fear of possible OMB action led agencies to modify rules they had previously adopted. OMB could, and did, both postpone and actively block regulations. Such regulations were placed in the 'black hole' of regulatory limbo as OMB, through its review power, indefinitely postponed promulgation" (Belsky, 1984:48). Because this influence occurs outside of the formal, public rule-making process required for most regulatory proposals, it is shielded from public scrutiny, and free of the strict judicial standards of documentation and due process required in formal rule-making. It has institutionalized, in the view of some scholars, the White House's "back door" influence on a rule-making process supposed to be free of covert participation by the chief executive or his subordinates.

Who or what got "hammered"?

Of the many "hammer" provisions in environmental legislation since the 1970s, strict compliance deadlines have been judged the least successful. The research literature is replete with examples, cited by partisans on all sides of the ideological debate over environmental regulation, to prove that deadlines routinely fail. As experience with environmental legislation increases, researchers have largely shifted from arguments over the efficacy of "action forcing" in achieving its stated objective—to force program completion within mandated periods—to arguments about the secondary benefits in action-forcing deadlines despite their failure.

Economists (almost always) and lawyers (usually) offer the bleakest appraisal of action-forcing deadlines. For different reasons, both tend to agree that action-forcing statutory commands are inherently flawed by failing to provide sufficient incentives for agencies and regulated interests to comply voluntarily with their provisions (Henderson and Pearson, 1978; Portney, 1978: chapters 1 and 2). The litany of alleged costs entailed in such predictable failure is usually assumed to greatly exceed any benefits. Among these costs: diminished agency credibility from repeated failures to meet compliance deadlines or to enforce them on regulated interests; litigation delaying agency implementation of the law; economic inefficiencies imposed upon regulated interests by unpredictability in enforcement of action-forcing laws; chronic agency resort to misinterpretation or evasion of the law in order to implement programs despite anticipated deadline failures; repeated congressional intervention in program implementation creating costly political externalities, and more. Shep Melnick's verdict is the epitaph others would apply to action-forcing: "The deadline has become a hollow symbol in search of tenable underpinning" (Melnick, 1983:128).

Not all researchers agree with these judgments. Some blame Congress for blunting the effectiveness of "action forcing" through excessive use. Richard N. L. Andrews, for instance, argues that EPA has been burdened with a congressionally created administrative "overload" (Andrews, 1979). Faced in rapid succession between 1970 and 1977 with responsibility for the Clean Air Act, Federal Water Pollution Control Act Amendments, the Safe Drinking Water Act, the Toxic Substances Control Act, and the Resource Conservation and Recovery Act, the agency was forced to set priorities among programs although it lacked formal authority to create such a comprehensive implementation agenda. It chose to concentrate first upon the major air and water pollution programs, leaving many deadlines in TSCA, RCRA, and the Safe Drinking Water Act deliberately unmet. From the perspective of the mid-1980s, Edward Woodhouse concluded, in a similar vein, that EPA's implementation of TSCA was impeded largely by forces "outside its control" (Woodhouse, 1985:501).

Many adverse judgments about the efficacy of action forcing were made before EPA and other environmental agencies had gained experience enough to make more constructive responses to mandatory deadlines. Stephen Cohen and Mark Tipermas, for example, have noted that EPA's earlier experience with program deadlines led it to anticipate problems in implementing the "Superfund" legislation of 1980. EPA began planning for Superfund implementation in advance of its passage so well that "it [was] possible to meet statutory deadlines, such as the promulgation of key regulations and the publication of a hazardous waste site response-priority list. Although the Reagan administration halted these efforts, they would have permitted the rapid implementation of superfund" (Cohen and Tipermas, 1983:56). And Jurgen Schmandt has argued that EPA is developing a promising organizational strategy for "integrated environmental management" of high-risk pollutants in response to the difficulties of dealing with single pollutants regulated under many different laws with different compliance deadlines (Schmandt, 1985).

Proponents of action forcing also argue that regulated interests and the regulatory agencies would achieve far less program compliance without the goad of compulsory deadlines—an assertion difficult to prove. Sometimes it is alleged that mandated deadlines give opportunity for proponents of regulation to use litigation as a means of forcing the pace of regulatory implementation. Even if unmet deadlines must be waived or recalculated, so the argument often runs, the threat of judicial intervention in agency decision-making encourages a better agency effort at program implementation than would be true without it. Although these arguments usually lack empirical confirmation, they have been persuasive to most environmental activists and their congressional allies.

Elsewhere in this book citizen participation is extensively reviewed. In discussing the impact of "hammer" provisions, however, it is useful to note a few widely accepted conclusions about the experience of federal environmental agencies with citizen involvement. The programs largely sponsored or supported by environmental agencies have endured a rapid transition from indifference through promotion to decline since 1970. Few agencies welcomed the newer forms of citizen involvement in administrative procedures, including intervenor funding, citizen "workshops" on new regulations, and more public hearings on proposed programs (Rosenbaum, 1976; Caldwell, Hayes, and MacWhirter, 1976). With the exception of the Corps of Engineers and OSHA, most federal environmental agencies provided, at best, indifferent support for these newer arrangements until the Carter administration (Strange, 1972; Cupps, 1977). For a brief period ending with Ronald Reagan's inauguration, the White House gave citizen participation a high priority, indicated by much greater agency resources and efforts expended on citizen involvement programs (Aaron, 1980; Tobias, 1982).

The Reagan administration's aversion to the newer forms of public participation was immediately evident in the thoroughness with which citizen involvement activities at EPA, OSM, NRC (Nuclear Regulatory Commission), OSHA, and the CPSC were practically eliminated within the administration's first six months. The political controversy provoked by early "regulatory reform" at EPA and OSM eventually compelled the Reagan administration to revive—but barely—citizen programs at EPA and OSM (Rosenbaum, 1983). The process of public review and comment required by NEPA for all EISs has been less affected by changing political seasons, and some observers have argued that the procedure has become a durable "early warning system" for environmental interests concerned with long-term implications of emerging agency policies (Caldwell, 1982:72). Today, the public involvement provisions of NEPA appear to be among the few public participation arrangements of the early 1970s with continuing vitality.

Judgments about the impact of citizen involvement on agency decision-making is fragmentary and mixed. Environmental groups had vigorously promoted citizen participation from a conviction they could use it to advantage. During its earliest years, EPA was able to use citizen participation activities to mobilize its environmentalist constituency in support of agency programs. Experiments with intervenor funding in administrative proceedings at EPA, like that at CPSC and OSHA, were generally judged to be helpful to the agency and valuable to environmental interests (Tobias, 1982). Citizen activities, largely organized through environmental groups, also had a strong influence on the content of numerous state implementation plans formulated in the early 1970s to implement the Clean Air Act (Sabatier, 1975). The Corps of Engineers in the middle 1970s promoted active and influential involvement programs, usually encouraged by environmental interests, in most district offices. Interest in these programs apparently waned in the latter 1970s and remained weak through the Reagan administration.

No environmental legislation written to date contains a more comprehensive provision for public involvement in its implementation than did SMCRA and its regulations. After an ambitious beginning under the Carter administration, however, OSM support for public participation in surface mine regulation at both state and federal levels was severely curtailed in the first Reagan administration and subsequently revived only slightly.

The most significant controversy of the 1980s over citizen involvement arises from public participation in the regulation of toxic waste sites. EPA and state agencies implementing TSCA, RCRA, and Superfund are required to provide public notice and public hearings on licensing of toxic waste sites and determinations of priority abandoned waste sites for cleanup. Many agency administrators, among others, believe that public involvement activities have intensified public distrust toward agencies responsible for toxic waste management. Public involvement allegedly favors the opponents of toxic waste depositories and waste sites, confuses and alarms the public about the risks involved in siting decisions, and generally makes scientifically safe location and management of toxic waste sites extremely difficult.

There is considerable evidence that public hearings and other involvement procedures have considerably slowed the pace of federal and state licensing of toxic waste storage and disposal facilities (Centaur Associates, 1979). Public hearings and other incidents of public controversy over scientific and technical data associated with toxic sites have probably encouraged public distrust, or confusion, toward government agencies and experts advocating specific siting decisions. But there is insufficient research to indicate how the quality of administrative decision-making has been influenced by these participation arrangements or whether public involvement is incompatible with timely and effective location and regulation of hazardous waste sites.

A New Administrative Agenda

Experience since the beginning of the environmental era now raises some fundamental questions about the appropriateness of the administrative structures and the quality of bureaucratic performance essential to achieve the nation's environmental goals. These issues, sometimes discussed but more often implied in the literature on environmental administration gradually accumulating since 1970, ought to head an agenda of research issues for environmental administration in the near future. In different ways, they emphasize that the time is ripe to use the inherited experience with environmental administration as a critical tool for appraisal and innovation in the decade ahead.

First, the difficulties in implementing major federal environmental programs since the 1970s are leading many observers to believe that effective environmental regulation requires, perhaps more than substantive changes in environmental laws, a major institutional restructuring of existing environmental agencies. The most commonly cited institutional flaws in the current design of federal environmental regulation are (a) a fragmentation of authority among too many separate and competitive agencies; (b) a tendency to force policy-making about major pollutants into a media-based organizational framework that impedes efficient and incisive approaches to the many pollution problems involving many different media; and (c) a need to create a greater institutional separation, leading to more political independence between the EPA and the presidency. Clearly, all these issues touch the EPA most directly; some are not new. The issue of EPA's organizational structure for dealing with major pollutants was raised when the agency was being designed in the early 1970s. Then, proponents of a media-based organizational structure, with separate components responsible for air, water, soil, and other pollution media, prevailed. It is the experience with "cross-media pollutants," such as acid rain or toxic substances, that raises the issue with fresh urgency.

The fragmentation problem, most often cited in regulating toxic and hazardous substances, became increasingly evident with the passage of TSCA and RCRA in the late 1970s. The independence of EPA regulatory procedures from excessive political manipulation and partisan intervention assumed major concern under the Reagan administration. This issue vastly transcends environmental affairs, however, because it raises important questions about the proper balance between agency independence and responsibility to the presidency. In broad perspective, it deals with the proper limits of the "administrative presidency" in an environmental context (Nathan, 1983). Nonetheless, the EPA experience of 1981–83 strongly suggests that the agency needs better structural and legal insulation between its scientific decision-making and ideological pressures originating in the White House.

Second, the literature on environmental administration is pervasively pessimistic about bureaucratic performance and capacities and seems to unite friend and foe of environmental regulation so otherwise divided. Typically, proponents of federal environmental programs enacted since 1970 tend to impute such failures to bureaucratic rigidities, the political power of regulated interests, congressional meddling in administrative affairs, and (since the Reagan presidency) the politicizing of environmental administration through the "administrative presidency." Critics of these programs, though equally likely to cite (different) bureaucratic rigidities for program failures, also commonly blame the "command and control" philosophy inherent in federal regulatory programs, the power of organized environmental groups, and the federal courts for program difficulties. Taken uncritically, this tacit consensus about program failures would seem a damning indictment of bureaucracy's role in federal environmental protection and a discouraging omen for the future. Yet there is empirical evidence that some programs, in some instances, have worked reasonably well—or, at least, that the environment has improved when the programs were operating (CEQ, 1981:21–32, 52, 57–59). It seems appropriate, in light of this bleak literature, to attack the issue directly and to encourage more research and writing that ask where programs have been successful and what bureaucratic factors can be discovered that distinguish between successful and unsuccessful program implementation.

Third, the literature of political science and closely related fields such as public administration contributes little to the understanding of most important issues concerning federal environmental administration. Most analytical writing about environmental policy and administration relevant to political science is produced by bureaucrats, former administrative officials, and consultants—primarily lawyers, economists, and others with experience in federal policy-making. Much of the writing about environmental administration involves partisan and philosophical debates about the relative virtues of various regulatory procedures. Notwithstanding the studies attempting to be more empirical and analytical, many of which have been cited, a great deal more is needed. A major institutional study of the EPA dealing critically with its structural inadequacies in the light of experience since 1970, for instance, would be welcome. Even good institutional histories dealing with the political experience of EPA, OSHA, OSM, or other important environmental agencies would be valuable.

Finally, it seems important to know if there are institutional "learning curves" in environmental administration. The environmental programs enacted by Congress since 1970 involve many new forms of regulation. The institutions implementing these programs are often new. Precedents and experience give no assistance in designing programs in many instances. The experience of environmental administration in the last several decades needs to be examined with attention to the capacity of institutions to change and innovate in response to experience—an approach that attacks, as well, the prevalent pessimism in much writing about environmental administration. One common criticism of environmental agencies since 1970 is that they are incapable of learning from their own behavior. "Environmental/regulatory agencies were not designed to carry on trial-and-error learning," conclude Eugene Bardach and Robert Kagan (Bardach and Kagan, 1982:184). Perhaps. The answer to the "learning curve" issue would take us a long way toward sound decisions about the need for institutional reforms in environmental administration. But the literature has yet to appear in satisfactory scope.

These issues are reminders that we are exceedingly early in the environmental era, that we have barely begun to ask the fundamental questions and assemble the necessary information to answer them. At the same time, the issues are a constant challenge to use the existing experience with environmental management more imaginatively and productively.

Some Propositions for Testing

This survey should suggest how ample are the opportunities for research about bureaucracy's impact on environmental administration and how many fundamental issues have yet to be carefully investigated. A number of what can be called "generic propositions" are suggested—broad theoretical issues amenable to numerous modifications and amplifications. Some of the more important include the following:

I. On the "environmental impact" process in the federal government:

A. Impact statements are likely to be least effective in traditional mission-oriented agencies, such as the Corps of Engineers or the Federal Highway Administration, where subgovernmental structures and distributive programs are well established.

B. Impact statements are likely to be influential in agency decision-making only when strong external oversight of the process is created through judicial, legislative, or White House action.

C. The EIS process has often been more politically important as an "early warning" system to alert organized interests to the environmental implications of agency decisions than as an influence on substantive agency decisions.

D. As the EIS process has become routinized in federal agencies, environmental interests have come to rely upon other procedures, such as litigation or public involvement activities, to influence environmental agencies.

II. On risk assessment procedures in environmental agencies:

A. Agency determinations concerning the degree of risk associated with potentially hazardous substances or technologies, and regulatory strategies for managing unacceptable risks, are always based upon multiple criteria including economic, political, scientific, and administrative considerations.

B. Regulators select from the many criteria that might be used to justify risk assessment and risk management decisions those criteria that are the most judicially defensible.

C. In administrative risk assessment procedures and judicial review of such procedures, scientists and other technical experts adopt professional opinions in technical controversies that are compatible with their political, economic, or ethical bias on such issues.

D. Scientific data almost never provide enough information to indicate how administrative decisions should be made during risk assessment procedures.

III. On the organization and performance of the EPA:

A. The institutional history of EPA will reveal that some programs have experienced a "learning curve" resulting in greater efficiency and effectiveness of operations over time.

B. The media-based organizational structure of the EPA inhibits efficient regulation by creating organizational rigidities and internal pluralistic power struggles that could be diminished through alternative organizational schemes such as substance-based regulatory units.

C. A major source of regulatory failure in EPA is a chronic insufficiency of financial and personnel resources.

D. The Reagan administration's efforts to achieve "regulatory relief" at

EPA seldom resulted in significant savings of money or more efficiency in regulation.

IV. On the Reagan administration's "regulatory reform" of environmental programs:

A. Under the Reagan administration, the President's Office of Management and Budget became an important influence in the substantive writing of environmental regulations and other policies in federal environmental agencies.

B. Benefit-cost analysis was not an important consideration in the writing and revision of environmental regulations during the Reagan administration.

C. "Regulatory reform" has resulted in a significant displacement of influence and authority in making environmental policy from the federal to state regulatory agencies.

D. Although controversy over "regulatory reform" was most intense during the first Reagan administration, the impact of such "reform" was significant during the second Reagan administration also.

9

The Courts and Environmental Policy

Lettie McSpadden Wenner

At the beginning of the environmental decade environmental activists made the conscious decision to take their demands to court. Many groups that lobbied Congress for new public laws controlling pollution and conserving natural resources believed they needed to monitor the administration of those laws and wrote into them provisions for citizen suits to help enforce the substantive requirements. Recognizing the success that economically powerless groups, such as the civil rights movement, had had in the judicial arena, many attorneys with environmental values argued that the courts offered the most promising forum for achieving their policy goals (Sax, 1971; Landau and Rheingold, 1971).

Since that time critics have argued that courts are peculiarly unsuited for making the tradeoffs necessary for comprehensive policy formulation (Glazer, 1975; Horowitz, 1977; Melnick, 1983). Alternative methods for resolving environmental conflicts, such as mediation, have been suggested (Bacow and Wheeler, 1984; Susskind et al., 1983). Supporters of courts as policy-makers, however, contend that courts are especially suited to uphold principles and values that are often lost sight of in the political arena (Chayes, 1976; Stone, 1974). It is the purpose of this chapter to examine the record of environmental policy-making in the courts for the last fifteen years and to suggest some additional types of research that might be undertaken in the future.

Modes of Judicial Research

Analysts of the judicial process in the United States are divided into two major categories. Traditional substantive interpreters of the law emphasize developing areas of law, many advocating a particular normative position regarding a given legal question. Because of its developing nature, environmental law has been subject to a great deal of interpretation by legal scholars in the 1970s and 80s. In recent years several law journals have been established that publish in the legal subfields of environmental law and natural resource management. Most of the research reviewed in this chapter falls into this category of substantive interpretation of landmark cases or categories of decisions defined by fairly narrow environmental topics.

In addition to exegesis of legal doctrine, nonenvironmental legal scholars have focused on the impact that court decisions have had on specific public policies (Johnson and Canon, 1984). These researchers have directed attention to landmark Supreme Court cases dealing with school desegregation (Rodgers and Bullock, 1976), defendants' rights (Canon, 1977), state/church relations (Birkby, 1966), and other civil liberties issues. A few environmental legal scholars have begun to follow this tradition, especially those interested in the impact of the National Environmental Policy Act (Anderson, 1973; Andrews, 1976; Liroff, 1976) and the Clean Air Act (Melnick, 1983).

Another group of scholars has, since the 1950s, attempted to explain and predict judicial behavior based on research models drawn from other social sciences. These judicial behaviorists have based their research on theories developed in other parts of the discipline, such as voter behavior and congressional policy-making. Many have directed their research toward individual justices of the U.S. Supreme Court and have postulated that public policy preferences of the men who have served on that court have been crucial in determining outcomes (Pritchett, 1948; Schubert, 1965, 1974). Others have argued that judicial philosophy or role theory (the judge's attitude toward the degree of restraint he should show for elected policy-makers) influences his decisions (Gibson, 1978).

Because of the limited number of justices who have served on the Supreme Court and cases decided yearly, students of that body have grouped all types of decisions together in order to develop a general measure of liberalism/conservatism. Some have divided this composite measure into two scales, cases involving civil liberties and those concerned with economics (Schubert, 1974); others split the civil liberties scale into individual freedom and equality scales (Spaeth, 1979). But with few exceptions (Dudley and Ducat, 1985), these studies have not broken down economic regulation, and it is this category into which the few environmental Supreme Court cases fall.

Students of judicial ideology have gone beyond demonstrating the consistency of individual judges' attitudes and have attempted to explain the origins of those values. Some have focused on the backgrounds from which justices and judges have come, demonstrating that Democratic judges and those with demographic profiles similar to Democratic voters tend to decide cases more liberally than do their Republican counterparts (Nagel, 1961; and Ulmer, 1985). Others have attempted to show that method of judicial selection (Watson and Downing, 1969) and especially the ideology of presidents who appoint judges is important in determining future court policy (Carp and Rowland, 1983).

In addition to variables at the individual judge level, other explanations have been suggested for variations in judicial policies. Group dynamics among judges on collegial courts appears to influence some judicial decisions (Murphy, 1964). Litigants and attorneys and their resources and strategy in litigation may have an impact on judicial outcomes. Some research has been done on specific interest groups' effects on policies made by courts, especially regarding civil rights (Vose, 1959; O'Connor, 1980). Other researchers have also pointed to the increased use of the courts by public interest groups (Orren, 1976), economic interest groups (O'Connor and Epstein, 1982), and environmental groups (Cook, 1980; Wenner, 1984). The socioeconomic and political context in which judges make their decisions has been shown to have some influence over outcomes, especially in civil rights cases (Giles and Walker, 1975) and draft protestor cases (Cook, 1977; Kritzer, 1978). Environmental cases' outcomes also appear to vary depending on the region in which the case is decided (Wenner, 1982). Despite the few exceptions, however, judicial behavioral studies have not been systematically linked to environmental legal doctrine. The latter has been extensive, however, and it is to that doctrinal analysis that we now turn.

Traditional Legal Research

The judicial branch has long been known as the third branch of government because its nonelective nature has relegated it to a subordinate position to the legislature and executive in a democratic political system. Yet their power to say "what the law is" (*Marbury v. Madison,* 1803) enables courts to overturn legislative actions whenever they offend the Constitution and to reverse administrative decisions whenever agencies abuse the power delegated by statute law. The law-defining power of the courts has long been a subject for controversy in our democratic society. Two forms this argument takes are: (1) a discussion about judicial restraint in applying constitutional principles and (2) deference to administrative discretion in interpreting laws.

In an administrative state, where technical expertise in policy areas such as the environment is crucial to understanding issues and making decisions, an increasingly large degree of policy-making power has been delegated to administrative agencies, not necessarily any more responsive to direct political control than courts. Legal commentators are divided in their opinion as to how much oversight courts should exercise over administrative discretion and how much freedom should be given to the experts who occupy administrative positions. One judge on the U.S. Court of Appeals for the D.C. Circuit, Harold Leventhal (1974), has argued that it is the courts' responsibility to guarantee that agencies take a "hard look" at all factors that should be considered when making their decisions. For agencies whose primary mission is distributing benefits or constructing public works, this hard look should emphasize environmental variables. For agencies engaged in regulating others' behavior in the name of the environmental or public health values, judicial review should focus on economic considerations.

NEPA Cases

The discussion about how much judicial review of administrative discretion is appropriate often takes place within the context of the National Environmental Policy Act (NEPA). In passing this law Congress attempted to reduce the first problem noted by Leventhal, the tendency of nonenvironmental agencies to overlook environmental values in making decisions. Formulators of NEPA hoped to achieve this result at two levels: through internal reform by forcing agencies to incorporate environmental values into their thinking, and through external oversight, by informing the public and other agencies about projects under consideration and eliciting comments from them. Evaluation of the effectiveness of NEPA has been mixed. Some observers have argued that writing environmental impact statements (EISs) for government projects has merely added to a process on which it makes no substantive impact (Fairfax, 1978). Others have observed some reform of the system (Liroff, 1976; Mazmanian and Nienaber, 1979).

It is at the second level, external reform, that the courts enter the process, because NEPA provides for citizen suits through which groups dissatisfied with the EIS process may sue any government agency for shirking its duty. Many who have analyzed the courts' impact argue that only the courts' insistence on strict application of the law in the early days of NEPA forced many agencies to write EISs at all, and to take seriously the information contained in them (Andrews, 1976; Liroff, 1976; Anderson, 1973). During the 1970s various federal courts struggled with procedural questions regarding NEPA: what constitutes a "major federal action" requiring an EIS, who should write it, when it should be written, and what kinds of projects are exempt (Claff, 1977; ABA Environmental Quality Committee, 1978).

Starting in the late 1970s, however, most commentators have noted a narrowing of the meaning of NEPA, brought about by certain Supreme Court precedents. In *Kleppe v. Sierra Club* (1976), the Supreme Court decided that an EIS is not required until there is some final federal action to review (Koshland, 1978). This decision reduced substantially the precedential value of *Calvert Cliffs v. AEC* (1972), through which the D.C. circuit had influenced many agencies to prepare EISs early in order to use those documents in planning. *Kleppe* also reduced the scope of EISs because it allowed the Department of Interior to write small EISs for each area to be strip mined without considering the cumulative impact of many such projects in one region. Some commentators greeted the *Kleppe* decision enthusiastically as providing a much needed corrective to premature EIS writing (Shafstrom, 1983). Others, including dissenting Justice Marshall, objected on the ground that if courts cannot control agency discretion until the project reaches its final stages, it will be too late to influence the vital planning process (McGarity, 1977).

In *Andrus v. Sierra Club* (1979) the Supreme Court continued to narrow the scope of NEPA by agreeing with the executive branch that the budget process was exempt from EIS requirements regardless of its impact on the environment (Shortsleeve, 1981). Two decisions—one each in the First and Second Circuits—allowing the leasing of sites in the outer continental shelf without considering the impact of oil production at those sites were regarded as setbacks for the environment (Fryer, 1979; Kameron, 1978). In *Defenders of Wildlife v. Andrus* (1979) the Ninth Circuit and later the D.C. Circuit concluded that a federal agency does not have to write an EIS when it considers whether or not to regulate state or private action with significant environmental impacts that it could legally control (Marek, 1980).

In conclusion, it appears that commentators in the early 1970s tended to view the courts' interpretation of NEPA as expanding its meaning and increasing public oversight of government actions. More recent cases, however, have considerably reduced the full disclosure aspect of NEPA, thereby diminishing the opportunity for oversight by opponents of public works projects. This tendency was initiated by the U.S. Supreme Court, which has taken a conservative view of most environmental legislation, and its precedents have considerably dampened lower federal courts' earlier enthusiasm for NEPA.

Nuclear Power Cases

The single NEPA case that has generated more commentary than any other is *Vermont Yankee v. NRDC* (1978), in which the Supreme Court overturned two District of Columbia Circuit decisions remanding Nuclear Regulatory Commission (NRC) decisions for inadequate treatment of environmental issues. Writing for a unanimous Supreme Court, Justice Rehnquist chastised the D.C. Circuit for interfering with NRC discretion and inserting its own policy preferences for that of an expert commission. Later the court issued two additional decisions, *Strycher Bay v. Karlen,* and *Baltimore Gas & Electric v. NRDC,* which made it even clearer that the high court considers NEPA's EIS-writing as a procedural requirement that requires no substantive content (Rubin, 1980).

Many comments in environmental law journals have tended to agree with Judge Bazelon's original D.C. Circuit decision in *Vermont Yankee* that would have required NRC to develop a complete record for courts to review in which intervenors would have been permitted to insert more of their substantive information opposing that of the agency (Raymond, 1979; Stewart, 1978; Edwards, 1980). Others agreed with the Supreme Court's unwillingness to allow the D.C. court to reprimand the NRC for regulatory leniency, arguing in favor of agency discretion and expertise (Byse, 1978; Breyer, 1978). One study attributed the decline of the nuclear industry partly to the ability of environmental groups to manipulate the judicial process in order to delay the permitting process and raise the costs of nuclear power (Cook, 1980).

Whatever their policy preference, however, commentators are in agreement that the net impact of *Vermont Yankee* has been to reduce the strictness with which NEPA is utilized to criticize agency actions. Some would remedy this situation by allowing other administrative agencies to provide oversight to NRC's activities—a policy suggestion first made and rejected when NEPA was being formulated (Liroff, 1976). Others would free lower federal courts from the strict procedural interpretation given NEPA by the Supreme Court (Davis, 1980; Goldsmith and Banks, 1983).

Vermont Yankee is only the most famous of Supreme Court decisions that favor nuclear power and the NRC over their critics. In *PANE v. NRC* the Supreme Court ruled that no EIS was necessary to discuss the psychological effects on residents near the disabled Three Mile Island plant when the second unit was reactivated (Jordan, 1984). The D.C. Circuit followed this general line of Supreme Court precedents when it decided there was no need for NRC to write EISs about exporting nuclear technology (Baer and Anderson, 1982).

Other cases concerning nuclear power have not involved NEPA. In *Duke Power Company v. Carolina Environmental Study Group* the Supreme Court declared constitutional the Price-Anderson act that relieved the nuclear industry of most of its liability for accidents (Varat, 1980). Although they differed about the extent to which lower federal courts should follow Supreme Court precedent, most commentators agreed that lower federal courts had originally increased their oversight of NRC decision-making. But the Supreme Court consistently rejected the importance of judicial oversight and insisted that lower courts reduce their second-guessing of the NRC's expertise (Johnson, 1978; Edwards, 1980).

While judicial oversight of NRC decision-making has tended to become more relaxed, the Supreme Court has recently allowed for increased state control of the nuclear power industry. Originally courts tended to interpret the Atomic Energy Act as preempting state control over any public health and safety matters because it assigned this responsibility to the Atomic Energy Commission (later NRC) (*Northern States Power v. Minnesota,* 1978). Nevertheless, traditional state authority to determine land use and economic need for additional power plants afforded them some control over siting individual plants within their jurisdictions. The passage of the Energy Reorganization Act in 1974, replacing the AEC with the NRC, and the 1977 amendments to the Clean Air Act, which gave EPA control over radioactive air pollutants, both reduced the exclusiveness of the NRC over nuclear safety and health concerns (Henderson, 1980). Finally, in 1983, the Supreme Court approved a California law banning further expansion of nuclear power in that state until the nuclear waste disposal problem is solved (*Pacific Gas and Electric v. California Natural*

Resources Commission). The value which the present Supreme Court assigns to states' rights appears in some cases to outweigh the importance of the exclusivity which the Court gives to NRC's control over nuclear power.

Water Pollution Cases

Pollution control laws differ from NEPA in the important sense that they do not attempt to control polluting activities of the federal government. Rather they have given to the U.S. Environmental Protection Agency (EPA) authority to control private and state activities to reduce their polluting effects. Hence judicial deference to agency discretion in these cases would appear to strengthen environmental interests, whereas judicial insistence on Leventhal's hard look would seem to favor critics of the control program.

The Clean Water Act (CWA; formerly, the Federal Water Pollution Control Act) originally set very ambitious goals: making the waterways of the U.S. "swimmable and fishable" by 1983 and free of any manmade pollutants by 1985. These goals, however, were gradually relaxed, first by the courts and later by Congress throughout the 1970s. Those who agree with such changes argue that they reflected a recognition of the need to consider the high costs to society of pollution control. Critics believe they represent an erosion of our commitment to public health goals. Whatever one's policy preference, however, it is generally agreed that recent changes in the law strike a new balance between economic and environmental values.

Eight years of litigation in the 1970s over Reserve Mining's dumping of taconite tailings into Lake Superior resulted in several decisions rendered by different federal and state courts and illustrates many of the problems of administering the Clean Water Act. The author of one case study concluded that the end of the case, a settlement worked out between the state of Minnesota and the corporation, was a classic case of balancing concern for public health with the economic well-being of several communities and their industry (Bartlett, 1980). Another study, financed by the industry, examined the same convoluted history and concluded that the on-land disposal solution agreed to by the court was not worth the cost to the company (Schaumberg, 1976). A third, a former EPA lawyer who had been involved in the litigation, interpreted the dismissal of the judge who had been sympathetic to public health arguments and the refusal of the Justice Department to continue the case as evidence of industry's capacity to influence the judicial process (Bastow, 1986).

Enforcement of the CWA occurs in two phases. In the first, EPA sets effluent standards for each industry based on current pollution reduction technology. In phase two, EPA or an EPA-authorized state agency issues a National Pollution Discharge Elimination System (NPDES) permit to each point source (municipal sewage treatment plant, or industrial plant) specifying the percentage reduction of each pollutant and the deadline for its achievement. In addition, variances may be granted to each source which postpone the deadline by which the reduction in pollution must be achieved, or reduce the requirement altogether (Rodgers, 1977; Schoenbaum, 1983).

Industry has challenged the discretion of EPA before federal courts at all of these stages. Industry attorneys began with procedural challenges, arguing that EPA had not provided an appropriate hearing or sufficient notice to interested parties to comment on the regulations. EPA was able to meet these challenges primarily by slowing its processes (McKinnon, 1979). Substantive challenges by industry were more difficult to meet, as all federal circuits insisted EPA demonstrate in its administrative record that it had taken Leventhal's hard look at all the legally relevant factors for setting effluent standards. The standards for old sources of water pollution were divided by the 1972 amendments into two levels, "best practicable" and "best available." The former was designed to be less strict and to require that the agency balance the cost to industry against the demonstrated benefits to the community brought about by cleaner water. In setting best-available treatment, EPA had only to consider cost along with other factors (*Appalachian Power v. Train,* 1976).

In *DuPont v. Train* (1977) the Supreme Court also required EPA to provide for variance procedures for both best-available and best-practicable treatment permits; only new source performance standards (NSPS) were to be exempt from the variance procedure (McKinnon, 1979). In 1977 Congress amended the CWA to replace the best-available technology with conventional and nonconventional treatment; only toxic pollutants are to be subject to best-available treatment (Voytko, 1977). EPA, however, has been slow to identify any pollutants as toxic and only agreed to name a few in order to settle a lawsuit against it by the Natural Resources Defense Council (*NRDC v. Agee,* 1976). Recent industrial challenges have been made to EPA's data base and its lack of understanding of the engineering problems in treatment processes. The decline in EPA administrative and research capacity in the 1980s gave industry's challenges, based both on economic costs and technical incapacity, even greater credibility in court.

Another major issue that has received attention from the courts is that concerning federal common law remedies available to private litigants. In the first 1972 *Illinois v. Milwaukee* case the Supreme Court appeared to give credence to the concept that individuals injured by pollutants that met current legislated standards would still have recourse to common law if they could demonstrate injury (Leybold, 1978). After several federal circuits had utilized this precedent to find a common law remedy in some cases (Weiland, 1980), the Supreme Court reversed the Seventh Circuit in *Illinois v. Milwaukee II* and declared that the 1972 amendments to the CWA had covered so comprehensively the subject of water pollution in the U.S. there was no need for any federal common law (Torti, 1981). At least one disapproving commentator argued that this misconstrued Congress's intent and gave legal imprimatur to actions that might have been illegal before the passage of the CWA (Collins, 1984). Thus Milwaukee could obtain multiple variances from the state of Wisconsin for repeated sewer overflows without any remedy for downstream users because it possessed a valid permit to discharge. Collins (1984) argued that Congress ought to put back into the CWA by amendment what the Court had eliminated through interpretation.

In 1981 commercial fishermen attempted to obtain damages for sewage that had reduced their ability to earn a livelihood, but the Supreme Court decided they had no private cause of action under the CWA (*Middlesex County Sewerage Authority v. National Sea Clammers*, 1981). Citizen suit provisions may be used only in cases where the public law has failed to protect the general public against water pollution damage (Manning, 1981). Neither federal common tort law nor the regulatory scheme devised by Congress appears to afford relief to individuals suffering property loss due to water pollution (Bleiweiss, 1983). Formerly private parties had used Section 1983 of the Civil Rights Act to assert rights given them under the Constitution and other federal laws. The Supreme Court's ruling in *Middlesex* appears to eliminate this protection for any laws with enforcement mechanisms unless Congress writes in a specific savings clause. Critics of the case argued withdrawing previous protection should require an affirmative act by Congress (Private, 1983).

Hazardous Waste Cases

One of the major problems of water pollution not covered by the CWA is groundwater contamination which stems from a number of sources, including spraying commercial poisons to control pests in agricultural and residential areas; injection of toxic wastes into deep wells; and drainage from landfills where toxic liquid and solid wastes are frequently deposited. Some commentators have tried to piece together a regulatory scheme to control such problems from existing laws, but most agree a more comprehensive law is needed at the federal level (Tripp, 1979; Dycus, 1984). The laws designed to address this problem most directly are the Resource Conservation and Recovery Act (RCRA), and the Comprehensive Emergency Response, Compensation, and Liability Act (CERCLA). Together these laws constitute a far from comprehensive scheme for controlling groundwater pollution (Rea, 1982), and a considerable legal commentary is being developed arguing about the merits and demerits of the present and proposed laws.

RCRA provides for the tracking of hazardous wastes from their generation through their transportation and disposal at special landfills designed to contain and monitor the leachate from these sites for thirty years. Few of the framers of the legislation believed in 1976 that monitoring toxic liquids left in metal containers underground for a limited time would solve the problem of contaminating the groundwater, and RCRA was substantially revised by the Congress in 1984. During the interval many interim permits for toxic waste dumps were issued, based on current practices at preexisting sites (Deutsch et al., 1983). However, little progress was made in the creation of more stringent permanent permits that would resolve the conflict between those who believe land burial constitutes a safe disposal technique for toxic wastes and those who wish to develop alternative methods, such as incineration and chemical fixation.

Two major problems remain. Communities have become increasingly reluctant to host hazardous waste sites because of publicity about leaks from abandoned waste disposal sites such as Love Canal (Wolf, 1980). Since EPA has failed to issue stringent permanent standards for operating sites, many states and localities have responded by simply refusing to allow any new hazardous landfills to be sited in their jurisdictions. Spokespersons for the disposal industry argue that a central authority (federal or state government) should be empowered to override local objections to new sites because toxic wastes are being produced at increasing rates. Others also concerned about the availability of storage space for toxic wastes argue that arbitration between developers of disposal sites and local authorities should be developed, as in the state of Massachusetts (Bacow and Milkey, 1982). Alternatively, or in addition, states might cooperate by forming interstate compacts and selecting regional sites for the most hazardous wastes, as are being developed for low-level radioactive wastes (Florini, 1982). At present there is an impasse between those who seek new sites and others who prefer to find alternatives to land disposal. Court action has been rare since there are few real standards to enforce at presently operating sites. However, there have been some case studies of particular sites (Wenner, 1987).

Under CERCLA the U.S. government was charged with identifying and cleaning up abandoned hazardous waste dumps that constitute a threat to public health. After doing so, the law provided that costs of cleanup could be recovered from those who owned the site and had profited from its operation. CERCLA left two major problems unaddressed. One was how liability was to be assessed among the several responsible parties (past and present owners of the site, producers and haulers of waste to the site). Congress refused to address this problem because of differences among its members about how strict the law should be. Some commentators have argued that federal courts should develop a federal common law to address this problem and should assign joint and several liability to all contributors to the problem. Under such a rule the government would be able to recover its costs for cleaning up such abandoned sites from any party it could prove contributed to the damage (Joint and Several Liability, 1982). Such writers argue that it is not possible to apportion responsibility for specific parts of the damage because of the mixed nature of the hazard. Applying joint and several liability would place the burden of demonstrating that damages could be divided among multiple tortfeasors on the defendant rather than forcing the plaintiff to show that the damage is indivisible (Luster, 1982–83).

One indication that federal courts may be willing to undertake the development of such common law occurred in a 1982 oil spill case. In *U.S. v. M/V Big Sam* the U.S. Court of Appeals for the Fifth Circuit ruled that both the vessel that caused the accident and the tanker that spilled the oil were jointly and separately liable for costs of cleanup. This was determined under federal maritime common law despite the fact that the CWA limits recovery of damages to the value of the vessel causing the spill. The Fifth Circuit, unlike the Supreme Court in *Illinois v. Milwaukee II,* decided that in order for Congress to preempt other federal remedies, it would have to do so affirmatively in the CWA (Brooks, 1983).

Another major gap in the comprehensiveness of CERCLA was the lack of any statutory remedy for persons suffering personal injury from abandoned waste sites such as Love Canal (Tauberman, 1983). Some commentators argued that because of the Supreme Court's rulings in water pollution cases there could be no development of federal common law in this area either. Victims would have to rely for any recovery on the varied liability rules of different state laws (Dore, 1981; Hinds, 1982). Other legal writers argued that strict liability (no need to demonstrate negligence or intent to do harm by the dumpers) should be applied by state courts in personal injury cases stemming from abnormally dangerous activities, that is, nonnormal land uses in inhabited areas (Baurer, 1980). Admittedly, however, state common law varies on this subject, and it will be difficult to establish a uniform common law throughout the U.S. without using federal common law (Dore, 1981). Both the issues of joint and several liability for multiple responsible parties and of private party injuries will doubtless be discussed at length in the federal and state courts unless or until Congress makes a more definitive statement of national policy than CERCLA now represents.

The primary means for cleaning up hazardous waste disposal sites rests with EPA, the responsible administrative agency. When EPA began to enforce the law, it chose to do so by utilizing an obscure part of CERCLA (section 106) designed for responses to emergency situations. It ignored the major remedial action provided in CERCLA which allows the government to clean up the area (section 107) and then recover costs from the responsible parties (section 102) (Dorge, 1984). Just why EPA chose this technique is unclear. One possible explanation is the fact that action under 106 is considered "voluntary" private cleanup and enables the agency to settle with the owner of the dump with minimal expense to both and minimal cleanup. Action under 107, however, requires uniform nationwide standards and liability; by avoiding use of this section of the law, EPA has reduced the effectiveness of CERCLA. Some judges have noted this result with critical comment (*U.S. v. Wade,* 1983; Wenner, 1984). By relying almost exclusively on section 106, EPA has placed the question of what constitutes cleanup squarely in the forum of the federal courts. The latter are faced with the task of fashioning a common law of hazardous waste cleanup, a result that contradicts the Supreme Court's preference for comprehensive statutory solutions (Dorge, 1984). The typical EPA response has been to dig up buried hazardous waste and move it to new locations. This policy, together with present RCRA regulations for landfilling wastes, has been interpreted to mean that wastes relocated from old dumps may create new Superfund sites in the future (Office of Technology Assessment, 1983).

Clean Air Cases

The single environmental issue about which the most legal research has been done is air pollution. The Clean Air Act (CAA) represents a regulatory scheme similar to that under the CWA with certain exceptions, the most important of which is the law's reliance on ambient air quality standards rather than emission treatment standards. National ambient air quality standards (NAAQS) were set by EPA after passage of the 1970 amendments of the CAA, and a multilayered method of achieving them was devised. Emissions from mobile sources (cars, trucks) are regulated nationally, but only major new stationary sources are regulated by state agencies under state implementation plans (SIPS), which vary with the ambient air conditions where they apply (Currie, 1980; Schoenbaum, 1982).

One issue raised early in the CAA's implementation was whether areas that were already in compliance with NAAQS were subject to regulation. Although some authors have argued that Health, Education, and Welfare (EPA's predecessor in the clean air field) originally intended to regulate attainment (clean) areas, the 1970 amendments to the CAA were interpreted by EPA to apply only to nonattainment (dirty) areas (Walker and Storper, 1978). Landmark litigation in the D.C. Circuit (*Sierra Club v. Ruckelshaus,* 1972) forced EPA to develop regulations to control emissions in attainment areas (Branagan, 1977). This decision survived on appeal when the Supreme Court, missing one justice, divided evenly on the vote to uphold (*Fri v. Sierra Club,* 1973).

One critic of this case argues it resulted in unnecessary and uneconomical waste of administrative resources in writing regulations (Melnick, 1983). Later these regulations were incorporated into the 1977 amendments to the CAA and gave rise to two different enforcement strategies depending on whether the air in a region was clean or dirty. Both involved the location of new sources of pollution. Siting major new sources in attainment areas depends on a review process to "prevent significant deterioration" (PSD) that shows the new emissions will not push the area over the increments in pollutants allotted to it. According to the original 1970 CAA, if nonattainment areas did not reach NAAQS by 1977, EPA could prevent new industrial plants from locating there.

To avoid this unpopular result, EPA in 1976 developed the concept of offsets—tradeoffs that enabled new sources to add to the pollution load in dirty areas by getting an old source in the same area to reduce its pollution load a greater amount (Landau, 1980b). The 1977 amendments to the CAA ratified this modification, and in 1979 EPA wrote regulations allowing industry to "bank" emission rights for later use if a new source was not available at the time an old source was retired (Emission Offset Banking, 1980).

A technique common to both attainment and nonattainment areas is the development of new source performance standards (NSPS) for all major plants within one industrial type. All of the NSPSs have been challenged when developed by EPA, just as CWA regulations were. Some of the most controversial were those developed for new fossil-fuel-fired electric power generators. In 1979 EPA settled on a strategy that required all major new generators to scrub the emissions from their stacks to reduce sulfur oxides on a sliding scale. This was accomplished only after an intense debate within and outside the agency over whether all emissions should be reduced equally (Ayers and Doniger, 1979) or whether a sliding scale should be developed depending on the sulfur content of the coal (Badger, 1979). The latter strategy was accepted and was criticized by some as being too responsive to industry pressure (Banks, 1981) and by others as too harsh and economically inefficient (Ackerman and Hassler, 1980, 1981). The latter argued that more sulfur reduction could be achieved less expensively by allowing the industry to determine its own strategy (substituting lower sulfur coal, for example). Agency spokespersons countered with arguments about the accuracy of the critics and the difficulties of policing different control techniques (Smith and Randle, 1981). The issue for critics on all sides was the appropriate role that courts should play in the process. Both sides hoped that the judiciary would force EPA to revise its strategy either to restrict industry further or to give it more discretion. However, the D.C. Circuit upheld EPA on this issue (*Sierra Club v. Costle,* 1981).

Questions about how much discretion should be given to EPA by Congress and how much freedom should be passed on to states and industry to determine their own pollution control strategies have been adjudicated in many forms under the CAA. Economists have long argued that pollution control can be achieved most efficiently by allowing industry to reduce easily treated emissions extensively in exchange for little or no treatment of emissions that are expensive to treat (Kneese and Schultz, 1972). The acceptance of offsets by EPA, Congress, and the courts was one method of accommodating such economic theory to the regulatory system of the CAA (Pedersen, 1980).

Another indication of the new emphasis on economic costs of pollution control is the concept of a bubble placed over a single industrial plant. Originally a stationary source of air pollution was defined to mean one smokestack, furnace, or other point source. Critics of the system, however, argued that such a definition tied industry to a fixed technology defined by EPA as the best available and eliminated the possibility of finding innovative methods for treating pollutants. Instead they favored considering entire industrial plants as one source and allowing for an increase in pollution from one part to be compensated for by phasing out or diminishing the emissions from another part of the "same source" through the idea of a bubble placed around the entire factory (Landau, 1980).

When EPA attempted to apply the bubble concept to modifications of old sources in nonattainment areas, the D.C. Circuit struck it down on the grounds that the CAA did not allow for such a definition of "source" (*ASARCO v. EPA,* 1978). Nevertheless, EPA went on to apply the bubble idea to old sources in attainment areas, and in *Alabama Power v. Costle,* 1979, the D.C. Circuit explicitly agreed to this strategy for old sources in clean areas (Del Calvo y Gonzalez, 1981). It still maintained the ban against using the bubble to avoid applying NSPSs in all areas. This decision was the result of a divided court in which some judges, such as Wright, preferred a stricter reading of the CAA, and others, such as Wilkey, wanted to liberalize it.

Thus an old plant in a clean area could add components to its facility without going through the PSD review process or applying best-available controls to it as long as an equivalent reduction in pollutants was achieved somewhere else in the facility. The two cases were incompatible according to some commentators and needed to be reconciled. Some argued that the bubble concept should be applied widely in both dirty and clean areas in order to reduce costs of pollution control (Landau, 1980b). Others felt that while the bubble was legitimate for clean areas, it should be prohibited in nonattainment areas because of the threat to human health that was not diminished by simply maintaining the status quo (EPA's Bubble, 1980). Others opposed the notion of bubbles altogether as affording industry a way out of applying the latest pollution control technology to its new plants, thus retarding the improvement of air quality around the country (Rodgers, 1977). The trend, however, within the agency and in federal courts has been to liberalize the definition of source and provide for trading emission reductions for increases both within the same industrial complex and between facilities.

In addition to accepting the bubble concept, in *Alabama Power v. Costle* the D.C. Circuit took a very hard look at other EPA regulations about attainment areas and made several modifications, most of which favored industry. Prevention of significant deterioration (PSD) is based on the idea that clean areas should be allowed to gradually increase their pollution levels based on the air quality in the region on a given date. Originally EPA wanted this date to be uniform throughout the country, but the D.C. Circuit ruled that each area could have a unique baseline date depending on when the first major new pollution source applied for a permit. Major source was defined by the court as plants emitting at least 100 to 250 tons of pollutants per year calculated according to how much the plants can emit with controls in place operating a limited workday, rather than the physical potential for all emissions, on which EPA had based its regulations (Floy, 1981).

Just as individual judges on the D.C. Circuit differed about the definition of "source" of pollution, so too have there been differences of opinion among the several circuits. One disagreement centered on EPA's discretion in designating nonattainment areas. Industry argued that this could be accomplished only after notice and comments under the Administrative Procedures Act. However, EPA finessed this process on the grounds that it did not have time to observe these procedures and meet the statutory deadline for getting SIPs in place. The Third, Fifth, and D.C. Circuits agreed with industry and set back EPA's implementation schedule two years in the process. The Sixth and Seventh, however, agreed with EPA, thus creating different target dates depending on the region of the country involved (Feldman, 1982). The Ninth Circuit agreed with EPA that it could use outside contractors to conduct inspections of plants, while the Tenth and Sixth said that only employees of EPA were empowered to perform this function (Simmons, 1983).

One problem arising from air pollution presently creating controversy in law journals is atmospheric deposition—sulfate and nitrate fallout which leads to acidification of lakes and soils. This problem has been exacerbated in recent years by the administration of the CAA. Requiring that concentrations of pollutants be reduced in local air-quality control regions led some dischargers to adopt a tall-stack strategy to disperse their emissions at a greater distance and thus avoid treating them. Originally many states wrote such techniques into their SIPs, and EPA acquiesced. A Fifth Circuit case struck down such SIPs (*NRDC v. EPA,* 1974) and Congress later ratified this decision through the 1977 amendments. Nevertheless, some degree of dispersion is still allowed to count in the cleanup, and many such tall stacks were built in the intervening period (Wetstone, 1980). This strategy and the increasing number of sources of sulfur and nitrogen oxides have led to increasing accumulations of acid rain in the eastern U.S. and Canada.

Those concerned about the problem tend to agree that the present CAA is unlikely to have any impact on acid rain in the near future. Only sulfur and nitrogen oxides are directly controlled by the law, not the sulfates and nitrates that compose acid rain because these form in the upper atmosphere. Ambient air quality standards apply only to air close to ground level where it can be said to have an effect on the health of people, not to atmospheric conditions (Hartman, 1983). The only legal remedy that appears to remain is the common law of nuisance, whose application has been weakened by the Supreme Court's denial of common law remedies where comprehensive statute regulation exists (Acid, 1982). Potential for change rests either on congressional action or on the slim possibility that environmental attorneys will succeed in convincing courts that the CAA does not represent a comprehensive legislated approach to air pollution.

Clearly there are many issues that remain to be resolved by the courts. The CAA has been attacked by environmental groups and industrial opponents alike. Each would like to see the courts rein in EPA when it believes its own policy preferences will be advanced in so doing. Both have been successful in obtaining some of their goals through the courts. Some commentators believe the courts have been overly concerned about environmental values to the detriment of the economy (Melnick, 1983). However, most recent legal commentary has focused on cases in which courts, like the executive branch, have demonstrated their concern that costs of pollution control not become excessive.

One analyst who disagrees with this conclusion is Melnick, who investigated in depth the impact of six different decisions (or groups of cases), and concluded that in each instance the courts had a deleterious impact on air pollution control policy. He does not base his criticism primarily on the courts' interpretation of the laws, but rather on the policy impact that their decisions have had. He argues that in most cases they have forced EPA to act more strictly than is practical; expend its limited resources on unimportant issues; and generally tie the hands of administrators who should be freer to make bargains with industry to get what is possible in the way of pollution reduction rather than stick to the unrealistic goals that Congress has set (Melnick, 1983).

Judicial Oversight: Conclusions

Comment about courts' interpretations of environmental policies in the early 1970s focused on the courts' insistence that the laws be strictly adhered to, oftentimes beyond the more relaxed interpretation of the agencies responsible for their administration. In some cases these interpretations led to amendments that increased the strictness of the law in question. At the same time, however, other amendments relaxed originally optimistic goals for reducing pollution. These legislated changes may have been due to political shifts in the country which led to an altered approach to environmental issues from the executive branch of government. These same factors, together with the increased litigation activity of industry, have influenced courts, too, to change their interpretations of the laws. Opinion among commentators continues to be divided between those who prefer greater or less regulation of the environment, and their perception of the courts' impacts is colored by their own policy preferences. Legal comment in the 1980s tends to center on judicial rulings that relax regulations and accept arguments against strict environmental controls.

All arguments about environmental law in court eventually come down to the issue of how much judicial oversight should be made of administrative decisions. In some cases the Supreme Court has appeared to favor extreme discretion for agencies on the ground that administrators understand the policy issues and technical problems better than anyone else, as in the nuclear power cases. In other situations involving agencies other than the NRC and laws other than the Atomic Energy Act, the high court has taken a more critical look at what the agencies have done. The latter reaction occurs frequently when the appellant bringing its case to the Court is industry, and the agency against whom the complaint is made is a health or environmental one.

One example of the Supreme Court's rejection of an agency's expert judgment occurred in 1980 when the Court agreed with the Fifth Circuit's remand of the Occupational Safety and Health Administration's (OSHA's) benzene standards for worker exposure (Linet and Bailey, 1981). The plurality of a divided court ruled that OSHA had not produced sufficient evidence to demonstrate that its standard was necessary to protect human health. Four justices, however, disagreed with this conclusion, but neither side was willing to address the crucial question of whether OSHA must produce a cost/benefit analysis to justify any of its decisions. Justice Rehnquist went so far as to revive the New Deal Court's argument that Congress had overdelegated its policy-making function to the executive branch (Rodgers, 1981). In comparing the *Vermont Yankee* case with the benzene case, it appears that at least a plurality of the justices is more willing to allow lower federal courts to review agency decisions when they are under challenge from industry on the grounds of cost rather than from the public on the grounds of safety or health.

Judges at all levels of the federal system recognize the problems of conducting oversight of expert agency decisions. They also differ regarding the appropriate balance to be made between economic costs and environmental/health values, and potential litigants obviously understand and use this information in seeking favorable forums for their cases (McGarity, 1980). Conscious of the problems of second-guessing expert agency decisions, judges have developed various strategies for coping with the problem. Judge Leventhal of the D.C. Circuit has argued for judges to have access to court-appointed scientific experts for assistance in understanding the conflicting testimony of adversarial expert witnesses. Others have argued the need for a "science court" composed of natural scientists to define the common ground among experts over controversies involving natural science phenomena (Kantrowitz, 1975; Martin, 1977). Certain of Judge Leventhal's colleagues, for example, Judge Bazelon of the D.C. Circuit, are more skeptical of expert judgments about uncertainty, and would prefer to insist on procedures designed to ensure that all opinions about an issue are incorporated into the agency decision-making process itself. Obviously attitudes about the importance of economic and health considerations and about the fallibility of experts vary among judges, as they do among other people. These values are often masked by a procedural discussion of the appropriate role that judges should play in reviewing agency decisions.

Some analysts argue that judges are singularly unsuited to make broad policy decisions because of their lack of expertise and the necessity for them to answer individual questions about particular cases (Horowitz, 1977; Melnick, 1983). Others caution against the dominance of technical experts and urge the continued use of lay judges to counterbalance the inequities that are certain to arise when there is an unrestrained technocracy controlling policy (Tribe, 1972; Yellin, 1983). As one student of the administrative process has indicated, the balance moves continually between a preference for substantively "correct" decisions reached by technical experts and democratically derived solutions with public participation encouraged and facilitated by the courts' insistence on due process (Shapiro, 1982).

At the present time this discussion about judicial oversight is complicated by the fact that agency values and positions have shifted in the last decade. Formerly expert judgments by agencies charged with maintenance of the public health and safety, such as EPA and OSHA, could be assumed to reflect an emphasis on those values. After the 1980 election and the shift within the executive branch to emphasize economic values and deregulation, such assumptions became problematic. Courts, too, including the D.C. Circuit, have experienced some change in personnel to reflect a more business-oriented ideology. Hence judicial decisions should not be expected to compensate for the change in executive branch orientation. Congress, on the other hand, has reacted against loosening enforcement of environmental laws by beginning to tighten up requirements in certain legislation, as in the RCRA amendments of 1984. Courts in the 1990s are likely to face ever more detailed laws pertaining to increasingly technical issues, as Congress attempts to delegate less discretion to the executive. This is only likely to heighten the differences among judges regarding their own opinions on these issues as all actors in the controversies seek their day in court.

Directions for Future Research

Doctrinal development of environmental law has been extensively treated in the last fifteen years; the above review constitutes only a sampling of the topics that have been addressed. Given the propensity for jurisprudents to write on developing areas of law, it seems likely that the newest laws, such as those dealing with hazardous and solid waste disposal issues, will continue to be emphasized. With few exceptions, however, there has been little effort to link this literature with general policy discussions. One promising area of research that could help to make this linkage is impact analysis, through which the effects of major landmark court decisions can be tracked in the broader political arena. This approach has been used in examining NEPA's impact (Anderson, 1973; Liroff, 1976) and that of the Clean Air Act (Melnick, 1983). It could be expanded to include other important laws in the pollution control field, tracing congressional responses to court decisions through legislative amendments and administrative responses through altered regulations. Some students of the congressional process regard court precedents as one major impetus for change. Students of the courts could consider court decisions as independent variables capable of making a difference in the policy-making process. The impact of important cases could also be traced at the local and state government levels where much environmental policy is being carried out today, as has been done in other areas of the law such as civil rights.

Even more evident by its absence is a link between doctrinal review and judicial behavior literature. Yet environmental law appears to be a prime candidate for such research. Many of the individual statutes were developed by organized groups with a conscious intent to use the courts to advance their causes. During the last ten years, however, industry's use of courts to slow the regulatory process has exceeded environmental groups' use of them for their policy goals (Wenner, 1982). Questions about the success of these groups in court seem particularly relevant to this area of the law and could be used to extend the general knowledge of judicial scholars about litigant influence on courts.

Another variable external to courts and judges, the socioeconomic and cultural context in which they make their decisions, also appears highly promising for explaining judicial behavior, just as it has for other policy-makers such as congressmen. Attorneys have long recognized variations among judges' attitudes toward particular legal questions and have forum-shopped accordingly. This tendency has been noted by environmental legal scholars (McGarity, 1980), as regional variations among court outcomes reflect congressional voting on the same issues (Wenner, 1982).

At the individual judge level, judicial philosophy regarding environmental values has gone largely unexamined. Yet there is a large untapped reservoir of information in the form of judges' opinions in the hundreds of environmental cases that have been adjudicated in the last fifteen years. Some judges may have developed worldviews that incorporate sensitivity to environmental values, and some, such as the late Supreme Court justice William O. Douglas, wrote extensively on the subject. Background characteristics that have proved useful in other areas of the law may also be demonstrated to affect judges' rulings on the environment (Grunbaum, 1974).

The Reagan administration adopted a conscious policy of appointing federal judges with conservative philosophies to match its own social values, especially regarding church/state relations and civil rights. Given the general linkage between environmental values and liberal causes, it would appear reasonable to hypothesize that these appointments will have an impact on the outcomes of environmental cases. A sufficient time lag has now occurred to enable researchers to compare the decisions of Reagan appointees to the bench with those of other judges, especially in the crucial D.C. Circuit. Indeed, the time appears ripe to gain insight into judicial behavior by examining environmental cases. Similarly, our understanding of the courts' contribution to environmental policy-making should be enhanced by greater utilization of judicial theory in future studies of environmental law.

10

Elites and Environmental Policy

Mark E. Rushefsky

The implication of the psychologists' work is that the public is not qualified to participate in decisions about the risks they will have to endure. The public pursues an informal, probably messy "logic" that the experts do not share.—Perrow (1984:320)

In this chapter we consider, review, and integrate several bodies of literature with one major purpose: to examine the role of elites in environmental decision-making. The topics to be explored include the policy process; risk policy as a focus for looking at environmental policy; the importance of elites in politics; belief systems; and the abundant literature on cognitive psychology and behavioral decision-making, both in general and particularly that body dealing with risk perception.

I develop a model that integrates these various bodies of scholarly knowledge. I do not suggest that the following review and critique is comprehensive. The relevant literature on cognitive psychology and behavioral decision-making, for example, is enormous, and the reader should consult several comprehensive bibliographic sources for further study (e.g., Covello et al., 1983; Otway and Thomas, 1982; Hohenemser and Kasperson, 1982; Cole and Withey, 1981). This review covers the essence of these fields and for our purposes will suffice. Additionally, I will suggest areas for further research at the end of this chapter.

Risk Policy

Environmental concerns have evolved since the heady days of the modern environmental movement, 1968 to 1972 (Rosenbaum, 1977). Early legislation concentrated on the impact of man's activities on the environment and the more obvious sources of pollution: air contaminants such as sulfur oxides and photochemical smog and water pollutants such as dissolved organic chemicals and pesticides (Rosenbaum, 1985). These were plainly hazards that affected many of us and our surroundings and were visible or had acute effects (seen in a relatively brief time). As we moved into the late 1970s and the 1980s, the center of concern shifted to a more difficult and tenuous problem. Information gathered earlier suggested the possibility that exposure to substances in the air, land, and water, in consumer products, and in the workplace might affect us years later. To make matters worse, we were exposed to those substances in small amounts, in parts per million or even parts per billion. The focus, in short, shifted from hazard (which affects all of us) to risk (which affects some of us) (Davis, 1984; Dietz and Rycroft, 1987; Rosenbaum, 1985; Rushefsky, 1986).[1]

Legislative and regulatory activity after 1975 began to have more and more of a risk focus. Early legislation, such as the Consumer Product Safety Act (1972), the Occupational Safety and Health Act (1970), and the Federal Insecticide, Fungicide, and Rodenticide Act (1972), incorporated risk concerns with other problems. Later legislation, such as the Toxic Substances Control Act (1976), the Resource Conservation and Recovery Act (1976), and the Comprehensive Environmental Response, Compensation, and Liability Act (Superfund) (1980), had primarily a risk concern. Thus in this chapter I examine elites and environmental policy as they relate to risk.[2]

Risk, according to Lowrance (1976:94) is "a measure of the probability and severity of adverse effects." Risk is thus a function of exposure to a substance and the severity of that exposure (both amount and time). To control risk (Conservation Foundation, 1984), two analytically separate activities may be engaged in, what Hadden (1984) calls the "two-stage process" of risk control. The first stage, the more scientific-technical based phase, is risk assessment, evaluating the risk from exposure to some activity or substance. The steps involved in risk assessment are well established (see Bazelon, 1979; Lave, 1982; National Research Council, 1983; Office of Technology Assessment, 1981; Rushefsky, 1986), though conducting a valid risk assessment is difficult. The information problems associated with this stage are daunting and necessitate the making of assumptions to bridge data gaps. For example, much of the testing is conducted on small rodents. The lack of human data requires that we make some assumptions as to how to extrapolate from animals to humans. Similarly, animal testing requires high doses, far beyond, in most cases, what humans are exposed to. Again, risk assessors have to extrapolate from those high doses to lower doses. The resultant uncertainties and the tenuous basis for these assumptions leads to conflict at this early stage of risk control. A few of the studies we will examine later look at differences between groups on these assumptions.

The second stage of risk control is risk management. Given an estimate of risk based on the risk assessment, how acceptable is that risk? A substantial risk may require regulation of exposure and possibly banning of the substance or activity. Low risk may require no action at all. This stage is equally as controversial as risk assessment, though the disagreements are more overtly political than in the prior stage. In actuality, it is difficult to separate the two stages (Hadden, 1984; Rushefsky, 1986).

An Integrated Policy Model

Figure 10.1 presents a model that provides a framework for integrating and considering the literature mentioned above. We begin with the bottom section, the policy process, based on Jones (1984:36; see also Anderson, 1984). The center of interest is on the critical role of problem identification in structuring the rest of the process.[3]

By Jones's formulation, problem identification consists of a variety of functional activities: perception, definition, aggregation, organization, representation, and agenda setting. The first two of these activities are the most important for our purposes. The other activities are directed at getting government to accept the results of perception and definition. In this early stage of the policy process (as well as many of the others), we can conceive of the process as clashes of different actors and groups over problem definitions. The actors or groups that can impose their definitions will emerge victorious. But as Lindblom points out (1980), problems are not out there waiting to be considered. Someone must define a set of events as a problem worthy of public attention. Jones writes:

> Perception is important in the policy process, therefore, because it conditions the definitions of problems. As used here, *perception* simply means the reception and registering of an event through sight, hearing, touch, and smell. Involved in that comprehension is an interpretation. Thus *perception refers to an event. Definition refers to a problem.* Something happens, someone perceives it in a particular way and defines it as a problem. (Jones, 1984:52, emphasis in original)

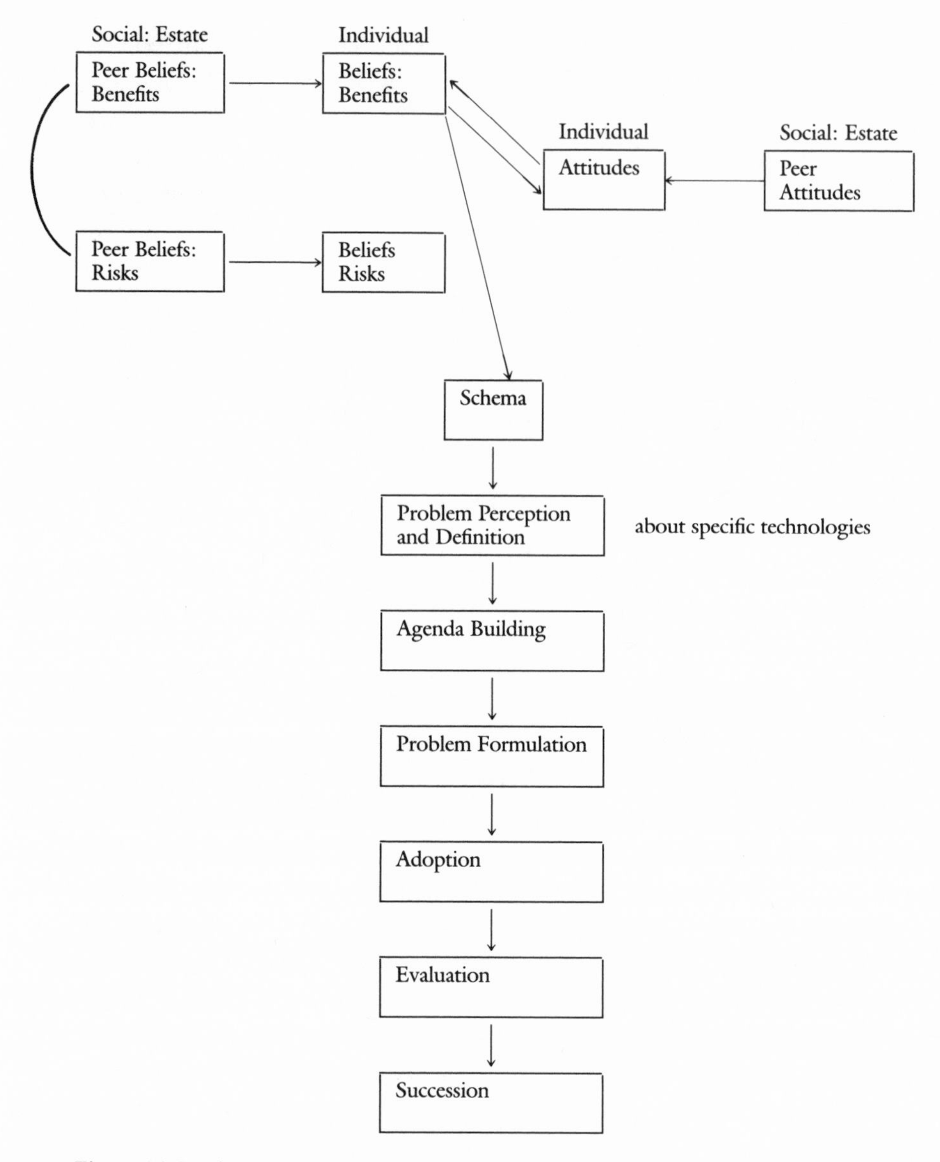

Figure 10.1 An Integrated Policy Model

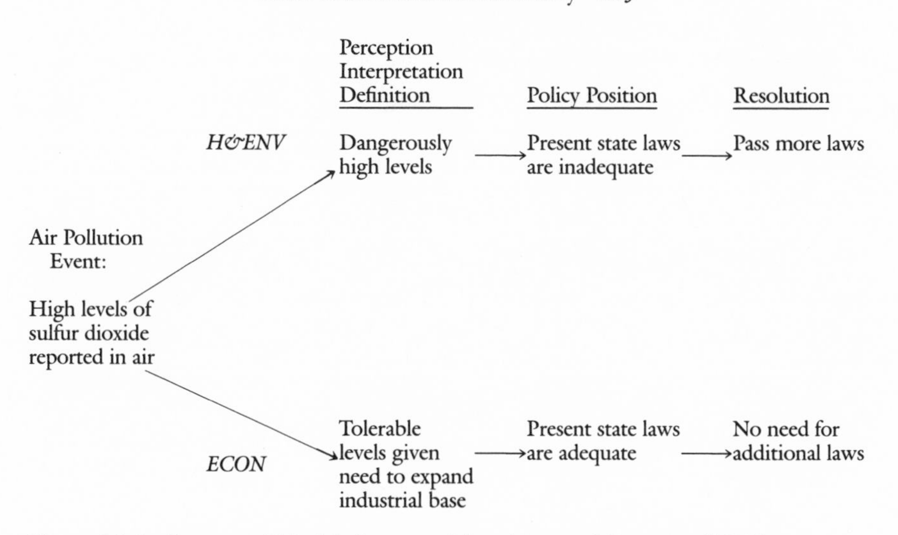

Figure 10.2 Perceptual Model. SOURCE: Maggiotto and Bowman (1982).

Perception is the registering of some event; definition is the interpretation of the meaning or significance of that event. Perception and definition lead to a particular set of possible solutions to the defined problem; they also eliminate other possible sets.

A study by Maggiotto and Bowman (1982) stressed the importance of perception and definition in structuring the subsequent course of policy-making. While their research was limited both as to substance (air pollution) and sample (Florida state legislators), their results do support and make explicit the thrust of this chapter. Maggiotto and Bowman hypothesized that perceptual screens (or ideologies, belief systems, or schemas) filter out information inconsistent with that screen. The authors saw two rival sets of problem formulations in hearings on air pollution: one stressed pollution as an environmental and health problem; the other saw pollution as largely an economic problem. The results of their survey led them to posit a perceptual model, linking events, perceptions, positions, and solutions (see figure 10.2). They described the model as follows:

> An event occurs in the environment and is perceived by the policy maker. Those who view air pollution from a health and environmental perspective see the incident as posing a threat, while those who view air pollution as a question of economics see the same event as tolerable given the alternative values which they hold. These conditional relationships pro-

> duce different policy resolutions because the event is evaluated in the context of what the state is already doing. Hence, state laws are either adequate or not, or should be changed or not, depending upon the conditional relationship between event and contextual interpretation of the event. (Maggiotto and Bowman, 1982:167–68)

Notice that the two problem definitions (health and environmental perspective, economic perspective) lead to different perspectives on government activity. One suggests an active government role, the other implies that no further involvement is necessary. This leads us to investigate how problems are identified and by whom.

Policy Elites

The chapter title gives us the answer to the "who" question: elites. There has been a long-running debate in political science (and sociology) over power structures, who governs, etc. (see references in Domhoff, 1983, and Dye, 1983). In simplified terms, we can distinguish between pluralist and elitist views. Pluralists maintain that no single elite or set of elites is overwhelmingly influential or participates alone in decision-making (see, for example, Dahl, 1967, 1982; Polsby, 1980). The elite theorists suggest that actors in institutional positions of power (both governmental and private) make most of the policy decisions or are highly influential (Domhoff, 1983; Dye, 1983; Mills, 1956). Both the elitist and pluralist schools of power say the same thing. The elitists by definition see only a few exercising power. But the pluralists also agree that only a few participate (though asserting that participation is considerably more fluid than the elitists say). In a sense, the pluralists confront what the early-twentieth-century Italian political scientist Roberto Michels (1962) called the "iron law of oligarchy." Even in those organizations that are committed to democratic procedures and wide participation (such as the European social-democratic parties that Michels studied), only the active minority participated over time.

But the elitist model has several variants. The elitist view mentioned above may be viewed as the "ruling elite model." This model is based on overall or societal power structures, but does not necessarily identify those who make decisions or are influential in specific policy areas. Other terms have been used to describe a set of elites in policy areas. Iron triangles, policy clusters, and subgovernments describe close relationships among congressional committees and subcommittees, executive branch agencies, and relevant interest groups. The terms suggest close relationships among these three groups of actors that make much of the policy decisions with little publicity.

Lowi's (1964) distinction between distributive, regulatory, and redistributive policy arenas, however, suggests that the iron triangles are more likely and stable in distributive policy than in the other two (see also Ripley and Franklin, 1984). While there certainly are elements of distributive policy in the enviromental area, that area is better characterized as regulatory. Heclo (1978) proposes the term "issue networks" to describe a more fluid flow of actors in and out of policy issues. Kingdon's model of agenda-building (1984) also suggests this fluidity. Perhaps the term most useful to us, or for any policy area, is the term "policy elite."

> The shift from disputes about the place of environmental policy in the political agenda to debates about the specifics of policy has generated a new group of policy specialists whose work centers on environmental health and safety. Unlike the power elite, who deal only with broad issues, these professionals do the daily work of the risk policy system. While they have more clout than does the average citizen, the policy elite is not as influential as the power elite. Unlike the power elite, they tend to specialize, focusing their energies on a limited set of related issues. By promoting or opposing policies, by developing and interpreting data and by administering programs, they shape regulation. Their work is what translates popular demand for environmental protection into action. . . . They are of special importance in those [policy systems] with a high scientific and technological content. (Dietz and Rycroft, 1987:13–14)

Problem identification (as well as the rest of the policy process pictured in figure 10.1) is thus the result of elite interaction. But which elites? Dye (1983) identifies a number of institutional bases, for example, government, the military, and the corporate sector. Hamlett's (1984) model of political estates is particularly helpful in identifying such estates. He identifies seven estates: corporate-managerial, executive, regulatory, congressional, academic-professional, organized labor, and consumerist-environmentalist. While there are certainly divisions within each estate, the leaders within each (elites) are appropriately identified as important participants in environmental policy-making. We agree with the pluralists that participation is fluid. For example, those in a particular area concerned with hazardous waste (the individuals within an estate) might not be the same individuals concerned about air pollution. But in general, this model does allow us to identify in broad terms the appropriate elites. Dietz and Rycroft's (1988) study of risk professionals included people from the following groups: executive branch agencies (especially the Environmental Protection Agency), congressional staff and support agencies, law and consulting firms, environmental organizations, corporations and professional and trade associations, research organizations (such as think tanks and universities), and a miscellaneous category (including labor groups and state and local governments).

Elite recruitment

One question that may be asked about elites is how they emerge: that is, how are people recruited into elite positions? Some obviously emerge because of their institutional positions in agencies, interest groups, and so on, though other paths to influence and power are available. Because environmental policy in general and risk policy in particular are so heavily dependent on science and technology and the uncertainties of science, it would stand to reason that scientists would become important political actors. In Goddell's words (1977) scientists become visible.

In the early years of the modern environmental movement Rachel Carson's *Silent Spring* (1962) demonstrated how a scientist could be influential in setting the policy agenda and making policy proposals. In later years, Samuel Epstein, in *The Politics of Cancer* (1978), has been a forceful spokesman for stringent regulation of carcinogens.

The most interesting example of scientist as political actor is Bruce Ames. A prominent researcher in cancer, Ames developed the first of the short-term tests to detect mutagens.[4] Recently, Ames has switched his position based on findings that naturally occurring causes of cancer are much more significant than synthetic chemicals. Ames's work and his activities as a political actor since then have been aimed at getting this new viewpoint accepted (Rushefsky, 1986).

Another nontraditional path to influence is the crusading free-lance writer. Edith Efron epitomizes this type. Her 1984 book *The Apocalyptics* was as controversial as *Silent Spring* two decades earlier. Whereas Carson emphasized risks posed by agricultural pesticides, Efron's work was a major attack on risk policy.

Perhaps the most interesting of paths to elite influence is the self-made actor. This is someone with little expertise in the area but who feels threatened by environmental hazards. Self-made actors seek redress for exposure to hazards. They try to mobilize their community and seek wider support from other political actors, including the media. Two examples illustrate this type.

The first example is Lois Gibbs of Niagara, New York. Niagara is the location of the infamous Love Canal, formerly a toxic waste dump that leaked into the surrounding neighborhood, including the school built on the site. Gibbs, concerned about the hazard and the lack of response by local and state officials, began a door-to-door survey of her neighbors to explore the extent of harm and to mobilize the community. A Love Canal Homeowners Association was formed, with Gibbs as its head, that pressured local, state, and federal officials to take action. Eventually, the state bought the inner ring of homes near the dump and took action to prevent further leakage (Levine, 1982).

The second example is from the other side of the country, Oregon. The hazard this time was the herbicide 2,4,5-T and its contaminant, dioxin (TCDD). Forests in rural Oregon were treated with the herbicide to reduce competition from surrounding brush. Several months after one of the applications, a resident of one of the nearby towns, Bonnie Hill, suffered a miscarriage. In talking with her neighbors, Hill noted a highly unusual number of miscarriages during the spring, when the spraying occurred. She and others then sought to stop the spraying, an effort that precipitated an emergency suspension of the herbicide by the Environmental Protection Agency in 1979 and an agreement by the major manufacturer, Dow Chemical, to cease production (Van Strum, 1983). Common citizens may thus have a dramatic impact on policy, but only when they make an extraordinary effort.

Elites and belief systems

The last question is the "how": how do elites (whose perceptions and interactions are critical) perceive environmental problems and act on those perceptions? The top of the model in figure 10.1 suggests how this might be done.[5] The model states that first there is interaction between an individual's beliefs and attitudes and, second, that an individual's beliefs and attitudes are affected by peer beliefs and attitudes. In our terminology peer beliefs and attitudes are estate beliefs and attitudes. The model as a whole (and this section of the model in particular) relates the social or societal level to the individual level; it has macro and micro dimensions.

The individual beliefs and attitudes form a schema, defined as a "preexisting assumption about the way the world is organized" (Singer, quoted in Axelrod, 1973:1248). Axelrod (1973:1248) writes: "When new information becomes available, a person tries to fit the new information into the pattern which he has used in the past to interpret information about the same situation. If new information does not fit very well, something has to give." Schema (also known as ideology, belief system, or perceptual screen) provides the basis by which an individual will perceive and define an event and possibly identify it as a problem that the public sector should confront.

A number of studies have looked at elites and belief systems, especially in the foreign policy area (Axelrod, 1973; Jarvis, 1976; Pruitt, 1965). There have also been a number of studies examining environmental belief systems of various groups. Constantini and Hanf (1972), in an early study, examined the relationship between variations in environmental concern and other environmental perceptions, background of decision-makers, and political and social psychological attitudes of elites in Lake Tahoe. Their descriptive study showed that there were considerable differences between those rating high on environmental concern and those rating low. For example, those rating high were more liberal and more cosmopolitan than those rating low.

Pierce and Lovrich (1980) compared the belief systems of several different groups in Idaho: general public, attentive publics, and state legislators. Their study, a particularly detailed and rich one, examined the cognitive consistency (what they call "constraint") of belief systems among the various groups. They did, indeed, find this consistency within belief systems. Pierce and Lovrich (1980:282) concluded, among other things, that:

> preservationist identification plays a significant role in environmental belief systems, acting as a general orientation around which other beliefs can be organized and interpreted. As in other policy domains, the environmental one is characterized by a single dimension along which a number of objects and beliefs can be arrayed, and which can be used to create links to other aspects of politics, such as the partisan and the ideological.

A recent study examined the "devil" hypothesis, again concentrating on environmental policy. In this case, the perceptions concerned opponents on environmental issues, rather than the issues themselves. In this sense the study is closer to the international relations literature cited above than the other environmental studies. Nevertheless, perception is the major concern. The study, by Hunter and Sabatier (1985), examined the extent to which members of interest groups overestimated the strength of their opponents (opponents as "devils") and underestimated their own strength. Their research confirmed the existence of the devil hypothesis.[6] They concluded that "the devil hypothesis has all the worst features of a positive feedback loop" (Hunter and Sabatier, 1985:22), thus leading to a cycle or spiral of suspicion and conflict (see also Jarvis, 1976, on this point).

One other work certainly deserves mention here: the three-country survey directed by Milbrath (1984). Milbrath's study investigated the extent to which a new environmental paradigm was taking root. He contrasts this paradigm with the older one, what he calls the dominant social paradigm, grounded in materialism. Based on his survey in Germany, England, and the United States (the latter in 1980 and 1982), Milbrath classifies the respondents into eight categories. At the extremes of the continuum are the rearguard (defending the dominant social paradigm) and the vanguard (promoting the new environmental paradigm). The middle group includes the establishment and nature conservationists. The sample of respondents includes environmentalists, the general public, labor leaders, elected and appointed officials, business leaders, and members from media groups. Milbrath sees a revolutionary change occurring as the new environmental paradigm begins to supplant the dominant social paradigm.

One note of caution has been raised by Lovrich et al. (1985). The new belief system as described by Milbrath, and indeed environmental belief systems commonly seen in the literature, may only be a Western phenomenon. Lovrich et al. compared the belief systems of environmental group members in the United States and Japan. They found considerable differences in belief systems, with American environmentalists more concerned about preservation and postmaterialism and supporting the new environmental paradigm, whereas the Japanese environmentalists interpreted environmental problems within a public health context.

Several recent studies have looked at attitudes of environmental elites. Lynn (1986) specifically examined the interplay of science and values discussed in risk policy. The controversy over OSHA's generic cancer regulations risk assumptions (see Rushefsky, 1986) led her to test the hypothesis "that regulatory values and other social and political values influenced the selection among scientific assumptions and, furthermore, that these regulatory values seemed linked to place of employment" (Lynn, 1986:40). She interviewed 136 industrial hygienists and occupational physicians employed in three settings, government, industry, and universities. Her overall finding confirmed the linkage among scientific beliefs, political values, and place of employment. Government scientists were more likely to be politically liberal and to choose protective scientific assumptions. Industry scientists were more likely to be politically conservative and to choose more risk-tolerant assumptions. University scientists were in between. Interestingly, though Lynn asks questions concerning risk assumptions, she does not rely on the literature on risk perception discussed below.

Rothman and Lichter (1987) explored the hypothesis offered by Douglas and Wildavsky (1982) that risk perception is related to a rejection of traditional values. They surveyed various leadership groups, covering some of the same types of groups discussed above but adding others such as national-media journalists, science journalists, military leaders, and television and motion picture entertainment creators. Rothman and Lichter tested five specific hypotheses, focusing on nuclear energy:

1. The relevant scientific community believes nuclear plants to be safe, and neither ideology nor economic interest plays a substantial role in their assessment.
2. Among other key leadership groups, by contrast, views about nuclear energy correlate with political ideology.
3. National media journalists are skeptical about nuclear safety.
4. Journalists inaccurately report the views of the relevant scientific community.
5. The views of other leadership groups on nuclear energy correlate highly with the news sources that they consider reliable. (Rothman and Lichter, 1987:385)

In general, their study supports both the specific hypotheses and the more general one.

The most recent of studies is that of Dietz and Rycroft (1987). Their study is a descriptive one of 223 risk professionals in the Washington, D.C. area. They argued that a descriptive study was necessary because of the lack of systematic and theoretical work in the area. Their study is structured around four perspectives as a way of understanding the risk professionals, all four of them relevant to our concerns. The first is the elite perspective, exploring the relationship between political power and personal background. The second is the class perspective, looking at the linkage between ideology, economic interests, and attempts to influence policy. The third perspective centers on the extent to which risk professionals are an establishment, representing institutional interests. The final perspective focuses on risk professionals as a community, examining linkages and communication.

Their findings both support and contradict some of the research previously discussed. For example, they found strong support for the Lynn (1986) hypothesis of the linkage between worldview and place of employment. Rothman and Lichter did not find this result among their scientists, suggesting methodological differences between these three studies (sampling and types of questions asked).

Dietz and Rycroft continued this inquiry by testing support for the dominant social paradigm and the new environmental paradigm that Milbrath (1982) discussed. In essence, this is the same question posed by Rothman and Lichter, in asking whether leadership groups rejected traditional values. In general, the Dietz/Rycroft study supports the view that risk professionals reject traditional values (dominant social paradigm) with the important exceptions of actors in the private sector. In contrast to Rothman and Lichter (as well as Douglas and Wildavsky), however, Dietz and Rycroft do not imply criticism of those supporting the new environmental paradigm. They argue that it is equally as possible that those who support the dominant social paradigm are Pollyannaish, denying the seriousness of environmental problems.

But more provocative is their point that we should "focus on the interplay between ideology and the strategy and tactics of actors in the policy system" (Dietz and Rycroft, 1988:51). Environmentalists initially raised alarms of environmental problems and engaged in protest-type activities. Over the years they have moderated the rhetoric and concentrated on specific issues. The private sector's original tactics were to deny the existence of a problem and then to deny the seriousness of risks, suggesting a focus on more serious concerns. Dietz and Rycroft's (1987) work stands virtually alone in suggesting a relationship between elite beliefs and tactics.

Risk Perception

One of the key questions of this chapter is how decision-makers perceive environmental risks and the relationship between those perceptions and decisions (activity). There is a large literature on risk perception, but very little of it has been applied to elites.

Origins of risk perception literature

The literature on risk perception has several different origins. In a sense, the most indirect origin is from the literature on financial risk. More specifically, the risk perception literature derives from behavioral decision theory.[7] Behavioral decision theory may be defined as the study of how people actually make decisions. Much of this stems from the work of Tversky and Kahneman (see Tversky and Kahneman, 1974, 1981, and McKean, 1985). In a series of papers, the two found that decision-making was a more problematic enterprise than first appeared. For example, they have shown that decisions people make are dependent on the context of the decision situation. That is, people are willing to make a less risky decision if it involves a possible gain or saving of lives but a more risky decision to prevent loss, whether of lives or in a gamble, even though the two situations are identical. They have also found that people have difficulty estimating small probabilities.

To deal with uncertainty, the defining characteristic of risk policy, people use certain heuristics or problem-solving methods. In perhaps their most famous article, Tversky and Kahneman (1974) discuss three of these heuristics: representativeness, availability, and anchoring. Representativeness means that people expect small samples to be representative of large samples. Availability means that things that are easily recalled are considered common. Anchoring means that people make adjustments to their estimates but the adjustments are usually insufficient.

Thus the literature on decision-making, through important work such as Tversky and Kahneman, raised critical questions about the rationality of people's decision-making ability. These questions coalesced in the environmental area when the risk of technologies became a political issue. Cole and Withey (1981) point out that the interest in the subject paralleled the expansion of participants in technology development from industry and agency to include the public. The *objective* assessments of risk did not correspond to the *subjective* assessments made by the public. Scholars became interested in the subjectivity of acceptable risk concepts. Acceptability of risk is clearly a political question; since perception of risk determined the acceptability of risk, the two were obviously related.

One can note in some of the risk perception literature this bias against risk judgments made by the general public and environmental groups. The single most important technology that stimulated this literature was nuclear power. Objective assessments of the risks from nuclear power were orders of magnitude lower than subjective assessments. Slovic, Fischhoff, and Lichtenstein (1979), in their studies of risk perception factors, have shown that nuclear power is essentially an outlier; it is both an unknown and dreaded risk and is judged as much more hazardous than any other technology. The bias that underlies much of the risk perception literature and its public policy implications can be seen in the following passage:

> Knowledge of the causal relationships between attitudes and beliefs is not only useful in formulating public policies that represent public views, but also may suggest implementation strategies for obtaining public support and acceptance of social policies. To illustrate, a government-sponsored effort to attempt to change attitudes directly about a new technology (e.g., use of breeder reactors) would have little effect if benefit and risk perceptions determined attitudes, but would have considerable influence if it were known that attitudes affected benefit and risk perceptions ("halo effect"). In the former case, focusing on the risks and benefits of a technology might be a more rational strategy. Indeed and furthermore, there may even be "halo" effects regarding risks and benefits; e.g., if the risk due to radioactivity is perceived to be high then all risks due to nuclear energy would be perceived high. Reducing public perceptions of the risk due to radioactivity would thus reduce all other perceived nuclear risks and possibly enhance simultaneously the perceived benefits of nuclear power. (Bajgier and Moskowitz, 1982:270)

That quote certainly indicates a bias: the public's perceptions about nuclear power are wrong and ought to be changed. In a similar mode and following from the Tversky-Kahneman heuristic of availability, Combs and Slovic (1979) analyzed the content of newspaper articles covering hazards. They showed that the press emphasized accidents rather than disease as a cause of death, even though the latter were far more important. If people use the availability heuristic, judging risk based on what they are familiar with, then the public will misperceive risk. The research questions thus have a hidden agenda, one that relates directly to politics: "What can be gained from research aimed ultimately at correcting misperceptions, and by whom?" (Otway and Thomas, 1982:75). The Rothman and Lichter (1987) study has this same tint

Table 10.1 Evaluated Technologies

Alcoholic beverages	High school and college football	Power mowers
Bicycles	Home appliances	Prescription antibiotics
Commercial aviation	Hunting	Railroads
Contraceptives	Large construction	Skiing
Electric power	Motor vehicles	Smoking
Fire fighting	Motorcycles	Spray cans
Food coloring	Mountain climbing	Surgery
Food preservatives	Nuclear power	Swimming
General (private) aviation	Pesticides	Vaccinations
Handguns	Police work	X-rays

SOURCE: Slovic et al. (1980).

with its focus solely on nuclear power and attempting to show the linkage between opposition to nuclear power and ideology.

There was one other seminal work that led to risk perception studies, a 1969 article by Chauncey Starr. Writing at the very beginning of the period when technologies, and nuclear energy in particular, were being questioned, Starr tried to develop an objective measure of acceptable risk by looking at those risks that had been accepted (and rejected) in the past. This approach, called revealed preferences, could then be applied to present efforts to judge the acceptability of technologies. Starr derived several "laws" of acceptable risk based on his data. Unfortunately, an attempt to replicate Starr's work was unsuccessful (Otway and Thomas, 1982). Starr's work was also criticized by Slovic and co-workers for enshrining the market and allowing past decisions to determine present and future ones.

Studying risk perception

While a number of scholars have contributed to the study of risk perception, the most prominent works have been those by Bruce Fischhoff, Sarah Lichtenstein, and Paul Slovic (and their associates), labeled here as the Decision Research group.[8] Slovic et al. (1979:18) describe the importance of risk perception studies from a policy perspective: "In order to be of assistance in the hazard management process, a theory of perceived risk must explain people's extreme aversion to some hazards, their indifference to others, and the discrepancies between these reactions and experts' recommendations."

Table 10.2 Extended List of Risk Characteristics

Affects me	Immediate	Not easily reduced
Catastrophic	Increasing	Not observable
Dread	Inequitable	Not preventable
Fatal	Involuntary	Uncontrollable
Future generations	Many exposed	Unknown to exposed
Global catastrophe	New	Unknown to science

SOURCE: Slovic et al. (1980).

The methodology of this group has remained the same through a series of studies. First, a small group of subjects is selected for participation, typically students or members of an attentive group such as the League of Women Voters. The participants are then asked to rate a series of activities and technologies (thirty or forty-five) for their perceived benefits, perceived risks, the acceptability of the current level of risk, and nine (or eighteen in a later study) dimensions of risk. Each technology is evaluated separately for each of these tasks, with the groups divided by whether they evaluated perceived risk or perceived benefit. Tables 10.1 and 10.2 list the technologies and the risk characteristics.

The subjects are then asked to do a comparative evaluation of risks and benefits of the technologies using a version of dimensional scaling (see Lodge and Tursky, 1979, on dimensional scaling). For example, the perceived benefits group was asked to order the technologies from least to most beneficial. Then, assigning a rating of 10 to the least beneficial, the other technologies are rated accordingly. To clarify the procedure, the following instructions were given (Fischhoff et al., 1978:131): "A rating of 12 indicates that the item is 1.2 times as beneficial as the least beneficial item (i.e., 20 percent more beneficial). A rating of 200 means that the item is 20 times as beneficial as the least beneficial item, to which you assigned a 10." The perceived risk group performs a similar task.

The subjects were asked to do a second task: judge the acceptability of the level of risk from the activities and substances. The choices given to the participants were

(a) "Could be riskier: it would be acceptable if it were __ times riskier"; (b) "It is presently acceptable"; and (c) "Too risky: to be acceptable, it would have to be __ times safer."

These ratings are then used to determine acceptable levels of risk.

The final task is to evaluate the thirty (or forty-five) activities or technologies on nine (or eighteen) seven-point scales (see table 10.2). Each technology is evaluated on each of the scales (or characteristics) of risk before the next technology is evaluated.

Slovic et al. employed the geometric mean to rate the activities and characteristics on the nine technologies. Nuclear power was rated the riskiest of the technologies on eight of the nine dimensions (and was a close second on the ninth). This is consistent with the origins of risk perception studies. The dimensions were then correlated with perceived risk and perceived benefit. None correlated with perceived benefit and only dread and severity correlated with perceived risk.

Other findings included: (1) the view that current levels of risk for many technologies were too high (unacceptable), (2) that there was little relationship between perceived risk and perceived benefits, (3) that there was a relationship between perceived benefit and acceptable level of risk (greater benefits permit higher acceptable levels of risk), and (4) that the nine characteristics were highly correlated and could be reduced to two dimensions or factors, one dimension representing new, involuntary, and poorly known technologies and the other reflecting certainty of death.[9] Their later study (Slovic et al., 1980) produced somewhat different results: using eighteen risk characteristics produced three factors: dread risk, familiarity, and number of people exposed.

One other part of the studies asked the participants to estimate the number of fatalities per year from the activity or technology. Those estimates were then compared with the actual number and with estimates by a group of experts. In another study (Lichtenstein et al., 1978), subjects were asked to make pairwise comparisons between two technologies or activities as causes of death. The subjects were able to do this with a moderate degree of accuracy. However, their estimates of the number of fatalities were dramatically misestimated; Slovic et al. (1979) interpret those findings within the framework of the availability heuristic discussed by Tversky and Kahneman. The estimates of technical experts were more or less the same as the actual numbers of fatalities.

Slovic et al. drew a number of important conclusions from these studies. People do not estimate frequencies very well, and their patterns of estimation are captured by the heuristics. People also tend to be overconfident of their guesses. One implication, which they do not necessarily draw, might be that the public ought to defer to expert judgment. However, the Decision Research group is not particularly sanguine about experts' abilities to make judgments.

In two articles, Fischhoff et al. examined the ability of technical experts to make risk decisions. In the earlier one (1982), part of a published symposium on "actual" versus "perceived" risk (the title expressing an important bias in risk perception studies), they investigated the extent to which expert perceptions were more accurate than lay or public perceptions. The manner of their presentation can be seen in their semihumorous suggestion to rename the title of the conference "The Analysis of Risks as Perceived by Ranking Scientists within their Field of Expertise vs. as Perceived by Anybody Else." They write:

> Although there are actual risks, nobody knows what they are. All that anyone does know about risks can be classified as perceptions. Those assertions that are typically called "actual risks" (or "facts" or "objective information") inevitably contain some element of judgment on the part of the scientists who produced them. The element is most minimal when judgment is needed only to assess the competence of a particular study conducted within an established paradigm. It grows as one needs to integrate results from diverse studies or to extrapolate results from a domain in which they are readily obtainable to another in which they are really needed (e.g., from animal studies to human effects). Judgment becomes all when there are no (credible) available data, yet a policy decision requires that some assessment of a particular fact be made. (Fischhoff et al., 1982:237)

They point out that experts and the public mean different things when talking about risk and mention an earlier study (Slovic et al., 1979, 1980), where expert risk assessments defined risk as annual fatalities. Lay experimental subjects, when asked to estimate annual fatalities, gave approximately similar results as experts. When asked to assess risk, then the lay public gave drastically different responses; thus risk to the public means something other than annual fatalities. The implication is not that the public is irrational but that it has a wider view of risk than resides in technical communities. I will return to this point later.

Further, the public and experts may be considering different problems when it comes to acceptable risk questions. Fischhoff et al. point out, as have others, that "one does not accept risks. One accepts options that entail some level of risk among their consequences. . . . The attractiveness of an option depends upon its full set of relevant positive and negative consequences" (Fischhoff et al., 1982:240).

In the second article, Fischhoff et al. (1983) examined ways in which expert judgments may be biased or inaccurate. They write that experts know things in their fields but, when forced to go outside or beyond their narrow fields, make the same errors of judgment as do nonexperts. Their errors include insensitivity to the sample size. In a rather illuminating passage, particularly for control of potentially hazardous chemicals, Fischhoff et al. note:

> Page (1981) has similarly shown the low power of representative toxicological studies. In designing such studies, one inevitably makes a tradeoff between avoiding false alarms (e.g., erroneously calling a chemical a carcinogen) and misses (e.g., erroneously calling a chemical a noncarcinogen). For any given false alarm rate, the smaller the sample size the larger the miss rate. Because scientists are typically most concerned about false alarms, that rate is usually set at some conventional value (e.g., .05). As a result, variations in sample size affect primarily the miss rate, with decreased samples leading to increased miss rates. In this way, wayward intuitions may lead to underpowered experimental designs that represent, perhaps inadvertently, a social policy that protects chemicals more than people. (Fischhoff et al., 1983:251)

Other expert judgment problems include hindsight bias and overconfidence in assessing the quality of their own judgments. The latter problem, overconfidence (i.e., underestimation of risk) includes (1) "failure to consider the ways in which human errors can affect technological systems"; (2) "overconfidence in current scientific knowledge"; (3) "failure to appreciate how technological systems function as a whole"; (4) "slowness in detecting chronic, cumulative effects"; (5) "failure to anticipate human response to safety measures"; and (6) "failure to anticipate 'common-mode failures.'"[10]

Though the Slovic, Fischhoff, and Lichtenstein research has dominated this area, in volume of publications if nothing else, others have also undertaken psychometric studies of risk perception. One of the most careful of these has been the work of Charles Vlek and Pieter-Jan Stallen (1981). A collection of twenty-six risky activities was presented to the subjects for various evaluations of risk. The dimensions by which they were evaluated included: riskiness, feelings of insecurity, amount of information, acceptability, imaginability of danger, catastrophic potential, personal avoidability of accident, probability of accident, and personal influence on choice.

One of their major findings was the similarity of the subjects' judgments about risk. Vlek and Stallen state that the risk characteristics reduced basically to one dimension, what they called "size of possible accident and degree of decisional control" (1981:247). Nuclear power again was rated high on this overall dimension. Vlek and Stallen not only used rather sophisticated quantitative techniques and rich measures of risk, benefit, etc., but they also looked at subgroup differences in a variety of aspects such as sex, professional class, and political inclination. They noted significant differences by professional classes:

> Administrators and top managers, industrial workers and craftsmen, employees in administrative, financial, and organizational jobs, and agricultural personnel, all consider the secondary dimension—"scale of production and/or distribution of benefits and size of potential accident"—to contribute positively to overall "acceptability." On the other hand, those having medical, social, scientific, and artistic professions consider activities with large-scale benefits and sizeable potential accidents as being less "acceptable." (Vlek and Stallen, 1981:261)

Harding and Eiser's (1984) risk perception studies differed from the Decision Research group work in two ways. First, whereas the Decision Research group defined risk for the subjects (in terms of annual fatalities), Harding and Eiser allowed the subjects to use whatever definition of risk they wanted. Second, the Decision Research group used the geometric mean as a way of summarizing their data and performed their analyses on the reported means. Harding and Eiser employed regression analysis; their rationale is that the use of means masks individual variation in risk perception; it tells us nothing about how individuals perceive risk and would make risk decisions. Regression analysis, Harding and Eiser asserted, permits the drawing of conclusions about individual behavior and perceptions. Some of their results support those of the Decision Research group, for example on the negative correlation between perceived risk and perceived benefit. Perhaps their most important finding relates to how the subjects were perceiving or defining risk. The definition that was produced from the analysis was the "perceived likelihood of mishap and the perceived likelihood of death as a consequence" (Harding and Eiser, 1984:140). This is a broader definition than the Decision

Research term employed. Though the Slovic group did offer a definition of risk, they were also aware, as the discussion of expert problems in judgment pointed out, that the public employed a different definition of risk than that used by technical experts.

Three more studies bear mentioning. Bajgier and Moskowitz (1982), using a form of regression analysis, examined the role of attitudes and beliefs in risk perception, and the interaction of attitudes and beliefs. Thomas et al. (1980), who have done work on energy issues, investigated a particularly important policy aspect of risk perception: the extent to which leaders correctly understood the public's views of the risks from nuclear energy. They found that the policy-makers had a more positive attitude toward nuclear power and underestimated the negative feelings of the public.

The last study is in many ways the most intriguing; it combines the work on risk perception with research on belief systems. Buss and Craik (1983) begin by suggesting that the work on worldviews (belief systems) suggests two polar ideological extremes: Worldview A, comprising a pro-growth, pro-technology, materialistic, and rationalistic conception, and Worldview B, stressing environmental concerns, redistribution of resources, decentralization, and participative decision-making. These polar positions correspond, roughly, to Milbrath's (1984) dominant social paradigm (Worldview A) and new environmental paradigm (Worldview B). After briefly reviewing the literature on risk perception, Buss and Craik offered the following research hypotheses (which support some of the work of Dietz and Rycroft [1988] and Lichter and Rothman [1987]):

> (1) Individuals differ with respect to their orientation toward policy issues across a variety of domains. . . .
>
> (2) These contemporary sociotechnological orientations have implications for the manner in which risk is perceived to be associated with various technologies and activities. Specifically, greater risk is perceived to be associated with technological activity by the Worldview B adherents than the Worldview A adherents.
>
> (3) Contemporary policy orientations are related to preferences for societal decision-making procedures; those who hold Worldview A will prefer decision procedures that rely on hard-headed rationality; in contrast, those who hold Worldview B will prefer decision procedures that are more participative (e.g., expressed preferences or political judgment).

(4) Adherence to a given worldview will be associated with generalized environmental dispositions. (Buss and Craik, 1983:262)

Buss and Craik employed a variety of measurement instruments to test these hypotheses on some 230 college undergraduates. For example, they employ the questionnaires used in the Fischhoff et al. (1978) study to assess technological risk perception. They added to the risk dimensions three new ones: personal perceived risk, uncertainty of risk, and the intrinsic nature of risk. The third hypothesis, mentioned above, concerned decision-making procedures. The six procedures included in the Buss and Craik questionnaires were cost-benefit analysis, expressed preferences, natural standards, political judgment, revealed preferences, and technical judgment.

In general, the results confirmed the hypotheses, though the strength of the relationships run from weak to modest. More importantly for our purposes, the Buss and Craik study extends the work of the cognitive psychologists and relates belief systems both to risk perception and to more general environmental concerns. Keeping in mind the preliminary nature of their research and the modest empirical support for the hypotheses, Buss and Craik's substantive and research conclusions add to our understanding of policy perception and the factors that may shape those perceptions:

> Our findings demonstrate the value of conceptualizing and measuring contemporary worldviews. It is evident that individuals do not come to terms with each and every technology that passes through the arena of public discourse. Instead, a more or less integrated orientation is fashioned and applied to specific instances. . . .
>
> Worldviews A and B also implicate the preferences of individuals for the procedures by which society should decide about acceptable levels of risk for technologies. Thus, persons holding to Worldview A tended to endorse the use of cost-benefit analysis, while those holding to Worldview B opt for expressed preferences. The worldviews entail differences not only in how risky technologies appear to be, but also in how society should go about dealing with the management of technological risks. The important implications of these findings regarding societal decision procedures would justify a more ambitious replication, employing fuller descriptions of each approach and a wider range of responses to them from research participants. (Buss and Craik, 1983)

Finally, in a third study, Slovic et al. (1982) discussed the results of the psychometric studies of risk perception (their own and others):

> We have learned that difficulties in understanding probabilistic processes, biased media coverage, misleading personal experiences, and the anxieties generated by life's gambles cause uncertainty to be denied, risks to be misjudged (sometimes overestimated and sometimes underestimated), and judgments of facts to be held with unwarranted confidence. Unfortunately, experts' judgments appear to be prone to many of the same biases as those of laypersons, particularly when experts are forced to go beyond the limits of available data and rely upon their intuitions. Research further indicates that disagreement about risk should not be expected to evaporate in the presence of evidence. Strong initial views are resistant to change because they influence the way that subsequent information is interpreted. New evidence appears reliable and informative if it is consistent with one's initial beliefs; contrary evidence tends to be dismissed as unreliable, erroneous, or unrepresentative. When people lack strong prior opinions, the opposite situation exists—they are at the mercy of the problem formulation. Presenting the same information about risk in different ways buffets their perspectives and their actions like a ship in a storm. (Slovic et al., 1982:85)

Other generalizations include: (1) that perceived risk is quantifiable and predictable; (2) that risk means different things to different people; (3) that groups agree on their evaluations of technologies along the risk dimensions; (4) that risk characteristics tend to be highly interrelated; (5) that characteristics associated with "dread risk" seem to correspond with laypersons' perceptions (or definitions) of risk; (6) that acceptability of risk is related to benefit perception and degree of voluntariness of risk; and (7) that unfamiliarity with the hazard seems to raise people's concerns.

The Decision Research group also pointed to some of the public policy implications of risk perception studies. One rather intriguing example concerned seat-belt usage. How a risk is presented affects perceptions of risk and behavior based on those perceptions. Their experiments have shown that if people are presented with the risks of driving without seat belts on a trip-by-trip basis, then they are unlikely to change their habits. However, if presented with the cumulative lifetime risk, behavioral change does occur (Slovic et al., 1982).

Conclusion

While the risk perception literature has made substantial research contributions, it nevertheless suffers from some faults. Some have already been mentioned. For example, the political agenda of the research lies in its origin, trying to explore the irrational basis for opposition to nuclear power (see Otway and Thomas, 1982). The review of the risk perception literature also suggests that very little of it has been applied to policy elites. This is true of the literature discussed as well as the three major studies discussed above (Dietz and Rycroft, 1988; Lichter and Rothman, 1987; Lynn, 1986). To the extent that they addressed risk issues, they involved risk assumptions but not risk perceptions.

There has also been little work on relating perceptions, ideology, employment, and so forth, with actual decisions. A reasonable assumption can be made that the linkage between beliefs and action is strong. More work needs to be done here. In addition, as the federal government eased its regulatory efforts during the Reagan administration, some of the policy focus shifted to the state level (see, for example, Bowman and Kearney, 1986). The risk perception literature, as well as the type of studies that Dietz and Rycroft have done, should be replicated at the state level. Here we could look at differences between policy elites at the federal and state levels and among the states.

There are other problems with the risk perception literature. The definition of risk used by the Decision Research group is especially narrow: the total risk of dying in a given year from an activity or substance. The problem with this emphasis on mortality is that it neglects morbidity, sub-lethal occurrences that may be the result of the same set of activities or technologies. The rate of morbidity greatly exceeds mortality rates. For example, more than 45,000 people died in motor vehicle accidents in 1975, but over *5 million people* were injured in such accidents during that year. Possible sub-lethal effects of technologies and activities include birth and genetic defects, cancer, injuries to various parts of the body, reproductive difficulties, and illnesses (see Rowe, 1977).

Their definition of risk may also be responsible for differences in lay judgments and expert judgments. Again, the Decision Research group recognized this possibility. When asked to estimate the number of fatalities, the lay members are moderately accurate. When asked to evaluate risk, then the differences between the two groups are substantial. As they pointed out, for experts risk may be synonymous with annual fatalities. For the lay public, it means something else (see also Perrow, 1984).

The implications of this discussion for risk perception are important. Much of the burden of risk perception (and decision-making) studies is that people in general do not make decisions rationally. Recall the Combs and Slovic (1979) study which suggested that the representative heuristic was at play in estimating fatalities, because newspapers emphasized injuries over disease. Yet if the subjects used a broader, richer concept of risk than the experts, the appropriate conclusion is that risk means something different to some than to others, not that some misperceive or are given misleading information.

Others have pointed out the problems with the one definition of risk. Vlek and Stallen (1980) offered six different definitions of risk. Lee (1981) indicated that for many people there are fates worse than death. Cole and Withey (1981) also suggested that perceived risk is a multidimensional study. Harding and Eiser (1984), in their risk perception study, allowed subjects to define risk for themselves.

Finally, Otway and Thomas (1982) indicated that the most useful findings are those that show differences in perceptions observed for different groups. The Vlek and Stallen study (1981) showed that the greatest disagreement among groups was on dimensions having the most policy implications. Thus, Otway and Thomas concluded (1982:78), "These results suggest to us that the lack of consensus among lay publics, (and thus the root of conflict) is centered on perception and meaning of control and organization of regulatory procedures, and on equitable distributions of benefits (rather than on riskiness per se)." Again, such questions ought to be addressed in relation to policy elites.

Ideally, risk perception studies would look at risk perception of a variety of different groups, distinguished at a minimum by the seven estates discussed earlier in this chapter. In effect, the risk perception studies have failed to answer our most important question: How does risk perception affect policy-making? And the elite studies have ignored the risk perception literature (with the partial exception of Rothman and Lichter [1987]).

In sum, we need to know how risk perceptions are formed, and how they affect policy-making toward risk. A comparative study, across the estates and between elites and the mass, would also address a fundamental problem of democratic politics: the linkage between the public, its representatives, and public policy (Luttbeg, 1981).

Part Three

Environmental Policy Outcomes

11

International Environmental Politics: A Theoretical Review of the Literature

Dimitris Stevis, Valerie J. Assetto, and Stephen P. Mumme

The politics of the international environment has only recently entered the study of international relations. Nonetheless, there is an impressive body of literature on various aspects. A substantial part of the literature examines the political and tactical requirements for a better environment or a better-managed environment. Another significant part examines the impact of environmental problems on relations among governments and other organizations. In the essay that follows we attempt a theoretically informed inventory of the literature. We hope that the criteria and classification used will offer themselves to cumulation, either in the direction of theory or in the direction of more comprehensive classification efforts.

In this discussion our definition of environment utilized is limited to activities which pollute, which transform the physical qualities of the biosphere, including irreparable damage to renewable resources, or which create situations hazardous to habitats and health. We do not include the utilization of resources except as this results in the above. In general, therefore, the concept of "environment" is not coterminous with the total context within which humans exist.

We have concentrated mainly on literature that deals with the above types of activities when they involve or are likely to involve two or more agents across state jurisdictions. Accordingly, we have also reviewed the literature which examines foreign-policy-making questions and domestic issues whose resolution is closely connected to international relations, for example, the export of hazardous materials.

We do not aim, however, at a comprehensive account of the literature on natural environmental developments, nor do we discuss technical writings, whether those are on economics or on the practical requirements and procedures for the application of environmental programs or measures. Moreover, within the literature on the politics or political economy of the international environmental issues, we have paid close attention to those sources which offer theoretical insights.

We have been lucky to have access to two useful and recent thematic reviews of international environmental developments and policies (Caldwell, 1984a; Dahlberg et al., 1985). We have undertaken, however, a systematic review of the literature since 1971. The year was chosen because the Stockholm Conference was just a year away and a variety of writings were published in the years 1971 and 1972 in anticipation or under its influence.

Although our goal is not a detailed bibliographic essay but, rather, a critical theoretical review, we have attempted to canvass as much of the available English-language literature as possible. While much of the problematic is that encountered in North America, we have paid close attention to the discussion of the relations between environment and economic development.

The literature may be broadly divided into that which is primarily substantive and that which is primarily theoretical. The substantive literature, in turn, may be subdivided into those writings which are primarily descriptive accounts and those which are informed by theoretical considerations.

Substantive Literature

A thematic presentation of the substantive literature on international environmental politics is a requisite first part. In line with our goals, the substantive literature we are interested in is that which deals with the political aspects of environmental issues. As indicated, many of the writings in this category may also deal with theoretical issues or may be informed by identifiable assumptions (e.g., Schneider, 1979; M'Gonigle and Zacher, 1979; Rochlin, 1979; Kay and Jacobson, 1983).

A first set of substantive literature consists of writings that examine the evolution of environmental concern and activities as a whole (e.g., Caldwell, 1972, 1984a; Dahlberg et al., 1985). These works offer a rounded view on environmental issues, while they may be informed by particular points of views or ends.

A second set consists of information and data compendia (e.g., *The Global 2000 Report,* 1980; Simon, 1981; Holdgate, Kassas, and White, 1982; OECD, 1985). These writings catalogue activities and resources and describe the state of the environment. They do reflect, however, different approaches to international environmental policy, such that they cannot be thought of as mere descriptions of political activities or natural developments.

A third, larger set consists of writings on particular environmental issues. These studies may be more or less comprehensive, that is, they may cover the natural developments, the historical background, the considerations and priorities of the interested parties, negotiations and other interactions among interested parties, the pertinent law, the involvement of regional or global organizations, as well as theoretical propositions, in an attempt to explain the present situation and forecast the future.

Various aspects of the marine environment have been the object of intensive negotiations and extensive academic research. There exists a substantial literature on marine pollution in general (e.g., Waldichuk, 1973, 1977, 1982; Lester, 1980; Johnston, 1981; Charney, 1982; Timagenis, 1980; Kindt, 1986). The collections tend to concentrate on the legal aspects of the issue; we have not found a comprehensive study of the politics of marine pollution.

Specific sources of pollution, such as land-based pollution, vessel pollution, and dumping and regional strategies, such as the UNEP (United Nations Environment Program) regional seas program, have received a great deal of attention.

The pollution of the seas from vessels is particularly controversial because of the significance of ocean trade and has received a great deal of attention (Bernhardt, 1980; Dempsey and Helling, 1980; Meese, 1982; Schneider, 1982; Khaier and Sebek, 1985; Wang, 1986). The study by M'Gonigle and Zacher (1979) offers both theoretical insights and a substantive overview of the question of oil pollution from tankers.

Dumping has also received a great deal of attention (e.g., Boehmer-Christiansen, 1983, 1986; Zepetello, 1985; Bewers and Garrett, 1987). There are no comprehensive analyses, however, except on the question of using the seabed for the burial of radioactive wastes (Deese, 1978; Miles, Lee, and Carlin, 1985).

The question of environmental impacts from offshore activities, such as mining and drilling, have also been examined (e.g., Goldie, 1972; Hardy, 1973/74; de Mestral, 1979). Although there are no comprehensive studies on the environmental effects of offshore resource activities, the study by Manners (1982) offers a thorough examination of the issues as related to the North Sea.

Land-based marine pollution has also been the object of study (e.g., McManus, 1982; Kildow, 1982; Kwiatkowska, 1984). Land-based pollution, along with vessel pollution, are at the heart of regional concerns over the environment. It is in the area of regional marine protection that we find a great deal of practical developments—through the UNEP Regional Seas Program—as well as a healthy amount of writing (e.g., Okidi, 1977; Thacher and Meith, 1980; Alheritiere, 1982; Boczek, 1984; Hayward, 1984).

In addition to the above more general writings, there is an increasing body of work on various regions, particularly the Mediterranean (e.g., Juda, 1979; Baruch, 1982; Saliba, 1983; Haas, 1986), but, also other regions (e.g., Thacher and Meith, 1982; Charney, 1982; Boczek, 1983; Joyner, 1984; Boehmer-Christiansen, 1984; Pathmarajah and Meith, 1985).

Finally, the relation of the Law of the Sea Convention and the regulation of the marine environment is ever present and has been the specific object of much research, much of it exegetic of the text (e.g., Kindt, 1980, 1986; Boyle, 1985).

The quality of air and the climate has been the object of increased attention due to the transnational effects of acid rain and other airborne substances. The question of acid rain in Europe and North America has attracted attention with respect to the questions of law (e.g., van Lier, 1981), with respect to its significance for the relations between neighboring countries (e.g., Davilla, 1972; Smith, 1983; Elsworth, 1984; Scott, 1986), with respect to its economics (e.g., Gilbert, 1982; Seigneur, 1987), and with respect to efforts at solving the problem (e.g., Cameron, 1982; Wetstone and Rosencranz, 1983; Brady and Scelle, 1985).

Related to the question of the quality of the air and the atmosphere is the question of climatic change. This issue has been the object of a comprehensive collection (Nanda, 1983). Within this issue, the question of environmental modification for military purposes was also the object of study during the 1970s (e.g., Samuels, 1973).

Yet another substantive issue that has generated a well-developed body of literature concerns management of water quality in international rivers and lakes. The problem of transboundary pollution and water quality in international drainage basins has produced a substantial commentary on the application of international law to the settlement of disputes related to transboundary surface and groundwater pollution (e.g., Utton, 1973a; Alheritiere, 1976; Caponera, 1985; Teclaff and Teclaff, 1979; Hayton, 1982; Kiss, 1985; Carroll, 1986). Additional studies focus on diplomacy, negotiation, and conflict management (e.g., Utton, 1976; LeMarquand, 1976, 1977; Mingst, 1981; Carroll, 1983, 1986;

Mumme, 1985)—while others concentrate on problems of administration and management (e.g., Fox, 1976; Carroll, 1986).

Some of the earliest efforts at international cooperation for ecological conservation occurred in the area of species preservation. Much has been written about the efforts of nongovernmental organizations (NGOs), and later, states and their attendant governmental agencies, to preserve migratory species that traveled beyond a single state's boundaries (de Klemm, 1972; McHugh, 1977; Scharff, 1977a and 1977b; Barnes, 1982; Birnie, 1985). The majority of the more current literature on species preservation focuses on the efforts of states and their affiliated organizations, both public and private, to formulate international conventions designed to protect and preserve various species of flora and fauna through agreements to limit state behavior (Boardman, 1981; Barnes, 1982; Caldwell, 1984a; Bordwin, 1985). Within this category, the literature on the preservation of whales is the most complete (Scharff, 1977a and 1977b; McHugh, 1977; M'Gonigle, 1980; Birnie, 1984, 1985).

Recently there has been a growing concern with the preservation of wildlife habitats, the degradation of which is seen as perhaps most threatening to endangered species and to human well-being (Tulchin, 1986). Issues of habitat preservation thus encompass much broader issues of environmental degradation, including marine pollution and land-use practices, such as deforestation. These issues have increased the already significant amount of controversy surrounding the species preservation question and bring into sharp contrast the divisions within this group of analysts. Specifically, the debate centers on the reconciliation of the needs and demands of humans and economic development with the needs of other species. There is a tension, yet to be resolved, between those who advocate enlightened management of species and habitat and those who argue that the crisis is so severe that nothing short of complete conservation, or restoration, will suffice to stem the growing tide of species extinction (Boardman, 1981).

Finally, there is an emerging literature specifically focused on the problem of transnational hazardous waste management. While this literature, insofar as water is concerned, somewhat overlaps the literature on transboundary water pollution, it is substantively broader gauged, including in its orbit themes of solid waste disposal, industrial toxic waste contamination, and problems related to radioactivity and nuclear waste, all resulting from the intensified use of high technologies in industry, health maintenance, and—most visible of all—energy production (e.g., Alston, 1978; Handl, 1978; Finn, 1983; Goldberg,

1985; Ramberg, 1986/87; Carter, 1987). Closely related to this body of literature, but substantially distinct in its focus on the environmental costs of thermonuclear war, is a growing body of literature addressing the hypothetical problem of nuclear winter (e.g., Thompson and Schneider, 1986; Sagan, 1985).

A fourth set of substantive writings consists of comprehensive legal compendia (e.g., Bleicher, 1972; Novak, 1976; Johnson, 1976; Kiss, 1976; Bothe et al., 1980; Lausche, 1982; Dupuy, 1985), theoretically informed legal studies (Schneider, 1979; Springer, 1983; Kiss, 1983), or studies of particular issues or cases whose primary aim is to present the extant regulations and law and/or the legal arguments of the interested parties (e.g., Alston, 1978; Boczek, 1983; Charney, 1982; Johnston, 1981). The volume of the legal literature is impressive. Most of it is exegetic of various documents and points of view. In dealing with questions of fundamental legal principles such as the "common heritage of mankind" (Kiss, 1983; de Klemm, 1985) or the constitution of a world public order (Schneider, 1979) or the political sources of international law (Wilson, 1974; Piper, 1979), writings in this category introduce a significant metalegal component.

A fifth category of substantive literature consists of accounts of the structure and operations of various organizations, meetings, and conferences related to international environmental politics. The organizations may be national (e.g., Johnson and Blake, 1979), regional (e.g., Burhenne and Schoenbaum, 1973; Hertzel, 1980; Wilcher, 1980), or global (e.g., Hargrove, 1972; Kay and Skolnikoff, 1972; Stein and Johnson, 1979; Boardman, 1981; Kay and Jacobson, 1983; Barkenbus, 1987). The work of various conferences has also been extensively covered (e.g., Berry, 1972; Sohn, 1973; M'Gonigle and Zacher, 1979; Timagenis, 1980).

Finally, there exists a growing literature dealing with the relations of economics and the environment. A major component of this body of literature is that which deals with the issue of environment and development (e.g., Pearson and Pryor, 1978; Riddell, 1981; Redcliff, 1984; Leonard, 1985; Pearson, 1975, 1985, 1987; Bartelmus, 1986). The literature on the relation between environment and development is inherently "theoretical," inasmuch as the concept of development is far from being one on which there is general agreement.

In addition to the question of the relationship between environment and development, there is also a more general body of work on economics and the environment that concentrates on the impact of environmental regulations on trade and investment (e.g., Baumel, 1971; Pearson, 1976, 1985, 1987; World Bank, 1975, 1978; Rubin and Graham, 1982).

Theoretical Literature

Two questions have directed this review. First, have theoretical propositions been used to study international environmental issues? Second, if so, what have been the scope and content of these theories? The first question requires no extended answer; environmental issues have attracted a fair amount of theorizing. The scope and content of these theories do require elaboration, however. Theories have been marshaled to map long-term developments, that is, to model the future, as well as to explicate discord and collaboration among the various interested parties. Moreover, a shift is recognized from the grand theorizing of the 1970s to the micro-theorizing of the 1980s. Overall, we have found that the literature of environmental politics may be subdivided into what we have labeled the contextual, situational, and futures categories. The meanings of these terms are elaborated below.

We have chosen to approach the literature by using three levels of analysis. The question of the levels of analysis is well known in international politics (Russett and Starr, 1985:13–17). We use levels only in order to facilitate classification rather than in order to establish the primacy of one over the other. While following Russett's and Starr's preference for including a multiplicity of factors in setting up their levels, we have not used the same scheme. Instead we are using the three levels of *agent, structure,* and *process,* which are defined rather broadly.

The first organizing level is that of *the agent*. As agents we will consider only purposeful social forces, entities or organizations, such as individuals, households, firms, interest groups, parties, nongovernmental organizations, governmental bureaucracies, governments, intergovernmental organizations (IGOs).

The second level is that of *structure*. We take the term *structure* to denote both the "architectonic" arrangement of agents and the long-term forces which affect this arrangement as well as the characteristics of the agents themselves. With respect to governments, structure can denote long-term relations with other governments, access to resources, internal organization, nature of political and economic systems, etc. With respect to firms, structure can denote internal organization, access to technology, geographic and sectoral deployment, etc. With respect to other organizations structure can denote internal organization and level of autonomy.

Finally, we also use the level of *process*. Process denotes the micro-behaviors of agents within the extant structural parameters, and includes the process and exigencies of conflict resolution, access to information, international conferences and negotiations.

Categories of theoretical writings

Our review of the literature has suggested a threefold division into what we have labeled *contextual, situational,* and *futures* literature. The distinction among these categories serves both a logistical and an analytic purpose. While they deal with the same subjects and are often founded upon the same theoretical assumptions, their temporal and spatial scopes are sufficiently different.

Contextual literature consists of writings that purport to situate the contemporary social world in a larger historical or ecological context. The first subset purports to uncover and map the diachronic trends and causes which have led us to the present conjuncture (e.g., Meadows et al., 1972; Mesarovic and Pestel, 1974; Simon, 1981). The second subset consists of macro-theoretical propositions that purport to explain social and political affairs in a larger synchronic context—and one of analytical and practical import (Deutch, 1977; Sprout and Sprout, 1971, 1978; Ophuls, 1977; Pirages, 1978, 1983). These works offer us an alternate way of looking at the social world and its workings. Consequently, they suggest additional or different variables, relations, and goals that both theorists and practitioners have to take into account. Nonetheless, beyond the common admonitions for an "ecological" approach, this literature diverges into different assumptions, theories, and goals.

Environmental issues—as we have defined them—are only one of the component elements of contextual literature. For the most part, these writings include resources, energy, population, and social structures.

Situational literature consists of writings that purport to explain or predict patterns and outcomes regarding international environmental activities and developments within a shorter temporal and spatial scope. Situational literature identifies specific agents and problems. It may be distinguished from contextual literature in that it deals with issues within an implicit or explicit context.

We feel that the distinction between contextual and situational literature is a useful one and one that has general validity. Propositions about the long-term impact of industrialization on the environment, for example, tell us little about the resolution of the acid rain question between the United States and Canada; similarly, ecopolitics does not automatically suggest which variables and causal paths account for hazardous waste disposal in the Atlantic, nor can geo/ecopolitical schemes account for particular policies. Contextual literature is most useful when it is used to alert us to additional factors that we may wish to take into consideration in resolving specific problems and with information about the limits to our capacities.

Futures literature may be subdivided into two types. Most prominent during the 1970s was the "global future" type (for a summary of futures literature see Soroos in Dahlberg et al., 1985:chap. 5). This type of futures literature is a component part of what we have called contextual literature. The second type of future-oriented literature is applied in nature. Accordingly it consists of proposals that are founded on present potentialities, in order to regulate or resolve an environmental issue. The UNEP strategy, other regional or bilateral agreements, and various functional conventions fit well within this type, which we consider to be adequately dealt with within what we have called situational literature.

Most of contextual literature includes strategic, normative, or predictive propositions on the future. These may be more or less detailed (e.g., Falk, 1971, and the World Order Models Project [WOMP]); they remain, however, at a high level of speculation or abstraction or are not applicable in the resolution of immediate problems. Situational literature also offers tactics, strategies, prescriptions, and predictions—which may be informed by the same priorities as contextual literature. The temporal frame of these elements, however, is of a shorter term and their purpose is application.

We have decided not to include a separate discussion of futures literature since there are explicit and implicit references to it throughout the presentation of the contextual and situational categories.

Theories and Assumptions from the Contextual Literature

Contextual literature attempts to identify the agents, structures, or processes that cause the environment—among other elements—to change or that establish the environment as a factor in thinking about human affairs, in general, and politics, in particular. With respect to the diachronic contextual literature, we may ask "What is the agent, process, or structure that best accounts for the state of the environment?" With respect to the synchronic contextual literature we may ask "What are the ways in which the environment relates to and influences agents, structures, and processes?"

The studies of the Club of Rome—and the school of diachronic thought and research that they have inspired (see summary and comparison in *The Global 2000 Report,* vol. 2, pts. 3 and 4)—constitute the most prominent example of contextual literature that attempts to establish the contemporary conjuncture as part and product of long-term processes. Similarly, opposing research (Simon, 1981; Simon and Kahn, 1984) is also part of this approach. What best accounts for deteriorating environmental quality according to the "pessimists" is the intensive use of the world around us in ways that do not take into account its limits. The "optimists," on the other hand, feel that humanity can avoid these limits, primarily through technology and productivity. Most prominent among the latter are those who advocate the solution of growth and those advancing the more extreme version of the view of the industrializing economies. In both the "optimist" and "pessimist" strains, the environment is only one of the major factors that are considered. As with the other components—demographics, resources, industry, and technology—environmental trends have both an exogenous and an endogenous dynamic. The environment is a dependent variable in that its quality improves or worsens as a result of changes in the other variables. The environment, however, is also an independent variable in that its transformation will feed into the other trends.

Much of the contemporary argument on limits has not acknowledged the less than satisfactory environmental standards, policies, and outcomes of the past (Bettman, 1974). Such evidence is not necessarily adverse to the argument of environmental catastrophes; there probably have been as many environmental catastrophes in historical times as there have been recuperations. It may be that the argument of a "final" catastrophe at a highly aggregated level has overshadowed the probability of major regional or partial catastrophes. Similarly, the arguments of the opponents when based on evidence of an equally "bad" past may be a valid critique of the projection of a final reckoning, but may not be construed as evidence that environmental problems will correct themselves.

Closely related to the limitarian problematic of the critical global predicament are the "lifeboat" and "one-world" images ("ethics") (Soroos, 1979). The "lifeboat" approach draws its historical and analytic inspirations from the dynamics of scarcity as set out in the "tragedy of the commons" dilemma (Hardin, 1968, 1986; Hardin and Baden, 1977). The "one-world" approach draws from the same pool of ideas but differs with respect to the solutions proposed. These two approaches can serve as a bridge between the mainly diachronic and mainly synchronic components of contextual literature.

Hardin's "tragedy of the commons" is predicated on the existence of limits to the goods that are available to the agents. In this sense, the choices of the agents are circumscribed by the "architecture" of the world in which they must operate. The applicability of the "tragedy of the commons" dilemma and of "lifeboat ethics" to the environment—as we have defined it—is not without its problems. When applied to resources, it has been a trenchant argument for property and state rights (Eckert, 1979); it is not clear, however, how property rights can effectively protect us from transboundary pollution. While property holders may clean up within their jurisdiction, there is no guarantee that they will choose cleaning up over production, before irreparable damage has taken place. On the other hand, and consistent with the theory, the problem could be solved through various transnational arrangements (Soroos in Dahlberg et al., 1985:chap. 4). Such a solution, however, would have to assume that the transboundary impacts of local activities imbue these activities with an internal logic that, in turn, conditions the responses of agents.

Another question that can be raised with respect to the "tragedy of the commons" dilemma is that of its historical veracity (Cox, 1985). If, in fact, the logic of the dilemma unfolds not as a result of the architectonics of the situation—limited resources accessible to benefit-maximizing agents—but as a result of long-term social transformations that herald the decline of agents and structure and their replacement by others, then the "commons" problematic may be misplaced. Accordingly, the issue raises the question of what agents would do if they were interested in increasing the size of their flocks but does not ask why they have flocks or why they may wish to increase their size.

The "one-world" image has taken the principles of scarcity and limits to imply that the only meaningful path for theory and action is one that accepts the unity of the world (e.g., Caldwell, 1972, 1974, 1984a; Falk, 1971; Boulding, 1966; Brown, 1978, 1981). The nature of the biosphere, moreover, further underscores the imperative of this unity. For the most part the writers in this vein do recognize the obstacles to change posed by the present characteristics of the world, particularly sovereign rights, uninformed values, and economic priorities. For these reasons they are interested in "rearranging" the world.

A theoretical strain that underlies the "one-world" image is that of the "steady-state" (Daly, 1973, 1980; Brown, 1978, 1981). The essential thrust is toward a systematic and large-scale restructuring of values and developmental and economic practices so that they do not lead to rapid entropy. The supporters of the "one-world"/"steady-state" image emphasize the need for political action; it is not clear, however, whether such action will be led by any specific social force other than people with new values. Nor have they dealt with the possibility that the breaking down of state boundaries or the adoption of new values may require dramatic transformations in all social relations, including property rights.

The "tragedy of the commons" and "steady-state" approaches offer us ways in which to think about the global predicament as it has appeared during the last two decades. In a somewhat different vein, the works of Harold and Margaret Sprout (1971, 1978), Dennis Pirages (1978, 1983), and Karl Deutch (1977), as well as those who have used the image of "spaceship Earth," seek to introduce an ecological perspective to the understanding of politics. Their similarities lie in the sharing of the idea of limits and their explicit efforts to locate politics within a larger context informed by a fusion of geopolitics and ecology. For them it is not adequate to consider only the traditional variables of politics—mostly exhausted as they are in other characteristics of the social world. Instead, it is necessary to place the social world within the context of technological capacities and natural resources, including environmental limits.

It is not justifiable, however, to consider all of the writers in this vein as internationalists, nor is there something inherent in ecopolitical literature that makes it applicable only to internationalist theory and analysis. Accordingly, the Sprouts have accentuated the geopolitical aspect of ecopolitics to suggest a strategy for the survival of the United States (Sprout and Sprout, 1978). It is perhaps this "procedural neutrality" of some ecopolitical thinking that distinguishes it from that which accepts the substantive inescapability of global ecological and environmental interdependence.

Situational Literature

Much of the prominent literature on the environment has been associated with what we have called contextual literature, and many of the major works were published in the seventies. Since then there has been something of a diminution in grand environmental theorizing. Environmental research, however, has not retreated below what it had been before the seventies. In fact, it would seem that environmental questions have entered the agenda of both states and political groups as well as academia—whether as a way of looking at the world or as specific areas of concern.

In dealing with situational literature we are attempting a theoretical classification of writings that have attempted to apply theory—whether informed by the mainstream international politics or ecopolitical writings—to specific environmental and environmentally relevant issues. In order to establish a theoretically informed classification, we aim at the identification of the agent, process, or structure that best accounts for the outcomes—including inaction—in dealing with environmental questions.

The level of the agent

At this level, analysis, prediction, and explanation are articulated around the *interests* and *behavior* of the agent. Accordingly, within this category we include literature that attempts to analyze the actions of agents as they seek to pursue their interests and as they respond to a variety of influences. At the level of the agent, the causal path and the theoretical account are articulated around the agents, rather than structural properties or the exigencies of process.

The "state"—when it refers to "country" or "state apparatus"—is not considered a purposeful agent. A country cannot act, except through the institutions of the state. Similarly, the "state apparatus" can only act through the government or various of its institutions. Moreover, the actions of a government or a bureaucracy may or may not aim at some "national interest," defined to mean a nonparticularistic interest. It is not justifiable, therefore, to consider governmental actions as symmetric or similar to each other. Moreover, governments and governmental bureaucracies—as well as other agents—also act within both a domestic and a global structure.

IGOs may be considered as mere instruments of states in a divided world; or they may be thought of as entities with potential, if limited, agency. It is in this sense that IGOs will be examined here, that is, as entities that are attempting to intervene autonomously in the global environmental process. IGOs as signal posts of some network of rules and expectations are dealt with as part of regimes.

International nongovernmental organizations (INGOs), such as the International Union for the Conservation of Nature, Friends of the Earth, or Greenpeace, and local parties, such as the Greens, with an international view of the environment, constitute a third layer of agents with purposeful input and impact on international environmental politics.

Finally, in our view, firms are not simply interest groups or INGOs. Both within most of the major economies and at a global level, firms control and deploy resources which few, if any, entities other than governments possess. These resources, in turn, are necessary not only to the firm but, also, to society at large. Finally, the transnational organizational deployment of firms seems unmatched, with the possible exception of the Catholic Church. It seems impossible to talk about the impact of economic interests, let us say in vessel-pollution or acid rain, without taking into account industry interests; and if these are not dealt with in literature we should consider it an area for more research.

Governments and bureaucracies. The distinction between government and bureaucracy facilitates the separation of those instances in which particular bureaucracies have a predominant impact on the shaping of a policy, perhaps in the face of governmental opposition. Accordingly it allows for the consideration of all shades of transnational policies.

The actions of governments and bureaucracies raise the question of what motivates them to act. Generally, governmental institutions will act in response to various interests as well as to their interpretation of their own interests and of the general interests of the country at large. To simply say that they will respond, however, may be an incomplete representation of reality. Institutions are also likely to be shaped in a way that will require them to act in particular directions. For example, the International Atomic Energy Agency is responsible for certain issues related to the safe use of nuclear energy; it is not, however, an opponent of nuclear energy. As a result, we cannot expect that it will advocate the abolition of nuclear energy.

The overall development and changes in environmental policy have received some attention in the United States, particularly with respect to the ideologically motivated priorities of the Reagan administration and the need for an environmentally informed foreign policy (e.g., Coan, Hillis, and McCloskey, 1974; Caldwell, 1984b; Benedict, 1986). Intragovernmental dynamics affecting international environmental politics have been examined with respect to the transboundary issues, such as those involving the United States and its neighbors or European countries (e.g., OECD, 1981; Carroll, 1983; Mumme, 1985; Fullenbach, 1981; Elsworth, 1984; Wetstone and Rosencranz, 1983). We have found no comprehensive studies, however, on the formation of the international environmental politics as an aspect of foreign policy.

One area where the institutions of the state are increasingly involved is that of energy. The production of energy constitutes one of the foremost causes of environmental risks (Kelley, 1977; Manners, 1982). There is a great deal of literature covering the issues of acid rain, water pollution, and radioactive wastes. In general this literature speaks to the priority of energy issues over environmental issues. There are no detailed analyses, however, of the societal dynamics that underlie this balance, nor of the inroads that some environmental concerns may have achieved.

The impact of military activities, where governments have a monopoly, has not been adequately studied, with the possible exceptions of nuclear explosions, nuclear winter, and weather modification. It is noteworthy, however, that military activities are often privileged in international instruments. For example, the 1972 London Dumping Convention does not affect military vessels.

Disasters and accidents are supposed to have an impact on the formation of such pressures, and international disasters are supposed to have an impact on shaping international policies. There are frequent references in the literature to the dramatic impact of disasters at sea on the growth of the international environmental concern. While disasters may in fact have a proximate effect, it is not clear that there is a causal relation between them and environmentalism. Perhaps "postindustrialist" arguments or arguments regarding the nonaesthetic costs of environmental degradation can shed more light on the subject. An extensive literature has emerged, however, dealing with the risks of the deployment of hazardous technologies (Shrader-Frechette, 1985; Perrow, 1984). The extension of this research to the international level could be quite productive.

The autonomous role of governmental institutions has not received a great deal of attention, perhaps because of the predominance of interest-group politics in the United States. It is interesting to note, also, that the impact of various interest groups on international environmental policy has received limited attention; there exists, however, an abundance of comparative and country studies (e.g., Enloe, 1975; Kelley, Stunkel, and Wescott, 1976; de

Bardelaben, 1985; Park, 1986). There is also a small literature on the implications of policies on the international environment (e.g., Azevedo, 1982; Gaines, 1982; Stowe, 1987).

Private firms and the environment. The impact of environmental developments on the economy—and thus on the firm—and the impact of the private firm on the environment are questions which have received increasing attention. During the emergence of environmental concerns in the early seventies, the core question was whether environmental costs in the industrial economies would lead to a flight of capital to the less industrialized world (e.g., Baumel, 1971; Koo, 1979). This possibility may not have come to pass (Rahmatullah, 1980); there is a substantial literature, however, on the impacts of environmental policies on trade (e.g., Pearson, 1976; Rubin and Graham, 1982; Galli, 1987).

The impact of firms on the policies of governments and bureaucracies does not exhaust their influence on international environmental policies. Multinational corporations can also operate outside of the jurisdiction of governments with demanding environmental standards. They can in fact reach agreements with governments that choose certain risky industries or less satisfactory standards. Such a collaboration may be thought of as an exercise in state sovereignty or as a means by the firm to transfer externalities to another market. In either case, such interactions constitute international environmental policy. A growing concern both with respect to the negative image of firms and with the need for higher environmental standards has produced an increasing body of literature (e.g., Pearson, 1985, 1987; Elkington, 1987).

International organizations—IGOs and INGOs. Up to the 1972 Stockholm Conference there was a great deal of discussion on the appropriateness of an environmental IGO or some other international or even supranational entity to coordinate and establish policy on the environment. The UNEP is not a supranational IGO and, in fact, it is no more than a coordinating program. Various IGOs, however, have continued to be involved in environmental policy, as part of their general responsibilities. A collection of studies by Kay and Jacobson (1983) offers one of the few systematic studies of environmental politics. More specifically it concentrates on the role and efficacy of IGOs, utilizing an analytic framework (Jacobson and Kay, 1983a). Among the findings of the eleven studies, as summarized by the editors, the efficacy of IGOs is greater when the issue is not controversial and uncertainty is low, costs are not very high, and individual states are unwilling to assume disproportionate costs. IGOs themselves, however, can enhance their impact by openness to new facts, competence, and dynamic leadership.

Another study (Hertzel, 1980) concentrates on the role of regional IGOs connecting the Western industrial states and concludes that IGOs are not themselves the cause of environmental cooperation but, rather, the facilitators of such cooperation. Within the constraints imposed by member states, these regional IGOs can facilitate learning and help push through national programs.

The role of economic IGOs has received attention, due to a large extent to the World Bank's emphasis on the environment (e.g., World Bank, 1975, 1978; Stein and Johnson, 1979; Horberry, 1985; Rich, 1985).

In general, IGOs may be a proximate cause of some environmental policy, but are not generally considered as autonomous policy-making agents at this point.

The role of INGOs has been the object of some research (Feraru in Dahlberg et al., 1985). As with IGOs, however, INGOs have been thought of as sources of information and knowledge.

The level of structures

In many instances the distinction between agent and structure is simply a matter of emphasis. Is it structure that determines the environmental policy of a less industrialized country, or is it the specific strategy and priorities of the government? Is it the necessary pursuit of profit that determines the actions of a firm or is it the particular management?

Nonetheless, we can point out two observations which justify the distinction between structure and agency. First, it is a distinction inherent in international relations theory, and thus in theoretical research on the environment. Second, there are, in fact, definite limits beyond which agents cannot go during specific historical periods. For example, it is not possible to have capitalism and continuous losses; nor is it possible to have both sovereign states and thoroughly autonomous IGOs.

State attributes. A number of structural characteristics have played a dominant role in the contextual literature. These characteristics we may call "state attributes" and include such characteristics as the level of industrialization or economic development, demographics, natural resources, and geopolitical position. Not all of these attributes, however, have been utilized to the same extent, nor received the same emphasis. A prominent set of attributes that has received extensive consideration is that of the level of economic development/industrialization and environmental politics.

The literature almost uniformly accepts the basic premise that a higher level of industrialization correlates with greater economic and strategic power. Within this context a second premise holds that the more industrialized states become, the greater their adverse impact on the environment, or pollution potential, will be. In what might be called the paradox of pollution, a corollary holds that those countries with greater pollution potential are those countries more likely to be concerned with quality of life, and the more likely to use their greater economic and strategic power domestically and within the international system to conserve and reclaim the environment. Theoretically, this relationship resembles the well-known thesis of a "demographic transition," suggesting that a threshold is reached at some point "X" in a state's industrialization, following which it exhibits a propensity to seek to ameliorate adverse environmental consequences following from industrialization. A number of subsidiary hypotheses may be drawn from these previous assumptions.

The most explicit statement of these relationships is found in the *Founex Report* on development and environment (1972), expressing the Third World governments' concern that the upcoming 1972 UN Conference on the Human Environment might prejudice the development prospects of the less industrialized countries by pressuring for restrictions on global industrialization. From this perspective the problem of economic development is seen as a basic impediment to the prospects of international environmental cooperation, but not necessarily an irreconcilable one (Woodhouse, 1972; Joyner and Joyner, 1974; Sunkel, 1980; Tolba, 1982; Bartelmus, 1986).

A number of studies have sought to examine aspects of this putative adversarial relationship between the more industrialized and less industrialized countries, focusing variously on (a) problems of export pollution, or externalities of industrialization, (b) international diffusion of innovation aimed at environmental amelioration, and (c) relationships of dependency and interdependency with respect to environmental protection in the international system. Virtually all of these studies either focus on specific issue areas (oceans, hazardous wastes, etc.) or on limited case studies or both (Cardoso, 1980; Mumme, 1985; Mumme, Bath, and Assetto, 1988).

Yet another genre of literature predicated on these assumptions seeks to evaluate global environmental trends and make policy recommendations at the binational, multilateral, and global levels. Because much of this literature is discussed in other contexts, only a couple of general references need be indicated here (Caldwell, 1984a; Biswas and Biswas, 1985).

The distribution of capacities. In dealing with questions of war and conflict many international theorists have found it useful to think of the world in terms of "anarchy." While anarchy does not mean the lack of overall order, it does mean the lack of a central political authority. Accordingly, states with unequal capacities are the last-instance determinants of their interests and goals. In turn, the outcomes in the interactions among states are best predicted by the systemwide distribution of power.

Applied to environmental politics, "structural realism" would suggest that environmental concerns are likely to be of secondary importance and that environmental policies will be determined by the structure of the system. If, for example, the most powerful state chooses to uphold environmental standards and pay for the costs, then important environmental policies will be pursued.

The merits of pure "structural realism" have been the object of debate for quite some time. There seems to be some common ground, however, between structural realists and both adversarial and sympathetic critiques. Structural realists are satisfied that their theory holds where it counts, meaning in questions of survival. Accordingly, the variability of outcomes in less consequential cases is not as significant, nor is it a major threat to the theory. From this starting point, there is no contradiction between them and the supporters of "complex interdependence" when arguing that in issues of lower priority outcomes may not be determined by the overall distribution of power. The outcome may not necessarily be adverse to environmental protection; that is, unilateral actions may be necessary or a major power, like the United States, may take the leadership in promoting environmental quality.

Pure structural-realist analysis has not been explicitly used in the analysis of environmental politics. It is ever present, however, as a background factor surfacing in references to the incompatibility of environmentalism with sovereignty.

Analyses emphasizing the issue-specific distribution of capacities, however, are more prominent (e.g., M'Gonigle and Zacher, 1979; Carroll, 1983). Accordingly, the capacities and intensity of interests of the participants in resolution of the issue may overdetermine the overall, bilateral, regional, or global distribution of power.

Regimes and institutions. We consider "regimes" to be an attempt to capture the processes that mediate between capacities and outcomes. Accordingly, generally acceptable principles do serve this analytic purpose, to the extent that they do have an impact on the resolution of problems. For example, the principle of "sovereign equality" has served important purposes in the post–World War II era, even though there is no specific IGO empowered to ensure that the principle is applied—perhaps the General Assembly comes the closest to fulfilling this role. Similarly, an international organization or an international agreement may also play the role of a "regime," even though they may not be associated with a variety of other mechanisms that could constitute an "ideal" regime.

While the concept of regime is frequently used in relation to environmental issues, there are no explicit attempts to find out the impact of regimes on outcomes. For this reason it is more useful to analyze the literature that deals with the formation and internal arrangements of environmental regimes. Our review has suggested a number of research questions that underlie the literature. A first question deals with the existence or not of "full-blown" regimes. A corollary to this question regards the methods by which regimes are created, for example, functionalism, negotiations, or imposition. A second question deals with the strategies preferable in the creation of environmental regimes. Within this set a prominent question deals with the relative merits and impacts of unilateral, regional, and global strategies and institutions on the formation of efficacious environmental policy. A third question deals with the existence of certain basic principles or imperatives around which law and organizations can be erected.

The question of the existence or not of regimes with respect to marine pollution has been dealt with by Boczek (1986) in an explicitly theoretical fashion. Young (1987) has dealt with regime formation with respect to the Arctic—which includes environment as one of the components. Boczek has concluded that a great variety of regimes are in place but that the evidence is still insufficient to establish their impacts on outcomes. Other accounts of regimes (e.g., Soroos, 1986; Dolman, 1981) offer "thick descriptions" of the various organizational and legal arrangements in a variety of areas, one of which is the environment.

The functionalist logic underlies much of the environmental literature; it is not always explicit, however. Accordingly, the question of the environment can be dealt with in a technical, nonpoliticized fashion and on an incremental basis. The debate over regional or international strategies is very much over functionalism or "politics." Mingst (1981) has explicitly challenged the functionalist argument; in her view, regime formation and functionalism constitute two distinct approaches to the understanding of environmental politics. Regime formation has the advantage that it recognizes the role of asymmetries and politics.

The regional-international controversy has attracted a great deal of attention—perhaps more in the seventies than now (Ward and Dubos, 1972; Kennan, 1970; Okidi, 1977). Hardin's (1986) objection to considering every issue as global does not solve the problem of what is truly global and what is not. Accordingly, we cannot use as our criterion of globality the physical properties of the environment alone. Pollution of the seas by oil is also a global problem, inasmuch as vessels navigate many seas. Standards for one region cannot be prepared without regard to other areas.

The regional seas program of the United Nations reflects both the technical and political obstacles to establishing global or regional standards. Articulated around the issues of transboundary and marine pollution, there has been a body of literature that examines the progress made primarily in North America, Europe, and the Mediterranean (Hayward, 1984; Haas, 1986). The discussion, however, is less and less on the relative merits of global or regional strategies.

Earlier on in the environmental debate there had been proposals for a global environmental agency, proposals which were negated by the Stockholm Conference. The issue, therefore, is no longer whether there should be an IGO—although that may happen in the future. Instead, the questions that are asked are whether unilateral actions may have a positive impact, what the determinants for reaching regional agreements are, and, finally, whether regional standards must be within some general global standards.

The question of regional versus global programs and standards, more than anything else, brings forth the question of "functionalism." The success of the functionalist strategy in the regional seas program of the UNEP remains to be seen.

The question of whether unilateral actions may catalyze system-wide changes has also been studied (Piper, 1979). Unilateralism may initiate an issue but it is hardly adequate to the creation of global policy.

Finally, there has been an extensive literature regarding the existence of basic principles on the basis of which environmental responsibilities and law should be established. Much of it deals with the foundations of transboundary responsibility and it seeks to establish the logic and limits of such expectations (Handl, 1975, 1980, 1986; Teclaff and Teclaff, 1985; Goetze, 1987). Another strain deals with the question of the "common heritage of mankind" and its applicability on environmental issues (Kiss, 1983; De Klemm, 1985). Finally, Schneider (1979)—but also, if in a less explicit fashion, Dahlberg et al. (1985) and Soroos (1986)—has used McDougal's "policy process" approach. Inasmuch as this approach requires the postulation of some global minimum standard, it is predicated upon a principle that ought to shape policy.

The level of process

The interactions between two or more agents may have their own dynamic. Accordingly, it is possible that agents participating in negotiations may have no reason not to reach an agreement that is related to the benefits and losses they expect on the particular issue. Agreement may not be reached, however, because of linkages or the nature of the decision-making process itself. It is known, for example, that the USSR abstained from the 1972 Stockholm Conference because of the East German question. This is a case of linkage that affected—to some degree—a major conference.

The study of process is more apparent in the examination of conferences, negotiations, and the resolution of conflict. There is a significant literature that describes conferences and outlines the views of particular participants (Berry, 1972; Sohn, 1973; Rowland, 1973; Timagenis, 1980). Moreover, there are a few studies that examine a variety of dynamics apparent in conferences (M'Gonigle and Zacher, 1979; Kindt, 1980; Bederman, 1986). One aspect that may require further study could be the impact of the size and complexity of conferences; it has been suggested, for example, that agreements on the Antarctic environment have been facilitated by the small number of participants (Krasner, 1985). Small conferences involving participants who share an interest in the issue are preferable to large conferences which may be held hostage to outsiders with unnecessary linkages. Depoliticized negotiations, that is, negotiations which involve noncontroversial issues or that can be reduced to technical discourse are also thought to be preferable. This approach, of course, is essentially functionalist.

The resolution of environmental conflict has also received increasing attention (Lake, 1977; Busterud, 1980; Mingst, 1982; Barnes, 1985; Dryzek and

Hunter, 1987). The use of mediation, rather than litigation or arbitration, has been considered desirable because it prevents confrontation and imposes fewer costs. Moreover, its unobtrusive nature makes it a better candidate for consideration by governments.

Conclusion

Our attempt has been to provide a theoretically informed inventory of the literature on international environmental issues. We have not sought to overload this essay with references but have provided enough to indicate the range of the literature.

We have found that the amount of writing on environmental issues has continued to grow. The character of the literature has changed, however, since the 1970s. During the 1970s much of the literature was contextual and programmatic. Contextual literature engaged in accounts of the diachronic sources of our present predicament. Situational literature consisted of proposals toward the reform of the structures that perpetuated these problems and of statements of the positions of the various agents and groups of countries on what should and could be done.

The diminution of grand-scale, often speculative theorizing is both positive and negative. It is positive inasmuch as it suggests that such an approach cannot continue defining the debate. It is negative inasmuch as it has not been replaced by more empirically informed theoretical proposals.

Such theoretical proposals do not need to map the whole environmental problematic. Nor do they need to cover whole areas, even though more such studies would be useful. The examination of particular events or developments, informed by explicit theories, would strengthen the further consideration of the environment as a theoretically significant issue in the study of international politics. It is interesting to note, in this respect, that the major international politics journals include a very small number of empirically grounded and theoretically informed articles. Most of the literature on the international environment is to be found in "trade" and international law journals.

While grand-scale theorizing has diminished, there has been a proliferation of literature on a great variety of environmental issues, most of it descriptive or presenting the views of particular agents. The increase in this literature is both useful and encouraging—as it indicates that environmental issues remain on the agenda. There is a risk, however, that the "critical" nature of environmental concern will dissipate into an "applied" attitude. Accordingly, environmental concerns may be equated solely with the management of the environment within the parameters of the extant values and relations.

In general, however, we have found that the amount of literature and information available represents an impressive foundation on which to build comprehensive, theoretically informed studies that can situate environmental studies in the midst of international politics discourse.

In closing, we would like to suggest a number of areas which could, and hopefully will, receive more or continuous attention. One such area is the role of overseas investment. In addition to the possibility of "pollution havens" it is also relevant to examine the degree to which investments abroad are environmentally sound. Complementarily, the conditions for the transfer of hazardous technology, such as chemical or nuclear technology, may also be a target for investigation.

The impact of growth on the environment along with the distributive impacts of economic deployment also require further study. The question of combining development and environment has been prominent since the beginning. Distributive impacts, however, have been examined mostly in terms of whole economies, rather than social groups, for example, indigenous people.

The operations and efficacy of transnational movements, such as Greenpeace and Friends of the Earth, and the spread of environmentally minded parties is another promising area. One aspect that may be worth examining is the degree to which these movements are included or excluded from global environmental decision-making. Such groups may be studied in addition and in comparison to IGOs and more traditional INGOs.

A fourth area that requires more research is that of the impact of military activities and armaments on the environment. While the scenarios on "nuclear winter" are on the agenda, there is comparatively little study of the impact of accidents, or of the environmental standards applicable to military industries.

The formation of foreign policy is also an area that requires continuous attention, particularly where domestic decisions will have an impact on the international deployment of firms, the military, financial or technological resources, or of various interest groups.

Finally, more explicit applications of various theories from international relations and political economy could also deliver interesting and useful results. The use of structural realism, regimes, or world systems, for example, can add both to our understanding of environmental politics and of the analytical and explanatory efficacy of those theories.

12

Alternative Views of the Environmental Problematic

John S. Dryzek and James P. Lester

The preceding chapters should make it abundantly clear that the environmental problematic is complex and multidimensional. Such complexity breeds variety in problem definitions and diagnoses, projections of environmental futures, evaluations of established means for coping with environmental problems, and prescriptions for policy and politics. Our intent in this chapter is to impose some order on this variety. We shall approach this task through reference to the fundamental worldviews which underpin diverse problem definitions and diagnoses, evaluations, and prescriptions. After enumerating and explicating these worldviews, we shall build upon them to outline several different scenarios for the environmental future. These scenarios constitute the possible contexts within which environmental policy will take effect—and to which the content of this policy should therefore be sensitive (cf. Dryzek, 1983b:357–61). But it should also be remembered that the scenarios could in part be created by environmental policy.

Imposing order is no easy task here. At first sight only a plethora of possibilities is evident, associated with both political organizations and movements and environmental intellectuals. Sometimes (and given the policy context this should come as no surprise) the line between political activism and intellectual cogitation is blurred.

If we begin our exploration with the environmentalists, we find a very broad church. The more conservative wing of extant environmentalism is home to business-sponsored groups such as the Club of Rome, and organizations like the Conservation Foundation which seek an accommodation with industrial society and the cooperation of the captains of industry in controlling pollution and promoting amenity. The environmentalist center is represented by groups such as the Sierra Club and Natural Resources Defense Council, which distrust industry but accept and utilize conventional channels of political action (lobbying, litigation, and campaign financing). More radical groups such as the Committees of Correspondence (representing an incipient Green movement of the sort that flourishes in West Germany) seek a different kind of politics, rejecting both the economic and political institutions of the status quo. Movements such as Earth First! and Greenpeace disdain politics altogether, pursuing direct action in obstructing the loggers of old-growth forests or harassing ocean waste dumpers.

Overlain on this conservative-radical dimension is variety in substantive concerns. Thus the Wilderness Society cares mostly about natural areas, while People for the Ethical Treatment of Animals is concerned only with the rights of individual creatures. More intricate is variety in the way groups view the environment. So while Friends of the Earth generally espouses a holistic, ecosystems view of man in the environment, the National Wildlife Federation conceives of the environment as a source of fish and game. And while the Sierra Club tends to stress amenity to humans, Earth First! is thoroughly misanthropic.

Of course, not all the political forces active on environmental issues can be located in the environmentalist camp. The opposition includes, not surprisingly, polluting and extracting industry, and—less stridently—labor and agricultural interests who care more about production and employment than a clean and healthy environment (see Hays, 1987:287–328). Beyond a few industry fronts, there is no antienvironmental interest group as such. However, the proliferating right-wing think tanks, conservative political entrepreneurs, and informal networks such as that surrounding the "Sagebrush Rebellion" of the early 1980s (which managed to propel several of its members into high federal office) are all active in this area.

The ecologists, economists, philosophers, and political scientists who think and write about environmental issues complicate matters further. A perusal of the journal *Environmental Ethics* will give some idea of the lively debates between partisans of different ethical positions. Some philosophers seek only to extend traditional anthropocentric ethical doctrines (such as utilitarianism, or rights-based reasoning) to environmental affairs (e.g., Goodin, 1983). The rights and interests of future generations are often central in such work (e.g., Sikora and Barry, 1978; Partridge, 1981). These doctrines can even be extended to the entities of the natural world; so Stone (1972) argues that rocks and trees as well as people have rights. But as well as applying human standards to nature, we can also apply nature's standards to humans: so

Wilson (1984) argues that biophilia, a love for the environment, is in fact inherent in our genes. It is also possible to discern in nature a source of values such as diversity and homeostasis (Lemons, 1981). Biocentric doctrines argue that nature has inherent value, irrespective of human interests and ascriptions. Deep ecologists, Heideggerians, ecofeminists, eco-Marxists, aesthetes, and eco-anarchists all add to this ferment. Ecological scientists often remind us of the need to take a holistic view of the environment (Commoner, 1972), though some ecologists are happily reductionistic.

The economic and political analyses which draw upon these ethical and scientific positions are equally varied. Some argue that ecological concerns demand a wholly new kind of rationality in policy-making (Dryzek, 1983a; Bartlett, 1986). Others feel that more familiar kinds of economic and political rationality are perfectly adequate guides to environmental policy (Baumol and Oates, 1975; McClosky, 1983). The resulting political prescriptions range from totalitarianism (Heilbroner, 1980) to the free market (Simon, 1981) to anarchism (Bookchin, 1982).

How, then, are we to make sense of this variety?

A Typology of Environmental Worldviews

We begin our construction of a typology of environmental worldviews by noting that people concerned with environmental affairs value different things. The two dominant traditions in Western political, social, and economic thought focus, respectively, on the individual and the community. Since the Enlightenment and the Industrial Revolution the individualist tradition has dominated, underpinning both market systems and liberal polyarchy, and, in the academy, contemporary economics and liberal constitutionalist political thought. The communitarian strain is manifested in classical conservatism and various kinds of socialism. Recent ecological concerns suggest that the community of interest can be biological as well as human, and so we can further divide our community category on this basis.

Regardless of where they locate value, thinkers can also be classified according to whether they favor centralized or decentralized solutions to environmental problems. Centralization obviously involves a major role for governmental institutions, and perhaps their consolidation across jurisdictions and functional areas. Decentralization implies suspicion of—and hostility toward—coordinated governmental action.

		LOCUS OF VALUE		
			Community	
		Individuals	Anthropocentric	Biocentric
LOCUS OF SOLUTIONS	Centralized	Hobbesians and Structural Reformers	Guardians	Reform Ecologists
	Decentralized	Free-market Conservatives	Social Ecologists	Deep Ecologists

Figure 12.1 A Taxonomy of Environmental Worldviews. SOURCE: Compiled by the authors.

Combining these two dimensions produces a six-celled typology which, we contend, captures the major modes of thought on environmental issues in recent years (see figure 12.1). We will now discuss each of these six cells, and then outline some uses for this taxonomy.

Hobbesians and structural reformers

One of the founders of modern liberal individualism was Thomas Hobbes. Hobbes believed, however, that unchecked individual appetites would lead to a disastrous "war of all against all." The solution, which benefited every individual, was political centralization in the person of an all-powerful sovereign. Hobbes's heirs today apply this logic to environmental problems. In this interpretation, unchecked desires lead to overuse and depletion of natural resources, and excessive pollution. The more prominent contemporary ecological Hobbesians include Garrett Hardin (1968) and Robert Heilbroner (1980), who both propose authoritarian central governance. Somewhat less draconian Hobbesian measures are advocated in Herman Daly's (1977) program for steady state economics. This program shares the normative individualism of contemporary market economics.[1] Daly envisages stationary levels of population, capital stock, and consumption, secured by a central government issuing birth licenses and depletion quotas for natural resources (which could both be traded). This government would also have to pacify the disadvantaged (no longer able to share in the rewards of growth) by redistributing wealth.

However, avowed Hobbesians constitute a small voice in contemporary environmental discourse. More numerous is a category we call the structural reformers. While generally advocating administrative centralization, these reformers are less apocalyptic in their perceptions than the Hobbesians, and more willing to tolerate the pluralistic aspects of the (liberal individualist) political status quo.

This group of political scientists and moderate environmentalists believes that continued tinkering with decision-making processes will suffice. Thus they typically propose more laws to regulate polluters, more funds for enforcement, and minor structural reforms (Passmore, 1974). Some of them argue that incremental changes in laws and social institutions to incorporate environmental quality into our political tradition are the most that can be hoped for at present (Bond, 1977). These reformers claim to be acting responsibly or realistically, and suggest that "extension, elaboration, and refinement of existing social and political traditions and attitudes" would best serve the environmental cause (Cahn, 1978).

For example, Lynton Caldwell (1974) argues that the development of new structures and procedures of planning and control is essential. A super-department of natural resources (a proposal made in the 1960s) would be a step in the right direction (Caldwell, 1974:108).[2]

Similarly, Walter Rosenbaum argues that several structural changes would greatly improve the Environmental Protection Agency's capabilities. First, the EPA should be insulated from direct White House manipulation by establishing a five- or seven-year term for the administrator. This arrangement would make it hard for presidents to change leadership quickly. Second, most of the EPA's middle and upper management positions, now populated by political appointees, should be made into permanent civil service positions and filled on the basis of professional competence. Third, the agency should have a permanent inspector general with the authority to initiate administrative or legal action against internal abuses of authority. Fourth, the EPA's scientific and technical decision-making should be subject to a mandatory five-year review by an external scientific panel, whose mission would be to evaluate the quality of technical information used and determine the degree of independence from political interference.[3]

James Lester (1983, 1985) established that a consolidated environmental bureaucracy at the state level greatly facilitated the responsible management of toxic wastes. In addition, a centralized structure for environmental policy-making was found to promote ocean pollution regulation within the advanced industrial countries of Western Europe (Lester, 1982).

A somewhat different kind of centralizing structural reform has been sponsored by the Conservation Foundation (see, e.g., Leonard, Davies, and Binder, 1977). The dialogue with industry which the Foundation sponsors might, if institutionalized, establish a kind of environmental corporatism, in which representatives of business, government, and environmental groups together would hammer out coordinated and coherent policy.

Guardians

The school of thought we classify as the guardians has more adherents than the Hobbesians, but is no less committed to political centralization. The political power of Plato's guardians was warranted by their philosophical knowledge. Here, we apply the term to any group whose claim to the monopolization of political power is grounded in some special expertise relevant to the determination of what is best for the environmental affairs of the community as a whole. Such claims can be based on scientific and technical knowledge, inherent intellectual capabilities, or ideology. By conventional classifications those who make these claims constitute a mixed bag of Marxists, technocrats, and classical conservatives. In the light of environmental concerns, these people turn out to be remarkably similar.

Those who espouse a technocratic guardianship include Alvin Weinberg (1972), who proposes a "permanent priesthood" of nuclear technologists to oversee and operate the vulnerable energy systems vital to society's future. William Ophuls would prefer to entrust political power to ecologists rather than nuclear engineers, and he speaks of the need for a "class of ecological mandarins" (Ophuls, 1977:163). Political ideology—more precisely, subscription to a postindustrial paradigm—is the key for Milbrath (1984), who wants environmental "prophets" to form the "vanguard" in a transition to a new society. Socialist and Marxist environmentalists (e.g., Stretton, 1976; Pryde, 1972) see capitalism as the problem, and the kind of central planning possible under socialism—committed, of course, to ecological goals—as the solution. The Socialist Environmental and Resources Association in the United Kingdom shares this perspective.

The writer who epitomizes the centralized, communitarian approach of the guardians is Ophuls. Though he is not without some Hobbesian proclivities, his favorite political philosopher is Edmund Burke. Burke's classical conservatism venerates an organic society composed for the most part of people with modest appetites and ambitions, governed by aristocrats born to rule. In this idiom, Ophuls disparages "individualistic" political, economic, and social philosophies in favor of "communalistic" alternatives (Ophuls, 1977:151–59), and favors rule by a "natural aristocracy" (Ophuls, 1977:226–27).

Reform ecologists

Our reform ecologists help populate the mainstream of American environmentalism. For present purposes we may define this category in terms of its intent to give ecological values a voice in the higher (central) levels of the existing political system. The values at issue here are not just the human, individualistic ones of clean air to breathe, clean water to drink, and picturesque scenery to enjoy, but also the biocentric and holistic ones of ecosystem integrity and stability. Obviously, different environmental groups balance anthropocentric and biocentric concerns in different proportions. Biocentric, communitarian concerns weigh rather heavily in Friends of the Earth and Earth Island Institute, moderately in the Sierra Club and Audubon Society, and hardly at all in the American Lung Association.

Reform ecologists are generally inattentive to the structure of economic and political institutions. This inattention is understandable, given that their intellectual backing comes not from social scientists, but rather from policy-oriented natural scientists. Prominent individuals include Eugene Odum (1983), Barry Commoner (1972), Paul Ehrlich (1968), and Lester Brown (1978). These authors all engage in exhortation on behalf of ecologically sound public policies, be it for wetland preservation, population stabilization, land management, or pollution control. While often constituting challenging and well-publicized contributions to policy debates, these exhortations are of limited interest to policy-oriented social scientists *qua* social scientists, simply because of their insensitivity to social, economic, and political factors.

Free market conservatives

In contrast to the reform ecologists, our next category, the free marketeers, is highly sensitive to institutional considerations. Three subgroups shelter under this intellectual umbrella: neoconservative regulatory reformers, new resource economists, and cornucopians. They are united by a faith in the essential rationality of self-regulating market systems, understood in terms of a capability to satisfy individual wants (including wants for environmental goods such as clean air). Conversely, they believe that government intervention in environmental problems has gone too far, and in erroneous directions, under the sway of false doctrines to boot. These marketeers prospered amid Reagan-era hostility to federal government; they also captured the intellectual high ground in the early to mid-1980s.

The neoconservative regulatory reformers advocate reduced environmental regulation on the grounds that regulations have meant high costs to business and hence higher inflation (Lester, 1983:12). They further argue that rules which set absolute standards (e.g., the Delaney Amendment, absolute ambient air quality standards) "run the risk of seriously reducing the profitability of many businesses and the entire performance of the American economy" (Williams and Matheny, 1983:79). It is claimed that independent regulatory agencies have become too powerful; and that regulatory agencies (especially the EPA) have become antibusiness as a result of their capture by self-styled public interest groups (Williams and Matheny, 1983:75–76). Thus the reformers argue that regulation should involve less in the way of punitive sanction, and more reliance on market-oriented incentives (e.g., tax credits for the installation of pollution control equipment).

More specifically, Murray Weidenbaum claims that excessive regulation increases paperwork (whose cost decreases capital formation), hurts smaller enterprises, and increases costs to consumers. He concludes that the net effect of regulation is negative: "the cure is worse than the disease" (Weidenbaum, 1979). He would prefer that business receive information and incentives rather than commands and sanctions from government. In short, the goal of environmental policy should be to "free the Fortune 500" from the shackles of government (Weidenbaum, 1983).

The new resource economists (e.g., Stroup and Baden, 1983; Simmons and Mitchell, 1984) attack federal land management policies rather than regulatory practices. They argue that widespread public ownership of land (especially in the American West) leads to inefficiency and abuse, because users of this land such as logging companies, cattle grazers, and backpackers push their interests by political means. There is thus an incentive for these users to seek—and for politicians and bureaucrats to grant—benefits in an irresponsible manner; that is, in a fashion insensitive to the total cost to society. For example, it is widely acknowledged that many federal timber sales take place at a net loss to society, for the cost to the Forest Service of constructing logging roads is less than the value of the trees harvested. To new resource economists, the solution is clear: privatization of the public lands. Private owners are disciplined by the market in a way that public land managers and interest groups are not. They have to be sensitive to the costs of their actions, and they will not engage in destructive or inefficient uses of the resources they control (including privatized scenic resources currently in national parks or wilderness areas).

The cornucopian free marketeers have more global aims and analyses. In essence, their argument is that no resource can ever run out if a competitive market order exists to stimulate the development of substitutes. Nor is there any need to worry about population growth, for more people means more problem solvers. And pollution can be ameliorated by technological changes that spontaneously make production cleaner as economies grow. The only possible obstacle to this rosy future is misguided government intervention—for example, of the sort that prolonged the energy crisis of the 1970s by regulating energy prices. The most provocative and prominent salesman of this new cornucopia is Julian Simon (1981; Simon and Kahn, 1984), though many economists share his views about resource availability (e.g., Barnett and Morse, 1963).

Social ecologists

The free market is not the only kind of decentralized political-economic system. There is also a vision associated with the libertarian left of the political spectrum which is averse to centralized governance, but prefers communal cooperation to competition. In an environmental context this vision is expressed in what we can call social ecology (to distinguish it from the biocentric perspective of deep ecology). The term social ecology is used by Murray Bookchin (1980, 1982), who also describes himself as an eco-anarchist. But we can also apply this term to other proponents of radically decentralized and nonhierarchical social formations, such as ecofeminists (Griffin, 1978; Merchant, 1980) and critical theorists (Dryzek, 1987a; Luke and White, 1985).

Murray Bookchin's many writings spell out the essential features of eco-anarchism. His hostility to the market is unequivocal:

> Any attempt to solve the environmental crisis within a bourgeois framework must be dismissed as chimerical. Capitalism is inherently anti-ecological. Competition and accumulation constitute its very law of life, a law which Marx pungently summarized in the phrase, "production for the sake of production." Anything, however hallowed or rare, "has its price" and is fair game for the marketplace. In a society of this kind, nature is necessarily treated as a mere resource to be plundered and

> exploited. The destruction of the natural world, far from being the result of mere hubristic blunders, follows inexorably from the very logic of capitalist production. (Bookchin, 1971:16–17)

The solution, according to Bookchin, is a classless, stateless, and decentralized society of the sort envisioned by socialists and anarchists. But he has no faith in the Marxist-Leninist program of vanguard revolution, seeking instead a spontaneous nonhierarchical transformation from the bottom up. His new society would feature small communities, humanistic technologies, unrepressed sexuality, communal solidarity, individual development, self-discipline, the elimination of toil, and the promotion of craftsmanship (Bookchin, 1971:78). Thus would be accomplished "the reconsideration of nature and human society in a new ecological sensibility and a new ecological society—a reharmonization of nature and humanity through a rehumanization of human with human" (Bookchin, 1982:11).

Ecofeminists share Bookchin's antipathy to hierarchy, but are more specific as to the location of this root of all evils. They claim that patriarchy in human society, or hierarchy based on gender, makes other dominations—including the domination of nature—possible. Thus it is foolish to talk of better environmental policy, or more harmonious, less exploitative relationships with the natural world, unless one first attacks patriarchy. Ecofeminists criticize other environmentalists, especially deep ecologists, for failing to recognize this basic truth (e.g., Salleh, 1984).

Critical theorists take their cue from a critique of modernity and the kind of instrumental and technical rationality it embodies (e.g., Habermas, 1984). They are sensitive to the questions of scale and community that preoccupy other social ecologists. However, they devote most of their attention to the kinds of political relationships that will obtain within and between communities. In this light, ecological values are inevitably unrealized in processes encumbered by the (instrumentally rational) pursuit of individual interest and the exercise of economic or political power. Such values will fare much better in processes built on free discourse among equals (Dryzek, 1987a:200–215; Dryzek, 1987b).

Deep ecologists

Deep ecologists differ from social ecologists in their relative inattention to and limited interest in human communities. Their avowed locus of value is the biotic community, independent of human ascriptions and purposes. Deep ecology's most well-known proponents are Naess (1973) and Devall and Sessions (1985), though their precursors include Thoreau and Leopold (1949). Contemporary exponents also include Dave Foreman of Earth First! and Fritjof Capra (1987), and literary figures such as Barry Lopez, Gary Snyder, and Edward Abbey. Devall and Sessions portray deep ecology as a loose agglomeration of Eastern spiritualism, the minority tradition in Western philosophy identified by Aldous Huxley, the worldview of American Indians, and scientific (systems) ecology. "Self-realization" and "biocentric equality" are central, but this involves "realization of the 'self-in-Self' where 'Self' stands for organic wholeness" (Devall and Sessions, 1985:255). While calling for "decentralized, non-hierarchical, fully democratic social structures" (Devall and Sessions, 1985:255), deep ecologists favor them for nature's sake, rather than for man's. Devall (1980:315) confesses that "the deep ecology movement does not have a fully articulated political-economic program." It rejects what it calls the "dominant worldview" of the domination of nature, unlimited resources for economic growth, high technology, and anthropocentrism. Yet the movement is not clearly revolutionary, or even clearly political. Some of its adherents advocate and practice a retreat from politics into actions and feelings toward nature which should be embodied in the everyday life of the individual and community. Indeed, deep ecology sometimes verges on a misanthropic denunciation of human rationality in favor of more intuitive or spiritual relationships with nature.

Our typology is now complete, but, like even the best taxonomy, it is not free from gaps and ambiguities. So, for example, we do not recognize biocentric individualists. While of limited political interest, such people do exist, in the form of animal rights philosophers and advocates (e.g., Regan, 1983). Moreover, there are some dimensions of controversy which our taxonomy does not cover. For example, among deep and social ecologists there is a persistent argument over what role—if any—an ecocentric spirituality should play.

Using the Typology

Our taxonomy can be put to work in several ways. First and most obviously, it can be used as a heuristic device to simplify a complex domain and to highlight key differences and similarities among environmental intellectuals. The environmental perspective is clearly not all of one mind, and some profound inconsistencies between different positions (e.g., Hobbesians and social ecologists) are emphasized by our typology. Our classifications define intellectual debate and dispute, but they also relate to real-world political and policy possibilities. We can predict what alliances are likely, and which ones would be fragile, unlikely, or problematical. For example, some of the problems faced by the Green movement (now well established in Europe, though just beginning in the United States) stem from its combination of social and deep ecology.

Second, we can employ the taxonomy to chart intellectual and political shifts over time. It is clear that recent years have witnessed a broad movement in the decentralized direction, be it toward the free market or the communitarian designs of social and deep ecologists. Around 1970 more centralized perspectives dominated.

Third, the typology can be used to criticize the work of environmental intellectuals. If a thinker is not readily located in one cell, we should look out for potentially fatal inconsistencies. For example, Ophuls (1977) combines aspects of Hobbesian authoritarianism, communalistic guardianship, and social and deep ecology. While presenting a provocative admixture, Ophuls offers no means for the reconciliation of these disparate parts. Similarly, Lovins (1977) seems to favor both the market and more communitarian decentralized forms. While his presentation is plausible, we might criticize it on the grounds that market systems always create imperatives of growth and profit which highly constrain any political-economic mechanisms with which they coexist (Lindblom, 1982). However, we do not rule out the possibility that creative thinking which transcends the categories in our typology may be productive—and even necessary.

Finally, we can employ the taxonomy to inform the construction of scenarios for the environmental future. And it is to this task we now turn.

Environmental Futures: Some Alternative Scenarios

Forecasting is a hazardous endeavor, in environmental affairs no less than elsewhere (note that almost no one predicted the energy crisis of the early 1970s). The scenarios for the next few decades which we enumerate here have some roots in the political and economic status quo, but they also draw upon the diagnoses, evaluations, and prescriptions of the schools of thought discussed in the earlier parts of this chapter. Thus they are not just empirical projections of likely futures. The scenario which obtains can also be determined in part by the choices of policy-makers, activists, and citizens—perhaps under the influence of one or more of the perspectives detailed above. Our four scenarios are summarized in table 12.1.

1. More of the same: pluralist democracy

One very likely possibility is that the status quo will change but marginally. Environmental policy will be negotiated through "interest group liberalism" (Lowi, 1969). More often than not, corporations and business groups will exercise greater influence on policy than environmental groups. Minor structural adjustments may strengthen environmental policy through new laws and more funds for the enforcement of existing laws. Business will continue to argue that the costs of environmental regulation outweigh the benefits to society, and will often succeed in preventing more stringent legislation.

The population of the United States will continue to spread westward and suburbia will continue to grow. Thus pollution will worsen in the West and Southwest. Problems that are currently acute in the Northeast (e.g., acid rain, hazardous waste) will show up in the sunbelt.

National policy will focus on the implementation of environmental legislation passed during the 1970s. Attempts will be made to generate more resources at the state and local levels, where taxes will increase dramatically in order to pay for cleanup activities. Federal fiscal retrenchment will continue.

Public opinion will favor environmental protection and exhibit a willingness to pay for such activities. At the same time, the public will resist radical institutional restructuring. Thus the EPA, state agencies, state and federal courts, city councils, and citizen advisory boards will continue to function as the primary institutions for dealing with environmental problems.

The status quo model prompts questions about both institutional capabilities and environmental conditions. It presupposes that existing institutions, especially those at the state and local level, are adequate for the task at hand. Although some states have markedly improved their capacity for dealing with environmental problems (Bowman and Kearney, 1986), others remain reluctant to engage these problems in constructive fashion (Lester, 1986). Will environmental conditions improve under this model? While some evidence suggests improvement in some cities of the Northeast (Jones, 1975), other evidence suggests deterioration in cities of the West and Southwest (Ballard

Table 12.1 Alternative Scenarios for the Environmental Future

	1. More of the Same	2. Laissez-Faire	3. Authoritarianism	4. Radical Decentralization
Worldview	Structural reform	Free market	Hobbesian/ Guardian	Deep or social ecology
Value Change	None	None	Frugality	Significant and multidimensional
Predominant Approach to Environmentalism	Public involvement	Incentives for private action	Elitist	Citizen involvement
Nature of Public Opinion	Moderate	Free-market conservative	Irrelevant	Radical
Attitudes toward High Technology	Ambivalent	Positive	Ambivalent or negative	Negative
Assumed Availability of Resources	Abundant	Abundant	Scarce	Scarce
Key Actors	Interest groups	Business	Technological or scientific elite	Citizens and communities
Institutional Implications	No change	Less government	Strong centralized government	Decentralization of authority
Primary Government Activity	More "end of pipe" regulations, lax enforcement	Deregulation and privatization	Direct control of production, pollution, and resource use	Innovative "front end" changes; stringent self-regulation; restructuring of government and production processes

SOURCE: Compiled by the authors.

and James, 1983). So it remains to be seen whether "more of the same" will result in environmental improvement or deterioration nationwide.

2. *Laissez-faire*

Our second scenario considers what might happen if (some) business dreams were to come true.[4] This laissez-faire model of the environmental future would see a government limited to providing incentives for market actors to restrict pollution and control resources in responsible fashion. For example, the federal government might provide greater tax writeoffs for private-sector pollution control expenditures. Washington might also prompt "clean" industries to locate in the Northeast by awarding them federal contracts. Beyond this minimal government constraint, the private sector will be free to determine efficient levels of pollution and rates of resource use. The market will respond by producing innovations to change polluting practices and ameliorate resource shortages.

Again, this scenario inspires several fundamental questions. Will the private sector indeed act responsibly? Can a set of incentives be devised by government to ensure that it does? Will business really internalize all the costs of production, and not impose many of those costs on the environment? Are the world's resources (including energy resources and the assimilative capacity of the environment) really unlimited? (For further discussion, see Dryzek, 1987a:67–87.)

3. *Authoritarianism*

Our third scenario is a grim one, rooted in the outlooks of Hobbesians and guardians. It envisages the rise of stringent and coercive authoritarian governance to cope with an environmental crisis by controlling population, pollution, and resource use. Proponents or predictors of this model usually envisage some kind of crisis or collapse precipitating a draconian response.

With extensive centralized planning, many decisions now made by individuals, communities, or the market would be made by government planners. Coercive controls would guarantee implementation, and some mix of incentives and directives would bring individual behavior into line with government objectives. An environmental "super-department" would be created at the federal level, and, inasmuch as any decentralized power remained, at the state level too (many states—e.g., New York—already have such a department).

Scenario 3 may not appear very plausible in the individualistic and decentralist American political culture. Moreover, it is far from clear that authoritarian centralization would lead to better environmental policy. The maintenance of central control can be costly in terms of the amount of coercion required; centralized bureaucracies are insensitive to their errors, and unlikely to correct them; and they can easily lose touch with changing conditions (Marcus, 1980:179). Most fundamentally, hierarchically administered systems cannot easily cope with circumstances of variability, uncertainty, and complexity—which almost define the realm of environmental problems (Dryzek, 1987a:88–109).

4. *Radical decentralization*

Our final scenario envisages a massive restructuring of social, economic, and political life, but in a diametrically opposed direction to that of scenario 3. Radical decentralization would embody the preferred future of social and deep ecologists: a human scale in technology, settlement patterns, and institutions, together with cooperative rather than hierarchical or competitive social organization. Communities would regulate themselves rather than be regulated by government, to the extent that it may be hard even to speak of environmental policy as such. However, proponents of this scenario also envisage bioregional authorities and confederal institutions for dealing with supra-local problems (e.g., long-distance pollution).

Along with major institutional transformations, radical decentralization would also require substantial change in social values, away from material consumption and aggressive competitiveness, and toward more cooperative and nonviolent ecological sensibilities. While such transformation might seem unlikely, some analysts (Milbrath, 1984; Cotgrove, 1982; Inglehart, 1977) detect a shift in public values away from material quantity and toward postindustrial concerns related to the quality of life experiences, aesthetics, and community. Irrespective of such incipient shifts in social values, one should not underestimate the resistance of the entrenched capitalist economic system, the individualistic American political culture, and a centralized (if mildly pluralistic) political system.

We should also mention one scenario which is not directly commensurable with the other four (and so does not appear in table 12.1). This scenario is a dystopia of ecological collapse: we overpopulate the planet, exhaust vital resources, and choke on pollution. Our economic and political systems fail, resulting in a barbaric Hobbesian state of nature. Such a prospect seems more remote today than in the early 1970s, when models of doom (e.g., Meadows et al., 1972) were both popular and plausible.

Conclusion

The possibilities enumerated in this final chapter are intended to stimulate thinking about the future of environmental politics and policy in the United States (and the developed world more generally). The politics of the environment, and what happens to our ecosystems as a result, will surely be affected by technological change, social forces, economic developments, and the individual values that people hold. But environmental politics, policies, and outcomes lie also within the realm of conscious and collective human choice. We hope that the intelligence with which such choices are made can be improved by a better understanding of the major actors and issues related to environmental affairs which we have sketched here.

Appendix A

Selected Statistics on Environmental Policy

The tables A.1–4 have been gathered to facilitate students' investigation into the comparative study of state environmental policy. Basically, two types of data exist: (1) state expenditure data and (2) nonfiscal data on the quality of state environmental programs. From 1969 to 1980, the Bureau of the Census collected statistics on environmental quality spending in the fifty American states. These reports were issued annually and were entitled *Environmental Quality Control* (Special Studies in State and Local Government). Unfortunately, budget cuts in the early 1980s curtailed this data collection effort. Nevertheless, the Council of State Governments (CSG) has begun an extensive data collection effort on state spending on environmental programs. At present the CSG has collected data for FY 1986 only (see table A.3). Data for the periods FY 1981–FY 1985 are still missing as is data for FY 1987–FY 1988. At some future date, the CSG expects to fill in the missing data for these years.

Other institutions, such as the Conservation Foundation and the Fund for Renewable Energy and the Environment (FREE) have begun to collect nonfiscal comparative state environmental policy data on the quality of states' environmental programs. One of the first such efforts was a study by the Conservation Foundation (see chapter 3, table 3.1). This study attempted to evaluate the quality of state efforts to protect the environment. Thus, the higher the score, the greater the commitment to environmental protection by the state. In 1987 (and every year thereafter), FREE gathers similar data in order to evaluate the stringency of state environmental protection programs (see table A.4). These data are subjective estimates of the quality of a state's programs but they are nevertheless a useful nonfiscal measure of state commitment to environmental protection. Once again, the higher the score, the greater the stringency of the state program.

Some of these data are included here for reference purposes so that the student can get a clear picture of their value. Careful researchers will want to update these data when they can, and when they cannot, use the best available data. In addition, students may want to write these organizations directly in order to obtain the complete documents that are referenced here.

Table A.1 State Expenditures for Environmental Quality Control

	1970 Per Capita Expenditure	1980 Per Capita Expenditure	1970–80 Percentage Change
Alabama	$ .46	$ 1.73	276%
Alaska	.51	36.16	6,990
Arizona	.49	4.14	745
Arkansas	.35	2.43	592
California	1.02	8.12	696
Colorado	.52	5.93	1,040
Connecticut	.51	5.65	1,008
Delaware	1.43	38.20	2,571
Florida	.41	1.96	378
Georgia	.50	4.33	766
Hawaii	.53	9.85	1,758
Idaho	.93	6.86	638
Illinois	.18	7.21	3,906
Indiana	.17	4.61	2,612
Iowa	.13	3.01	2,215
Kansas	.36	2.03	464
Kentucky	.72	4.21	485
Louisiana	.69	2.40	248
Maine	.74	7.89	966
Maryland	.67	11.22	1,575
Massachusetts	1.35	11.10	722
Michigan	.30	5.90	1,867
Minnesota	.36	5.69	1,481
Mississippi	.38	1.73	355
Missouri	.28	4.97	1,675
Montana	.77	6.57	753
Nebraska	.23	3.70	1,509
Nevada	.90	4.07	352
New Hampshire	.95	23.01	2,322
New Jersey	.45	5.48	1,118
New Mexico	.57	5.60	882
New York	.72	9.51	1,221
North Carolina	.72	4.32	500
North Dakota	.41	3.46	744
Ohio	.28	35.28	12,500
Oklahoma	.37	2.42	554

Table A.1 State Expenditures for Environmental Quality Control

	1970 Per Capita Expenditure	1980 Per Capita Expenditure	1970–80 Percentage Change
Oregon	.97	8.78	805
Pennsylvania	.41	4.94	1,105
Rhode Island	.43	12.22	2,742
South Carolina	.60	3.34	457
South Dakota	.39	4.01	928
Tennessee	.16	3.76	2,250
Texas	.49	2.33	376
Utah	.44	2.57	484
Vermont	1.37	13.83	909
Virginia	.66	3.00	355
Washington	.98	9.24	843
West Virginia	.67	6.11	812
Wisconsin	.89	8.40	844
Wyoming	1.06	5.85	452

SOURCE: U.S. Dept. of Commerce, Bureau of the Census, *Environmental Quality Control,* FY 1970; FY 1980 (Numbers 61 and 103).

Table A.2 State Government Environmental Quality Control Expenditure: Fiscal Year 198

State	Population, 1980[1]	Expenditure (thousands of dollars	
			Direct
		Total	Total
Total	225,867,174	1,661,810	1,116,36
Alabama	3,890,061	6,726	6,72
Alaska	400,481	14,483	6,27
Arizona	2,717,866	11,258	11,21
Arkansas	2,285,513	5,546	4,59
California	23,668,562	192,092	113,07
Colorado	2,888,834	17,131	12,54
Connecticut	3,107,576	17,548	9,95
Delaware	595,225	22,739	21,65
Florida	9,739,992	19,119	19,11
Georgia	5,464,265	23,644	12,64
Hawaii	965,000	9,509	9,10
Idaho	943,935	6,480	3,61
Illinois	11,418,461	82,339	30,43
Indiana	5,490,179	25,325	8,85
Iowa	2,913,387	8,773	5,86
Kansas	2,363,208	4,796	4,79
Kentucky	3,661,433	15,403	15,36
Louisiana	4,203,972	10,108	10,00
Maine	1,124,660	8,871	4,17
Maryland	4,216,446	47,324	27,09
Massachusetts	5,737,037	63,657	39,06
Michigan	9,258,344	54,639	23,32
Minnesota	4,077,148	23,194	15,11
Mississippi	2,520,638	4,372	3,98
Missouri	4,917,444	24,428	6,58
Montana	786,690	5,172	4,11
Nebraska	1,570,006	5,804	2,88
Nevada	799,184	3,252	2,20
New Hampshire	920,610	21,187	5,01
New Jersey	7,364,158	40,382	33,55

Expenditure (thousands of dollars)			Per capita expenditure (dollars)		
Direct					
urrent eration	Capital outlay	Intergov-ernmental	Total	Direct	Intergov-ernmental
77,078	439,288	545,444	7.36	4.94	2.41
6,725	1	—	1.73	1.73	—
6,128	142	8,213	36.16	15.66	20.51
10,997	219	42	4.14	4.13	.02
4,512	83	951	2.43	2.01	.42
11,101	1,976	79,015	8.12	4.78	3.34
10,602	1,939	4,590	5.93	4.34	1.59
9,600	354	7,594	5.65	3.20	2.44
3,587	18,068	1,084	38.20	36.38	1.82
18,399	720	—	1.96	1.96	—
12,644	—	11,000	4.33	2.31	2.01
2,837	6,268	404	9.85	9.44	.42
3,496	115	2,869	6.86	3.83	3.04
29,371	1,059	51,909	7.21	2.66	4.55
8,672	178	16,475	4.61	1.61	3.00
5,827	34	2,912	3.01	2.01	1.00
4,598	198	—	2.03	2.03	—
14,646	722	35	4.21	4.20	.01
9,976	30	102	2.40	2.38	.02
3,926	245	4,700	7.89	3.71	4.18
24,350	2,742	20,232	11.22	6.43	4.80
26,810	12,252	24,595	11.10	6.81	4.29
22,529	798	31,312	5.90	2.52	3.38
14,775	335	8,084	5.69	3.71	1.98
3,712	276	384	1.73	1.58	.15
6,377	204	17,847	4.97	1.34	3.63
3,705	407	1,060	6.57	5.23	1.35
2,775	112	2,917	3.70	1.84	1.86
2,061	143	1,048	4.07	2.76	1.31
4,763	253	16,171	23.01	5.45	17.57
30,442	3,112	6,828	5.48	4.56	.93

Table A.2 *Continued*

State	Population, 1980[1]	Expenditure (thousands of dolla	
			Direc
		Total	Total
New Mexico	1,299,968	7,285	3,9
New York	17,557,288	167,031	68,8
North Carolina	5,874,429	25,383	13,5
North Dakota	652,695	2,261	2,2
Ohio	10,797,419	380,976	366,6
Oklahoma	3,025,266	7,319	6,6
Oregon	2,632,663	23,111	13,7
Pennsylvania	11,866,728	58,654	38,8
Rhode Island	947,154	11,576	7,8
South Carolina	3,119,208	10,411	10,1
South Dakota	690,178	2,768	2,6
Tennessee	4,590,750	17,278	14,5
Texas	14,228,383	33,208	32,6
Utah	1,461,037	3,755	3,6
Vermont	511,456	7,075	3,8
Virginia	5,346,279	16,054	15,4
Washington	4,130,163	38,181	14,9
West Virginia	1,949,644	11,906	7,3
Wisconsin	4,705,335	39,524	13,0
Wyoming	470,816	2,753	2,7

Note: The detail for per capita expenditure may not add to total due to rounding.

[1]Bureau of the Census, *1980 Census of Population and Housing,* Advance Reports, PHC 80-V, March 19
excludes Americans living overseas and the District of Columbia.

Expenditure (thousands of dollars)			Per capita expenditure (dollars)		
Direct					
[C]urrent [op]eration	Capital outlay	Intergov-ernmental	Total	Direct	Intergov-ernmental
3,737	194	3,354	5.60	3.02	2.58
40,608	28,233	98,190	9.51	3.92	5.59
13,166	394	11,823	4.32	2.31	2.01
1,980	281	—	3.46	3.46	—
21,126	345,552	14,298	35.28	33.96	1.32
6,249	386	684	2.42	2.19	.23
12,198	1,574	9,339	8.78	5.23	3.55
34,404	4,455	19,795	4.94	3.27	1.67
7,324	514	3,738	12.22	8.28	3.95
9,805	304	302	3.34	3.24	.10
2,646	38	84	4.01	3.89	.12
14,303	285	2,690	3.76	3.18	.59
31,244	1,424	540	2.33	2.30	.04
3,102	517	136	2.57	2.48	.09
3,297	514	3,264	13.83	7.45	6.38
14,982	437	635	3.00	2.88	.12
14,777	206	23,198	9.24	3.63	5.62
6,986	396	4,524	6.11	3.79	2.32
12,526	521	26,477	8.40	2.77	5.63
2,675	78	—	5.85	5.85	—

Represents zero.

URCE: U.S. Department of Commerce, Bureau of the Census, *Environmental Quality Control,* FY 1980.

Table A.3 State Environmental Expenditures: Fiscal Year 1986

Ranked by Total Environmental Expenditures		Ranked by Per Capita Expenditures		Ranked by % State Environmental Expenditures of Total State Expenditures	
1. California	$1,199,938,000	Alaska	$326.00	Wyoming	15.00
2. Pennsylvania	332,549,763	Wyoming	135.33	Oregon	4.44
3. Wisconsin	260,289,169	South Dakota	75.90	South Dakota	4.31
4. New York	227,274,090	Montana	69.55	California	3.53
5. New Jersey	200,750,000	Wisconsin	55.31	Idaho	3.49
6. Illinois	181,897,000	Idaho	51.97	Montana	3.46
7. Michigan	173,007,900	California	50.70	Alaska	3.00
8. Florida	171,267,941	Oregon	49.01	New Hampshire	2.89
9. Washington	160,334,318	Delaware	47.74	Wisconsin	2.79
10. Alaska	130,973,900	Vermont	42.94	Pennsylvania	2.71
11. Oregon	129,052,806	Washington	38.80	Vermont	2.39
12. Missouri	123,279,074	New Hampshire	32.41	Missouri	1.96
13. Massachusetts	122,313,035	North Dakota	31.08	Washington	1.91
14. Texas	100,921,072	Pennsylvania	28.03	Mississippi	1.83
15. Ohio	92,169,500	New Jersey	27.25	North Dakota	1.82
16. Kentucky	88,448,194	Rhode Island	26.16	West Virginia	1.60
17. Virginia	87,316,466	Missouri	25.07	Delaware	1.57
18. Maryland	85,748,214	Utah	24.60	Kentucky	1.51
19. North Carolina	77,193,938	New Mexico	24.59	Nevada	1.41
20. Minnesota	73,482,950	Mississippi	24.38	New Jersey	1.39
21. Louisiana	73,079,329	Kentucky	24.16	Utah	1.36
22. Tennessee	70,911,499	West Virginia	23.68	Massachusetts	1.32
23. Georgia	68,986,592	Maine	22.31	Colorado	1.30
24. Colorado	64,319,886	Colorado	22.26	Michigan	1.25
25. Wyoming	63,604,967	Nevada	21.77	New Mexico	1.25
26. Mississippi	61,453,623	Massachusetts	21.32	Rhode Island	1.23
27. Alabama	60,252,564	Maryland	20.33	Maine	1.21
28. Montana	54,739,315	Hawaii	19.21	Tennessee	1.18
29. South Dakota	52,450,000	Michigan	18.68	Illinois	1.14
30. South Carolina	50,018,484	Minnesota	18.03	Louisiana	1.12
31. Idaho	49,063,734	Florida	17.57	Nebraska	1.09
32. Iowa	47,090,046	Louisiana	17.38	Iowa	1.07
33. Indiana	46,551,743	Virginia	16.33	Maryland	1.06
34. West Virginia	46,183,752	Iowa	16.16	Virginia	1.04
35. Oklahoma	43,892,933	South Carolina	16.02	North Carolina	1.04

Table A.3 *Continued*

Ranked by Total Environmental Expenditures		Ranked by Per Capita Expenditures		Ranked by % State Environmental Expenditures of Total State Expenditures	
36. Arizona	41,287,553	Illinois	15.92	Alabama	0.99
37. Connecticut	38,666,000	Alabama	15.47	Florida	0.98
38. Utah	35,947,156	Tennessee	15.45	South Carolina	0.97
39. New Mexico	32,046,123	Arizona	15.19	Arizona	0.95
40. Kansas	30,445,137	North Carolina	14.62	Connecticut	0.89
41. Arkansas	30,372,330	Oklahoma	14.51	Arkansas	0.88
42. New Hampshire	29,850,570	Nebraska	13.32	Minnesota	0.88
43. Delaware	28,359,508	Arkansas	13.29	Kansas	0.87
44. Maine	25,096,481	New York	12.94	Oklahoma	0.85
45. Rhode Island	24,767,942	Kansas	12.88	Georgia	0.83
46. Vermont	21,944,786	Georgia	12.63	Hawaii	0.72
47. Nebraska	20,918,705	Connecticut	12.44	Indiana	0.69
48. North Dakota	20,293,798	Ohio	8.54	Ohio	0.60
49. Hawaii	18,540,533	Indiana	8.48	Texas	0.55
50. Nevada	17,413,195	Texas	7.09	New York	0.54

SOURCE: Council of State Governments, *Resource Guide to State Environmental Management* (Lexington, Ky.: Council of State Governments, 1988).

Table A.4 States' Commitment to Environmental Protection

	Air Programs	Soil Conservation Programs	Groundwater Programs	Hazardous Waste Programs	Solid Waste Programs	Renewable Energy & Energy Conservation	Total	Rank
AL	3	3	2	3	3	2	16	26
AK	7	3	3	2	2	1	18	25
AZ	7	3	7	5	2	3	27	19
AR	1	3	2	5	3	4	18	25
CA	10	3	7	9	9	10	48	2
CO	4	6	4	3	4	3	24	21
CT	9	6	9	4	9	7	44	4
DE	1	8	6	3	4	2	24	21
FL	7	4	9	8	6	7	41	7
GA	4	5	7	4	3	3	26	20
HI	4	4	3	2	2	4	19	24
ID	2	1	6	1	2	6	18	25
IL	7	9	5	7	7	6	41	7
IN	6	5	4	6	7	8	36	10
IA	5	10	5	5	7	7	39	8
KS	2	5	8	8	4	2	29	17
KY	7	3	1	6	8	3	28	18
LA	5	3	3	7	2	1	21	23
ME	3	6	7	6	6	8	36	10
MD	3	8	7	6	6	4	34	12
MA	6	4	8	9	6	8	41	7
MI	8	7	8	9	8	3	43	5
MN	5	6	5	9	9	4	38	9
MS	1	3	2	4	2	2	14	28
MO	5	6	7	8	1	4	31	15
MT	2	5	6	3	1	6	23	22
NE	4	6	6	2	6	7	31	15
NV	2	6	4	2	2	7	23	22
NH	6	5	5	7	5	4	32	14
NJ	9	6	7	10	10	5	47	3
NM	1	2	8	5	1	6	23	22
NY	5	5	10	8	8	7	43	5
NC	8	7	8	6	6	7	42	6
ND	1	3	4	2	3	3	16	26
OH	8	8	4	5	5	4	34	12

Table A.4 *Continued*

	Air Programs	Soil Conservation Programs	Groundwater Programs	Hazardous Waste Programs	Solid Waste Programs	Renewable Energy & Energy Conservation	Total	Rank
OK	5	5	5	4	7	3	29	17
OR	6	2	7	5	7	8	35	11
PA	8	6	5	5	3	5	32	14
RI	6	4	6	4	7	3	30	16
SC	6	5	7	5	2	6	31	15
SD	1	8	6	2	2	4	23	22
TN	3	3	4	7	5	7	29	17
TX	7	2	2	5	3	7	26	20
UT	3	4	3	2	1	3	16	26
VT	3	3	5	6	4	7	28	18
VA	8	7	6	2	3	7	33	13
WA	8	1	6	5	5	3	29	17
WV	2	5	2	4	1	1	15	27
WI	9	8	8	7	8	9	49	1
WY	1	3	8	1	2	1	16	26

SOURCE: Scott Ridley, *The State of the States, 1987* (Washington, D.C.: Fund for Renewable Energy and the Environment, 1987).

Appendix B

State Institutional Capacity: Data and Sources

Environmental Indicators:

1. Voting record of state's congressional delegation on environmental and energy issues. Awarded: 0–4 points. Based on League of Conservation Voters ranking—0–20, 0 pts.; 21–40, 1 pt.; 41–60, 2 pts.; 61–80, 3 pts.; 81–100, 4 pts. Source: *How Congress Voted on Energy and the Environment, 1982 Directory* (Washington, D.C.: League of Conservation Voters, 1982).

2. Existence of state environmental impact statement process. Awarded: 0, 2, or 4 points. No statement, 0 pts.; limited statement, 2 pts.; comprehensive statement, 4 pts. Source: Nicholas A. Robinson, "SEQRA's Siblings: Precedents from Little NEPAs in Sister States," *Albany Law Review* 46 (1982): 1155.

3. State planning director's ranking of priority given environmental protection by state legislature. Awarded: 0–4 points. Source: Richard A. Mann and Mike Miles, "State Land Use Planning: The Current Status and Demographic Rationale," *American Planning Association Journal* 45 (January 1979): 48, 52–53.

4. Existence of state income tax check-off for wildlife and fisheries programs. Awarded: 0–1 point. Sources: *National Wildlife* (August–September 1983): 31; *Nongame Newsletter,* publication of the Nongame Wildlife Association of North America (Summer 1983): 3.

5. Per capita environmental-quality-control expenditures. State expenditures primarily for planning, regulation, and enforcement, and technical and financial assistance related to air, water, and land pollution. Awarded: 0–6 points. $0.00–$1.99, 0 pts.; $2.00–$3.99, 1 pt.; $4.00–$5.99, 2 pts.; $6.00–$7.99, 3 pts.; $8.00–$9.99, 4 pts.; $10.00–$11.99, 5 pts.; $12.00 and greater, 6 pts. Source: U.S. Department of Commerce, Bureau of the Census, *1982 State and Metropolitan Area Data Book* (Washington, D.C.: U.S. Government Printing Office, 1982).

6. Existence of EPA-authorized state program for hazardous-waste control under the Resource Conservation and Recovery Act. Awarded: 0–2 points. No authorization, 0 pts.; Phase I interim authorization, 1 pt.; Phase II interim authorization, 2 pts. Source: *Environmental Quality 1982* (Washington, D.C.: U.S. Government Printing Office, 1982), p. 125.

7. Existence of one umbrella state environmental agency with responsibility for any three of air, water, noise, and hazardous-waste pollution. Awarded: 0–1 point. Source: *World Environmental Directory,* 4th ed. (Silver Spring, Md.: Business Publishers, 1980), pp. 395–428.

8. Existence of tax breaks for residential and nonresidential use of solar energy. Awarded: 0–2 points. Source: Information sheets on tax breaks for residential solar systems and nonresidential uses of solar energy, Conservation and Renewable Energy Inquiry and Referral Service (formerly the National Solar Heating and Cooling Information Center).

9. Existence of state protection of wild, scenic, or recreation rivers. Awarded: 0–2 points. No protection, 0 pts.; administrative protection, 1 pt.; legislative protection, 2 pts. Sources: State Wild and Scenic River Programs: 1980 (Albany: New York Department of Environmental Conservation, State Rivers Program, June 1981); Bureau of Outdoor Recreation, Report No. 43 (Spring 1977), cited in Jon A. Kusler, *Regulating Sensitive Lands* (Cambridge, Mass.: Ballinger, 1980), p. 35.

10. Per capita expenditures for noise-control programs. Expenditures for the development of regulations through enforcement. Awarded: 0–2 points. No expenditures, 0 pts.; more than 0.0–1.0 cents, 1 pt.; more than 1.0 cents, 2 pts. Source: *Environmental Quality 1979:* 10th Annual Report of the Council on Environmental Quality (Washington, D.C.: U.S. Government Printing Office), p. 556.

Land-Use Indicators:

11. Existence of critical-area legislation protecting wetlands or endangered-species habitat. Awarded: 0–2 points. Source: *Environmental Quality 1979:* 10th Annual Report of the Council on Environmental Quality (Washington, D.C.: U.S. Government Printing Office), p. 490.

12. Per capita expenditures for state parks. Expenditures for agency operating budgets and fixed capital outlays. Awarded: 0–2 points. Less than $1.50, 0 pts.; $1.50–$4.00, 1 pt.; more than $4.00, 2 pts. Sources: *1982 Annual Information Exchange* (Santa Fe, N.M.: National Association of State Park Directors), p. 10; U.S. Department of Commerce, Bureau of the Census, *1982 State and Metropolitan Area Data Book* (Washington, D.C.: U.S. Government Printing Office), p. 448, table C, item 6.

13. Existence of state power-plant siting law with an environmental review process. Awarded: 0–3 points. No such law or process, 0 pts.; environmental review process, 1 pt.; power-plant siting law, 2 pts.; both law and process, 3 pts. Source: *1981* NARUC *Annual Report on Utility and Carrier Regulation* (Washington, D.C.: National Association of Regulatory Utility Commissioners), p. 671.

14. Existence of state requirements for comprehensive land-use plans and consistency of land-use decisions. Awarded: 0–4 points. No requirements, 0 pts.; optional or limited comprehensive planning or limited consistency requirement, 1 pt. each; mandatory comprehensive planning or nonlimited consistency, 2 pts. each. Source: Edith Netter, ed., *Land Use Law: Issues for the 1980s* (Washington, D.C.: American Planning Association, February 1981), pp. 77–80.

15. Existence of environmental protection as a stated goal in state land-use law. Awarded: 0–2 points. Source: Richard A. Mann and Mike Miles, "State Land Use Planning: The Current Status and Demographic Rationale," *American Planning Association Journal* 45 (January 1979): 48, 54–55.

16. Existence of state surface-mine reclamation program approved under the Surface Mining Control and Reclamation Act (SMCRA). Awarded: 0–3 pts. No approved state program, 0 pts.; conditionally approved program, 1 pt.; fully approved program, 2 pts.; 1 additional point awarded if state law before enactment of the SMCRA covered all minerals, regulated water flow and quality, and had requirements for conserving and replacing topsoil. Sources: U.S. Department of the Interior, Report to the House Committee on Appropriations on the Regulatory Program of the Office of Surface Mining (April 23, 1983); Edgar A. Imhoff, Thomas O. Friz, and James R. La Fevers, *A Guide to State Programs for the Reclamation of Surface Mined Areas,* U.S. Geological Survey Circular No. 731 (Washington, D.C.: U.S. Government Printing Office, 1976).

17. Existence of state floodplain law regulating development in floodways and floodplains.

Awarded: 0–2 points. No regulation, 0 pts.; regulation of floodways, 1 pt.; regulation of floodplains, 2 pts. Sources: U.S. Army Corps of Engineers, *Perspective on Flood Plain Regulations for Flood Plain Management* (Washington, D.C.: U.S. Government Printing Office, June 1976), pp. 90–101; *Environmental Quality 1979*: 10th Annual Report of the Council on Environmental Quality (Washington, D.C.: U.S. Government Printing Office), p. 490.

18. Existence of specific state land-use policies or laws. Fourteen land-use variables were analyzed to determine the extent of state involvement in land-use decision-making. Award: 0–6 points. Based on Dillard composite score—0–1 policies or laws, 0 pts.; 2–3, 1 pt.; 4–5; 2 pts.; 6–7, 3 pts.; 8–9, 4 pts.; 10–11, 5 pts.; 12–14, 6 pts. Source: Jan E. Dillard, "State Land-Use Policies and Rural America," in Robert Browne and Dan Hadwiger, eds., *Rural Policy Problems: Changing Dimensions* (Lexington, Mass.: Lexington Books, 1982).

19. Adoption of an aesthetic rationale, standing alone, to support use of the police power. Awarded: 0–2 points. Rejection of aesthetics only rationale or no reported court cases, 0 pts.; adoption of rationale based on court dictum, 1 pt.; adoption of rationale based on court holding, 2 pts. Sources: Samuel Bufford, "Beyond the Eye of the Beholder: A New Majority of Jurisdictions Authorize Aesthetic Regulation," *Univeristy of Missouri-Kansas City Law Review* 48 (1980): 125; Clan Crawford, Jr., "The Metromedia Impact," *Zoning and Planning Law Reports* 6, no. 2 (February 1983).

20. Per capita expenditures for natural resources, parks and recreation, sewerage, sanitation, and housing and urban renewal. "Natural resources" include conservation and development of agriculture, fish and game, forestry, and other soil and water resources; "sanitation" includes street cleaning, collection and disposal facilities and services; "housing" covers housing and redevelopment projects and any promotion or support of private housing and redevelopment activities. Awarded: 0–2 points. Less than $30.00, 0 pts.; $30.00–$59.99, 1 pt.; $60.00 and greater, 2 pts. Source: U.S. Department of Commerce, Bureau of the Census, *1982 State and Metropolitan Area Data Book* (Washington, D.C.: U.S. Government Printing Office), pp. 513, table C, item 1113, and 448, item 6.

21. Existence of EPA-approved state solid (nonhazardous) waste management plan under the Resource Conservation and Recovery Act. Awarded: 0–2 points. No plan or in draft stage, 0 pts.; plans adopted by state and submitted to EPA for approval, 1 pt.; plan approved or partially approved by EPA, 2 pts. Source: *Environmental Quality 1982:* 13th Annual Report of the Council on Environmental Quality (Washington, D.C.: U.S. Government Printing Office), p. 121.

22. Existence of agricultural preservation tools. Includes agricultural districting, enabling legislation for agricultural zoning, and purchase or transfer of development rights. Awarded: 0–3 points. Source: *Farmland*, newsletter of the American Farmland Trust, 3, no. 2 (1983): 4.

23. Existence of a state register of historic places or recognition of conservation restrictions. A conservation restriction is a less-than-fee property interest, including a restriction, easement, covenant, or condition. Awarded: 0–2 points. Sources: James P. Beckwith, Jr., "Preservation Law 1976–80: Faction, Property Rights, and Ideology," *North Carolina Central Law Journal* 11 (1980): 276; Comment, "Conservation Restrictions: A Survey," *Connecticut Law Review* 8 (1975–76): 383.

Notes

1 Introduction

1 The role played by Lynton K. Caldwell in drafting the legislation for the National Environmental Policy Act (NEPA) of 1969 deserves special mention. His role in environmental policy formation is unique and illustrates a nonpartisan role by a political scientist in public affairs. Readers interested in the formulation of this act should see his *Science and the National Environmental Policy Act: Redirecting Policy through Procedural Reform* (University of Alabama Press, 1983).

2 The first reference by a political scientist to the concept of *environment* as contrasted to *conservation* in public policy is found in Lynton K. Caldwell, "Environment: A New Focus for Public Policy," *Public Administration Review* (September 1963).

3 This research collection is directed primarily toward theory development and is thus closer to the latter position; however, many of the contributors are also actively concerned with practical issues of environmental protection and support efforts to provide a better physical environment.

4 A recent example of a study that is directed toward an analysis of institutional dilemmas is John S. Dryzek, *Rational Ecology: Environment and Political Economy* (Oxford: Basil Blackwell, 1987).

2 The Conservation and Environmental Movements: An Historical Analysis

Author's Note:

I entered the field of natural resources/environment when I became a member of the Program Staff, Office of the Secretary, Department of the Interior, in July 1951. Being in the secretary's office, I had duties related to all of Interior's bureaus and quickly detected the interest of senior professionals in the National Park Service in finding out whether I was a preservationist and, in the Bureau of Reclamation, etc., whether I was a traditional conservationist. Their interest appeared to reflect much more than bureaucratic rivalry. Rather strong identification with the correctness of their respective ideologies and basic values was evident. Later experiences fully confirmed this initial experience. Indoctrination reflected in policy positions and use of symbolic language was complete on both sides. Traditional conservation doctrine and vocabulary were then clearly dominant within the department.

Assistance in the preparation of this chapter was provided by the following persons who reviewed various drafts: Stewart L. Udall, Charles H. Stoddard, Harold C. Jordahl, Jr., James P. Lester, and Michael A. Gheleta. Responsibility for emphasis and accuracy of the final version, of course, is entirely the responsibility of the author.

1 I became a member of the immediate staff of Secretary Udall in late January 1961. He and other staff were immediately confronted by the apparent fact that the White House had ordered that all White House mail on natural resources matters should be sent to Udall for preparation of replies. This was true regardless of whether the incoming letter related solely to natural resource responsibilities of the Department of Agriculture, the Army Corps of Engineers, etc. Given the awkwardness of this situation and the volume of mail, we had to get the White House routing order changed. The change was made so that we received only the mail relating to general natural resources policy issues, general resource factual questions, and, of course, letters relating to Interior directly. The lead policy role of Secretary Udall was not changed and was largely accepted, throughout the Kennedy-Johnson years.

2 Charles Stoddard was introduced to Udall in early December 1960 by Congressman Henry Reuss of Wisconsin. On December 10, 1960, Stoddard supplied Udall with a document entitled "National Resources Programs and Policy Suggestions." Under priority legislative proposals, Stoddard listed bills on wilderness preservation, pollution control, a council of advisers on natural resources, and youth conservation. He stated that these bills were suggestions of the Democratic National Committee's advisory committee on natural resources (on which he had served) and the recent Democratic platform. He then went on to state other suggestions of his own for legislative consideration as well as administrative measures relating to both the Department of the Interior and the Department of Agriculture. His own first legislative proposal involved federal financial assistance to states and municipalities to acquire land and develop park facilities.

Udall apparently found Stoddard's thinking compatible with his own. Stoddard became the director of the central policy development staff (later called the Resources Program Staff) in late January 1961. He reported directly to Udall.

Stoddard had known Secretary Freeman previously, but he had been more closely associated with George Selke, a top assistant to Freeman. Stoddard and I were close professional and personal friends at Resources for the Future, starting in 1955.

When I became the assistant director to Stoddard in early February 1961, I was well acquainted with Elmer Staats, dating back to the period 1951–1955 when he served as a career professional on the Interior secretary's central staff. Although President Kennedy and I were members of the class of 1940 at Harvard College, we never met as students or when Kennedy was president. However, I had long known Kermit Gordon (a Harvard-connected Kennedy appointee to the Council of Economic Advisers) and Richard Neustadt, a Kennedy adviser, Harvard professor, and author of ***Presidential Power*** (Neustadt, 1980), as well as Arthur Maass, a Harvard professor of government.

Of the initial top officials and staff within the Interior, Secretary Udall had only been closely associated previously with his special assistant, Orren Beaty, and his solicitor, Frank Barry.

3 In the rapidly developing period of major policy change of the 1960s, involving political messages and speeches, as well as writings attempting to summarize what was going on, an important semantic problem was identified in 1964. Until then "natural resources" were viewed as the appropriate words to refer to the domain of concern. At that time staff of

Secretary Udall (and possibly others about the same time) recognized that "resources" was too restrictive. It appeared to refer only to specific things found useful and available to man (e.g., timber, minerals, and water). Moreover, "natural" was becoming inappropriate because emerging policies emphasized landscape gardening, screening junkyards, etc. "Environment," meaning all that is external to people, was recognized as the domain of ecology and taken to be the most appropriate term for the domain of concern. Natural resources were seen as a subset of the environment.

With *The Quiet Crisis* (Udall, 1963) as a policy direction, "environmental quality" became the expressed goal of what President Johnson called the new conservation. How soon this symbolic expression became widely used cannot be said without detailed research. With respect to use of the term *environment,* however, I might say that I spoke as a substitute for Secretary Udall at a conference of Zonta International, Washington, D.C., on the "environmental revolution," October 10, 1964.

4 I believe that presidential messages have more importance in the process than the literature of political science would appear to have recognized. As political parties have declined in importance as bearers of ideological identity and in other ways, the special message is a substitute or a supplement. In the presidencies of Kennedy, Johnson, Nixon, Ford, and Carter they were taken very seriously. Richard Goodwin, speech writer for President Johnson, was very able and worked brilliantly, long, and hard on such messages. Quite apart from their utility in the exercise of public leadership, building public support by the president, and giving guidance to the Congress, they have a very important function that is easily overlooked: they represent "the program of the president." Internally, cabinet officers and others work hard to get policies and programs legislated or implemented that are important to them. If included in messages, they can rightfully consider them marching orders from the president, which helps to overcome bureaucratic barriers.

5 In interviews with White House officials in 1978 I became impressed with their anxiety that the Carter administration might become labeled as in favor of "no-growth."

4 Public Opinion and Environmental Policy

This chapter is a revised version of a paper, originally titled "Two Decades of Public Concern for Environmental Quality: Up, Down and Up Again," presented at the annual meeting of the American Sociological Association, New York, August 1986.

1 Logically, one could also divide the "anti-environmental" segment of the public into the active, attentive, and sympathetic orbits, although the "counter-environmental movement" has never been sufficiently well organized to allow one to make these distinctions meaningfully (see, e.g., Albrecht, 1972, and Morrison, 1973, on the counter-environmental movement).

2 Perhaps the most egregious example is Lowe et al. (1980:441). These authors base their argument that environmental concern did *not* decline between 1970 and 1973 (when the NORC data they analyze became available) on the basis of "a review of several of the Gallup Opinion Indexes published during that period." However, as noted previously, the Gallup MIP data peaked in 1970 with 10 percent, and then gradually declined, standing at 4 percent in late 1972, before Gallup went to a *two*-MIP question format. Even with the latter format, environmental problems disappeared from the Gallup MIP lists in 1974. The only specific Gallup data Lowe et

al. cite are two surveys of college students which included MIP-type questions. These surveys showed that environment declined from sixth in 1970 to eleventh in 1971 among college students, clearly contradicting their argument!

3 Further evidence that concern about energy adequacy did not have a direct impact on environmental concern is presented in Viladas (1974) and the Dunlap et al. (1979) panel study discussed above. Also, the percents providing "neutral" responses or responding "Don't Know" for this item and the subsequent items in table 4.3 are reported in Dunlap (1987).

4 A review of the *Gallup Opinion Index* throughout the seventies reveals that environmental problems reappeared on the MIP list only once after 1973, with 4 percent in May 1977.

5 For example, two recent analyses of the state of public concern with environmental quality through the seventies came to differing conclusions in this regard, with Lake (1983:232) concluding that "it has defied the issue-attention cycle" and Anthony (1982:19) noting that despite its continued strength, "there is also nothing . . . to suggest that Downs' analysis was basically wrong."

6 In 1984 two-thirds of the sample was given the old format, "improving and protecting the environment," and one-third was given the new format, "the environment." Of those given the old format, 58.5 percent said "too little" was being spent and 6.5 percent said "too much," while of those given the new format 56.7 percent said "too little" and 8.4 percent said "too much." In 1985 approximately half of the sample received each format. The figures for the old format were 56.4 percent "too little" and 8.0 percent "too much," and for the new format they were 60.4 percent "too little" and 7.2 percent "too much." Finally, in 1986 the approximately one-half of the sample that received the old format responded 59.4 percent "too little" and 5.2 percent "too much," while the half that received the new format responded 57.5 "too little" and 7.2 percent "too much." Because the results obtained with the two formats are reasonably close, and do not vary systematically (i.e., the old format produced a higher "pro-environment" response in 1984 and 1986, but not in 1985), table 4.3 reports results for the entire samples with the formats combined. In contrast, Gillroy and Shapiro (1986:273) report results only for the subsamples receiving the old format.

7 Additional trend data from a Business Week/Harris Poll survey (1983) confirm this trend, although they are not reported in enough detail to be included in table 4.3. Harris found that support for making the Clean Air Act "stricter" increased from 29 percent in 1981 to 47 percent in 1983, while support for making the Clean Water Act "stricter" rose from 52 to 61 percent during the same time period.

8 The only exception is in the case of energy-environment tradeoffs, as in 1982 slightly over a third of the public favored ensuring an adequate supply of energy even if doing so entailed "taking some risks with the environment." However, in view of the increasingly "pro-environment" trends observed with the other items and given the current situation of ample energy (at least in the eyes of consumers), it seems likely that current support for energy adequacy versus environmental quality would be much lower than in 1982.

9 For more detail on public reaction to Reagan's environmental policies see Mitchell (1984b) and Dunlap (1987).

10 For a compatible explanation grounded in social-psychological theory, see Heberlein's (1972) application of norm-activation theory to environmental issues and the recent revision of this theoretical model by Stern et al. (1987). Simply put, this model posits increases in environmental concern as a function of (1) increases in the awareness of the negative consequences of environmental problems for humans and (2) increases in the acceptance of personal responsibility for environmental protection. The latter variable, in turn, varies inversely with the

assumption that others—such as the government—are responsible for environmental protection.

11 Yet, it should be noted that even during the EPA and Watt controversies environmental problems never reappeared on the MIP lists, suggesting once again the overly stringent nature of MIP items as measures of salience.

12 Of particular note is the development that in recent years environmental problems have been linked with a wide range of technological accidents (e.g., Three Mile Island, Bhopal, Chernobyl, and numerous spills of hazardous materials in truck and railroad accidents). The technological hazards dimension has clearly enlarged the scope and ambiguity of "environmental problems."

13 For example, Opinion Research Corporation surveys (summarized in Roper Center, 1983:36–37) have found that 73 percent of the public believe government should play a "major role" and 23 percent believe it should play a "minor role" in "protecting the environment," while only 3 percent believe it should play "no role" (with 2 percent "don't know"), and also that when asked whether "protecting the environment" should be more public, about as it is, or more private, fully 62 percent believe it should be more public, 25 percent about as is, and only 8 percent more private (with 5 percent "don't know").

14 Obviously this is an ex post facto explanation, but the 1990s will allow for tests of its plausibility.

15 Of course, given the absence of public opinion data, it is impossible to prove that during earlier eras, such as the first conservation movement, a large proportion of Americans did *not* place a high value on environmental protection, worry about resource limits, and so forth. However, historical analysts (e.g., Whisenhunt, 1974) have seen the dominant ethos as largely void of environmental concern until the recent rise of environmentalism.

16 In contrast, simply having respondents *rate* individual items in a list of problems, issues, etc. without having to make choices between them, as with the NORC spending items, would *not* constitute a measure of salience.

17 For more detail on the Harris-Ladd debate see Mitchell (1984b:64–67) and Anthony (1982:19).

18 I want to caution against generalizing from Reagan's reelection and the data reviewed above on the self-reported electoral impact of environmental issues to the conclusion that environmental issues have little political significance. First, as Mitchell (1984b:67–70) notes, environmental activists and PACs can provide significant resources (labor, money, etc.) to political campaigns. In fact, environmentalists frequently claim to have affected the outcome of targeted campaigns (e.g., Ades, 1987; Kraft, 1984:46). Second, in some campaigns environmental issues are so important to voters that they clearly affect the outcome. For example, Brock Adams's upset of Slade Gorton in the 1986 race for the U.S. Senate is commonly attributed to Adams's staunch opposition to locating the nation's first permanent nuclear waste repository in Washington—a position shared by an overwhelming majority of state residents. It is easy to envision how state and local campaigns might be heavily influenced by local environmental issues such as the proposed location of a toxic waste site or even a less hazardous garbage landfill. This suggests that being seen as "anti-environmental" may well constitute a political liability for many candidates, and "make the difference" in some elections. Third, it should be emphasized that referenda and initiatives designed to protect environmental quality have generally fared well at the ballot box over the years, with election results apparently reflecting the pro-environment sentiment found in polls (Lake, 1983).

19 This illustrates a point implicit in the distinction between the direction/degree and the

salience/intensity of public opinion: If a minority of the public sees an issue as important and feels intensely about it, they may be active enough (writing letters, making phone calls, signing petitions, etc.) to have an effect on policy even though a majority of the public holds the opposite opinion—but not strongly enough to act on it. In fact, Schuman and Presser's (1981:chap. 9) results concerning attitudes toward gun permits and abortion illustrate how the "passionate" views of the anti-gun permit and anti-abortion forces have made them successful beyond their numbers. Clearly I have not been able to report trend data on the intensity of environmental opinions. However, given that environmental problems are more likely to be seen as threatening the health and well-being of humans now than in the past, it may be that pro-environmental opinions are held somewhat more intensely now than in the seventies.

10 Elites and Environmental Policy

1 For a discussion of the distinction between risk and hazard, see Okrent (1980).

2 There are, of course, other areas of environmental concern besides risk policy, such as acid rain and cross-media pollution.

3 I am indebted to one of the peer reviewers for pointing this out.

4 Mutagens are chemicals that act on genetic material. This is important because carcinogens are frequently, though not always, mutagens. Thus the Ames test is one of a series of screens for detecting potential carcinogens.

5 This section of the model is based on Bajgier and Moskowitz (1982).

6 A weakness of the study is that Hunter and Sabatier (1985) offer no objective way of evaluating the strength of different interest groups. While their results do show that the most extreme opponents make the most extreme judgments, the labeling of those judgments as over- or under-estimating is a relative one.

7 There has also been considerable theoretical work on decision theory. See, for example, Machina (1987).

8 Their work is part of an integrated community of policy scholars conducting research on risk, the environment, and decision-making. Fischhoff was a student of Tversky's and Kahneman's and, with Slovic and Lichtenstein, established a private research firm, based in Oregon, called Decision Research. In a sense, one can envision the empirical work of the Decision Research group as the working out of the theories of their mentors (see McKean, 1985). A further linkage is the funding. Much of the Decision Research work has been funded by a National Science Foundation program focusing on risk, a program directed by Vincent Covello and Joshua Menkes. The money has been granted to a group at Clark University (including Christoph Hohenemser, Roger Kasperson, and Robert Kates) that has also been doing work on risk assessment and risk management. The Clark University group, in turn, subcontracted out the risk perception work to Decision Research.

9 These are labeled by Vlek and Stallen (1981) as technological risk and severity of consequences.

10 These errors are all part of what Perrow (1984) calls "normal accidents."

12 Alternative Views of the Environmental Problematic

1 Most economists would regard Daly's notions as unorthodox and esoteric, but this judgment holds only through reference to the narrow standards of the economics profession.

2 Although Professor Caldwell was one of the first to make this structural argument, his views have evolved considerably over the past few years. Specifically, he now believes that although structural and procedural innovations are necessary, the primary need is for a fundamental reordering of public beliefs and values. Institutional changes will inevitably follow from such a value change among the citizenry.

3 Other political scientists such as Dean Mann, Phillip Foss, Norman Wengert, Helen Ingram, Michael Kraft, Henry Caulfield, Gregory Daneke, Alfred Marcus, and James P. Lester have also argued for relatively minor structural changes.

4 Note, however, that many businesses—especially large ones—have a vested interest in government controls that restrict competition. It is noteworthy that Milton Friedman, one of the best-known market advocates, characterizes big business as one of the foremost enemies of the market.

References

1 Introduction

Barke, Richard. 1986. *Science, Technology, and Public Policy.* Washington, D.C.: Congressional Quarterly Press.

Caldwell, Lynton K. 1970. *Environment: Challenge to Modern Society.* Garden City, N.Y.: Natural History Press.

Hofferbert, Richard. 1974. *The Study of Public Policy.* Indianapolis, Ind.: Bobbs-Merrill.

Jones, Charles O. 1972. "From Gold to Garbage: A Bibliographic Essay on Politics and the Environment." *American Political Science Review* 66:588–95.

Kraft, Michael E. 1974. "Environmental Politics and American Government: A Review Essay." In Stuart Nagel, ed., *Environmental Politics.* New York: Praeger.

Lester, James P. 1986. "New Federalism and Environmental Policy," *Publius* 16:149–65.

Lester, James P., and Ann O'M. Bowman. 1983. *The Politics of Hazardous Waste Management.* Durham, N.C.: Duke University Press.

Lowrance, William W. 1976. *Of Acceptable Risk.* Los Alton, Calif.: William Kaufman, Inc.

Lundqvist, L. J. 1978. "The Comparative Study of Environmental Politics: From Garbage to Gold." *International Journal of Environmental Studies* 12:89–97.

Mann, Dean E. 1980. "Symposium on Environmental Policy: An Introduction." *Policy Studies Journal* 9:322–25.

Mann, Dean E., Geoffrey Wandesforde-Smith, and Lennart Lundqvist. 1975. "Environmental Policy." In Stuart Nagel, ed., *Policy Studies in America and Elsewhere.* Lexington, Mass.: Lexington Books.

Sabatier, Paul A., and Geoffrey Wandesforde-Smith. 1979. "Major Sources on Environmental Politics, 1974–1977: The Maturing of a Literature." *Policy Studies Journal* 7:592–604.

Sprout, Harold, and Margaret Sprout. 1973. "Symposium on Environmental Policy and Political Science Fields." *Policy Studies Journal* 1:192–95.

2 The Conservation and Environmental Movements: An Historical Analysis

Albright, N. (as told to Robert Cahn). 1985. *The Birth of the National Park Service: The Founding Years, 1913–1933.* Salt Lake City, Utah: Howe Brothers.

Arnold, R. 1982. *At the Eye of the Storm: James Watt and the Environmentalists.* Chicago: Regnery Gateway.

Baker, R. A. 1985. "The Conservation Congress of Anderson and Aspinal, 1963–64." *Journal of Forest History* 29, no. 3 (July 1985): 104–19.

Barney, G. O., ed. 1977. *The Global 2000 Report*. New York: Thomas Crowell.

Bates, J. L. 1957. "Fulfilling American Democracy: The Conservation Movement, 1907–1921." *Mississippi Valley Historical Review* 44.

Blue Book. 1955. *Report of the Presidential Advisory Committee on Water Resources Policy*. Washington, D.C.: GPO.

Brown, H. 1954. *The Challenge of Man's Future*. New York: Viking Press.

Burford, A. 1985. *Rocky Mountain News*, December 6.

Burns, J. M. 1978. *Leadership*. New York: Harper & Row.

Caulfield, H. P., Jr. 1959. "The Living Past in Federal Power Policy." In *Annual Report* of Resources for the Future, Inc., Washington, D.C.

———. 1973. "Federal Guidelines for Water Resource Project Evaluation." In *Environmental Impact on Rivers*, edited and published by H. W. Shen. Fort Collins, Colo.

———. 1984. "U.S. Water Resources Development Policy and Intergovernmental Relations." In Allanheld, *Western Public Lands: The Management of Natural Resources in a Time of Declining Federalism*. Totowa, N.J.: Rowman.

Cawley, R. M. 1981. "The Sagebrush Rebellion." Ph.D. diss., Colorado State University.

Cogan, J. M. 1982. "Flowing Free: The Development of the Wild and Scenic Rivers Act." MA thesis, Colorado State University, pp. 36–37.

Commoner, B. 1971. *The Closing Circle: Man, Nature, and Technology*. New York: Alfred A. Knopf.

Daly, H. E., ed. 1973. *Toward a Steady-State Economy*. San Francisco: W. H. Freeman.

DeBell, G. 1970. *The Environmental Handbook*. New York: Ballantine.

Fausold, M. L. 1961. *Gifford Pinchot: Bull Moose Progressive*. Syracuse: Syracuse University Press.

Georgescu-Roegen, N. 1971. *The Law of Entropy and the Economic Process*. Cambridge, Mass.: Harvard University Press.

Green Books, 1950 and 1958. These publications were products of the Subcommittee on Benefits and Costs, Federal Interagency River Basin Committee, *Proposed Practices for Economic Analysis of River Basin Projects* (Washington, D.C.: GPO, 1950), and the Subcommittee on Evaluation Standards, Interagency Committee on Water Resources, *Proposed Practices for Economic Analysis of River Basin Projects* (Washington, D.C.: GPO, 1958).

Hays, S. P. 1959. *Conservation and the Gospel of Efficiency: The Progressive Conservation Movement, 1890–1920*. Cambridge, Mass.: Harvard University Press, p. 5.

———. 1982. "From Conservation to Environment: Environmental Politics in the United States since World War II." *Environmental Review* 6, no. 2:24.

Hickel, W. J. 1972. *Who Owns America?* Philadelphia: Coronet Communications Paperback Library, pp. 8–9.

Highsmith, R. M., Jr., J. G. Jensen, and R. D. Rudd. 1962. *Conservation in the United States*. Chicago: Rand McNally.

Hooker, F. 1986. Article on "At Home with David Freeman." *Denver Post Magazine*, August 10, 1986, p. 9.

Ise, J. 1961. *Our National Park Policy: A Critical History*. Baltimore: Johns Hopkins University Press, for Resources for the Future.

Jordahl, H. C., Jr. 1986. Letter to author dated April 8, 1986.

King, J. 1959. *The Conservation Fight: From Theodore Roosevelt to the Tennessee Valley Authority*. Washington, D.C.: Public Affairs Press.

Lovins, A. B. 1977. *Soft Energy Paths: Toward a Durable Peace*. Cambridge, Mass.: Friends of the Earth International and Ballinger.

Lowi, T. J. November 1971. *Four Systems of Policy, Politics, and Choice*. Syracuse, N.Y.: Inter-University Case Program, IC P#110.

Maass, A. 1983. *Congress and the Common Good*. New York: Basic Books, pp. 114–16.

McConnell, G. 1954. "The Conservation Movement Past and Present." *Western Political Quarterly* 7:463–78.

McGee, W. J. 1909. "Water as a Resource." *The Annals* (American Academy of Political and Social Science).

———. 1911. "The Conservation of Natural Resources." In *Proceedings of the Mississippi Valley Historical Association, 1909–1910*, vol. 3, p. 378. Cedar Rapids, Iowa: Torch Press.

McGregor, D. 1960. *Leadership and Motivation*. Cambridge, Mass.: MIT Press.

Maddox, J. 1972. *The Doomsday Syndrome*. New York: McGraw-Hill.

Mason, E. S. 1958. "The Political Economy of Resource Use." In *Perspectives on Conservation*, ed. Henry Jarrett. Baltimore: Johns Hopkins University Press, for Resources for the Future.

Morgan, R. J. 1965. *Governing Soil Conservation: Thirty Years of the New Decentralization*. Baltimore: Johns Hopkins University Press, for Resources for the Future.

Nelson, G. 1985. "Days of Earth." In *The Living Wilderness*, Summer 1983, p. 56.

Neustadt, R. E. 1980. *Presidential Power: The Politics of Leadership from FDR to Carter*. New York: John Wiley & Sons.

Olson, M., and H. H. Landsberg, eds. 1973. *The No-Growth Society*. New York: W. W. Norton.

Ophuls, W. 1977. *Ecology and the Politics of Scarcity: A Prologue to a Political Theory of the Steady State*. San Francisco: W. H. Freeman.

ORRC Report. 1962. *Outdoor Recreation for America*. A Report to the President and the Congress by the Outdoor Recreation Resources Review Commission, January 1962.

Pinchot, G. 1910. *The Fight for Conservation*. Republished in 1967 by the University of Washington Press, Seattle.

———. 1947. *Breaking New Ground*. New York: Harcourt, Brace & World.

Quarles, J. 1976. *Cleaning Up America: An Insider's View of the Environmental Protection Agency*. Boston: Houghton Mifflin.

Reich, C. 1970. *The Greening of America*. New York: Random House.

Richardson, E. 1958. "The Politics of Conservation Issues, 1896–1913." Ph.D. diss., University of California, Los Angeles.

Rosenbaum, W. A. 1973. *The Politics of Environmental Concern*. New York: Praeger.

Schlesinger, A. M., Jr. 1965. *A Thousand Days: John F. Kennedy in the White House*. Boston: Houghton Mifflin.

Schumacker, E. F. 1973. *Small Is Beautiful: Economics as if People Really Mattered*. New York: Harper & Row.

Smith, F. E. 1966. *The Politics of Conservation*. New York: Random House.

Statistical Abstract of the United States. 1985. Washington, D.C.: Department of Commerce, Bureau of the Census.

Stoddard, C. H. 1982. *Looking Forward: Planning America's Future*. New York: Macmillan.

———. 1985. Letter from Charles Stoddard to author dated October 9, 1985.

Stratton, O., and P. Sirotkin. 1959. *The Echo Park Controversy*, no. 46 in Inter-University Case Program. Indianapolis: Bobbs-Merrill.

Strong, D. H. 1970. "The Rise of American Esthetic Conservation: Muir, Mather, and Udall." *National Parks Magazine* 44, no. 269: February.

Udall, S. L. 1963. *The Quiet Crisis*. New York: Holt, Rinehart & Winston.
———. 1968a. *The New Conservation Era, 1964–1968*. Washington, D.C.: Yearbooks of the U.S. Department of the Interior.
———. 1968b. *1976: Agenda for Tomorrow*. New York: Harcourt, Brace & World.
———. 1985. An unpublished essay (as of 1985) on "The Rich Legacy of Rachel Carson."
U.S. Senate Select Committee. January 1961. *Report of the Senate Select Committee on National Water Resources,* Report No. 29, 87th Cong., 11th sess.
U.S. Supreme Court. 1978. *Tennessee v. Hill,* 98 S. Ct. 2279.
Van Hise, C. R. 1910. *The Conservation of Natural Resources in the United States*. New York: Macmillan.
Vig, N. J., and M. E. Kraft. 1984. *Environmental Policy in the 1980s: Reagan's New Agenda*. Washington, D.C.: Congressional Quarterly Press.
Wengert, N. 1962. "The Ideological Basis of Conservation and Natural Resources Policies and Programs." *The Annals* (American Academy of Political and Social Sciences, Philadelphia) 344:65–75.
White House Conference. 1965. *Beauty for America*. Proceedings of the White House Conference on Natural Beauty, May 24–25. Washington, D.C.: GPO.
Zeigler, L. H., and G. W. Peak. 1972. *Interest Groups in American Society.* 2d ed. Englewood Cliffs, N.J.: Prentice-Hall.

3 Federalism and Environmental Policy

Advisory Commission on Intergovernmental Relations. 1980. *Changing Public Attitudes on Governments and Taxes*. Washington, D.C.: GPO.
———. 1981. *Protecting the Environment: Politics, Pollution, and Federal Policy.* Washington, D.C.: GPO.
———. 1984. *Regulatory Federalism: Policy, Impact, Process, and Reform*. Washington, D.C.: GPO.
Andrews, Richard N. L., and Terrence K. Pierson. 1985. "Local Control or State Override: Experiences and Lessons to Date." *Policy Studies Journal* 14:90–99.
Arnold, R. D. 1979. *Congress and the Bureaucracy.* New Haven, Conn.: Yale University Press.
Beer, Samuel. 1973. "The Modernization of American Federalism." *Publius* 3:53–102.
Bowman, Ann. 1985. "Hazardous Waste Management: An Emerging Policy Area Within an Emerging Federalism." *Publius* 15:131–44.
Bowman, Ann, and Richard C. Kearney. 1986. *The Resurgence of the States*. Englewood Cliffs, N.J.: Prentice-Hall.
Break, George. 1979. *Financing Government in a Federal System*. Washington, D.C.: Brookings Institution.
Caulfield, Henry. 1984. "U.S. Water Resources Policy: Past, Present, and Future." In John G. Francis and Richard Ganzel, eds., *Western Public Lands: The Management of Natural Resources in a Time of Declining Federalism*. Totowa, N.J.: Rowman & Allanheld.
Conlan, Timothy, and David B. Walker. 1983. "Reagan's New Federalism: Design, Debate, and Discord." *Intergovernmental Perspective* 8:6–22.
Council of State Governments. 1984–85. *The Book of the States*. Lexington, Ky.: Council of State Governments.
Crotty, Patricia. 1987. "The New Federalism Game: Primacy Implementation of Environmental Policy." *Publius* 17:53–67.
Culhane, Paul. 1984. "Sagebrush Rebels in Office: Jim Watt's Land and Water Politics." In

Norman J. Vig and Michael E. Kraft, eds., *Environmental Policy in the 1980s: Reagan's New Agenda*. Washington, D.C.: Congressional Quarterly Press.

Davis, Charles. 1985. "Perceptions of Hazardous Waste Policy Issues among Public and Private-Sector Administrators." *Western Political Quarterly* 38:447–63.

Davis, Charles, and James P. Lester. 1987. "Decentralizing Federal Environmental Policy: A Research Note." *Western Political Quarterly* 40:555–65.

Derthick, Martha. 1974. *Between Nation and State*. Washington, D.C.: Brookings Institution.

Dye, Thomas, and Dorothy Davidson. 1981. "State Energy Policies: Federal Funds for Paper Programs." *Policy Studies Review* 1:255–62.

———. 1974. "The New Federalism: Can the States Be Trusted?" *The Public Interest* 35:89–102.

Elazar, Daniel. 1984. *American Federalism: A View from the States*. 3d ed. New York: Harper & Row.

Fawcett, James. 1986. "Redefining Local Government Power: The Influence of Informal Powers in Challenging Joint Implementation of a State Coastal Plan." *Policy Studies Review* 6:330–39.

Francis, John G., and Richard Ganzel, eds. 1984. *Western Public Lands: The Management of Natural Resources in a Time of Declining Federalism*. Totowa, N.J.: Rowman & Allenheld.

Getz, Malcolm, and Benjamin Walter. 1980. "Environmental Policy and Competitive Structure: Implications of the Hazardous Waste Management Program." *Policy Studies Journal* 9:404–14.

Glendening, Parris, and Mavis Mann Reeves. 1984. *Pragmatic Federalism*. 2d ed. Pacific Palisades, Calif.: Palisades Publishers.

Goetze, David, and C. K. Rowland. 1985. "Explaining Hazardous Waste Regulation at the State Level." *Policy Studies Journal* 9:111–22.

Gormley, William. 1987. "Intergovernmental Conflict on Environmental Policy: The Attitudinal Connection." *Western Political Quarterly* 40:285–303.

Hadden, Susan, Joan Veillette, and Thomas Brandt. 1983. "State Roles in Siting Hazardous Waste Disposal Facilities." In James P. Lester and Ann O'M. Bowman, eds., *The Politics of Hazardous Waste Management*. Durham, N.C.: Duke University Press.

Harrigan, John. 1980. *Politics and Policy in States and Communities*. Boston: Little, Brown.

Hebert, F. Ted, and Deil Wright. 1982. "State Administrators: How Representative? How Professional?" *State Government* 55:22–28.

Hedge, David, and Donald Menzel. 1985. "Loosening the Regulatory Ratchet: A Grassroots View of Environmental Deregulation." *Policy Studies Journal* 13:599–606.

Jones, Charles. 1976. "Regulating the Environment." In Herbert Jacob and Kenneth Vines, eds., *Politics in the American States*. 3d ed. Boston: Little, Brown.

Kamieniecki, Sheldon, Robert O'Brien, and Michael Clarke. 1986. "Environmental Policy and Aspects of Intergovernmental Relations." In J. Edwin Benton and David R. Morgan, eds., *Intergovernmental Relations and Public Policy*. Westport, Conn.: Greenwood Press.

Kearney, Richard. 1983. "Resurgence of the States." Paper presented at the Annual Meeting of the Western Political Science Association, Seattle.

Kneese, Allen, and Charles Schultze. 1975. *Pollution, Prices, and Public Policy*. Washington, D.C.: Brookings Institution.

Kraft, Michael E., Bruce B. Clary, and Richard J. Tobin. 1985. "The Impact of New Federalism on State Environmental Policy: The Midwestern Great Lakes States." Southwestern Political Science Association Conference Paper.

Lamare, James. 1981. *Texas Politics: Economics, Power, and Policy*. New York: West Publishing Company.

Lee, Robert D. 1979. *Public Personnel Systems*. Baltimore: University Park Press.

Lester, James P. 1986. "New Federalism and Environmental Policy." *Publius* 16:149–65.

Lester, James P., James Franke, Ann Bowman, and Kenneth Kramer. 1983. "Hazardous Wastes, Politics, and Public Policy: A Comparative State Analysis." *Western Political Quarterly* 36:257–85.

Levine, Charles, and Paul Posner. 1981. "The Centralizing Effects of Austerity on the Intergovernmental System." *Political Science Quarterly* 96:63–88.

Lopach, James. 1984. "The Supreme Court and Resource Federalism." In John G. Francis and Richard Ganzel, eds., *Western Public Lands*. Totowa, N.J.: Rowman & Allenheld.

Mazmanian, Daniel, and Paul Sabatier. 1983. *Implementation and Public Policy*. Glenview, Ill.: Scott Foresman.

Menzel, Donald. 1983. "Redirecting the Implementation of a Law: The Reagan Administration and Coal Surface Mining Regulation." *Public Administration Review* 43:411–20.

Mitnick, Barry. 1980. "Incentive Systems in Environmental Regulation." *Policy Studies Journal* 9:379–94.

Morell, David, and Christopher Magorian. 1982. *Siting Hazardous Waste Facilities*. Cambridge, Mass.: Ballinger.

Mushkatel, Alvin, and Dennis Judd. 1981. "The States' Role in Land Use Policy." *Policy Studies Review* 1:263–74.

Nathan, Richard, and Fred Doolittle. 1983. *The Consequences of Cuts: The Effects of the Reagan Domestic Program on State and Local Governments*. Princeton, N.J.: Princeton University Press.

———. 1985. "Federal Grants: Giving and Taking Away." *Political Science Quarterly* 100:53–74.

National Governors' Association. 1982. *The State of the States: Management of Environmental Programs in the 1980's*. Washington, D.C.: National Governors' Association.

Nice, David. 1984. "Cooperation and Conformity among the States." *Polity* 26:494–505.

———. 1987. "State Participation in Interstate Compacts." *Publius* 17:69–83.

Price, Kent. 1982. *Regional Conflict and National Policy*. Washington, D.C.: Resources for the Future.

Reagan, Michael. 1985. "Intergovernmental Implementation of Partial Preemption Regulatory Programs: Can National Policy Effectively Channel State Administration?" Paper presented at the Annual Meeting of the American Political Science Association.

Rickleen, Laura Stiller. 1982–83. "Negotiating Superfund Settlement Agreements." *Boston College Environmental Affairs Law Review* 10:697–714.

Riker, William. 1964. *Federalism*. Boston: Little, Brown.

Rosenbaum, Walter A. 1981. *Energy, Politics, and Public Policy*. Washington, D.C.: Congressional Quarterly Press.

Rowland, C. K., and Roger Marz. 1982. "Gresham's Law: The Regulatory Analogy." *Policy Studies Review* 1:572–80.

Schooler, Dean, and Helen Ingram. 1981. "Water Resource Management." *Policy Studies Review* 1:243–54.

Selznick, Phillip. 1949. *TVA and the Grass Roots*. Berkeley and Los Angeles: University of California Press.

Shapek, Raymond. 1980. "The Intergovernmental Personnel Program and Management Capacity." *Public Personnel Management* 9:75–85.

Walker, David. 1983. "A Perspective on Intergovernmental Relations." In Richard Leach, ed., *Intergovernmental Relations in the 1980's*. New York: Marcel Dekker.

———. 1981. *Toward a Functioning Federalism*. Cambridge: Winthrop.

Walzer, Norman, and Samuel Gove. 1981. "State Finance and Taxing Policies." *Policy Studies Review* 1:335–46.

Warren, Charles. 1982. "State Governments' Capacity: Continuing to Improve." *National Civic Review* 71:234–58.

Weinberg, Martha. 1977. *Managing the State*. Cambridge, Mass.: MIT Press.

Wells, Donald. 1982. "Site Control of Hazardous Waste Facilities." *Policy Studies Review* 1:728–35.

Willbern, York. 1959. "The States as Components in an Areal Division of Powers." In Arthur Maas, ed., *Area and Power: A Theory of Local Government*. New York: Free Press.

Wright, Deil. 1982. *Understanding Intergovernmental Relations*. 2d ed. Monterey, Calif.: Brooks/Cole.

4 Public Opinion and Environmental Policy

Ades, Susan. 1987. "The Environment Wins." *Environmental Action* 18:17–19.

Albrecht, Stan L. 1972. "Environmental Social Movements and Counter-Movements: An Overview and an Illustration." *Journal of Voluntary Action Research* 1:2–11.

Alter, Jonathan, Mary Hager, and Thomas M. DeFrank. 1984. "Ronald Reagan as Mr. Clean." *Newsweek* 104 (July 23): 48.

Anthony, Richard. 1982. "Polls, Pollution, and Politics: Trends in Public Opinion on the Environment." *Environment* 24 (May): 14–20, 33–34.

Axelrod, Regina S. 1984. "Energy Policy: Changing the Rules of the Game." In N. J. Vig and M. E. Kraft, eds., *Environmental Policy in the 1980s: Reagan's New Agenda*. Washington, D.C.: Congressional Quarterly Press.

Baldwin, Deborah. 1977. "Environmentalists Open the Revolving Door." *Environmental Action* 9 (June): 13–25.

Bernstein, Marver H. 1955. *Regulating Business by Independent Commission*. Princeton: Princeton University Press.

Bloomgarden, Kathy. 1983. "Managing the Environment: The Public's View." *Public Opinion* 6 (February/March): 47–51.

Business Week/Harris Poll. 1983. "A Call for Tougher—Not Weaker—Antipollution Laws." *Business Week*, no. 2774 (January 24): 87.

Buttel, Frederick H. 1975a. "Class Conflict, Environmental Conflict, and the Environmental Movement: The Social Bases of Mass Environmental Beliefs, 1968–1974." Ph.D. diss., University of Wisconsin—Madison.

———. 1975b. "The Environmental Movement: Consensus, Conflict, and Change." *Journal of Environmental Education* 7:53–63.

Cambridge Reports, Inc. 1986. "Paying for Environmental Quality." *Bulletin on Consumer Opinion*, no. 112.

Conservation Foundation. 1980. "Environmentalists Savor Past, Look Anxiously Ahead." *Conservation Foundation Letter* (January–February), 1–16.

Davies, J. Clarence, III. 1977. "The Greening of American Politics." *Wilson Quarterly* 1:85–97.

Downs, Anthony. 1972. "Up and Down with Ecology: The 'Issue-Attention Cycle.'" *Public Interest* 28:38–50.

Dunlap, Riley E. 1985. "Public Opinion: Behind the Transformation." *EPA Journal* 11 (July/August): 15–17.

———. 1987. "Polls, Pollution, and Politics: Public Opinion on the Environment in the Reagan Era." *Environment* 29 (July/August): 6–11, 32–37.

Dunlap, Riley E., and Don A. Dillman. 1976. "Decline in Public Support for Environmental Protection: Evidence from a 1970–1974 Panel Study." *Rural Sociology* 41:382–90.

Dunlap, Riley E., and Kent D. Van Liere. 1977. "Further Evidence of Declining Public Concern with Environmental Problems: A Research Note." *Western Sociological Review* 8:108–12.

———. 1978. "The 'New Environmental Paradigm': A Proposed Measuring Instrument and Preliminary Results." *Journal of Environmental Education* 9:10–19.

Dunlap, Riley E., and Michael Patrick Allen. 1976. "Partisan Differences on Environmental Issues: A Congressional Roll-Call Analysis." *Western Political Quarterly* 29:384–97.

Dunlap, Riley E., and Richard P. Gale. 1972. "Politics and Ecology: A Political Profile of Student Eco-activists." *Youth and Society* 3:379–97.

Dunlap, Riley E., Kent D. Van Liere, and Don A. Dillman. 1979. "Evidence of Decline in Public Concern with Environmental Quality." *Rural Sociology* 44:204–12.

Edelman, Murray. 1964. *The Symbolic Uses of Politics*. Urbana: University of Illinois Press.

Erskine, Hazel. 1972a. "The Polls: Pollution and Industry." *Public Opinion Quarterly* 36:263–80.

———. 1972b. "The Polls: Pollution and Its Costs." *Public Opinion Quarterly* 36:120–35.

Fanning, Odom. 1975. *Man and His Environment: Citizen Action*. New York: Harper & Row.

Farhar, Barbara C., Charles T. Unseld, Rebecca Vories, and Robin Crews. 1980. "Public Opinion about Energy." *Annual Review of Energy* 5:141–72.

Funkhouser, G. Ray. 1973. "The Issues of the Sixties: An Exploratory Study in the Dynamics of Public Opinion." *Public Opinion Quarterly* 33:62–75.

Gillroy, John M., and Robert Y. Shapiro. 1986. "The Polls: Environmental Protection." *Public Opinion Quarterly* 50:270–79.

Goodman, John L. 1983. *Public Opinion during the Reagan Administration*. Washington, D.C.: Urban Institute Press.

Harris, Louis. 1982. "Big Shift in Single-Issue Voting Expected This Fall." *The Harris Survey* no. 20:1–4.

———. 1983. "EPA Investigation Seriously Hurts Reagan Administration." *The Harris Survey* no. 24:1–4.

———. 1984. "Reagan vs. Mondale on the Issues." *The Harris Survey* no. 80:1–4.

———. 1985. "Expectations High for Reagan's Second Term." *The Harris Survey* no. 7:1–3.

Haskell, Elizabeth H., and Victoria S. Price. 1973. *State Environmental Management: Case Studies of Nine States*. New York: Praeger.

Heberlein, Thomas A. 1972. "The Land Ethic Realized: Some Social Psychological Explanations for Changing Environmental Attitudes." *Journal of Social Issues* 28:79–87.

Holden, Constance. 1980. "The Reagan Years: Environmentalists Tremble." *Science* 210:988–91.

Hornback, Kenneth E. 1974. "Orbits of Opinion: The Role of Age in the Environmental Movement's Attentive Public, 1968–1972." Ph.D. diss., Michigan State University.

Hornback, Kenneth E., and Denton E. Morrison. 1975. "The Role of Public Opinion in Social Movement Evolution." Paper presented at the annual meeting of the American Sociological Association, New York.

Keeter, Scott. 1984. "Problematical Pollution Polls: Validity in the Measurement of Public Opinion on Environmental Issues." *Political Methodology* 10:267–91.

Kenski, Henry C., and Margaret Corgan Kenski. 1984. In N. J. Vig and M. E. Kraft, eds., *Environmental Policy in the 1980s: Reagan's New Agenda*. Washington, D.C.: Congressional Quarterly Press.

Key, V. O., Jr. 1961. *Public Opinion and American Democracy.* New York: Alfred A. Knopf.

Kraft, Michael E. 1984. "A New Environmental Policy Agenda: The 1980 Presidential Campaign and Its Aftermath." In N. J. Vig and M. E. Kraft, eds., *Environmental Policy in the 1980s: Reagan's New Agenda.* Washington, D.C.: Congressional Quarterly Press.

Ladd, Everett Carl. 1982. "Clearing the Air: Public Opinion and Public Policy on the Environment." *Public Opinion* 5 (February/March): 16–20.

Lake, Laura M. 1983. "The Environmental Mandate: Activists and the Electorate." *Political Science Quarterly* 98:215–33.

Lane, Robert E., and David O. Sears. 1964. *Public Opinion.* Englewood Cliffs, N.J.: Prentice-Hall.

Lowe, George D., Thomas K. Pinhey, and Michael D. Grimes. 1980. "Public Support for Environmental Protection: New Evidence from National Surveys." *Pacific Sociological Review* 23:423–45.

McEvoy, James, III. 1972. "The American Concern with Environment." In W. R. Burch, Jr., N. H. Cheek, Jr., and L. Taylor, eds., *Social Behavior, Natural Resources, and the Environment.* New York: Harper & Row.

Mauss, Armand L. 1975. *Social Problems as Social Movements.* Philadelphia: Lippincott.

Milbrath, Lester W. 1984. *Environmentalists: Vanguard for a New Society.* Albany, N.Y.: SUNY Press.

Mitchell, Robert Cameron. 1979. "Silent Spring/Solid Majorities." *Public Opinion* 2 (August/September): 16–20.

———. 1980. "Public Opinion on Environmental Issues." In *Council on Environmental Quality: The Eleventh Annual Report of the CEQ.* Washington, D.C.: GPO.

———. 1984a. "Moving Backwards vs. Moving Forwards: Motivations for Collective Action." Paper presented at the Annual Meeting of the American Sociological Association, San Antonio.

———. 1984b. "Public Opinion and Environmental Politics in the 1970s and 1980s." In N. J. Vig and M. E. Kraft, eds., *Environmental Policy in the 1980s: Reagan's New Agenda.* Washington, D.C.: Congressional Quarterly Press.

Mitchell, Robert Cameron, and J. Clarence Davies III. 1978. "The United States Environmental Movement and Its Political Context: An Overview." Discussion Paper D–32. Washington, D.C.: Resources for the Future.

Morrison, Denton E. 1973. "The Environmental Movement: Conflict Dynamics." *Journal of Voluntary Action Research* 2:74–85.

———. 1980. "The Soft, Cutting Edge of Environmentalism: Why and How the Appropriate Technology Notion is Changing the Movement." *Natural Resources Journal* 20:275–98.

Murch, Arvin. 1974. "Who Cares about the Environment? The Nature and Origins of Environmental Concern." In Arvin W. Murch, ed., *Environmental Concern.* New York: MSS Information Corporation.

National Opinion Research Center. 1986. *General Social Surveys, 1972–1986: Cumulative Codebook.* Chicago: National Opinion Research Center.

Nimmo, Dan D., and Charles M. Bonjean. 1972. "Introduction." In D. D. Nimmo and C. M. Bonjean, eds., *Political Attitudes and Public Opinion.* New York: David McKay.

Odum, Eugene P. 1970. "The Attitude Revolution." In *Editors of "The Progressive": The Crisis of Survival.* New York: William Morrow.

Peters, B. Guy, and Brian W. Hogwood. 1985. "In Search of the Issue-Attention Cycle." *Journal of Politics* 47:238–53.

Pierce, John C., Kathleen M. Beatty, and Paul R. Hagner. 1982. *The Dynamics of American Public Opinion.* Glenview, Ill.: Scott, Foresman.

Roper Center. 1983. *American Public Opinion and Public Policy on the Environment*. Storrs, Conn.: Roper Center, University of Connecticut.

Rosa, Eugene. 1978. "The Public and the Energy Problem." *Bulletin of the Atomic Scientists* 34 (April): 5–7.

Sabatier, Paul, and Daniel Mazmanian. 1980. "The Implementation of Public Policy: A Framework of Analysis." *Policy Studies Journal* 8:538–60.

Schnaiberg, Allan. 1973. "Politics, Participation, and Pollution: 'The Environmental Movement.'" In J. Walton and D. E. Carns, eds., *Cities in Change: Studies on the Urban Condition*. Boston: Allyn & Bacon.

———. 1980. *The Environment: From Surplus to Scarcity*. New York: Oxford University Press.

Schoenfeld, A. Clay, Robert F. Meier, and Robert J. Griffin. 1979. "Constructing a Social Problem: The Press and the Environment." *Social Problems* 27:38–61.

Schuman, Howard, and Stanley Presser. 1981. *Questions and Answers in Attitude Surveys*. New York: Academic Press.

Shabecoff, Philip. 1985. "A Successful Revolution." *Resources* (Resources for the Future) no. 81:2.

Spector, Malcolm, and John I. Kitsuse. 1977. *Constructing Social Problems*. Menlo Park, Calif.: Cummings.

Stanfield, Rochelle L. 1984a. "Reagan's Environmental Record Not the Issue It Was Predicted to Be." *National Journal* 16 (October 6): 1874–75.

———. 1984b. "Ruckelshaus and Clark Seek to Blunt Environmental Lobby's Political Swords." *National Journal* 16 (June 30): 1256–60.

Stern, Paul C., Thomas Dietz, and J. Stanley Black. 1987. "Support for Environmental Protection: The Role of Moral Norms." *Population and Environment* 8:204–22.

Szasz, Andrew. 1986. "The Process and Significance of Political Scandals: A Comparison of Watergate and the 'Sewergate' Episode at the Environmental Protection Agency." *Social Problems* 33:202–17.

Thompson, Roger. 1985. "Environmental Conflicts in the 1980s." *Editorial Research Reports* 1 (February 15): 122–44.

Trop, Cecile, and Leslie L. Roos, Jr. 1971. "Public Opinion and the Environment." In L. L. Roos, Jr., ed., *The Politics of Ecosuicide*. New York: Holt, Rinehart & Winston.

Van Liere, Kent D., and Riley E. Dunlap. 1983. "Cognitive Integration of Social and Environmental Beliefs." *Sociological Inquiry* 53:333–41.

Vig, Norman J., and Michael E. Kraft. 1984. "Environmental Policy from the Seventies to the Eighties." In N. J. Vig and M. E. Kraft, eds., *Environmental Policy in the 1980s: Reagan's New Agenda*. Washington, D.C.: Congressional Quarterly Press.

Viladas Co., J. M. 1974. *Impact of the Fuel Shortage on Public Attitudes toward Environmental Protection*. Washington, D.C.: U.S. Environmental Protection Agency.

Watts, Nicholas, and Geoffrey Wandesforde-Smith. 1980. "Postmaterialist Values and Environmental Policy Change." *Policy Studies Journal* 9:346–58.

Whisenhunt, Donald W. 1974. *The Environment and the American Experience*. Port Washington, N.Y.: Kennikat Press.

Yankelovich, Daniel, and Bernard Lefkowitz. 1980. "The Public Debate on Growth: Preparing for Resolution." *Technological Forecasting and Social Change* 17:95–140.

5 Interest Groups and Environmental Policy

Anderson, Charles W. 1977. "Political Design and the Representation of Interests." *Comparative Politics* 10, no. 1:127–52.

Andrews, Richard N. L. 1980. "Class Politics or Democratic Reform: Environmentalism and American Political Institutions." *Natural Resources Journal* 20:221–41.

Berry, Jeffrey M. 1984. *The Interest Group Society.* Boston: Little, Brown.

Chubb, John. 1983. *Interest Groups and the Bureaucracy.* Stanford, Calif.: Stanford University Press.

Colby, Peter W. 1983. "The Organization of Public Interest Groups." *Policy Studies Journal* 11, no. 4:699–708.

Daneke, Gregory A., Margot W. Garcia, and Jerome Delli Priscoli, eds. 1983. *Public Involvement and Social Impact Assessment.* Social Impact Assessment Series, No. 9. Boulder, Colo.: Westview Press.

Downing, Paul B., and Gordon L. Brady. 1981. "The Role of Citizen Interest Groups in Environmental Policy Formation." In Michelle White, ed., *Nonprofit Firms in a Three-Sector Economy.* COUPE Papers on Public Economics. Washington, D.C.: Urban Institute.

Esch, Mary. 1985. "New Audubon Head Watches More Politics Than Birds." *News Tribune,* Tacoma, Washington, September 8, 1985, p. D–12.

Evans, Brock. 1980. "The Importance of Appointments." *Sierra* 65:22–23.

Frohlich, Norman, Joe A. Oppenheimer, and Oran R. Young. 1971. *Political Leadership and Collective Goods.* Princeton, N.J.: Princeton University Press.

Gendlin, Frances. 1982. "A Talk with Mike McCloskey, Executive Director of the Sierra Club." *Sierra* 67:36–41.

———. 1983. "Mike McCloskey: Taking Stock, Looking Forward." *Sierra* 68:45, 126–27.

Gottlieb, Bob, and Margaret FitzSimmons. 1986. "A New Environmental Politics?" Paper presented at the conference on International Green Movements.

Hansen, John Mark. 1985. "The Political Economy of Group Leadership." *American Political Science Review* 79, no. 1:79–96.

Hassler, Gregory L., and Karen O'Conner. 1986. "Woodsy Witchdoctors versus Judicial Guerrillas: The Role and Impact of Competing Interest Groups in Environmental Litigation." *Boston College Environmental Affairs Law Review* 13, no. 4:487–520.

Hayes, Michael T. 1983. "Interest Groups: Pluralism or Mass Society." In Burdett A. Cigler and Allan J. Loomis, eds., *Interest Group Politics.* Washington, D.C.: Congressional Quarterly Press.

Keller, Bill. 1981. "The Trail of the 'Dirty Dozen.'" *Congressional Quarterly* 39:510.

Langton, Stuart, ed. 1984. *Environmental Leadership.* Lexington, Mass.: Lexington Books.

Lester, James P., and Ann O'M. Bowman. 1983. *The Politics of Hazardous Waste Management.* Durham, N.C.: Duke University Press.

Loomis, Burdett A., and Allan J. Cigler. 1983. "Introduction: The Changing Nature of Interest Group Politics." In Allan J. Cigler and Burdett A. Loomis, eds., *Interest Group Politics.* Washington, D.C.: Congressional Quarterly Press.

Los Angeles Times, December 27, 1984, p. 3 ff.

Los Angeles Times, December 22, 1986, p. 1 ff.

Los Angeles Times, April 23, 1987, p. 3 ff.

McFarland, Andres. 1983. "Public Interest Lobbies versus Minority Factions." In Allan J. Cigler and Burdett A. Loomis, eds., *Interest Group Politics.* Washington, D.C.: Congressional Quarterly Press.

Mann, Dean E. 1975. "Political Incentives in U.S. Water Policy: Relationship between Distributive and Regulatory Politics." In Mathew Holden, Jr., and Dennis L. Dresang, eds., *What Government Does.* Beverly Hills, Calif.: Sage Publications.

———. 1985. "Democratic Politics and Environmental Policy." In Sheldon Kamieniecki, Robert O'Brien, and Michael Clarke, eds., *Controversies in Environmental Policy.* Albany: State University of New York Press.

Milbrath, Lester W. 1984. *Environmentalists: Vanguard for a New Society.* Albany: State University of New York Press.

Mitchell, Robert Cameron. 1978. "The Public Speaks Again: A New Environmental Survey." *Resources,* Resources for the Future, N. 60 September–November 1978.

———. 1984a. "Moving Backwards vs. Moving Forwards: Motivations for Collective Action." Paper presented at annual meeting of the American Sociological Association, San Antonio.

———. 1984b. "Public Opinion and Environmental Politics." In Norman J. Vig and Michael E. Kraft, *Environmental Policy in the 1980s: Reagan's New Agenda.* Washington, D.C.: Congressional Quarterly Press.

———. 1985. "From Conservation to Environmental Movement: The Development of the Modern Environmental Lobbies." Discussion Paper, QE85–12, Washington, D.C.: Resources for the Future, June 1985.

Morrison, Denton E., and Riley E. Dunlap. 1986. "Environmentalism and Elitism: A Conceptual and Empirical Analysis." *Environmental Management* 10, no. 5:581–89.

Mosher, Lawrence. 1980. "Environmentalists Question Whether to Retreat or Stay on the Offensive." *National Journal* 12 (December 13): 2116–21.

O'Hare, Michael, Lawrence Bacow, and Debra Sanderson. 1983. *Facility Siting and Public Opposition.* New York: Van Nostrand Reinhold.

Olson, Jr., Mancur. 1965. *The Logic of Collective Action.* Cambridge, Mass.: Harvard University Press.

Portnoy, Paul. 1984. "The Benefits and Costs of Regulatory Analysis." In V. Kerry Smith, *Environmental Policy-making under Reagan's Executive Order.* Chapel Hill: University of North Carolina Press.

Rheem, Donald L. 1987. "Environmental Action." Series in *Christian Science Monitor,* January 13, 14, 15, pp. 17 and 19.

Roe, David. 1984. *Dynamos and Virgins.* New York: Random House.

Salisbury, Robert H. 1984. "Interest Representation: The Dominance of Institutions." *American Political Science Review* 78, no. 1:64–76.

Selznich, Philip. 1957. *Leadership in Administration.* New York: Harper & Row.

Sierra, magazine published by Sierra Club, various issues, 1980–84.

Smith, V. Kerry. 1984a. "A Theoretical Analysis of the Green Lobby." *American Political Science Review* 79, no. 1:137–47.

———. 1984b. "Environmental Policy-Making under Executive Order 11191: An Introduction." In V. Kerry Smith, *Environmental Policy-making under Reagan's Executive Order.* Chapel Hill: University of North Carolina Press.

Stanfield, Rochelle L. 1985. "Environmental Lobby's Changing of the Guard Is Part of Movement's Evolution." *National Journal,* June 18, pp. 1350–53.

Utrup, Kathryn Ann. 1979. "How Sierra Club Members See Environmental Issues." *Sierra,* 64 (March/April 1979): 14–18.

Walker, Jack. 1983. "Origins and Maintenance of Interest Groups in America." *American Political Science Review* 77, no. 2:390–404.

Wall Street Journal, November 20, 1986.

Wasby, Stephen. 1983. "Interest Group Litigation in an Age of Complexity." In Allan J. Cigler and

Burdett A. Loomis, eds., *Interest Group Politics*. Washington, D.C.: Congressional Quarterly Press.
Weber, Max. 1966. *The Theory of Social and Economic Organization*. New York: Free Press.
Wenner, Lettie M. 1982. *The Environmental Decade in Court*. Bloomington: Indiana University Press.
Zeckhauser, Richard. 1981. "Preferred Policies When There Is a Concern for Probability of Adoption." *Journal of Environmental Economics and Management* 8:215–37.

6 Party Politics and Environmental Policy

Alexander, Herbert. 1984. *Financing Politics: Money, Elections, and Political Reform*. 3d ed. Washington, D.C.: Congressional Quarterly Press.
Arrandale, Tom. 1983. *The Battle for Natural Resources*. Washington, D.C.: Congressional Quarterly Press.
Brownstein, Ronald, and Nina Easton. 1982. *Reagan's Ruling Class*. Washington, D.C.: Presidential Accountability Group.
Calvert, Jerry. 1979. "The Social and Ideological Basis of Support for Environmental Legislation: An Examination of Public Attitudes and Legislative Action." *Western Political Quarterly* 22:327–37.
———. 1982. "Linking Citizen Preferences to Legislative Choices: The Role of Political Parties." *State and Local Government Review* 14:68–74.
Cohen, Richard. 1982. "Rating Congress: A Guide to Separating the Liberals from the Conservatives." *National Journal* 14:800–810.
Congressional Quarterly Weekly Report. 1984. 42 (October 27): 2809–14.
Crenson, Matthew. 1971. *The Un-Politics of Air Pollution: A Study of Non-Decisionmaking in the Cities*. Baltimore: Johns Hopkins University Press.
Culhane, Paul. 1984. "Sagebrush Rebels in Office: Jim Watt's Land and Water Policies." In Norman Vig and Michael Kraft, eds., *Environmental Policy in the 1980s: Reagan's New Agenda*. Washington, D.C.: Congressional Quarterly Press.
Dunlap, Riley, and Michael Allen. 1976. "Partisan Differences on Environmental Issues: A Congressional Roll Call Analysis." *Western Political Quarterly* 19:384–97.
Dunlap, Riley, and Richard Gale. 1974. "Party Membership and Environmental Politics: A Legislative Roll Call Analysis." *Social Science Quarterly* 55:670–90.
Engelbert, Ernest. 1961. "Political Parties and Natural Resources Policies: An Historical Evaluation." *Natural Resources Journal* 1:224–56.
Francis, John. 1984. "Environmental Values, Intergovernmental Politics, and the Sagebrush Rebellion." In John Francis, ed., *Western Public Lands: The Management of Natural Resources in a Time of Declining Federalism*. Totowa, N.J.: Rowan & Allenheld.
Keefe, William, and Morris Ogul. 1985. *The American Legislative Process: Congress and the States*. 6th ed. Englewood Cliffs, N.J.: Prentice-Hall.
Kenski, Henry, and Margaret Kenski. 1981. "Partisanship, Ideology, and Constituency Differences on Environmental Issues in the U.S. House of Representatives and Senate, 1973–1978." In Dean Mann, ed., *Environmental Policy Formation*. Lexington, Mass.: D. C. Heath.
———. 1984. "Congress against the President: The Struggle over the Environment." In Vig and Kraft, eds., *Environmental Policy in the 1980s*.
Kraft, Michael. 1984. "A New Environmental Agenda: The 1980 Presidential Campaign and Its Aftermath." In Vig and Kraft, eds., *Environmental Policy in the 1980s*.

Lash, Jonathan et al. 1984. *A Season of Spoils: The Reagan Administration's Attack on the Environment*. New York: Pantheon Books.
Lester, James. 1980. "Partisanship and Environmental Policy: The Mediating Influence of State Organizational Structures." *Environment and Behavior* 12:101–31.
Mazmanian, Daniel, and Paul Sabatier. 1981. "Liberalism, Environmentalism, and Partisanship in Public Policy-Making: The California Coastal Commissions." *Environment and Behavior* 13:361–84.
Mitchell, Robert. 1984. "Public Opinion and Environmental Politics in the 1970s and 1980s." In Vig and Kraft, eds., *Environmental Policy in the 1980s*.
Monroe, Alan. 1983. "American Party Platforms and Public Opinion." *American Journal of Political Science* 27:27–42.
Ritt, Leonard, and John Ostheimer. 1974. "Congressional Voting on Ecological Issues." *Environmental Affairs* 3, no. 3:459–72.
Rosenbaum, Walter. 1985. *Environmental Politics and Policy*. Washington, D.C.: Congressional Quarterly Press.
Schattschneider, Elmer. 1960. *The Semisovereign People*. New York: Holt, Rinehart & Winston.
Schneider, William. 1983. "Party Unity on Tax, Spending Issues—Less in House, More in Senate." *National Journal* 15:936–52.
———. 1984. "Democrats, Republicans Move Further apart on Most Issues in the 1983 Session." *National Journal* 16:904–20.
Vig, Norman. 1984. "The President and the Environment: Revolution or Retreat?" In Vig and Kraft, eds., *Environmental Policy in the 1980s*.
Vig, Norman, and Michael Kraft. 1984. "Environmental Policy from the Seventies to the Eighties." In Vig and Kraft, eds., *Environmental Policy in the 1980s*.

7 Congress and Environmental Policy

Some of the research summarized here was supported by a grant from the National Science Foundation, Division of Policy Research and Analysis, NSF, PRA 800 7228. Additional support was provided by the Dirksen Congressional Center for an ongoing study of congressional leadership on technological risk management. I would like to thank Jolene Anderson for her assistance in updating and revising an earlier draft of this chapter and Tamara Crockett for reading and commenting on the manuscript.

Aberbach, Joel D. 1979. "Changes in Congressional Oversight." *American Behavioral Scientist* 22:493–515.
Ackerman, Bruce A., and William T. Hassler. 1981. *Clean Coal/Dirty Air*. New Haven, Conn.: Yale University Press.
Bartlett, Robert V. 1984. "The Budgetary Process and Environmental Policy." In Norman J. Vig and Michael E. Kraft, eds., *Environmental Policy in the 1980s: Reagan's New Agenda*. Washington, D.C.: Congressional Quarterly Press.
Bauer, Raymond A., Ithiel de Sola Pool, and Lewis A. Dexter. 1972. *American Business and Public Policy*. 2d ed. Chicago: Aldine-Atherton.
Bernstein, Robert A., and Stephen R. Horn. 1981. "Explaining House Voting on Energy Policy." *Western Political Quarterly* 34:235–45.
Berry, Jeffrey M. 1977. *Lobbying for the People: The Political Behavior of Public Interest Groups*. Princeton, N.J.: Princeton University Press.
———. 1984. *The Interest Group Society*. Boston: Little, Brown.

Brooks, Harvey. 1985. "Technology Assessment and Environmental Impact Assessment." In Committee on Scholarly Communication with China, *U.S.-China Conference on Science Policy*. Washington, D.C.: National Academy Press.

Burnham, David. 1985. "Five House Chairmen Assail Budget Office Role." *New York Times*, June 29, p. 1.

Chubb, John E. 1983. *Interest Groups and the Bureaucracy: The Politics of Energy*. Stanford, Calif.: Stanford University Press.

Cook, Mary Etta, and Roger H. Davidson. 1985. "Deferral Politics: Congressional Decision Making on Environmental Issues in the 1980s." In Helen M. Ingram and R. Kenneth Godwin, eds., *Public Policy and the Natural Environment*. Greenwich, Conn.: JAI Press.

Cooley, Richard A., and Geoffrey Wandesforde-Smith, eds. 1970. *Congress and the Environment*. Seattle: University of Washington Press.

Davidson, Roger. 1981. "Subcommittee Government: New Channels for Policy Making." In Thomas E. Mann and Norman J. Ornstein, eds., *The New Congress*. Washington, D.C.: American Enterprise Institute.

Davidson, Roger H., and Walter J. Oleszek. 1981. *Congress and Its Members*. Washington, D.C.: Congressional Quarterly Press.

Davies, J. Clarence, and Barbara S. Davies. 1975. *The Politics of Pollution*. 2d ed. Indianapolis: Bobbs-Merrill.

Davis, David Howard. 1985. "Energy Subsystems and Congress: A Review of Recent Literature." Paper presented at the annual meeting of the American Political Science Association, New Orleans.

Davis, Joseph A., and Nancy Green. 1984. "Bhopal Tragedy Prompts Scrutiny by Congress." *Congressional Quarterly Weekly Report*, December 22, pp. 3147–48.

Dunlap, Riley E., and Michael Patrick Allen. 1976. "Partisan Differences on Environmental Issues: A Congressional Roll-Call Analysis." *Western Political Quarterly* 29:384–97.

Dunlap, Riley E. 1987. "Public Opinion on the Environment in the Reagan Era." *Environment* 29:6–11, 32–37.

Eads, George C., and Michael Fix. 1984. *Relief or Reform? Reagan's Regulatory Dilemma*. Washington, D.C.: Urban Institute.

Edwards, George C. 1980. *Presidential Influence in Congress*. San Francisco: W. H. Freeman.

Fenno, Richard F. 1973. *Congressmen in Committees*. Boston: Little, Brown.

———. 1978. *Home Style: Representatives in Their Districts*. Boston: Little, Brown.

Ferejohn, John A. 1974. *Pork Barrel Politics: Rivers and Harbors Legislation, 1947–1968*. Stanford, Calif.: Stanford University Press.

Foss, Philip O. 1960. *Politics and Grass*. Seattle: University of Washington Press.

Fowler, Linda L., and Ronald G. Shaiko. 1983. "The Influence of Environmental Activists on Senate Roll Call Decisions." Paper presented at the annual meeting of the American Political Science Association, Chicago, April.

Fox, Harrison W., Jr., and Susan Webb Hammond. 1977. *Congressional Staffs*. New York: Free Press.

Gibbons, John H., and Holly L. Gwin. 1985. "Technology and Governance." *Technology in Society* 7:333–52.

Goldenberg, Edie N., and Michael W. Traugott. 1984. *Campaigning for Congress*. Washington, D.C.: Congressional Quarterly Press.

Goodwin, Craufurd D., ed. 1981. *Energy Policy in Perspective*. Washington, D.C.: Brookings Institution.

Green, Harold P. 1986. "The Role of Congress in Risk Management." *Environmental Law Reporter* 16:10220–23.

Gurr, Ted Robert. 1985. "On the Political Consequences of Scarcity and Economic Decline." *International Studies Quarterly* 29:51–75.

Hammond, Susan Webb, Arthur G. Stevens, Jr., and Daniel P. Mulhollan. 1983. "Congressional Caucuses: Legislators and Lobbyists." In Allan J. Cigler and Burdett A. Loomis, eds., *Interest Group Politics*. Washington, D.C.: Congressional Quarterly Press.

———. 1985. "Informal Congressional Caucuses and Agenda Setting." *Western Political Quarterly* 38:583–605.

Ingram, Helen M., and Dean E. Mann. 1983. "Environmental Protection Policy." In Stuart S. Nagel, ed., *Encyclopedia of Policy Studies*. New York: Marcel Dekker.

Ingram, Helen M., and R. Kenneth Godwin, eds. 1985. *Public Policy and the Natural Environment*. Greenwich, Conn.: JAI Press.

Ingram, Helen M., and Scott Ullery. 1980. "Policy Innovation and Institutional Fragmentation." *Policy Studies Journal* 8, no. 5:664–82.

Ingram, Helen M., Nancy K. Laney, and John R. McCain. 1980. *A Policy Approach to Political Representation: Lessons from the Four Corners States*. Washington, D.C.: Johns Hopkins University Press, for Resources for the Future.

Jacobson, Gary C. 1987. *The Politics of Congressional Elections*. 2d ed. Boston: Little, Brown.

Jennings, M. Kent. 1969. "Legislative Politics and Water Pollution Control, 1956–1961." In Frederick N. Cleaveland, ed., *Congress and Urban Problems*. Washington, D.C.: Brookings Institution.

Jones, Charles O. 1972. "From Gold to Garbage: A Bibliographical Essay on Politics and the Environment." *American Political Science Review* 66:588–95.

———. 1974. "Speculative Augmentation in Federal Air Pollution Policy-Making." *Journal of Politics* 36 (May): 438–64.

———. 1975. *Clean Air: The Policies and Politics of Pollution Control*. Pittsburgh: University of Pittsburgh Press.

———. 1979. "Congress and the Making of Energy Policy." In Robert Lawrence, ed., *New Dimensions to Energy Policy*. Lexington, Mass.: Lexington Books.

———. 1981. "Congress and the Presidency." In Thomas E. Mann and Norman J. Ornstein, eds., *The New Congress*. Washington, D.C.: American Enterprise Institute.

Katz, James Everett. 1984. *Congress and National Energy Policy*. New Brunswick, N.J.: Transaction Books.

Kau, James B., and Paul H. Rubin. 1979. "Public Interest Lobbies: Membership and Influence." *Public Choice* 34, no. 1:45–54.

Kenski, Henry C., and Margaret Corgan Kenski. 1981. "Partisanship, Ideology, and Constituency Differences on Environmental Issues in the U.S. House of Representatives and Senate: 1973–1978." In Dean E. Mann, ed., *Environmental Policy Formation*. Lexington, Mass.: Lexington Books.

———. 1984. "Congress Against the President: The Struggle over the Environment." In Norman J. Vig and Michael E. Kraft, eds., *Environmental Policy in the 1980s*. Washington, D.C.: Congressional Quarterly Press.

King, Anthony, ed. 1983. *Both Ends of the Avenue: The Presidency, the Executive Branch, and Congress in the 1980s*. Washington, D.C.: American Enterprise Institute.

Kingdon, John W. 1981. *Congressmen's Voting Decisions*. 2d ed. New York: Harper & Row.

———. 1984. *Agendas, Alternatives, and Public Policy*. Boston: Little, Brown.

Kraft, Michael E. 1973a. "Congressional Attitudes toward the Environment: Attention and Issue-Orientation in Ecological Politics." Ph.D. diss., Yale University.

———. 1973b. "Ecological Politics and American National Government." *Policy Studies Journal* 1, no. 4:238–44.

———. 1981. "Congress and National Energy Policy: Assessing the Policymaking Process." In Regina S. Axelrod, ed., *Environment, Energy, Public Policy: Toward a Rational Future.* Lexington, Mass.: Lexington Books.

———. 1982. *Risk Analysis in the Legislative Process: Congress and Risk Management Decisionmaking.* Redondo Beach, Calif.: J. H. Wiggins, prepared for the National Science Foundation, Policy Research and Analysis Division.

———. 1983. "Population Policy." In Stuart S. Nagel, ed., *Encyclopedia of Policy Studies.* New York: Marcel Dekker.

———. 1984. "A New Environmental Policy Agenda: The 1980 Presidential Campaign and Its Aftermath." In Vig and Kraft, eds., *Environmental Policy in the 1980s.* Washington, D.C.: Congressional Quarterly Press.

Kraft, Michael E., and Norman J. Vig. 1984. "Environmental Policy in the Reagan Presidency." *Political Science Quarterly* 99, no. 3:415–39.

Laney, Nancy, and Helen Ingram. 1981. "The Disincentives for Policy Leadership in Energy and the Environment: The Structure of Voter Opinion." In Regina C. Axelrod, ed., *Environment, Energy, Public Policy.* Lexington, Mass.: Lexington Books.

Lave, Lester B. 1981. *The Strategy of Social Regulation.* Washington, D.C.: Brookings Institution.

Lester, James P. 1980. "Domestic Structure and International Technological Collaboration: Ocean Pollution Regulation." *Ocean Development and International Law* 8, no. 4:299–335.

Litan, Robert E., and William D. Nordhaus. 1983. *Reforming Social Regulation.* New Haven, Conn.: Yale University Press.

Loomis, Burdett A. 1981. "Congressional Caucuses and the Politics of Representation." In Lawrence C. Dodd and Bruce I. Oppenheimer, eds., *Congress Reconsidered.* 2d ed. Washington, D.C.: Congressional Quarterly Press.

Lundqvist, Lennart J. 1980. *The Hare and the Tortoise: Clean Air Policies in the United States and Sweden.* Ann Arbor: University of Michigan Press.

McConnell, Grant. 1966. *Private Power and American Democracy.* New York: Alfred Knopf.

McFarland, Andrew W. 1976. *Public Interest Lobbies: Decision Making on Energy.* Washington, D.C.: American Enterprise Institute.

———. 1984. *Common Cause: Lobbying in the Public Interest.* Chatham, N.J.: Chatham House.

Malbin, Michael J. 1980. *Unelected Representatives: Congressional Staff and the Future of Representative Government.* New York: Basic Books.

———. 1981. "Delegation, Deliberation, and the New Role of Congressional Staff." In Thomas E. Mann and Norman J. Ornstein, eds., *The New Congress.* Washington, D.C.: American Enterprise Institute.

Mann, Dean E., ed. 1981. *Environmental Policy Formation.* Lexington, Mass.: Lexington Books.

———. 1982. *Environmental Policy Implementation.* Lexington, Mass.: Lexington Books.

Mayhew, David. 1974. *Congress: The Electoral Connection.* New Haven, Conn.: Yale University Press.

Meier, Kenneth J. 1985. *Regulation: Politics, Bureaucracy, and Economics.* New York: St. Martin's Press.

Milbrath, Lester W. 1984. *Environmentalists: Vanguard for a New Society.* Albany: State University of New York Press.

Murphy, James T. 1974. "Political Parties and the Porkbarrel: Party Conflict and Cooperation in House Public Works Committee Decision Making." *American Political Science Review* 68 (March): 169–85.

Nagel, Stuart S., ed. 1974. *Environmental Politics*. New York: Praeger.

Ogul, Morris S. 1981. "Congressional Oversight: Structures and Incentives." In Lawrence C. Dodd and Bruce I. Oppenheimer, eds., *Congress Reconsidered*. 2d ed. Washington, D.C.: Congressional Quarterly Press.

Ophuls, William. 1977. *Ecology and the Politics of Scarcity*. San Francisco: W. H. Freeman.

Oppenheimer, Bruce I. 1974. *Oil and the Congressional Process*. Lexington, Mass.: Lexington Books.

———. 1980. "Policy Effects of U.S. House Reform: Decentralization and the Capacity to Resolve Energy Issues." *Legislative Studies Quarterly* 5:5–30.

———. 1981. "Congress and the New Obstructionism: Developing an Energy Program." In Lawrence C. Dodd and Bruce I. Oppenheimer, eds., *Congress Reconsidered*. 2d ed. Washington, D.C.: Congressional Quarterly Press.

Orfield, Gary. 1975. *Congressional Power: Congress and Social Change*. New York: Harcourt Brace Jovanovich.

Ornstein, Norman J. 1981. "The House and the Senate in a New Congress." In Thomas E. Mann and Norman J. Ornstein, eds., *The New Congress*. Washington, D.C.: American Enterprise Institute.

Paehlke, Robert. 1989. *Environmentalism and the Future of Progressive Politics*. New Haven, Conn.: Yale University Press.

Peabody, Robert L. 1981. "Research on Congress: The 1970s and Beyond." *Congress and the Presidency* 9, no. 1:1–15.

Polsby, Nelson W. 1984. *Political Innovation in America: The Politics of Policy Initiation*. New Haven, Conn.: Yale University Press.

Portney, Paul R., ed. 1984. *Natural Resources and the Environment: The Reagan Approach*. Washington, D.C.: Urban Institute.

Price, David E. 1985. "Congressional Committees in the Policy Process." In Lawrence C. Dodd and Bruce I. Oppenheimer, eds., *Congress Reconsidered*. 3d ed. Washington, D.C.: Congressional Quarterly Press.

Riddlesperger, James W., Jr., and James D. King. 1982. "Energy Votes in the U.S. Senate, 1973–1980." *Journal of Politics* 44:838–47.

Rieselbach, Leroy N. 1983. "The Forest for the Trees: Blazing Trails for Congressional Research." In Ada W. Finifter, ed., *Political Science: The State of the Discipline*. Washington, D.C.: American Political Science Association.

Ripley, Randall B. 1969. "Congress and Clean Air: The Issue of Enforcement, 1963." In Frederick N. Cleaveland, ed., *Congress and Urban Problems*. Washington, D.C.: Brookings Institution.

Ripley, Randall B., and Grace A. Franklin. 1984. *Congress, the Bureaucracy, and Public Policy*. 3d ed. Homewood, Ill.: Dorsey Press.

Ritt, Leonard, and John Ostheimer. 1974. "Congressional Voting on Ecological Issues." *Environmental Affairs* 3, no. 3:459–72.

Rodgers, William H., Jr. 1980. "Benefits, Costs, and Risks: Oversight of Health and Environmental Decisionmaking." *Harvard Environmental Law Review* 4:191–226.

Rosenbaum, Walter A. 1985. *Environmental Politics and Policy*. Washington, D.C.: Congressional Quarterly Press.

Sanders, M. Elizabeth. 1981. *The Regulation of Natural Gas*. Philadelphia: Temple University Press.

Schlozman, Kay Lehman, and John T. Tierney. 1986. *Organized Interests and American Democracy*. New York: Harper & Row.

Sierra Club. 1987. "Scorecard." *Sierra* 72 (January/February): 16–17.

Smith, Steven S., and Christopher J. Deering. 1984. *Committees in Congress*. Washington, D.C.: Congressional Quarterly Press.

Smith, V. Kerry, ed. 1984. *Environmental Policy under Reagan's Executive Order: The Role of Benefit-Cost Analysis*. Chapel Hill: University of North Carolina Press.

Sundquist, James L. 1968. *Politics and Policy: The Eisenhower, Kennedy, and Johnson Years*. Washington, D.C.: Brookings Institution.

———. 1981. "Congress, the President, and the Crisis of Competence in Government." In Lawrence C. Dodd and Bruce I. Oppenheimer, eds., *Congress Reconsidered*, 2d ed. Washington, D.C.: Congressional Quarterly Press.

Temples, James R. 1980. "The Politics of Nuclear Power: A Subgovernment in Transition." *Political Science Quarterly* 95:239–60.

Vig, Norman J., and Michael E. Kraft, eds. 1984a. *Environmental Policy in the 1980s: Reagan's New Agenda*. Washington, D.C.: Congressional Quarterly Press.

———. 1984b. "Environmental Policy from the Seventies to the Eighties." In Vig and Kraft, eds., *Environmental Policy in the 1980s*. Washington, D.C.: Congressional Quarterly Press.

Vogler, David J. 1984. *The Politics of Congress*, 4th ed. Boston: Allyn-Bacon.

Wayne, Stephen J. 1978. *The Legislative Presidency*. New York: Harper & Row.

Whiteman, David. 1982. "The Impact of Technology Assessment: Congress and the Office of Technology Assessment." In David M. O'Brien and Donald A. Marchand, eds., *The Politics of Technology Assessment: Institutions, Processes, and Policy Disputes*. Lexington, Mass.: Lexington Books.

———. 1985. "The Fate of Policy Analysis in Congressional Decision Making: Three Types of Use in Committees." *Western Political Quarterly* 38:294–311.

Wilson, James Q. 1980. "The Politics of Regulation." In Wilson, ed., *The Politics of Regulation*. New York: Basic Books.

Wright, Gerald C., Jr., Leroy N. Rieselbach, and Lawrence C. Dodd, eds. 1986. *Congress and Policy Change*. New York: Agathon Press.

8 The Bureaucracy and Environmental Policy

Aaron, Joan B. 1980. "Citizens' Participation at Government Expense." In Charles R. Foster, ed., *Comparative Public Policy and Citizen Participation*. New York: Pergamon Press.

Advisory Commission on Intergovernmental Relations. 1980. *Citizen Participation in the American Federal System*. Washington, D.C.: Advisory Commission on Intergovernmental Relations.

Anderson, Frederick R. 1973. *NEPA in the Court*. Baltimore: Johns Hopkins University Press.

———. 1974. "The National Environmental Policy Act." In Erica L. Dolgin and Thomas G. P. Guilbert, eds., *Federal Environmental Law*. St. Paul, Minn.: West Publishing.

Andrews, Richard N. L. 1976. *Environmental Policy and Administrative Change*. Lexington, Mass.: Lexington Books.

———. 1979. "Environment and Energy: Implications of Overloaded Agendas." *Natural Resources Journal* 19, no. 3:487–504.

———. 1982. "Cost-Benefit Analysis as Regulatory Reform." In Daniel Swartzman, Richard A.

Liroff, and Kevin G. Croke, eds., *Cost-Benefit Analysis and Environmental Regulations*. Washington, D.C.: Conservation Foundation.

———. 1984a. "Deregulation: The Failure at EPA." In Norman J. Vig and Michael E. Kraft, eds., *Environmental Policy in the 1980s*. Washington, D.C.: Congressional Quarterly Press.

———. 1984b. "Economics and Environmental Decisions, Past and Present." In V. K. Smith, ed., *Environmental Policy under Reagan's Executive Order: The Role of Benefit-Cost Analysis*. Chapel Hill: University of North Carolina Press.

Baden, John, and Richard L. Stroup, eds. 1981. *Bureaucracy and the Environment*. Ann Arbor: University of Michigan Press.

Bardach, Eugene, and Lucian Pugliaiesi. 1977. "The Environmental Impact Statement and the Real World." *Public Interest* 49 (Fall): 22–38.

Bardach, Eugene, and Robert A. Kagan. 1982. *Going by the Book: The Problem of Regulatory Unreasonableness*. Philadelphia: Temple University Press.

Bardach, Eugene, and Robert A. Kagan, eds. 1982. *Social Regulation*. New Brunswick, N.J.: Transaction Books.

Bartlett, Robert V. 1984. "The Budgetary Process and Environmental Policy." In Vig and Kraft, eds., *Environmental Policy in the 1980s*.

Belsky, Martin H. 1984. "Environmental Policy Law in the 1980s: Shifting Back the Burden of Proof." *Ecology Law Quarterly* 12, no. 1:1–88.

Caldwell, Lynton K. 1978. "The Environmental Impact Statement: A Misused Tool." In Ravinder Jain and Bruce Hutchings, eds., *Environmental Impact Analysis*. Urbana: University of Illinois Press.

———. 1982. *Science and the National Environmental Policy Act: Redirecting Policy through Procedural Reform*. Tuscaloosa: University of Alabama Press.

Caldwell, Lynton K., Lynton R. Hayes, and Isabel M. MacWhirter, eds. 1976. *Citizens and the Environment*. Bloomington: University of Indiana Press.

Centaur Associates. 1979. *Siting of Hazardous Waste Management Facilities and Public Opposition*. Washington, D.C.: U.S. Environmental Protection Agency. Doc. No. SW–809.

Clark, Edwin H., II. 1984. "Reaganomics and the Environment: An Evaluation." In Vig and Kraft, eds., *Environmental Policy in the 1980s*.

Cohen, Linda. 1979. "Innovation and Atomic Energy: Nuclear Power Regulation, 1966–Present." *Law and Contemporary Problems* 43, no. 1:43–66.

Cohen, Stephen. 1984. "Defusing the Toxic Time Bomb: Federal Hazardous Waste Programs." In Vig and Kraft, eds., *Environmental Policy in the 1980s*.

Cohen, Steven, and Marc Tipermas. 1983. "Superfund: Preimplementation Planning and Bureaucratic Politics." In James P. Lester and Ann O'M. Bowman, eds., *The Politics of Hazardous Waste Management*. Durham, N.C.: Duke University Press.

Conservation Foundation. 1982. *The State of the Environment*. Washington, D.C.: Conservation Foundation.

———. 1984a. *Controlling Cross-Media Pollutants*. Washington, D.C.: Conservation Foundation.

———. 1984b. *The State of the Environment*. Washington, D.C.: Conservation Foundation.

Council on Environmental Quality (CEQ). *Environmental Quality*. Washington, D.C.: U.S. Government Printing Office. Issued annually.

Crandall, Robert W., and Lester B. Lave, eds. 1981. *The Scientific Basis of Health and Safety Regulation*. Washington, D.C.: Brookings Institution.

Cupps, Steven D. 1977. "Emerging Problems of Citizen Participation." *Public Administration Review* 37, no. 5:457–87.

Daneke, Gregory A. 1984. "Whither Environmental Regulation?" *Journal of Public Policy* 4, no. 2:139–51.

Davies, J. Clarence. 1983. "Environmental Institutions and the Reagan Administration." In Vig and Kraft, eds., *Environmental Policy in the 1980s.*

Dolgin, Erica L., and Thomas G. P. Guilbert, eds. 1974. *Federal Environmental Law.* St. Paul, Minn.: West Publishing.

Doniger, David. 1978. *The Law and Policy of Toxic Substances Control.* Baltimore: Johns Hopkins University Press.

Doniger, David, Richard Liroff, and N. Dean. 1978. *An Analysis of Past Federal Efforts to Control Toxic Substances.* Washington, D.C.: Environmental Law Institute.

Dorfman, Robert. 1982. "The Lessons of Pesticide Regulation." In Wesley A. Magat, ed., *Reform of Environmental Regulation.* Cambridge, Mass.: Ballinger.

Downing, Paul B., and James N. Kimball. 1982. "Enforcing Pollution Control Laws in the U.S." *Policy Studies Journal* 11, no. 1:55–65.

Dreyfus, Daniel A., and Helen M. Ingram. 1976. "The National Environmental Policy Act: A View of Intent and Practice." *Natural Resources Journal* 16, no. 2:243–62.

Dunlop, Thomas. 1981. *DDT: Scientists, Citizens, and Public Policy.* Princeton, N.J.: Princeton University Press.

Edgcomb, John D. 1983. "Co-operative Federalism and Environmental Protection: The Surface Mining Control and Reclamation Act of 1977." *Tulane Law Review* 58, no. 1:299–341.

Edmunds, Stahrl W. 1981. "Environmental Policy: Bounded Rationality Applied to Unbounded Ecological Problems." In Dean E. Mann, ed., *Environmental Policy Formation.* Lexington, Mass.: Lexington Books.

Environmental Law Institute. 1981. NEPA *in Action: The Experience of Nineteen Federal Agencies.* Washington, D.C.: Council on Environmental Quality.

Foster, Charles R., ed. 1980. *Comparative Public Policy and Citizen Participation.* New York: Pergamon Press.

Friesma, H. Paul, and Paul J. Culhane. 1976. "Social Impact, Politics, and the Environmental Impact Statement Process." *Natural Resources Journal* 16, no. 2:339–56.

Gaeuterer, Greg et al. 1983. "Federal Agencies in the Context of Transition." *Public Administration Review* 43, no. 5:421–32.

Goetze, David. 1981. "The Shaping of Environmental Attitudes in Air Pollution Control Agencies." *Public Administration Review* 41, no. 4:423–30.

Green, Harold P. 1977. "Cost-Risk Benefit Assessment and the Law: Introduction and Perspective." *George Washington Law Review* 45, no. 5:901–10.

Greenwood, Ted. 1984. "The Myth of Scientific Incompetence of Regulatory Agencies." *Science, Technology, and Human Values* 9, no. 11:83–96.

Grubb, W. Norton, Dale Whittington, and Michael Humphries. 1984. "The Ambiguities of Benefit-Cost Analysis: An Evaluation of Regulatory Impact Analyses under Executive Order 12291." In V. Kerry Smith, ed., *Environmental Policy under Reagan's Executive Order.* Chapel Hill: University of North Carolina Press.

Hadden, Susan, ed. 1984. *Risk Analysis, Institutions, and Public Policy.* Port Washington, N.Y.: Associated Faculty Press.

Harris, Richard A. 1985. *Coal Firms under the New Social Regulation.* Durham, N.C.: Duke University Press.

Havender, William R. 1981. "Politicians Make Bad Scientists." *Regulation* 5, no. 6:46–48.

———. 1982. "Assessing and Controlling Risks." In Eugene Bardach and Robert A. Kagan, eds., *Social Regulation*. New Brunswick, N.J.: Transaction Books.

Henderson, J. A., and R. N. Pearson. 1978. "Implementing Federal Environmental Policies: The Limits of Aspirational Command." *Columbia Law Review* 78, no. 7:1429–70.

Hedge, D. M., and D. C. Menzel. 1985. "Loosening the Regulatory Ratchet: A Grassroots View of Environmental Deregulation." *Policy Studies Journal* 13, no. 3:599–606.

Hill, William W., and Leonard Ortolano. 1976. "Effects of NEPA's Review and Comment Process on Water Resource Planning." *Water Resources Research* 12:1039–99.

House, Peter W., and Roger D. Shull. 1985. *Regulatory Reform: Politics and the Environment*. Lanham, Md.: Abt Associates and University Press of America.

Ingram, Helen, and J. R. McCain. 1977. "Federal Water Resource Management: The Administrative Setting." *Public Administration Review* 35, no. 5:448–55.

Ingram, Helen, and Scott Ullery. 1977. "Public Participation in Environmental Decisionmaking." In F. T. Koppock and W. R. D. Sewell, eds., *Public Participation in Planning*. New York: John Wiley.

Jain, Ravinder, and Bruce Hutchings, eds. 1978. *Environmental Impact Analysis*. Urbana: University of Illinois Press.

Johnson, N. Bruce. 1981. "The Environmental Costs of Bureaucratic Governance: Theory and Cases." In Baden and Stroup, eds., *Bureaucracy and the Environment*.

Jones, Charles O. 1974. "Speculative Argumentation in Federal Air Pollution Policy-Making." *Journal of Politics* 36, no. 2:438–64.

———. 1975. *Clean Air: The Policies and Politics of Pollution Control*. Pittsburgh: University of Pittsburgh Press.

Kasper, Raphael. 1977. "Cost-Benefit Analysis in Environmental Decision-Making." *George Washington Law Review* 45, no. 5:1013–24.

Kimm, Victor J., Arnold M. Kuzmack, and David W. Schnare. 1981. "Waterborne Carcinogens: A Regulator's View." In Crandall and Lave, eds., *The Scientific Basis of Health and Safety Regulation*.

Kneese, Allen V., and Charles L. Schultze. 1974. *Pollution, Prices, and Public Policy*. Washington, D.C.: Brookings Institution.

Koppock, F. T., and W. R. D. Sewell, eds. 1977. *Public Participation in Planning*. New York: John Wiley.

Kraft, Michael E. 1982. "The Use of Risk Analysis in Federal Regulatory Agencies: An Exploration." *Policy Studies Review* 1, no. 4:666–75.

Lake, Laura. 1982. *Environmental Regulation*. New York: Praeger.

Lave, Lester. 1982. *Quantitative Risk Assessment in Regulation*. Washington, D.C.: Brookings Institution.

———. 1983. "Specifying Risk Goals: Inherent Problems with Democratic Institutions." *Risk Analysis* 3, no. 3:207–16.

Leone, R. 1977. "The Real Costs of Regulation." *Harvard Business Review* 55, no. 6:122–36.

Lester, James P., and Ann O'M. Bowman, eds. 1983. *The Politics of Hazardous Waste Management*. Durham, N.C.: Duke University Press.

Levin, Michael H. 1982. "Getting There: Implementing the 'Bubble' Policy." In Bardach and Kagan, eds., *Social Regulation*.

Liroff, Richard A. 1976. *A National Policy for the Environment*. Bloomington: Indiana University Press.

———. 1980. "NEPA: Where Have We Been and Where Are We Going?" *Journal of the American Planning Association* 46, no. 2:154–61.

———. 1981. "NEPA Litigation in the 1970s: A Deluge or a Dribble?" *Natural Resources Journal* 21, no. 2:315–30.

Lowrance, William W. 1976. *Of Acceptable Risk.* Los Altos, Calif.: William Kaufmann.

Lynn, Frank M. 1986. "The Interplay of Science and Values in Assessing and Regulating Environmental Risks." *Science, Technology, and Human Values* 11, no. 2:40–50.

McDermott, J. E. 1980. "Improving EPA: New Regulations of the Council on Environmental Quality." *Boston College Environmental Affairs Law Review* 8, no. 1:89–118.

McGarity, Thomas. 1983. "Media-Quality, Technology, and Cost-Benefit Balancing Strategies for Health and Environmental Regulation." *Law and Contemporary Problems* 46, no. 3:159–73.

———. 1985. "The Use of Regulatory Analysis in the Decisionmaking Process." *Report to the U.S. Administrative Conference on Regulatory Impact Analysis in Federal Regulatory Agencies.* Washington, D.C.: U.S. Administrative Conference.

Magat, Wesley A. 1979. "The Effects of Environmental Regulation on Innovation." *Law and Contemporary Problems* 43, no. 1:4–25.

Magat, Wesley A., ed. 1982. *Reform of Environmental Regulation.* Cambridge, Mass.: Ballinger.

Mandelker, Daniel. 1981. *Environment and Equity.* New York: McGraw-Hill.

Mann, Dean E., ed. 1981. *Environmental Policy Formation.* Lexington, Mass.: Lexington Books.

Marcus, Alfred A. 1980. *Promise and Performance.* Westport, Conn.: Greenwood Press.

Marcus, Alfred A., F. A. Morris, and P. Sommers. 1982. "Alternative Arrangements for Cost Effective Pollution Abatement: The Need for Implementation Analysis." *Policy Studies Review* 1, no. 3:477–83.

Matheny, Albert R., and Bruce A. Williams. 1981. "Scientific Disputes and Adversary Procedures in Policy-Making." *Law and Policy Quarterly* 3, no. 3:341–64.

Mazmanian, Daniel A., and Jeanne Nienaber. 1979. *Can Organizations Change?* Washington, D.C.: Brookings Institution.

Mazur, Alan. 1981. *The Dynamics of Technical Controversy.* Washington, D.C.: Communications Press.

Melnick, R. Shep. 1983. *Regulation and the Courts: The Case of the Clean Air Act.* Washington, D.C.: Brookings Institution.

———. 1984. "Pollution Deadlines and the Coalition of Failure." *Public Interest* 75:123–34.

Menzel, Donald C. 1983. "Redirecting the Implementation of a Law: The Reagan Administration and Coal Surface Mining Regulation." *Public Administration Review* 43, no. 5:411–20.

Middleton, John T. 1981. "Sulfur Dioxide: A Regulator's View." In Crandall and Lave, eds., *The Scientific Basis of Health and Safety Regulation.*

Miller, Alan, et al. 1976. "The National Environmental Policy Act." *Environmental Law Reporter,* March 1976, 50020–29.

Nagel, Stuart S., ed. 1974. *Environmental Politics.* New York: Praeger.

Nathan, Richard P. 1983. *The Administrative Presidency.* New York: John Wiley.

National Research Council, Commission on Life Sciences. 1983. *Risk Assessment in the Federal Government: Managing the Process.* Washington, D.C.: National Academy Press.

Nelkin, Dorothy. 1984. *Controversy: Politics of Technical Decisions.* 2d ed. Beverly Hills: Sage Publications.

Nelson, Robert H. 1984. "Economic Analysis in Public Rangeland Management." In John G. Francis and Richard Ganzel, eds., *Western Public Lands.* Totowa, N.J.: Rowman & Allenheld.

Ortolano, Leonard, et al. 1978. *Environmental Considerations in Three Infrastructure Planning Agencies*. Report IPM-6. Department of Civil Engineering, Stanford University.

Ozawa, Connie. 1982. "Targeting the NEPA Process." *Environmental Impact Assessment Review* 3, no. 1:102–8.

Palmer, John L., and Isabel Sawhill, eds. 1984. *The Reagan Record*. Cambridge, Mass.: Ballinger.

Portney, Paul R. 1984. "Natural Resources and the Environment: More Controversy Than Change." In John L. Palmer and Isabel Sawhill, eds., *The Reagan Record*. Cambridge, Mass.: Ballinger.

Portney, Paul R., ed. 1978. *Current Issues in U.S. Environmental Policy*. Baltimore: Johns Hopkins University Press.

Regens, James L., Thomas M. Dietz, and Robert W. Rycroft. 1983. "Risk Assessment in the Policy Making Process: Environmental Health and Safety Protection." *Public Administration Review* 43, no. 2:137–45.

Rosenbaum, Walter A. 1974. "The End of Illusion: NEPA and the Limits of Judicial Review." In Stuart S. Nagel, ed., *Environmental Politics*. New York: Praeger.

———. 1978. "Public Involvement as Reform and Ritual: The Development of Federal Participation Programs." In Stuart Langton, ed., *Citizen Participation in America*. Lexington, Mass.: Lexington Books.

———. 1983. "The Politics of Public Participation in Hazardous Waste Management." In Lester and Bowman, eds., *The Politics of Hazardous Waste Management*.

Runge, Carlisle F. 1983. "Risk Assessment and Environmental Analysis." *Natural Resources Journal* 23, no. 3:683–96.

Rushefsky, Mark E. 1984. "The Misuse of Science in Governmental Decisionmaking." *Science, Technology, and Human Values* 9, no. 3:47–59.

Sabatier, Paul A. 1975. "Social Movements and Regulatory Agencies: Toward a More Adequate—and Less Pessimistic—Theory of 'Clientele Capture.'" *Policy Sciences* 6, no. 3:301–42.

———. 1977. "Regulatory Policy-Making: Toward a Framework of Analysis." *Natural Resources Journal* 17, no. 3:415–57.

Sabatier, Paul, and Geoffrey Wandesforde-Smith. 1979. "Major Sources in Environmental Politics, 1974–77: The Maturing of the Literature." *Policy Studies Journal* 7, no. 3:592–604.

Schmandt, Jurgen. 1984. "Regulation and Science." *Science, Technology, and Human Values* 9, no. 1:23–38.

———. 1985. "Managing Comprehensive Rule Making: EPA's Plan for Integrated Environmental Management." *Public Administration Review* 45, no. 2:309–18.

Schroeder, Christopher. 1984. "The Evolution of Federal Toxics Policy." Paper presented at the Conference on the Evolution of American Environmental Politics, the Wilson Center, Smithsonian Institution, Washington, D.C., June 28–30.

Smith, V. Kerry, ed. 1984. *Environmental Policy under Reagan's Executive Order: The Role of Benefit-Cost Analysis*. Chapel Hill: University of North Carolina Press.

Strange, John H. 1972. "The Impact of Citizen Participation on Public Administration." *Public Administration Review* 32 (Special Issue): 457–70.

Swartzman, Daniel. 1982. "Cost-Benefit Analysis in Environmental Regulation." In Swartzman, Liroff, and Croke, eds., *Cost-Benefit Analysis and Environmental Regulations*.

Swartzman, Daniel, Richard A. Liroff, and Kevin G. Croke, eds. 1982. *Cost-Benefit Analysis and Environmental Regulations*. Washington, D.C.: Conservation Foundation.

Taylor, Serge. 1984. *Making Bureaucracies Think: The Environmental Impact Statement Strategy of Administrative Reform*. Stanford, Calif.: Stanford University Press.

Tobias, Carl W. 1982. "Of Public Funds and Public Participation: Resolving the Issue of Agency Authority to Reimburse Public Participants in Administrative Proceedings." *Columbia Law Review* 82, no. 5:906–55.

U.S. Congress, General Accounting Office (GAO). 1981. EPA *Slow in Controlling* PCBs. Report No. CED-82–21 (December 30, 1981).

———. 1982. *A Market Approach to Air Pollution Control Could Reduce Compliance Costs without Jeopardizing Clean Air Goals.* Report No. PAD-82–15 (March 23, 1982).

———. 1983. *Delays in* EPA*'s Regulation of Hazardous Air Pollutants.* Report No. GAO/RCED-83–199 (August 26, 1983).

———. 1983. *Interim Report on Inspection, Enforcement, and Permitting Activities at Hazardous Waste Facilities.* Report No. GAO/RCED-83–241 (September 21, 1983).

———. 1984. *Cost-Benefit Analysis Can Be Useful in Assessing Environmental Regulations, Despite Limitations.* Report No. GAO/RCED-84–62 (April 6, 1984).

———. 1984. EPA*'s Efforts to Identify and Control Harmful Chemicals in Use.* Report No. GAO/RCED-84–100 (June 13, 1984).

Vig, Norman J., and Michael E. Kraft, eds. 1984. *Environmental Policy in the 1980s.* Washington, D.C.: Congressional Quarterly Press.

Vogel, David. 1986. *National Styles of Regulation: Environmental Policy in Great Britain and the U.S.* Ithaca, N.Y.: Cornell University Press.

Wandesforde-Smith, Geoffrey, et al. 1975. "Projects, Policies, and Environmental Impact Assessment." *Policy Studies Journal* 4, no. 1:81–90.

Wenner, Lettie McSpadden. 1982. *The Environmental Decade in Court.* Bloomington: University of Indiana Press.

White, Laurence J. 1982. "U.S. Mobile Source Emissions Regulation: The Problems of Implementation." *Policy Studies Journal* 11, no. 1:77–87.

Whittington, Dale, and W. Norton Grubb. 1984. "Economic Analysis in Regulatory Decisions: The Implications of Executive Order 12291." *Science, Technology, and Human Values* 9, no. 1:63–71.

Wichelman, Allan F. 1976. "Administrative Implementation of the National Environmental Policy Act of 1969." *Natural Resources Journal* 16, no. 2:263–300.

Williams, Deborah Lee. 1979. "Benefit-Cost Assessment in Natural Resources Decisionmaking." *Natural Resources Lawyer* 11, no. 4:761–96.

Woodhouse, Edward J. 1985. "External Influences on Productivity: EPA's Implementation of TSCA." *Policy Studies Journal* 4, no. 3:497–503.

Yellin, Joel. 1983. "Who Shall Make Environmental Decisions?" *American Statistician* 37, no. 4:362–66.

Zimmerman, Rae. 1982. "Formation of New Organizations to Manage Risk." *Policy Studies Review* 1, no. 4:736–47.

9 The Courts and Environmental Policy

ABA Environmental Quality Committee. 1978. Annual Review of Significant Activities. *Natural Resources Lawyer* 12:51–81.

"Acid Precipitation: Can the CAA Handle It?" 1982. *Boston College Environmental Affairs Law Review* 9:687–744.

"Acid Precipitation: Limits of the Clean Air Act." 1983. *Syracuse Law Review* 34:619–56.

Ackerman, Bruce A., and William T. Hassler. 1981. "Beyond the New Deal." *Yale Law Journal* 90:1412–34.

Anderson, Frederick. 1973. NEPA *in the Courts*. Washington, D.C.: Resources for the Future.

Andrews, Richard N. L. 1976. *Environmental Policy and Administrative Change*. Lexington, Mass.: Lexington Books.

Ayres, Richard E., and David D. Doniger. 1979. "NSPS for Power Plants II: Consider the Law." *Harvard Environmental Law Review* 3:63–83.

Bacow, David, and James R. Milkey. 1982. "Overcoming Local Opposition to Hazardous Waste Facilities: The Mass Approach." *Harvard Environmental Law Review* 6:265–305.

Badger, Daniel B., Jr. 1979. "New Source Standard for Power Plants I: Consider the Costs." *Harvard Environmental Law Review* 3:48–62.

Baer, David K., and Keith Anderson. 1982. "NRDC v. NRC: Environmental Review and Nonproliferation Policy in Nuclear Exports." *George Washington Journal of International Law and Economics* 16:579–603.

Banks, William C. 1981. "EPA Bends to Industry Pressure on Coal NSPS—and Breaks." *Ecology Law Quarterly* 9:67–117.

Bartlett, Robert. 1980. *The Reserve Mining Controversy*. Bloomington: Indiana University Press.

Bastow, Thomas F. 1986. *"This Vast Pollution. . . ."* Washington, D.C.: Green Fields Books.

Baurer, Theodore. 1980. "Love Canal: Common Law Approaches to a Modern Tragedy." *Environmental Law* 11:133–60.

Bazelon, David I. 1977. "Coping with Technology through the Legal Process." *Cornell Law Review* 62:817–32.

———. 1981. "Science and Uncertainty: A Jurist's View." *Harvard Environmental Law Review* 5:209–15.

Birkby, Robert H. 1966. "The Supreme Court and the Bible Belt." *Midwest Journal of Political Science* 10:304–19.

Bleiweiss, S. J. 1983. "Federal Regulation and the Federal Common Law of Nuisance: A Proposed Standard of Preemption." *Harvard Environmental Law Review* 7:41–70.

Breyer, Stephen. 1978. "Vermont Yankee and the Court's Role in the Nuclear Energy Controversy." *Harvard Law Review* 91:1833–45.

Brooks, Jon Schuyler. 1983. "Slick Maneuvering: The Fifth Circuit Finds Liability for Oil Pollution Exists outside the Federal Water Pollution Control Act—*U.S. v. M/V Big Sam*." *Maritime Lawyer* 8:171–98.

Byse, Clark. 1978. "Vermont Yankee and the Evolution of Administrative Procedure." *Harvard Law Review* 91:1823–32.

Canon, Bradley C. 1977. "Taking Advantage of a Quasi-experimental Situation: The Impact of Mapp." *American Politics Quarterly* 5:5–15.

Carp, Robert, and C. K. Rowland. 1983. *Policy Making and Politics in the Federal District Courts*. Knoxville: University of Tennessee Press.

Chayes, Abraham. 1976. "The Role of Judges in Public Law Litigation." *Harvard Law Review* 89:1281–1316.

Claff, Cindy, et al. 1977. "Federal Environmental Litigation in 1977: NEPA." *Harvard Environmental Law Review* 2:199–240.

"The Clean Water Act and Related Developments in the FWPC Program during 1977." 1977. *Harvard Environmental Law Review* 2:103–26.

Collins, Michael. 1984. "The Dilemma of the Downstream State: The Untimely Demise of

Federal Common Law Nuisance." *Boston College Environmental Affairs Law Review* 11:297–412.

Cook, Beverly B. 1977. "Public Opinion and Federal Judicial Policy." *American Journal of Political Science* 21:567–600.

Cook, Constance Ewing. 1983. *Nuclear Power and Legal Advocacy*. Lexington, Mass.: Lexington Books.

Currie, David P. 1979. "Relaxation of Implementation Plans under the 1977 CAA Amendments." *Michigan Law Review* 78:155–76.

———. 1980a. "Direct Federal Regulation of Stationary Sources under the CAA." *University of Pennsylvania Law Review* 128:1389–1466.

———. 1980b. "Nondegradation and Visibility under the CAA." *California Law Review* 68:48–57.

David, Christopher, et al. 1977. "The Clean Air Act Amendments of 1977: Away from Technology Forcing?" *Harvard Environmental Law Review* 2:1–102.

Davis, Kenneth Culp. 1980. "Administrative Law and the Vermont Yankee Opinion." *Utah Law Review* 87:3–17.

Del Calvo y Gonzalez, Jorge A. 1981. "Markets in Air: Problems and Prospects of Controlled Trading." *Harvard Environmental Law Review* 5:377–430.

Del Luca, Patrick. 1981. "The Clean Air Act: A Realistic Assessment of Cost-Effectiveness." *Harvard Environmental Law Review* 5:184–203.

Deutsch, Stuart L., A. Dan Tarlock, and Richard L. Robbin. 1983. "Analysis of Regulations under RCRA." *Washington University Journal of Urban and Contemporary Law* 25:145–202.

Dore, Michael. 1981. "The Standard of Civil Liability for Hazardous Waste Disposal Activity: Some Quirks of Superfund." *Notre Dame Lawyer* 57:260–84.

———. 1983. "A Commentary on the Use of Epidemiological Evidence in Demonstrating Cause-in-fact." *Harvard Environmental Law Review* 7:429–48.

Dudley, Robert, and Craig Ducat. 1985. "Recent Voting Patterns on the Burger Court in Economics Cases." Paper presented at the Western Political Science Association, Las Vegas, Nevada.

Edwards, Katherine B. 1980. "NRC Regulations." *Texas Law Review* 58:355–91.

"Emission Offset Banking: Accommodating Industrial Growth with Air Quality Standards." 1980. *University of Pennsylvania Law Review* 128:937–85.

"Environmental Impact Statements: Instruments for Environmental Protection or Endless Litigation?" 1983. *Fordham Urban Law Journal* 11:527–66.

"The EPA's Bubble Concept after *Alabama Power*." 1980. *Stanford Law Review* 32:943.

Fairfax, Sally. 1978. "Disaster in the Environmental Movement." *Science* 199:743–50.

"Federal Common Law of Nuisance No Longer a Remedy." 1981. *Thurgood Marshall Law Review* 7:354–63.

Feldman, Steven L. 1982. "The Administrative Procedure Act's Notice and Comment Requirements: 'Good Cause' for Further Delay in the Implementation of the CAA?" *Boston College Environmental Affairs Law Review* 9:549–622.

Florini, Karen L. 1982. "Issues of Federalism in Hazardous Waste Control: Cooperation or Confusion?" *Harvard Environmental Law Review* 6:307–37.

Floy, Kent R. 1981. "Prevention of Significant Deterioration of Air Quality—the Regulations after *Alabama Power*." *Boston College Environmental Affairs Law Review* 9:13–61.

Fryer, R. Alan. 1979. "*CLF v. Andrus* and Oil Drilling on Georges Bank: The First Circuit Attempts to Balance Conflicting Interests." *Boston College Environmental Affairs Law Review* 21:201–97.

Gibson, J. 1978. "Judges' Role Orientations, Attitudes, and Decisions: An Interactive Model." *American Political Science Review* 72:911–24.

Giles, M., and T. Walker. 1975. "Judicial Policy Making and Southern School Segregation." *Journal of Politics* 37:917–36.

Glazer, Nathan. 1975. "Toward an Imperial Judiciary?" *The Public Interest* 41:104–23.

Goldsmith, Richard I., and William C. Banks. 1983. "The Supreme Court and Environmental Values." *Harvard Environmental Law Review* 7:1–40.

Grunbaum, Werner. 1974. "Judicial Attitudes toward Environmental Quality in Federal and State Courts." Paper presented at Midwest Political Science Association Meeting, Chicago, Illinois.

Henderson, George B. 1980. "The Nuclear Choice: Are Health and Safety Issues Preempted?" *Boston College Environmental Affairs Law Review* 8:821–72.

Hinds, Richard. 1982. "Liability under Federal Law for Hazardous Waste Injuries." *Harvard Environmental Law Review* 6:1–34.

Horowitz, Donald. 1977. *The Courts and Social Policy.* Washington, D.C.: Brookings Institution.

Johnson, Charles A., and Bradley C. Cannon. 1984. *Judicial Policies: Implementation and Impact.* Washington, D.C.: Congressional Quarterly Press.

Johnson, Thomas C. 1978. "The Energy Crisis: 'Reasonable Assurances' of Safety in the Regulation of Nuclear Power Facilities." *University of Detroit Journal of Urban Law* 55:371–407.

"Joint and Several Liability for Hazardous Waste Releases under Superfund." 1982. *Virginia Law Review* 68:1157–95.

Jordan, William S. 1984. "Psychological Harm after PANE: NEPA's Requirements to Consider Psychological Damage." *Harvard Environmental Law Review* 8:55–88.

Kameron, Matthew A. 1979. "Offshore Oil Development and the Demise of NEPA." *Boston College Environmental Affairs Law Review* 7:121–35.

Koshland, William. 1978. "The Scope of the Program EIS Requirement: The Need for a Coherent Judicial Approach." *Stanford Law Review* 30:767–802.

Kritzer, Herbert. 1978. "Political Correlates of the Behavior of Federal District Judges." *Journal of Politics* 40:25–57.

Landau, Jack. 1980a. "*Alabama Power v. Costle:* End to Controversy over PSD." *Environmental Law* 10:585–642.

———. 1980b. "Economic Dream or Environmental Nightmare? The Legality of the 'Bubble Concept' in Air and Water Pollution Control." *Boston College Environmental Affairs Law Review* 8:741–81.

Landau, Norman J., and Paul D. Rheingold. 1971. *The Environmental Law Handbook.* New York: Ballantine.

Leventhal, Harold. 1974. "Environmental Decisionmaking and the Role of the Courts." *University of Pennsylvania Law Review* 122:509.

Leybold, Dennis. 1978. "Federal Common Law: Judicially Established Effluent Standards as a Remedy in Federal Nuisance Actions." *Boston College Environmental Affairs Law Review* 7:293–315.

Linet, Martha, and Paul Bailey. 1981. "Benzene, Leukemia, and the Supreme Court." *Journal of Public Health Policy* 2:115–36.

Liroff, Richard A. 1976. *A National Policy for the Environment:* NEPA *and Its Aftermath.* Bloomington: Indiana University Press.

———. 1980. "NEPA—Where Have We Been and Where Are We Going?" *American Planning Association Journal* 46:154–61.

Luster, Elizabeth T. 1982/83. "The Comprehensive Environmental Response, Compensation, and Liability Act of 1980; Is Joint and Several Liability the Answer to Superfund?" *New England Law Review* 18:179–87.

McGarity, Thomas D. 1977. "The Courts, the Agencies, and NEPA Threshold Issues." *Texas Law Review* 55:801–87.

———. 1980. "Multiparty Forum Shopping for Appellate Review of Administrative Action." *University of Pennsylvania Law Review* 129:302–76.

McKinnon, James E. 1979. "The FWPCA-Industrial Challenges to Effluent Limits." *Boston College Environmental Affairs Law Review* 7:545–66.

Marek, Howard R. 1980. "NEPA." *Texas Law Review* 58:393–413.

Marnell, Mark F. 1981. "EPA's Responsibilities under RCRA: Administrative Law Issues." *Ecology Law Quarterly* 9:555–78.

Mazmanian, Daniel, and Jeanne Nienaber. 1979. *Can Organizations Change: Environmental Protection, Citizen Participation, and the Corps of Engineers*. Washington, D.C.: Brookings Institution.

Melnick, Rowell Shep. 1983. *Regulation and the Courts: The Case of the Clean Air Act*. Washington, D.C.: Brookings Institution.

"*Middlesex County Sewerage Authority v. National Sea Clammers*." 1981. *Environmental Law* 12:197–229.

Murphy, Walter. 1964. *Elements of Judicial Strategy*. Chicago: University of Chicago Press.

Nagel, S. 1961. "Political Party Affiliation and Judges' Decisions." *American Political Science Review* 55:843–50.

O'Connor, K., and L. Epstein. 1983. "The Rise of Conservative Interest Group Litigation." *Journal of Politics* 45:479–89.

O'Connor, Karen. 1980. *Women's Organizations' Use of the Courts*. Lexington, Mass.: Lexington Books.

Office of Technology Assessment. 1983. *Technologies and Management Strategies for Hazardous Waste Control*. Washington, D.C.: Government Printing Office.

"Opening the Door to Earlier Judicial Review of EISs." 1983. *University of Colorado Law Review* 55:99–124.

Orren, K. 1976. "Standing to Sue: Interest Group Conflict in the Federal Courts." *American Political Science Review* 70:723–41.

Pedersen, William F., Jr. 1981. "Why the Clean Air Act Works Badly." *University of Pennsylvania Law Review* 129:1059–1109.

Pritchett, H. 1948. *The Roosevelt Court*. New York: Macmillan.

"Private Right of Action: Common Law of Nuisance." 1983. *New York Law School Law Review* 28:195–220.

Raymond, James F. 1979. "A *Vermont Yankee* in King Burger's Court: Constraints on Judicial Review under NEPA." *Boston College Environmental Affairs Law Review* 7:629–64.

Rea, Raymond. 1982. "Hazardous Waste Pollution: Need for Different Statutory Approach." *Environmental Law* 12:443–68.

Rodgers, Harrell R., and Charles S. Bullock III. 1972. *Law and Social Change: Civil Rights Laws and Their Consequences*. New York: McGraw-Hill.

Rodgers, William H. 1977. *Environmental Law*. Handbook Series. St. Paul, Minn.: West Publishing.

———. 1980. "Benefits, Costs, and Risks: Oversight of Health and Environmental Decisionmaking." *Harvard Environmental Law Review* 4:191–226.

———. 1981. "Judicial Review of Risk Assessments: The Role of Decision Theory in Unscrambling the Benzene Decision." *Environmental Law* 11:301–20.

Rubin, Hal. 1980. "Is It Cheaper to Litigate than Mitigate?" *Cry California* 10:31–35.

Sax, Joseph L. 1971. *Defending the Environment*. New York: Knopf.

Schaumburg, Frank D. 1976. *Judgment Reserved: A Landmark Environmental Case*. Reston, Va.: Reston Publishing.

Schoenbaum, Thomas J. 1981. *Environmental Policy Law*. New York: Foundation Press.

Schoenbrod, David. 1983. "Limits and Dangers of Environmental Mediation." *New York University Law Review* 58:1453–76.

Schubert, G. 1965. *The Judicial Mind*. Evanston, Ill.: Northwestern University Press.

———. 1974. *The Judicial Mind Revisited*. New York: Oxford University Press.

Shapiro, Martin. 1982. "On Predicting the Future of Administrative Law." *Regulation*, May/June, pp. 18–25.

Shea, Thomas E. 1981. "The Judicial Standard for Review of EIS Threshold Decisions." *Boston College Environmental Affairs Law Review* 9:63–101.

Shortsleeve, Catherine Finnegan. 1981. "*Andrus v. Sierra Club:* No Effective Environmental Review in the Federal Budget Process." *Boston College Environmental Affairs Law Review* 9:205–43.

Smith, Lowell, and Russell Randle. 1981. "Comment on 'Beyond the New Deal.'" *Yale Law Journal* 90:1398–1411.

Spaeth, H. 1979. *Supreme Court Policy Making*. New York: W. H. Freeman.

Speth, Gus. 1980–81. "Global Energy Futures and the Carbon Dioxide Problem." *Boston College Environmental Affairs Law Review* 9:1–11.

Squires, Mary P. 1979. "Restricted Judicial Review Provisions of the CAA—Denial of Due Process." *Harvard Environmental Law Review* 8:119–52.

Stewart, Richard. 1978. "*Vermont Yankee* and the Evolution of Administrative Procedure." *Harvard Law Review* 91:1805–45.

Stone, Christopher D. 1974. *Should Trees Have Standing?* Los Altos, Calif.: William Kaufman.

Susskind, Lawrence, David Bacow, and Michael Wheeler. 1983. *Resolving Environmental Regulatory Disputes*. Cambridge, Mass.: Schenkman Publishing.

Terziev, Alexandra J. 1981. "PSD: New Regulations and Old Problems." *Harvard Environmental Law Review* 5:130–52.

Thompson, Edward, Jr. 1977. "Section 404 of the FWPCA Amendments of 1977." *Harvard Environmental Law Review* 2:177–296.

Tribe, Laurence. 1972. "Policy Science: Analysis or Ideology." *Philosophy and Public Affairs* 2:56–72.

Tripp, James T. B., and Adam B. Jaffee. 1979. "Preventing Groundwater Pollution: Towards a Coordinated Strategy to Protect Critical Recharge Zones." *Harvard Environmental Law Review* 3:1–47.

Ulmer, S. Sidney. 1985. "Are Social Background Models Time Bound?" Paper presented at Midwest Political Science Association Meeting, Chicago, Illinois.

"Variable Justifiability and the Duke Power Case." 1980. *Texas Law Review* 58:273–327.

Vose, Clement. 1959. *Caucasians Only*. New York: Knopf.

Walker, Richard, and Michael Storper. 1978. "Erosion of the CAA of 1970: A Study in the Failure of Government Regulation and Planning." *Boston College Environmental Affairs Law Review* 7:189–257.

Watson, Richard A., and Ronald C. Downing. 1969. *The Politics of the Bench and Bar*. New York: Wiley.

Weiland, Robert A. 1980. Enforcement under RCRA of 1976." *Boston College Environmental Affairs Law Review* 8:641–78.

Wenner, Lettie M. 1982. *The Environmental Decade in Court*. Bloomington: Indiana University Press.

———. 1983. "Interest Group Litigation and Environmental Policy." *Policy Studies Journal* 11:671–83.

———. 1984. "Judicial Oversight of Environmental Regulation." In *Environmental Policy in the 1980s*, ed. Norman Vig and Michael Kraft. Washington, D.C.: Congressional Quarterly Press.

———. 1987. *Commercial Landfilling of Hazardous Wastes in Illinois*. Urbana, Ill.: Institute of Government and Public Affairs.

Wetstone, Gregory. 1980. "Air Pollution Control Laws in North America and the Problem of Acid Rain and Snow." *Environmental Law Reporter* 10:50001–20.

Williams, Bruce A., and Albert R. Matheny. 1984. "Testing Theories of Social Regulation: Hazardous Waste Regulation in the American States." *Journal of Politics* 46:428–58.

Wolf, Sidney M. 1980. "Public Opposition to Hazardous Waste Sites: Self-defeating Approach to National Hazardous Waste Control under Subtitle C of RCRA of 1976." *Boston College Environmental Affairs Law Review* 8:463–540.

Wooley, David R., and John Wappett. 1982. "Cumulative Impacts and the Clean Air Act: An Acid Rain Strategy." *Albany Law Review* 47:37–61.

Yellin, Joel. 1983. "Science, Technology, and Administrative Government Reform." *Yale University Law Journal* 97:327–40.

10 Elites and Environmental Policy

Ames, Bruce N. 1983. "Dietary Carcinogens and Anticarcinogens." *Science* 221 (September): 1256–65.

Anderson, James E. 1984. *Public Policy-Making*. 3d ed. New York: Holt, Rinehart & Winston.

Axelrod, Robert. 1973. "Schema Theory: An Information Processing Model of Perception and Cognition." *American Political Science Review* 68 (December): 1248–66.

Bajgier, Steve M., and Herbert Moskowitz. 1982. "An Interactive Model of Attitude and Risk/Benefit Formation Regarding Social Issues." *Policy Sciences* 14 (June): 257–78.

Bazelon, David L. 1979. "Risk and Responsibility." *Science* 205 (July): 277–80.

Bloomgarden, Kathy. 1983. "Managing the Environment: The Public's View." *Public Opinion* 6 (March): 47–51.

Bowman, Ann O'M., and Richard C. Kearney. 1986. *The Resurgence of the States*. Englewood Cliffs, N.J.: Prentice-Hall.

Buss, David M., and Kenneth H. Craik. 1983. "Contemporary Worldviews: Personal and Policy Implications." *Journal of Applied Social Psychology* 13 (May–June): 259–80.

Carson, Rachel. 1962. *Silent Spring*. Boston: Houghton Mifflin.

Cole, Gerald A., and Stephen B. Withey. 1981. "Perspectives on Risk Perceptions." *Risk Analysis* 1 (June): 143–63.

Colglazier, William, Jr., and Michael Rice. 1983. "Media Coverage of Complex Technological Issues." In Dorothy S. Zinberg, ed., *Uncertain Power: The Struggle for a National Energy Policy*. New York: Pergamon Press.

Combs, B., and Paul Slovic. 1979. "Causes of Death: Biased Newspaper Coverage and Biased Judgments!" *Journalism Quarterly* 56:837–43.

Conservation Foundation. 1984. *State of the Environment: An Assessment at Mid-Decade*. Washington, D.C.: Conservation Foundation.

Costantini, Edmond, and Kenneth Hanf. 1972. "Environmental Concern and Lake Tahoe: A Study of Elite Perceptions, Backgrounds, and Attitudes." *Environment and Behavior* 4 (June): 209–42.

Covello, Vincent T., et al. 1982. "Risk Analysis, Philosophy, and the Social and Behavioral Sciences: Reflections on the Scope of Risk Analysis Research." *Risk Analysis* 2 (June): 53–58.

Covello, Vincent T., et al., eds. 1983. *The Analysis of Actual Versus Perceived Risks*. New York: Plenum Press.

Crouch, Edmond A. C., and Richard Wilson. 1982. *Risk/Benefit Analysis*. Cambridge, Mass.: Ballinger.

Dahl, Robert A. 1967. *Pluralist Democracy in the United States*. Chicago: Rand McNally.

———. 1982. *Dilemmas of Pluralist Democracy*. New Haven, Conn.: Yale University Press.

Davis, Earon S. 1984. "Public Perception: The Environment Is 'Moving.'" *Environmental Forum* 3 (December): 29–33.

Dery, David. 1984. *Problem Definition in Policy Analysis*. Lawrence: University Press of Kansas.

Dietz, Thomas, and Robert W. Rycroft. 1988. *The Risk Professionals*. New York: Russell Sage.

Doll, Richard, and Richard Peto. 1981. *The Causes of Cancer: Quantitative Estimates of Avoidable Risks of Cancer in the United States Today*. Oxford: Oxford University Press.

Domhoff, G. William. 1983. *Who Rules America Now? A View for the '80s*. Englewood Cliffs, N.J.: Prentice-Hall.

Douglas, Mary, and Aaron Wildavsky. 1982. *Risk and Culture: An Essay on the Selection of Technological and Environmental Dangers*. Berkeley and Los Angeles: University of California Press.

Dye, Thomas R. 1983. *Who's Running America; The Reagan Years*. 3d ed. Englewood Cliffs, N.J.: Prentice-Hall.

Efron, Edith. 1984. *The Apocalyptics: Cancer and the Big Lie*. New York: Simon & Schuster.

Environmental Protection Agency. 1980. *Dioxins*. Cincinnati, Ohio: Office of Research and Development, U.S. Environmental Protection Agency.

Epstein, Samuel S. 1978. *The Politics of Cancer*. San Francisco: Sierra Club Books.

Fischhoff, Baruch. 1977. "Cost Benefit Analysis and the Art of Motorcycle Maintenance." *Policy Sciences* 8 (June): 177–202.

Fischhoff, Baruch, and Don MacGregor. 1983. "Judged Lethality: How Much People Seem to Know Depends upon How They Are Asked." *Risk Analysis* 3 (December): 229–36.

Fischhoff, Baruch, et al. 1978. "How Safe Is Safe Enough? A Psychometric Study of Attitudes towards Technological Risks and Benefits." *Policy Sciences* 9 (April): 127–52.

———. 1979. "Weighing the Risks." *Environment* 21 (May): 17–20, 32–38.

———. 1982. "Lay Foibles and Expert Fables in Judgments about Risk." *American Statistician* 36 (August): 240–55.

———. 1983. "'The Public' vs. 'The Experts': Perceived vs. Actual Disagreements about Risks of Nuclear Power." In Vincent T. Covello et al., *The Analysis of Actual versus Perceived Risks*. New York: Plenum Press.

———. 1984. "Defining Risk." *Policy Sciences* 17 (October): 123–39.

Forgus, Ronald H., and Lawrence E. Melamed. 1976. *Perception: A Cognitive-Stage Approach*. New York: McGraw-Hill.

Goodell, Rae. 1977. *The Visible Scientists*. Boston: Little, Brown.

Hadden, Susan G. 1984. "Introduction: Risk Policy in American Institutions." In Susan G.

Hadden, ed., *Risk Analysis, Institutions, and Public Policy.* Port Washington, N.Y.: Associated Faculty Press.

Hamlett, Patrick W. 1984. "Understanding Technological Development: A Decisionmaking Approach." *Science, Technology, and Human Values* 9 (Summer): 33–46.

Harding, Christina M., and J. Richard Eiser. 1984. "Characterizing the Perceived Risks and Benefits of Some Health Issues." *Risk Analysis* 4 (June): 131–41.

Hawkes, Glenn R., et al. 1984. "Assessing Risk: A Public Analysis of the Medfly Eradication Program." *Public Opinion Quarterly* 48 (September): 443–51.

Heclo, Hugh. 1978. "Issue Networks and the Executive Establishment." In Anthony King, ed., *The New American Political System.* Washington, D.C.: American Enterprise Institute.

Hogarth, Robin M. 1980. *Judgment and Choice: The Psychology of Decision.* New York: John Wiley & Sons.

Hohenemser, Christoph, and Jeanne X. Kasperson, eds. 1982. *Risk in the Technological Society.* Boulder, Colo.: Westview Press.

Hohenemser, C., R. W. Kates, and P. Slovic. 1983. "The Nature of Technological Hazard." *Science* 220 (April 22): 378–84.

Hunter, Susan, and Paul Sabatier. 1985. "The Devil Hypothesis: Perceptions and Misperceptions of Opponents." Paper presented at the 1985 annual meeting of the Western Political Science Association, Las Vegas, March 28–29.

Jarvis, Robert. 1976. *Perceptions and Misperceptions in International Relations.* Princeton, N.J.: Princeton University Press.

Jones, Charles O. 1984. *An Introduction to the Study of Public Policy.* 3d ed. Monterey, Calif.: Brooks/Cole.

Kasperson, Roger. 1983. "The Neglect of Social Risk Assessment in Energy Policymaking." In Zinberg, ed., *Uncertain Power.*

Kingdon, John W. 1984. *Agendas, Alternatives, and Public Policies.* Boston: Little, Brown.

Ladd, Everett C. 1982. "Clearing the Air: Public Opinion and Public Policy on the Environment." *Public Opinion* 5 (February/March): 16–20.

Lave, Lester B., ed. 1982. *Quantitative Risk Assessment in Regulation.* Washington, D.C.: Brookings Institution.

Lee, T. R. 1981. "The Public's Perception of Risk and the Question of Irrationality." *Proceedings of the Royal Society of London* 376 (April 30): 5–16.

Levine, Adeline Gordon. 1982. *Love Canal: Science, Politics, and People.* Lexington, Mass.: D. C. Heath.

Lichtenstein, Sarah, et al. 1978. "Judged Frequency of Lethal Events." *Journal of Experimental Psychology: Human Learning and Memory* 4 (November): 551–78.

Lindblom, Charles E. 1980. *The Policymaking Process.* 2d ed. Englewood Cliffs, N.J.: Prentice-Hall.

Lodge, Milton, and Bernard Tursky. 1979. "Comparisons between Category and Magnitude Scaling of Political Opinions Employing SRC/CPS Items." *American Political Science Review* 73 (March): 50–66.

———. 1980. "Workshop on the Magnitude Scaling of Political Opinion in Survey Research." *American Journal of Political Science* 25 (May): 376–419.

Lovrich, Nicholas, Jr., et al. 1985. "Belief Structures of Japanese and American Environmental Interest Group Members." Prepared for delivery at the 1985 annual meeting of the Western Political Science Association, Las Vegas, March 28–30.

Lowi, Theodore J. 1964. "American Business, Public Policy, Case-Studies, and Political Theory." *World Politics* 16 (July): 677–715.

Luttbeg, Norman R., ed. 1981. *Public Opinion and Public Policy: Models of Political Linkage*. 3d ed. Itasca, Ill.: F. E. Peacock, Inc.

Lynn, Frances M. 1986. "The Interplay of Science and Values in Assessing Environmental Risk." *Science, Technology, and Human Values* 11 (Spring): 40–50.

Machina, Mark J. 1987. "Decision-Making in the Presence of Risk." *Science* 236 (May 1): 537–43.

McKean, Kevin. 1985. "Decisions, Decisions." *Discovery* 6 (June): 22–31.

MacLean, Douglas. 1982. "Risk and Consent: Philosophical Issues for Centralized Decisions." *Risk Analysis* 2 (June): 59–67.

Maggiotto, Michael A., and Ann Bowman. 1982. "Policy Orientations and Environmental Regulation: A Case Study of Florida's Legislators." *Environment and Behavior* 14 (March): 155–70.

March, James G., and Herbert A. Simon. 1958. *Organizations*. New York: John Wiley & Sons.

Martin, L. John. 1981. "Science and the Successful Society." *Public Opinion* 4 (June/July): 16–19, 55–56.

Meyer, Marshall W., and Kenneth A. Solomon. 1984. "Risk Management of Local Communities." *Policy Sciences* 16 (February): 245–65.

Michels, Robert. 1962. *Political Parties: A Sociological Study of the Oligarchical Tendencies of Modern Democracies*. New York: Free Press; first published in 1915.

Milbrath, Lester W. 1984. *Environmentalists: Vanguard for a New Society*. Albany: State University Press of New York.

Mills, C. Wright. 1956. *The Power Elite*. New York: Oxford University Press.

Moates, Danny R., and Gary M. Schumacher. 1980. *An Introduction to Cognitive Psychology*. Belmont, Calif.: Wadsworth.

Morgan, M. Granger, et al. 1984. "Powerline Frequency Electric and Magnetic Fields: A Pilot Study of Risk Perception." *Risk Analysis* 5 (June): 139–49.

National Research Council. 1983. *Risk Management in the Federal Government: Managing the Process*. Washington, D.C.: National Academy Press.

Nelkin, Dorothy, and Michael S. Brown. 1984. *Workers at Risk: Voices from the Workplace*. Chicago: University of Chicago Press.

Office of Technology Assessment. 1981. *Assessment of Technologies for Determining Cancer Risks from the Environment*. Washington, D.C.: Office of Technology Assessment.

Okrent, David. 1980. "Comment on Societal Risk." *Science* 208 (April 25): 372–75.

O'Riordan, Timothy. 1982. "Risk-Perception Studies and Policy Priorities." *Risk Analysis* 22 (June): 95–100.

Otway, Harry J., and Kerry Thomas. 1982. "Reflections on Risk Perception and Policy." *Risk Analysis* 2 (June): 69–82.

Otway, Harry J., and Detlof Von Winterfeldt. 1982. "Beyond Acceptable Risk: On the Social Acceptability of Technologies." *Policy Sciences* 14 (June): 247–56.

Perrow, Charles. 1984. *Normal Accidents: Living with High-Risk Technologies*. New York: Basic Books.

Pierce, John C., and Nicholas Lovrich, Jr. 1980. "Belief Systems Concerning the Environment: The General Public, Attentive Publics, and State Legislators." *Political Behavior* 2:259–86.

Pokorny, Gene. 1979. "Living Dangerously . . . Sometimes." *Public Opinion* 2 (June/July): 10–13.

Polsby, Nelson W. 1980. *Community Power and Political Theory*. 2d ed. New Haven, Conn.: Yale University Press.

Pruitt, Dean G. 1965. "Definition of the Situation as a Determinant of International Action." In

Herbert C. Kelman, ed., *International Behavior: A Social-Psychological Analysis*. New York: Holt, Rinehart & Winston.

Reinhold, Robert. 1983. "A.M.A. Disavows Jab at Dioxin Reports." *New York Times* (July 1).

Reissland, John, and Vaughan Harries. 1979. "A Scale for Measuring Risks." *New Scientist* 83 (September): 809–11.

Ripley, Randall B., and Grace A. Franklin. 1984. *Congress, the Bureaucracy, and Public Policy*. 3d ed. Homewood, Ill.: Dorsey Press.

Rothman, Stanley, and S. Robert Lichter. 1982. "The Nuclear Energy Debate: Scientists, the Media, and the Public." *Public Opinion* 5 (August/September): 47–51.

———. 1987. "Elite Ideology and Risk Perception in Nuclear Energy Policy." *American Political Science Review* 81 (June): 383–404.

Rowe, William D. 1977. *An Anatomy of Risk*. New York: John Wiley & Sons.

Rushefsky, Mark E. 1986. *Making Cancer Policy*. Albany: State University of New York Press.

Schneider, William. 1983. "Elite and Public Opinion: The Alliance's New Fissure?" *Public Opinion* 6 (February/March): 5–8, 51.

Sclove, Richard. 1983. "Energy Policy and Democratic Theory." In Zinberg, ed., *Uncertain Power*.

Siderstrom, E. Jonathan, et al. 1984. "Risk Perception in an Interest Group Context: An Examination of the TMI Restart Issue." *Risk Analysis* 4 (September): 231–44.

Sjoberg, Lennart. 1979. "Strength of Belief and Risk." *Policy Sciences* 11 (August): 39–57.

Slovic, Paul, et al. 1979. "Rating the Risks." *Environment* 21 (April): 14–20, 36–39.

———. 1980. "Facts and Fears: Understanding Perceived Risk." In R. C. Schwing and W. A. Albers, Jr., eds., *Societal Risk Assessment: How Safe Is Safe Enough*. New York: Plenum Press.

———. 1981a. "Perceived Risk: Psychological Factors and Social Implications." *Proceedings of the Royal Society of London* 376 (April 30): 17–34.

———. 1981b. "Characterizing Perceived Risk." In R. W. Kates and C. Hohenemser, eds., *Technological Hazard Management*. Cambridge, Mass.: Oegleschlager, Gunn, & Hain.

———. 1982. "Why Study Risk Perception?" *Risk Analysis* 2 (June): 83–93.

Spangler, Miller B. "The Role of Interdisciplinary Analysis in Bridging the Gap between the Technical and Human Sides of Risk Assessment." *Risk Analysis* 2 (June): 101–14.

Stanfield, Rochelle L. 1985. "Assessing the Risk." *National Journal* 17 (June): 1495.

Starr, Chauncey. 1969. "Social Benefit versus Technological Risk." *Science* 165 (September): 1232–38.

Starr, Chauncey, and Chris Whipple. 1982. "Risks of Risk Decisions." In Christoph Hohenemser and Jeanne X. Kasperson, eds., *Risk in the Technological Society*. Boulder, Colo.: Westview Press.

Thomas, Kerry. 1981. "Comparative Risk Perception: How the Public Perceives the Risks and Benefits of Energy Systems." *Proceedings of the Royal Society of London* 376 (April 30): 35–50.

Thomas, Kerry, et al. 1980. "Nuclear Energy: The Accuracy of Policy Makers' Perceptions of Public Beliefs." *Behavioral Science* 25 (September): 332–44.

Tversky, Amos, and Daniel Kahneman. 1974. "Judgment under Uncertainty: Heuristics and Biases." *Science* 185 (September): 1124–31.

———. 1981. "The Framing of Decisions and the Psychology of Choice." *Science* 211 (January): 453–58.

Van Liere, Kent D., and Riley E. Dunlap. 1981. "Environmental Concern: Does It Make a Difference How It's Measured?" *Environment and Behavior* 13 (November): 651–76.

Van Strum, Carol. 1983. *A Bitter Fog: Herbicides and Human Rights*. San Francisco: Sierra Club Books.

Vlek, Charles, and Pieter-Jan Stallen. 1980. "Rational and Personal Aspects of Risk." *Acta Psychologica* 45 (August): 273–300.

———. 1981. "Judging Risks and Benefits in the Small and in the Large." *Organizational Behavior and Human Performance* 28 (October): 235–71.

Von Winterfeldt, Detlof, and Ward Edwards. 1981. "Cognitive Components of Risk Ratings." *Risk Analysis* 1 (December): 277–87.

———. 1984. "Patterns of Conflict about Risk Technologies." *Risk Analysis* 4 (March): 55–68.

Weinberg, Alvin M. 1984. "Letter: Diet and Cancer." *Science* 224 (May 18): 659.

———. 1985. Review: "*The Apocalyptics* by Edith Efron." *Environment* 27 (January/February): 28–30.

Wilson, Richard. 1979. "Analyzing the Daily Risks of Life." *Technology Review* 81 (February): 40–46.

Yankelovich, Daniel. 1983. "The Failure of Consensus." In Zinberg, ed., *Uncertain Power.*

Zinberg, Dorothy S., ed. 1983. *Uncertain Power: The Struggle for a National Energy Policy.* New York: Pergamon Press.

11 International Environmental Politics: A Theoretical Review of the Literature

Abbreviations:

NRJ (*Natural Resources Journal*)

ELQ (*Environmental Law Quarterly*)

OD and IL (*Ocean Development and International Law*)

Ocean Yearbook (Elisabeth Mann Borgese and Norton Ginsburg, eds., *Ocean Yearbook.* Chicago: University of Chicago Press)

Alheritiere, Dominique. 1976. "International Cooperation and Inland Waters: The Influence of Federalism." *NRJ* 16, no. 4:903–22.

———. 1982. "Marine Pollution Control Regulation: Regional Approaches." *Marine Policy* 6, no. 3:162–74.

Alston, Philip. 1978. "International Regulation of Toxic Chemicals." *ELQ* 7, no. 2:397–456.

Azevedo, Mary Patricia. 1982. "Trade in Hazardous Substances: An Examination of U.S. Legislation." In Seymour J. Rubin and Thomas R. Graham, eds., *Environment and Trade.* Montclair, N.J.: Allanheld, Osmun.

Barkenbus, Jack N. 1987. "Nuclear Safety and the Role of International Organizations." *International Organization* 41, no. 3:475–90.

Barnes, Bruce E. 1985. "Environmental Mediation: A Tool for Resolving International Environmental Disputes in the 'Pacific Way.'" In Rene-Jean Dupuy, ed., *The Future of the International Law of the Environment.* Dordrecht: Martinus Nijhoff Publishers.

Barnes, James N. 1982. "The Emerging Convention on the Conservation of Antarctic Marine Living Resources: An Attempt to Meet the New Realities of Resource Exploitation in the Southern Ocean." In Jonathan Charney, ed., *The New Nationalism and the Use of the Common Spaces.* Totowa, N.J.: Allanheld, Osmun.

Bartelmus, Peter L. 1986. *Environment and Development.* Reading, Mass.: Allen & Unwin.

Baruch, Boxer. 1982. "Mediterranean Pollution: Problems and Responses." *OD and IL* 10, no. 3/4:315–56.

Baumel, William J. 1971. *Environmental Protection, International Spillovers, and Trade.* Stockholm: Almquist & Wiksell.

Bederman, David J. 1986. "Dead in the Water: International Law, Diplomacy, and Compensation for Chemical Pollution at Sea." *Virginia Journal of International Law* 26, no. 2:484–514.

Benedict, Richard E. 1986. "The Environment on the Foreign Policy Agenda." *ELQ* 13, no. 2:171–80.

Bernhardt, J. 1980. "A Schematic Analysis of Vessel-Source Pollution: Prescriptive and Enforcement Regimes in the Law of the Sea Conference." *Virginia Journal of International Law* 20, no. 2:265–311.

Berry, Stephen, et al. 1972. "What Happened in Stockholm: A Special Report." *Science and Public Affairs: Bulletin of the Atomic Scientists* 28 (September): 16–56.

Bettman, Otto L. 1974. *The Good Old Days—They Were Terrible.* New York: Random House.

Bewers, J. M., and C. J. R. Garrett. 1987. "Analysis of Issues Related to Sea Dumping of Radioactive Wastes." *Marine Policy,* 11, no. 2:105–24.

Birnie, Patricia. 1984. "The International Organization of Whales." *Denver Journal of International Law and Policy* 13, no. 2–3:309–33.

———. 1985. "The Role of Developing Countries in Nudging the International Whaling Commission from Regulating Whaling to Encouraging Nonconsumptive Uses of Whales." *ELQ* 12, no. 4:937–76.

Biswas, Margaret R., and Asit K. Biswas. 1985. "The Global Environment: Past, Present, Future." *Resources Policy* 11, no. 1:25–42.

Bleicher, Samuel A. 1972. "An Overview of International Environmental Regulation." *ELQ* 2, no. 1:1–90.

Boardman, Robert. 1981. *International Organization and the Conservation of Nature.* Bloomington: Indiana University Press.

Boczek, Boleslaw Adam. 1983. "The Protection of the Antarctic Ecosystem: A Study in International Environmental Law." *OD and IL* 13, no. 3:347–425.

———. 1984. "Global and Regional Approaches to the Protection and Preservation of the Marine Environment." *Case Western Reserve Journal of International Law* 16, no. 1:39–70.

———. 1986. "The Concept of Regime and the Protection of the Marine Environment." In Elisabeth Mann Borgese and Norton Ginsburg, eds., *Ocean Yearbook 6.* Chicago: University of Chicago Press.

Boehmer-Christiansen, Sonja. 1983. "Dumping Nuclear Waste into the Sea: International Control and the Role of Science and Law." *Marine Policy* 7, no. 1:25–36.

———. 1984. "Marine Pollution Control in Europe: Regional Approaches, 1972–1980." *Marine Policy* 8, no. 1:44–55.

———. 1986. "An End to Radioactive Waste Disposal 'at Sea.'" *Marine Policy* 10, no. 2:119–31.

Bordwin, Harold J. 1985. "The Legal and Political Implications of the International Undertaking on Plant Genetic Resources." *ELQ* 12, no. 4:1053–70.

Bothe, Michael, project coordinator. 1980. *Trends in Environmental Policy and Law.* Gland, Switzerland: International Union for the Conservation of Nature and Natural Resources.

Boulding, Kenneth E. 1966. "The Economics of the Coming Spaceship Earth." In H. Jarrett, ed., *Environmental Quality in a Growing Economy.* Baltimore: Johns Hopkins University Press.

Boyle, Alan E. 1985. "Marine Pollution under the Law of the Sea Convention." *American Journal of International Law* 79, no. 2:347–72.

Brown, Lester. 1978. *The Twenty-Ninth Day: Accommodating Human Needs and Numbers to the Earth's Resources.* New York: W. W. Norton.

———. 1981. *Building a Sustainable Society.* New York: W. W. Norton.

Burhenne, Wolfgang E., and Thomas J. Schoenbaum. 1973. "The European Economic Community and the Management of the Environment: A Dilemma." *NRJ* 13, no. 3:494–502.

Busterud, John. 1980. "Mediation: The State of the Art." *The Environmental Professional* 2:34–39.

Caldwell, Lynton K. 1972. *In Defense of Earth: International Protection of the Biosphere.* Bloomington: Indiana University Press.

———. 1974. "The Coming Polity of Spaceship Earth." In Robert T. Roelofs, Joseph N. Crowley, and Donald L. Hardesty, eds., *Environment and Society.* Englewood Cliffs, N.J.: Prentice-Hall.

———. 1984a. *International Environmental Policy.* Durham, N.C.: Duke University Press.

———. 1984b. "The World Environment: Reversing U.S. Policy Commitments." In Norman J. Vig and Michael E. Kraft, eds., *Environmental Policy for the 1980s: Reagan's New Agenda.* Washington, D.C.: Congressional Quarterly Press.

Caponera, Dante A. 1985. "Patterns of Cooperation in International Water Law." *NRJ* 25, no. 3:563–89.

Cardoso, Fernando F. 1980. "Development and the Environment: The Brazilian Case." *CEPAL Review* 12 (December): 111–28.

Caroll, John. 1983. *Environmental Diplomacy: An Examination and a Prospective of Canadian–U.S. Transboundary Environmental Relations.* Ann Arbor: University of Michigan Press.

Carroll, John E. 1986. "Water Resources Management as an Issue in Environmental Diplomacy." *NRJ* 26, no. 2:207–20.

Carter, Luther J. 1987. *Nuclear Imperatives and Public Trust: Dealing with Radioactive Waste.* Washington, D.C.: Resources for the Future.

Charney, Jonathan, ed. 1982. *The New Nationalism and the Use of the Common Spaces: Issues in Marine Pollution and the Exploitation of Antarctica.* Totowa, N.J.: Allanheld, Osmun.

Coan, Eugene V., Julia Hillis, and Michael McCloskey. 1974. "Strategies for International Environmental Action: The Case for an Environmentally Oriented Foreign Policy." *NRJ* 14, no. 1:87–102.

Council on Environmental Quality and the Department of State. 1980. *The Global 2000 Report to the President: Entering the Twenty-First Century.* Washington, D.C.: Government Printing Office.

Cox, Susan Jane Buck. 1985. "No Tragedy of the Commons." *Environmental Ethics* 7 (Spring): 49–61.

Dahlberg, Kenneth A., et al. 1985. *Environment and the Global Arena: Actors, Values, Policies, and Futures.* Durham, N.C.: Duke University Press.

Daly, Herman, ed. 1973. *The Steady-State Economy.* San Francisco: W. H. Freeman.

———. 1980. *Economics, Ecology, Ethics: Essays toward a Steady-State Economy.* San Francisco: W. H. Freeman.

Davilla, Guillermo H. 1972. "Air Pollution Control on the United States–Mexico Border: International Considerations." *NRJ* 12, no. 4:545–50.

de Bardelaben, Joan. 1985. *The Environment and Marxism-Leninism: The Soviet and East German Experience.* Boulder, Colo.: Westview Press.

Deese, David A. 1978. *Nuclear Power and Radioactive Waste: A Seabed Disposal Option?* Lexington, Mass.: Lexington Books.

De Klemm, Cyrille. 1972. "The Conservation of Migratory Animals through International Law." *NRJ* 12, no. 2:255–70.

———. 1985. "Le Patrimoine naturel de l'humanite." In Dupuy, ed., *The Future of the International Law of the Environment.*

de Mestral, A. L. C. 1979. "The Prevention of Pollution of the Marine Environment from Offshore Mining and Drilling." *Harvard International Law Journal* 20, no. 3:469–518.

Dempsey, Paul Stephen, and Lisa L. Helling. 1980. "Oil Pollution by Ocean Vessels—An Environmental Tragedy: The Legal Regime of Flags of Convenience, Multilateral Conventions, and Coastal States." *Denver Journal of International Law and Policy* 10, no. 1:37–87.

Deutsch, Karl W., ed. 1977. *Ecosocial Systems and Ecopolitics: A Reader on Human and Social Implications of Environmental Management in Developing Countries*. Paris: UNESCO.

Dolman, Anthony G. 1981. *Resources, Regimes, and World Order*. New York: Pergamon Press.

Dryzek, John S., and Susan Hunter. 1987. "Environmental Mediation for International Problems." *International Studies Quarterly* 31, no. 1:87–102.

Dupuy, Rene-Jean, ed. 1985. *The Future of the International Law of the Environment*. Workshop, the Hague, November 12–14 1984. Hague Academy of International Law/UN University. Dordrecht, The Netherlands: Martinus Nijhoff Publishers.

Eckert, Ross D. 1979. *The Enclosure of Ocean Resources: Economics and the Law of the Sea*. Stanford, Calif.: Hoover Institute Press.

Elkington, John. 1987. *The Green Capitalists: Industry's Search for Environmental Excellence*. London: Victor Gollancz.

Elsworth, Steve. 1984. *Acid Rain in the U.K. and Europe*. London: Pluto Press.

Enloe, Cynthia H. 1975. *The Politics of Pollution in Comparative Perspective*. New York: David McKay.

Falk, Richard. 1971. *This Endangered Planet: Prospects and Proposals for Human Survival*. New York: Random House.

Finn, Daniel P. 1983. "Nuclear Waste Management Activities in the Pacific Basin and Regional Cooperation on the Nuclear Fuel Cycle." *Ocean Development and International Law* 13, no. 2:213–46.

Founex Report. 1972. *Development and Environment*. Report and working papers of a panel of experts convened by the secretary-general of the United Nations Conference on the Human Environment (Founex, Switzerland, June 4–12, 1971). Paris: Mouton.

Fox, Irving. 1976. "Institutions for Water Management in a Changing World." *NRJ* 16, no. 4:743–58.

Fullenbach, Josef. 1981. *European Environmental Policy: East and West*. London: Butterworths.

Gaines, Sanford E. 1982. "The Extraterritorial Reach of U.S. Environmental Legislation and Regulations." In Rubin and Graham, eds., *Environment and Trade*.

Galli, Craig D. 1987. "Hazardous Exports to the Third World: The Need to Abolish the Double Standard." *Columbia Journal of Environmental Law* 12, no. 1:71–90.

The Global 2000 Report. See Council on Environmental Quality.

Goetze, David. 1987. "Indentifying Appropriate Institutions for Efficient Use of Common Pools." *NRJ* 27, no. 1:187–200.

Goldberg, Karen A. 1985. "Efforts to Prevent Misuse of Pesticides Exported to Developing Countries: Progressing beyond Regulation and Notification." *ELQ* 12, no. 4:1025–52.

Goldie, L. F. E. 1972. "Pollution and Liability Problems Connected with Deep-Sea Mining." *NRJ* 12, no. 2:172–81.

Haas, Peter. 1986. "Coordinated Pollution Control in the Mediterranean: The Mediterranean Action Plan." Unpublished manuscript.

Handl, Gunther. 1975. "Territorial Sovereignty and the Problem of Transnational Pollution." *AJIL* 69, no. 1:50–76.

———. 1978. "An International Legal Perspective on the Conduct of Abnormally Dangerous

Activities in Frontier Areas: The Case of the Siting of Nuclear Power Plants." *ELQ* 7, no. 1:1–50.

———. 1980. "State Liability for Accidental Transnational Environmental Damage by Private Persons." *AJIL (American Journal of International Law)* 74, no. 3:525–65.

———. 1986. "Binational Uses of Transboundary Air Resources: The International Entitlement Issue Reconsidered." *NRJ* 26, no. 3:405–68.

Hardin, G., and J. Baden, eds., 1968. "The Tragedy of the Commons." *Science* 162:1243–48.

———. 1977. *Managing the Commons*. San Francisco: W. H. Freeman.

———. 1986. *Filters against Folly: How to Survive Despite Economists, Ecologists, and the Merely Eloquent*. New York: Penguin.

Hardy, Michael. 1973/74. "Offshore Development and Marine Pollution." *OD and IL* 1, no. 3:239–73.

Hargrove, John L., ed. 1972. *Institutions and the Global Environment*. Dobbs Ferry, N.Y.: Oceana Publications.

Hayton, Robert D. 1982. "The Law of International Aquifers." *NRJ* 22, no. 1:71–94.

Hayward, Peter. 1984. "Environmental Protection: Regional Approaches." *Marine Policy* 8, no. 2:106–19.

Hertzel, Nancy K. 1980. *Environmental Cooperation among Industrial Countries: The Role of Regional Organizations*. Washington, D.C.: University Press of America.

Holdgate, Martin W., Mohammed Kassas, and Gilbert F. White, with the assistance of David Surgeon. *The World Environment, 1972–1982: A Report by the* UNEP. Dublin: Tycooly International Publishing.

Horberry, Hohn. 1985. "The Accountability of Development Assistance Agencies: The Case of Environmental Policy." *ELQ* 12, no. 4:817–70.

Jacobson, Harold K., and David A. Kay. 1983a. "A Framework for Analysis." In Kay and Jacobson, eds., *Environmental Protection*.

———. 1983b. "Conclusions and Policy." In Kay and Jacobson, eds., *Environmental Protection*.

Johnson, Bo. 1976. *International Environmental Law*. Stockholm: LiberFörlag.

Johnson, Brian, and Robert O. Blake. 1979. *The Environmental Policies, Programs, and Performances of the Development Assistance Agencies of Canada, the Federal Republic of Germany, the Netherlands, Sweden, the United Kingdom, and the United States*. Washington, D.C.: International Institute for Environment and Development.

Johnston, Douglas M., ed. 1981. *The Environmental Law of the Sea*. Gland, Switzerland: International Union for the Conservation of Nature and Natural Resources.

Joyner, Christopher. 1984. "Oceanic Pollution and the Southern Ocean: Rethinking the International Legal Implications for Antarctica." *NRJ* 24, no. 1:1–40.

Joyner, Christopher C., and Nancy D. Joyner. 1974. "Global Eco-Management and International Organizations: The Stockholm Conference and Problems of Cooperation." *NRJ* 14, no. 4:533–56.

Juda, Lawrence. 1978. "Negotiating a Treaty on Environmental Warfare: The Convention on Environmental Warfare and Its Impact upon Arms Control Negotiations." *International Organization* 32 (Autumn): 975–91.

———. 1979. "The Regional Approach to Control Pollution in the Mediterranean Sea." *Ocean Management* 5, no. 2:125–50.

Kay, David A., and Eugene B. Skolnikoff, eds. 1972. *World Eco-Crisis*. Madison: University of Wisconsin Press.

Kay, David A., and Harold K. Jacobson, eds. 1983. *Environmental Protection: The International Dimension*. Totowa, N.J.: Allanheld, Osmun.

Kelley, Donald. 1977. *The Energy Crisis and the Environment: An International Perspective*. New York: Praeger.

Kelley, Donald R., Kenneth R. Stunkel, and Richard R. Wescott. 1976. *The Economic Superpowers and the Environment: The United States, the Soviet Union, and Japan*. San Francisco: W. H. Freeman.

Kennan, George F. 1970. "To Prevent a World Wasteland: A Proposal." *Foreign Affairs* 46, no. 3:401–13.

Khaier, Rouchdy, and Victor Sebek. 1985. "New Trends in Compensation for Oil Pollution Damage: Amoco Cadiz Legal Proceedings and the 1984 Diplomatic Conference on Liability and Compensation." *Marine Policy* 9, no. 4:269–79.

Kildow, Judith T. 1982. "Political and Economic Dimensions of Land-Based Sources of Marine Pollution." In Charney, ed., *The New Nationalism*.

Kindt, John W. 1980. "The Effect of Claims by Developing Countries on LOS International Marine Pollution Negotiations." *Virginia Journal of International Law* 20, no. 2:313–45.

———. 1986. *Marine Pollution and the Law of the Sea*. Buffalo, N.Y.: W. S. Hein.

Kiss, Alexander C. 1976. *Survey of Current Developments in International Environmental Law*. Switzerland: International Union for the Conservation of Nature and Natural Resources.

———. 1983. "La Notion de patrimoine commun de l'humanite." In Academie de Droit International, *Recueil des Cours, 1982,* vol. 175, III. The Hague: Martinus Nijhoff Publishers.

———. 1985. "The Protection of the Rhine against Pollution." *NRJ* 25, no. 3:613–38.

Koo, Anthony Y. C., et al. 1979. *Environmental Repercussions on Trade and Investment*. East Lansing, Mich.: MSU International Business and Economic Studies.

Krasner, Stephen. 1985. *Structural Conflict: The Third World Against Global Liberalism*. Berkeley and Los Angeles: University of California Press.

Kwiatkowska, Barbara. 1984. "Marine Pollution from Land-Based Sources: Current Problems and Prospects." *Ocean Development and International Law* 14, no. 3:315–35.

Lake, Laura. 1977. "Mediating Environmental Disputes." *Eckistics* 44:164–70.

Lausche, Barbara J. 1982. UNEP *Environmental Law In-Depth Review 1981: A Presentation by Subject Areas*. Berlin: Erich Schmidt Verlag.

LeMarquand, David. 1976. "Politics of International River Basin Cooperation and Management." *NRJ* 16, no. 4:883–902.

———. 1977. *International Rivers: The Politics of Cooperation*. Vancouver: Westwater Research Centre.

Leonard, Jeffrey H., ed. 1985. *Divesting Nature's Capital: The Political Economy of Environmental Abuse in the Third World*. New York: Holmes & Meier.

Lester, James P. 1980. "Domestic Structure and International Technology Collaboration: Ocean Pollution Regulation." *OD and IL* 8:299–335.

M'Gonigle, R. Michael. 1980. "The 'Economizing' of Ecology: Why Big, Rare Whales Still Die." *ELQ* 9, no. 1:119–238.

M'Gonigle, R. Michael, and Mark W. Zacher. 1979. *Pollution, Politics, and International Law: Tankers at Sea*. Berkeley and Los Angeles: University of California Press.

McHugh, J. L. 1977. "Rise and Fall of World Whaling: The Tragedy of the Commons Illustrated." *Journal of International Affairs* 31, no. 1:23–33.

McManus, Robert J. 1982. "Legal Aspects of Land-Based Sources of Marine Pollution." In Charney, ed., *The New Nationalism*.

Manners, Ian R. 1982. *North Sea Oil and Environmental Planning: The United Kingdom Conference.* Austin: University of Texas Press.

Meadows, Donella H., Dennis L. Meadows, Jorgen Randers, and William W. Behrens. 1972. *The Limits to Growth.* New York: Signet.

Meese, Sally A. 1982. "When Jurisdictional Interests Collide: International, Domestic, and State Efforts to Prevent Vessel Source Oil Pollution." *OD and IL* 12, no. 1/2:71–139.

Mesarovic, Mihajlo, and Eduard Pestel. 1974. *Mankind at the Turning Point.* New York: E. P. Dutton.

Miles, Edward L., Kai N. Lee, and Elaine Carlin. 1985. *Nuclear Waste Disposal under the Seabed: Assessing the Policy Issues.* Berkeley, Calif.: Institute of International Studies.

Mingst, Karen A. 1981. "The Functionalist and Regime Perspectives: The Case of Rhine River Cooperation." *Journal of Common Market Studies* 20, no. 2:161–73.

———. 1982. "Evaluating Public and Private Approaches to International Disputes: Statist and Transnational Solutions to Acid Rain Pollution." *NRJ* 22, no. 1:5–20.

Morse, Edward L. 1977. "Managing International Commons." *Journal of International Affairs* 33, no. 1:1–33.

Mumme, Stephen P. 1985. "State Participation in Foreign Policy-Making: The Case of Water-Related Environmental Disputes along the United States–Mexico Border." *Western Political Quarterly* 38, no. 4.

Mumme, Stephen P., C. Richard Bath, and Valerie Assetto. 1988. "Political Development and Mexican Environmental Policy." *LARR* (*Latin American Research Review,* 1988).

Nanda, Ved P., ed. 1983. *World Climate Change: The Role of International Law and Institutions.* Boulder, Colo.: Westview Press.

OECD. 1981. *Transfrontier Pollution and the Role of States.* Paris: OECD.

———. 1982. *Economic and Ecological Interdependence.* Paris: OECD.

———. 1985. *The State of the Environment 1985.* Paris: OECD.

Okidi, Charles Odidi. 1977. "Toward Regional Arrangements for Regulation of Marine Pollution: An Appraisal of Options." *OD and IL* 4, no. 1:1–25.

Ophuls, William. 1977. *Ecology and the Politics of Scarcity.* San Francisco: W. H. Freeman.

Orr, David W., and Marvin Soroos, eds. 1979. *The Global Predicament: Ecological Perspectives on World Order.* Chapel Hill: University of North Carolina Press.

Park, Chris, ed. 1986. *Environmental Policies: An International Review.* London: Croom Helm.

Pathmarajah, Meera, and Nikki Meith. 1985. "A Regional Approach to Marine Environmental Problems in East Africa and the Indian Ocean." *Ocean Yearbook* 5:162–91.

Pearson, Charles S. 1975. *International Environment Policy: The Economic Dimension.* Baltimore: Johns Hopkins University Press, Studies in International Affairs Number 25.

———. 1976. *Implications for the Trade and Investment of Developing Countries of United States Environmental Controls.* New York: United Nations.

———. 1985. *Down to Business: Multilateral Corporations, the Environment, and Development.* Washington, D.C.: World Resources Institute.

Pearson, Charles S., ed. 1987. *Multinational Corporations, Environment, and the Third World.* Durham, N.C.: Duke University Press.

Pearson, Charles S., and Anthony Pryor. 1978. *Environment: North and South: An Economic Interpretation.* New York: John Wiley & Sons.

Perrow, Charles. 1984. *Normal Accidents: Living with High-Risk Technology.* New York: Basic Books.

Piper, Don C. 1979. "Unilateral Acts of States with Regard to Environmental Protection." In Orr and Soroos, eds., *The Global Predicament*.

Pirages, Dennis. 1978. *Global Ecopolitics: The New Context for International Relations*. North Scituate, Mass.: Duxbury Press.

———. 1983. "The Ecological Perspective in the Social Sciences." *ISQ* 27, no. 3:243–55.

Rahmatullah, Khan. 1980. "Redeployment of Industries to Developing Countries—Environmental Considerations." In Bothe, ed., *Trends in Environmental Policy and Law*.

Ramberg, Bennett. 1986/87. "Learning from Chernobyl." *Foreign Affairs* 65, no. 2:304–28.

Redcliff, Michael. 1984. *Development and Environmental Crisis: Red or Green Alternatives?* London: Methuen.

Rich, Bruce M. 1985. "The Multilateral Development Banks, Environmental Policy, and the United States." *Ecology Law Quarterly* 12, no. 4:681–746.

Riddell, R. 1981. *Ecodevelopment, Economics, Ecology, and Development: An Alternative to Growth-Imperative Models*. New York: St. Martin's Press.

Rochlin, Gene I. 1979. *Plutonium, Power, and Politics: International Arrangements for the Disposition of Spent Nuclear Fuel*. Berkeley and Los Angeles: University of California Press.

Ross, Charles R. 1972. "International Sovereignty in International Environmental Decisions." *NRJ* 12, no. 2:242–54.

Rowland, Wade. 1973. *The Plot to Save the World: The Life and Times of the Stockholm Conference on the Human Environment*. Toronto: Clarke, Irwin.

Rubin, Seymour J., and Thomas R. Graham, eds. 1982. *Environment and Trade: The Relation of International Trade and Environmental Policy*. Totowa, N.J.: Allanheld, Osmun.

Russett, Bruce, and Harvey Starr. 1985. *World Politics: The Menu for Choice*. New York: W. H. Freeman.

Sagan, Carl. 1985. "Nuclear Winter: A Report from the World Scientific Community." *Environment* 27, no. 8:12–15, 38–39.

Saliba, Louis J. 1983. "Mediterranean Pollution: Health-Related Aspects." *Marine Policy* 7, no. 2:109–17.

Samuels, J. W. 1973. "International Control of Weather Modification Advances: Peril or Policy." *NRJ* 13, no. 2:327–42.

Scharff, James E. 1977a. "The International Management of Whales, Dolphins, and Porpoises: An Interdisciplinary Assessment (Part I)." *ELQ* 6, no. 3:323–428.

———. 1977b. "The International Management of Whales, Dolphins, and Porpoises: An Interdisciplinary Assessment (Part II)." *ELQ* 6, no. 4:571–638.

Schneider, Jan. 1979. *World Public Order of the Environment: Towards an International Ecological Law and Organization*. Toronto: University of Toronto Press.

———. 1982. "Prevention of Pollution from Vessels; or, Don't Give Up the Ship." In Charney, ed., *The New Nationalism*.

Scott, Anthony. 1986. "The Canadian-American Problem of Acid Rain." *NRJ* 26, no. 2:337–58.

Shrader-Frechette, K. S. 1985. *Science Policy, Ethics, and Economic Methodology*. Dordrecht, The Netherlands: D. Reidel.

Siegneur, Christian. 1987. "Economic Aspects of International Air Pollution Control Policies." *IJES* (*International Journal of Environmental Studies*) 29:297–306.

Simon, Julian J. 1981. *The Ultimate Resource*. Princeton, N.J.: Princeton University Press.

Simon, Julian J., and Herman Kahn, eds. 1984. *The Resourceful Earth*. Oxford: Basil Blackwell.

Smith, George P., II. 1983. "Acid Rain: Transnational Perspectives." *New York Law School Journal of International and Comparative Law* 4:459–502.

Sohn, Louis B. 1973. "The Stockholm Declaration on the Human Environment." *Harvard International Law Journal* 14 (Summer): 423–515.

Soroos, Marvin S. 1979. "Lifeboat Ethics versus One-Worldism in International Food and Resource Policy." In Orr and Soroos, eds., *The Global Predicament.*

———. 1986. *Beyond Sovereignty: The Challenge of Global Policy.* Columbia: University of South Carolina Press.

Springer, Allen I. 1983. *The International Law of Pollution: Protecting the Global Environment in a World of Sovereign States.* Westport, Conn.: Quorum Books.

Sprout, Harold, and Margaret Sprout. 1971. *Toward a Politics of the Planet Earth.* New York: Van Nostrand Reinhold.

———. 1978. *The Context of Environmental Politics: Unfinished Business for America's Third Century.* Lexington: University Press of Kentucky.

Stein, Robert E., and Brian Johnson. 1979. *Banking on the Biosphere? Environmental Procedures and Practices of Nine Multilateral Development Agencies.* Lexington, Mass.: D. C. Heath.

Stowe, Robert C. 1987. "United States Foreign Policy and the Conservation of Natural Resources: The Case of Tropical Deforestation." *NRJ* 27, no. 1:55–101.

Sunkel, Osvaldo. 1980. "The Interaction between Styles of Development and the Environment in Latin America." *CEPAL Review* 12 (December): 15–51.

Teclaff, Ludwik A., and Eileen Teclaff. 1979. "Transboundary Groundwater Pollution: Summary and Trends." *NRJ* 19, no. 3:629–68.

———. 1985. "Transboundary Toxic Pollution and the Drainage Basin Concept." *NRJ* 25, no. 3:589–612.

Thacher, Peter S., and Nikki Meith. 1980. "Approaches to Regional Marine Problems: A Progress Report on UNEP's Regional Sea Program." *Ocean Yearbook* 2:153–82.

———. 1982. "The Caribbean Example." *Ocean Yearbook* 3:223–57.

Thompson, Starley L., and Stephen H. Schneider. 1986. "Nuclear Winter Reappraised." *Foreign Affairs* 64, no. 5:981–1005.

Timagenis, Gregorios J. 1980. *International Control of Marine Pollution.* New York: Oceana Publications.

Tolba, Mostafa Kamal. 1982. *Development without Destruction: Evolving Environmental Perceptions.* Dublin: Tycooly International Publishers.

Tuclhin, Joseph S., ed. 1986. *Habitat, Health, and Development: A New Way of Looking at Cities.* Boulder, Colo.: Lynne Rienner Publishers.

Utton, Albert E. 1973. "International Water Quality Law." *NRJ* 13, no. 2:282–314.

———. 1976. "Managing the International Environment." *NRJ* 16, no. 3:597–600.

van Lier, Irene H. 1981. *Acid Rain and International Law.* Toronto: Bunsel Environmental Consultants.

Waldichuk, Michael. 1973. "International Approach to the Marine Pollution Problem." *Ocean Management* 1, no. 3:211–61.

———. 1977. "Control of Marine Pollution: An Essay Review." *OD and IL* 4, no. 3:269–96.

———. 1982. "An International Perspective on Global Marine Pollution." In Virginia K. Tippie and Dana R. Kester, eds., *Impact of Marine Pollution on Society.* New York: Praeger.

Wang, Cheng-Pang. 1986. "A Review of the Enforcement Regime for Vessel-Source Oil Pollution Control." *OD and IL* 16, no. 4:305–37.

Ward, Barbara, and René Dubos. 1972. *Only One Earth: The Care and Maintenance of a Small Planet.* London: Penguin/Andre Deutch.

Wetstone, Gregory S., and Armin Rosencranz. 1983. *Acid Rain in Europe and North America:*

National Responses to an International Problem. Washington, D.C.: Environmental Law Institute.

Wilcher, Marshall E. 1980. *Environmental Cooperation in the North Atlantic Area.* Washington, D.C.: University Press of America.

Wilson, Clifton E. 1974. "Environmental Policy and International Law." In Stuart S. Nagel, ed., *Environmental Politics.* New York: Praeger.

Woodhouse, Edward J. 1972. "Revisioning the Future of the Third World: An Ecological Perspective on Development." *World Politics* 25, no. 1:1–34.

World Bank. 1975. *Environment and Development.* Washington, D.C.: World Bank.

———. 1978. *Environmental Considerations for the Industrial Development Sector.* Washington, D.C.: World Bank.

Young, Oran R. 1987. "'Arctic Waters': The Politics of Regime Formation." *OD and IL* 18, no. 1:101–14.

Zeppetello, Marc A. 1985. "National and International Regulation of Ocean Dumping: The Mandate to Terminate Marine Disposal of Contaminated Sewage Sludge." *ELQ* 12, no. 3:619–64.

12 Alternative Views of the Environmental Problematic

Ballard, Steven C., and Thomas E. James. 1983. *The Future of the Sunbelt: Managing Growth and Change.* New York: Praeger.

Barnett, Harold J., and Chandler Morse. 1963. *Scarcity and Growth: The Economics of Natural Resource Availability.* Baltimore: Johns Hopkins University Press, for Resources for the Future.

Bartlett, Robert V. 1986. "Ecological Rationality: Reason and Environmental Policy," *Environmental Ethics* 8:221–39.

Baumol, William J., and Wallace E. Oates. 1975. *The Theory of Environmental Policy.* Englewood Cliffs, N.J.: Prentice-Hall.

Bond, Richard. 1977. "Salvationists, Utilitarians, and Environmental Justice." *Alternatives* 6:123–35.

Bookchin, Murray. 1971. *Post-Scarcity Anarchism.* San Francisco: Ramparts Press.

———. 1980. *Toward an Ecological Society.* Montreal: Black Rose.

———. 1982. *The Ecology of Freedom: The Emergence and Dissolution of Hierarchy.* Palo Alto, Calif.: Cheshire.

———. 1987. "Social Ecology versus 'Deep' Ecology: A Challenge for the Ecology Movement." *Green Perspectives* 4 and 5:1–23.

Bowman, Ann O'M., and Richard Kearney. 1986. *The Resurgence of the States.* New York: Harper & Row.

Brown, Lester R. 1978. *The Twenty-ninth Day.* New York: W. W. Norton.

Cahn, Robert. 1978. *Footprints on the Planet.* New York: Universe Books.

Caldwell, Lynton K. 1972. "Environmental Quality as an Administrative Problem." *Annals of the American Academy of Political and Social Science* 400:103–15.

Capra, Fritjof. 1987. "Deep Ecology: A New Paradigm." *Earth Island Journal* 2, no. 4:27–30.

Commoner, Barry. 1972. *The Closing Circle.* New York: Bantam.

Cotgrove, Stephen. 1982. *Catastrophe or Cornucopia: The Environment, Politics, and the Future.* New York: John Wiley.

Daly, Herman E. 1977. *Steady-State Economics.* San Francisco: Freeman.

Devall, Bill. 1980. "The Deep Ecology Movement." *Natural Resources Journal* 20:299–322.

Devall, Bill, and George Sessions. 1985. *Deep Ecology*. Salt Lake City, Utah: Peregrine Smith.

Dryzek, John S. 1983a. "Ecological Rationality." *International Journal of Environmental Studies* 21:5–10.

———. 1983b. "Don't Toss Coins in Garbage Cans: A Prologue to Policy Design." *Journal of Public Policy* 3:345–68.

———. 1987a. *Rational Ecology: Environment and Political Economy*. Oxford and New York: Basil Blackwell.

———. 1987b. "Discursive Designs: Critical Theory and Political Institutions." *American Journal of Political Science* 31:656–79.

Ehrlich, Paul. 1968. *The Population Bomb*. New York: Ballantine.

Goodin, Robert E. 1983. "The Ethics of Destroying Irreplaceable Assets." *International Journal of Environmental Studies* 21:55–66.

Griffin, Susan. 1978. *Women and Nature*. New York: Harper & Row.

Habermas, Jurgen. 1984. *The Theory of Communicative Action I: Reason and the Rationalization of Society*. Boston: Beacon Press.

Hardin, Garrett. 1968. "The Tragedy of the Commons." *Science* 162:1243–48.

Hays, Samuel P. 1987. *Beauty, Health, and Permanence: Environmental Politics in the United States, 1955–1985*. New York: Cambridge University Press.

Heilbroner, Robert L. 1980. *An Inquiry into the Human Prospect: Updated and Reconsidered for the 1980s*. New York: W. W. Norton.

Inglehart, Ronald. 1977. *The Silent Revolution: Changing Values and Political Styles Among Western Publics*. Princeton, N.J.: Princeton University Press.

Jones, Charles O. 1975. *Clean Air: The Policies and Politics of Pollution Control*. Pittsburgh: University of Pittsburgh Press.

Lemons, J. 1981. "Cooperation and Stability as a Basis for Environmental Ethics." *Environmental Ethics* 3:219–30.

Leopold, Aldo. 1949. *A Sand County Almanac*. Oxford: Oxford University Press.

Lester, James P. 1982. "Technology, Domestic Structures, and Ocean Pollution Regulation." In Dean E. Mann, ed., *Environmental Policy Implementation*. Lexington, Mass.: Lexington Books.

———. 1985. "Hazardous Waste and Policy Implementation: The Subnational Role." *Hazardous Waste and Hazardous Materials* 2:381–97.

———. 1986. "New Federalism and Environmental Policy." *Publius* 16:149–65.

Lester, James P., et al. 1983. "Hazardous Wastes, Politics, and Public Policy: A Comparative State Analysis." *Western Political Quarterly* 36:257–85.

Lindblom, Charles E. 1982. "The Market as Prison." *Journal of Politics* 44:324–36.

Lovins, Amory B. 1977. *Soft Energy Paths: Toward a Durable Peace*. New York: Harper & Row.

Lowi, Theodore J. 1969. *The End of Liberalism*. New York: W. W. Norton.

Luke, Timothy, and Stephen K. White. 1985. "Critical Theory, the Informational Revolution, and an Ecological Path to Modernity." In John Forester, ed., *Critical Theory in Public Life*. Cambridge, Mass.: MIT Press.

McClosky, H. J. 1983. *Ecological Ethics and Politics*. Totowa, N.J.: Rowman & Littlefield.

Marcus, Alfred A. 1980. *Promise and Performance: Choosing and Implementing Environmental Policy*. Westport, Conn.: Greenwood Press.

Meadows, Donella H., et al. 1972. *The Limits to Growth*. New York: Universe Books.

Merchant, Carolyn. 1982. *The Death of Nature: Women, Ecology, and the Scientific Revolution*. San Francisco: Harper & Row.
Milbrath, Lester W. 1984. *Environmentalists: Vanguard for a New Society.* Albany, N.Y.: State University of New York Press.
Naess, Arne. 1973. "The Shallow and the Deep, Long-Range Ecology Movement." *Inquiry* 16:95–100.
Odum, Eugene P. 1983. *Basic Ecology.* Philadelphia: Saunders.
Ophuls, William. 1977. *Ecology and the Politics of Scarcity.* San Francisco: W. H. Freeman.
Partridge, Ernest, ed. 1981. *Responsibilities to Future Generations.* Buffalo, N.Y.: Prometheus Books.
Passmore, John. 1974. *Man's Responsibility to Nature: Ecological Problems and Western Traditions.* New York: Scribner's.
Pryde, Philip R. 1972. "The Quest for Environmental Quality in the USSR." *American Scientist* 60:739–45.
Regan, Tom. 1983. *The Case for Animal Rights.* Berkeley and Los Angeles: University of California Press.
Salleh, Ariel Kay. 1984. "Deeper than Deep Ecology: The Eco-Feminist Connection." *Environmental Ethics* 6:339–45.
Sikora, R. I., and Brian Barry, eds. 1978. *Obligations to Future Generations.* Philadelphia: Temple University Press.
Simmons, Randy T., and William C. Mitchell. 1984. "Politics and the New Resource Economics." *Contemporary Policy Issues* 5:1–13.
Simon, Julian. 1981. *The Ultimate Resource.* Princeton, N.J.: Princeton University Press.
Simon, Julian, and Herman Kahn, eds. 1984. *The Resourceful Earth.* Oxford and New York: Basil Blackwell.
Stone, Christopher D. 1972. "Should Trees Have Standing? Toward Legal Rights for Natural Objects." *Southern California Law Review* 45:450–501.
Stretton, Hugh. 1976. *Capitalism, Socialism, and the Environment.* Cambridge: Cambridge University Press.
Stroup, Richard, and John Baden. 1983. *Natural Resources: Bureaucratic Myths and Environmental Management.* Cambridge, Mass.: Ballinger.
Weidenbaum, Murray L. 1979. *The Future of Business Regulation: Private Action and Public Demand.* New York: Amacon.
———. 1983. "Free the Fortune 500." In Theodore D. Goldfarb, ed., *Taking Sides: Clashing Views on Environmental Controversies.* Guildford, Conn.: Dushkin.
Weinberg, Alvin M. 1972. "Social Institutions and Nuclear Energy." *Science* 177:27–34.
Wilson, Edward O. 1984. *Biophilia.* Cambridge, Mass.: Harvard University Press.

About the Editor

James P. Lester is Professor of Political Science at Colorado State University. He is the coeditor of *The Politics of Hazardous Waste Management* (Duke University Press, 1983) and *Dimensions of Hazardous Waste Politics and Policy* (Greenwood Press, 1988).

About the Contributors

Valerie Assetto is Associate Professor of Political Science at Colorado State University. Professor Assetto received her Ph.D. in political science from Rice University in 1984. She co-authored an article in *The Latin American Research Review* and has published a book entitled *The Soviet Bloc and the International Monetary Fund* (Westview Press, 1988).

Jerry W. Calvert is Professor and Head of Political Science at Montana State University. Professor Calvert received his Ph.D. from Washington State University in 1972. He has published articles in several political science journals, including the *Western Political Quarterly.*

Henry P. Caulfield is Professor Emeritus of Political Science at Colorado State University. Dr. Caulfield received his B.S. and M.P.A. degrees at Harvard University in 1940 and 1949 respectively. He has published extensively in the natural resources politics and policy field.

Charles E. Davis is Professor of Political Science at Colorado State University. He received his Ph.D. from the University of Houston in 1977. He has authored or co-authored articles in *Polity, Western Political Quarterly, Policy Studies Review,* and *Public Administration Quarterly,* among others.

John S. Dryzek is Associate Professor and Chair of Political Science at the University of Oregon. He received his Ph.D. from the University of Maryland in 1981. He has authored or co-authored numerous articles in the area of environmental politics and policy. His most recent book is entitled *Rational Ecology: Environment and Political Economy* (Basil Blackwell, 1987).

Riley E. Dunlap is Professor of Sociology and Rural Sociology at Washington State University. He has written numerous articles on public attitudes toward environmental issues, the environmental movement, and environmental politics. In addition, he served as chair of the American Sociological Association's section on environmental sociology.

Helen M. Ingram is Professor of Political Science at the University of Arizona. She received her Ph.D. in public law and government from Columbia University. Her area of expertise is public policy, particularly natural resource and environmental policy. She is past president of the Policy Studies Organization and is treasurer of the American Political Science Association. She has written numerous articles on the policy process and environmental policy. Her most extensive work is *A Policy Approach to Political Representation: Lessons from the Four Corners States* (Johns Hopkins Press, 1980).

Michael E. Kraft is Professor of Political Science and Public Affairs at the University of Wisconsin-Green Bay. He received his Ph.D. from Yale University in 1973. He is the coeditor of *Environmental Policy in the 1980s: Reagan's New Agenda* (Congressional Quarterly Press, 1984), and has written widely on environmental politics, regulation, risk analysis, and other policy issues.

Dean E. Mann is Professor of Political Science at the University of California at Santa Barbara. He is the former chairman of the department and has published extensively in the area of public policy and American government, especially water resource policy issues. In addition, he is past president of the Policy Studies Organization and is the current editor of the *Western Political Quarterly.*

Stephen Mumme is Associate Professor of Political Science at Colorado State University. He received his Ph.D. from the University of Arizona in 1982. He has authored or co-authored numerous articles on environmental politics and policy, many of which have appeared in such journals as *Western Political Quarterly, Publius,* and *Policy Studies Journal,* among others.

Walter A. Rosenbaum is Professor of Political Science at the University of Florida. He received his Ph.D. from Princeton University in 1964. He has written numerous books and articles concerning energy policy, environmental policy, and related topics. His most recent books include *Environmental Politics and Policy* (Congressional Quarterly Press, 1985) and *Energy, Politics, and Public Policy* (Congressional Quarterly Press, 1986). He has also been a staff member to the U.S. Environmental Protection Agency and Fellow at the Woodrow Wilson Center of the Smithsonian Institution.

Mark E. Rushefsky is Professor of Political Science at Southwest Missouri State University. He received his Ph.D. from SUNY-Binghamton in 1977. He has contributed chapters to several books and has published in such journals as *Policy Studies Journal, Policy Studies Review,* and *Politics and the Life Sciences,* among others. His most recent book is *Making Cancer Policy* (SUNY Press, 1986).

Dimitris Stevis is Assistant Professor of Political Science at New Mexico State University. He received his Ph.D. from the University of Arizona in 1987 and is currently interested in issues relating to technology and international politics.

Lettie McSpadden Wenner is Professor and Chair of Political Science at Northern Illinois University. She received her Ph.D. from the University of Wisconsin in 1972. She has published extensively in the area of judicial politics and environmental policy. Her most recent book is entitled *The Environmental Decade in Court* (Indiana University Press, 1982).

Index

Library of Congress Cataloging-in-Publication Data
Environmental politics and policy : theories and evidence/edited by
James P. Lester.
p. cm.
Bibliography: p.
Includes index.
ISBN 0–8223–0938–6.—ISBN 0–8223–0942–4 (pbk.)
1. Environmental policy—United States. I. Lester, James P.,
1944–.
HC110.E5E49879 1989
363.7′05′0973—dc20 89–35743 CIP